ECONOMIC FORECASTING FOR BUSINESS:
Concepts and Applications

John J. McAuley

Vice President
Applied Portfolio Modeling
Chemical Bank
and
Adjunct Assistant Professor
Fordham University

Prentice-Hall, Inc., Englewood Cliffs, NJ 07632

Library of Congress Cataloging in Publication Data

McAuley, John J., [date]
 Economic forecasting for business.

 Includes bibliographical references and index.
 1. Business forecasting—Statistical methods.
I. Title.
HD30.27.M36 1986   658.4′0355   85-6548
ISBN 0-13-231556-4

Editorial/production supervision and interior design: Susan Fisher
Cover design: Diane Saxe
Manufacturing buyer: Ed O'Dougherty

Printed in the United States of America

10 9 8 7 6 5 4 3 2

ISBN 0ı-13-231556-4   0ı

Prentice-Hall International (UK) Limited, *London*
Prentice-Hall of Australia Pty. Limited, *Sydney*
Prentice-Hall Canada Inc., *Toronto*
Prentice-Hall Hispanoamericana, S.A., *Mexico*
Prentice-Hall of India Private Limited, *New Delhi*
Prentice-Hall of Japan, Inc., *Tokyo*
Prentice-Hall of Southeast Asia Pte. Ltd., *Singapore*
Editora Prentice-Hall do Brasil, Ltda., *Rio de Janeiro*
Whitehall Books Limited, *Wellington, New Zealand*

To Kath

CONTENTS

PART IV: APPLICATIONS: BUSINESS FORECASTING

PREFACE

Economic forecasting has attained increasing importance in business management since the 1960s. This evolution has provided a rich opportunity for economists to apply both economic theory and expert judgments on economic conditions to the construction of forecasts of future economic developments, which in turn serve as inputs to management decisions. While the demand and opportunities for economic forecasters in business have been growing for more than two decades, academic training specifically aimed at this role is a more recent development.

I have observed the split between conventional economic training and the needs of the novice business economic forecaster from two vantage points. Fifteen years of experience as a business economic forecaster has highlighted the need for—and difficulty of—bridging the gap between academic theory and economic forecasting in a business setting. At the same time, ten years at Fordham University, teaching applied macroeconomics and forecasting to undergraduates intent on a business career, have refined my views on how this gap has been narrowed.

This book is intended to provide the aspiring business forecaster with both a conceptual framework of the process of economic forecasting in a business environment, and with practical examples of how the principal types of business forecasts are prepared. Existing books on forecasting have often been of two extreme types, which this book attempts to link. One extreme consists of anthologies of articles on aspects of forecasting. While these books provide useful supplementary material, the lack of a unified theme makes them less useful as a core text. At the other extreme are texts on applied econometrics, which are strong on theory, but fail to provide a methodological approach to its application. A distinctive feature of this text is that, using standard economic theory and statistical techniques, it takes the reader through a series of real-world forecasts. Moreover, the need to keep models simple—in particular, to economize on the use of explanatory variables, which have themselves to be forecast—is stressed. In addition, it is strongly emphasized that forecasting is not a mechanistic application of statistical and econometric techniques to economic theory. By using actual forecast examples (largely for 1982 and 1983), the existence and size of errors between forecast and actual values are vividly shown. The special role of the economist's judgment in modifying forecast model results is, thus, stressed again and again. No text can demonstrate error-proof forecasting methods for all situations under all economic conditions. More important, I have found that students—and, indeed, practicing forecasters—may learn more from forecasts that are less than perfect than from made-up examples that never err.

The text is mainly aimed at advanced undergraduates and graduate students who will shortly embark on business careers. While stressing the role of the business economic forecaster, it is hoped the text will also help future business managers, who will use the economic forecasts of others, to understand and implement them more effectively. It is also hoped that the book will be useful to active economists and managers who have lately felt the need to understand in a more systematic way the process of economic forecasting. The student should have had at least two semesters of economic theory—both macro- and microeconomics—and, preferably, at least one semester of intermediate macroeconomics. In addition, two semesters of statistics and/or econometrics would be useful. Familiarity with, and access to, a computer is also desirable.

Part I of the text provides the reader with an introduction to the fundamental concepts of economic forecasting. Chapter 1 discusses why, what, how, and for whom business economists forecast. Chapter 2 offers a brief discussion of the theoretical underpinnings of economic forecasting. This chapter is not intended to be a substitute for macro- and microeconomic course work. Experience has shown, however, that while students may be well prepared in their theory courses, they are often unsure of how to translate theory to the actual workings of the economy. Thus, reviewing the most essential aspects of theory at the outset of the text allows this material to be integrated into the applications chapters more easily. In addition, this chapter stresses the importance of a theoretical model as the basis for *economic* forecasting. Chapter 3 offers a detailed discussion of the sources and nature of the main measures of macroeconomic activity. A detailed knowledge of the composition and features of economic measures is necessary if one is to forecast them. Moreover, experience using this material in the management training program of the Capital Markets Group at Chemical Bank has demonstrated its value to the general business manager who may have to react to economic announcements in an operational setting. Chapter 4 offers an overview of statistical methods in forecasting, including analysis of time series, simple regression analysis, multiple regression analysis, and error analysis and forecast evaluation. As is the case with Chapter 2, this chapter is more a review than an exhaustive treatment of these topics. Nevertheless, a review of the key topics is likely to be of help to the student and provides a framework within which to discuss applications in the rest of the text. These fundamental concepts are applied to five important types of economic forecasts used in business in the remainder of the text. These seven chapters should be viewed as parts of an integrated whole. Part II, consisting of Chapters 5, 6, and 7, examines forecasts of the main measures of specific economic activities. Extensive attention is paid to analysis of each economic process and the appropriate technique for forecasting the process. In many businesses, a forecast of a specific indicator may be vital to forecasting the firm's basic activity. A broader use of indicator forecasting is to derive inputs to a general macroeconomic forecast.

Part III looks at more fully integrated macroeconomic forecasting over longer time horizons. Chapter 8 addresses the topic of medium-term macroeconomic forecasting. The approach follows a sequential, recursive forecast model of the Gross National Product and its major components. Chapter 9 is concerned with financial forecasting. An extensive discussion of the financial sectors, their interrelationships, and the role of monetary policy is followed by a cross section of financial forecasting approaches. An example of an interest rate forecasting model is then developed. Chapter 10 deals with long-term forecasting, its differences from medium-term forecasting, and its uses. A basic long-term forecasting model is then described.

Chapter 11 discusses firm and industry forecasting. The chapter first establishes some guidelines to insure economic forecasts will be useful to management. Six varied case studies of industry-specific forecasts are then discussed. This discussion reinforces the role of an overall macroeconomic forecast as the basis for forecasting those measures of greatest interest to a particular firm. The cases provide examples of the range of interests of different types of business. Finally, the chapter concludes with guidelines on forecast presentation.

This project, like most, turned out to be lengthier and more challenging than I had forecast at the start. Its completion was aided by many people, all of whom deserve thanks. My past students at Fordham University have willingly suffered the role of preview audiences and enjoyed the role of critics. In particular, Margaret Millard and Verna Challenger made many helpful suggestions. Dominick Salvatore, Chairman of the Department of

Economics at Fordham University, has provided guidance and support. I owe a debt to former teachers, particularly Eugene Diulio and Edward Dowling, S.J., at Fordham; Frank McGrath, now at Iona College; and Emily Sun at Manhattan College. For the past eleven years, Frederick W. Deming, Senior Vice President and Chief Economist at Chemical Bank, has acted as a mentor, for which I am grateful. Other colleagues at Chemical whose patience and help has been great and whose criticisms were appreciated, in the end, are Carl A. Batlin, Steven Edelson, Jeffrey R. Leeds, Robert D. Sbarra, Thomas J. Spitznas, Karen Wasserman, and Robert B. Wooster. Former colleagues who allowed me to pick their brains include M. Desmond Fitzgerald, now at the City University of London; Thomas W. Moore, now at Tampa Electric Co.; Michael P. Niemira, now at Paine Webber; Thomas P. O'Toole, now at City Federal Savings and Loan; and James P. Winder, now at The Bank of New York. Nereida Gonzalez provided able (and cheerful) research assistance. Mrs. Shalane Kinney and Johnny Rivera did a superb job of transforming scribbles into a manuscript. The suggestions of outside reviewers Robert A. Meyers, Professor and Associate Dean at the University of California at Berkley; Professor David T. Levy at Rutgers University; and Ronald F. Rost at the Board of Governors of the Federal Reserve System made this a better book than it otherwise would have been. Linda Frascino and Susan Fisher at Prentice-Hall saw the project through to completion.

Finally, because not least, my wife Kathryn Felton McAuley fulfilled the roles of economic colleague, reviewer, critic, and supporter, for all of which I am grateful.

John J. McAuley

1

OVERVIEW
*Why, what, how,
and for whom business
economists forecast*

Economic forecasting plays an important role in the process of business management. One of management's most difficult tasks is to make decisions about the conduct of a business in the uncertain future. Consider three situations.

I.   A bank wishes to settle on the best funding strategy for the next six months so as to maximize the spread between the interest rate(s) at which it borrows and the interest rate(s) at which it lends.

II. A carpet manufacturer desires to know the number of new homes that will be built in the coming year because experience has shown there is a close relationship between new home building and the demand for carpets.

III. An electric company must determine the growth in demand for electricity in its service area over the next decade in order to plan its capital expansion.

Each of these situations shares a need to know something about future economic conditions in order to make operational decisions. Thus, a forecast of relevant economic conditions should be an important input to the decision making process. A forecast is not simply a prediction, however, but rather is a statement about future conditions based on a number of explicit assumptions. This distinction is important; by stating that some outcome results from certain other assumed conditions, the forecaster is supplying the user of the forecast results—the person who has to reach a business decision based on the forecast—with the criteria for accepting, rejecting, or modifying the forecast. A prediction, on the other hand, presents the decision maker with a take it or leave it choice: there are no bases for believing the outcome, or for making minor changes.

The three situations described above show the extent to which forecasts can vary in terms of detail, time horizon, and specificity. In the first case, a detailed macroeconomic forecast with explicit assumptions about monetary and fiscal policy is required. While the amount of forecast detail is great the time horizon is short. The focus of the carpet manufacturer is narrower; a variety of macroeconomic forecasts may result in the same level of housing starts over the next year, and thus, differences in many other details can be ignored. Indeed, the economist may accept a macroeconomic forecast prepared by another individual or group to derive a specific forecast for carpet demand. In evaluating the carpet demand forecast the final user (the decision maker) can examine the underlying economic forecast to question its reasonableness. The case confronting the electric company is different in two ways. First, the forecast horizon is much longer. This lessens the importance of short-term policy changes, but also results in a less detailed forecast. Second, since the forecast relates to a region, a national macroeconomic forecast will be of only limited help. A national forecast solution may be helpful, however, in highlighting the differences between the national and regional economies. It should be noted that in all three of these cases the economic forecast is only one input into the business decision making process. A forecast is not an end in itself, but rather a means to an end—a policy decision.

This chapter affords an overview of the economic forecasting process in a business environment by providing partial answers to the questions: why, what, how, and for whom business economists forecast.

WHY BUSINESS ECONOMISTS FORECAST

In recent years it has become increasingly apparent that one feature of the more successful businesses is better information. This ranges from information about the best sources of raw material and the most suitable production process to how best to communicate with customers, and to prospects for the future. The key function in modern business is that of the decision maker. That is, the person or group which receives all this information, processes it, and constructs a policy based on it.

Economic forecasts are one vital part of this information flow. The forecast should provide the decision maker with just the information needed to make an informed decision. As noted above, this information involves more than a mere prediction of some "bottom-line" value, such as sales, or price. A complete forecast should also state the assumptions upon which it was based. This permits the user of the forecast to accept, reject, or modify the results based on some specific difference. It also means that, even if the specific forecast results are rejected, the exercise need not have been futile. Quite likely the reason for rejecting the forecast is contained in the underlying assumptions, and altering the assumptions may lead to a new, acceptable forecast result. Indeed, the process of studying a forecast may prove a valuable exercise for management, in that it can focus more clearly on a critical unknown—and the associated risks—in the outlook.

The economist should also be careful to avoid supplying too much information. It must be remembered that the purpose of the forecast is to provide the business manager with the input needed to make an informed decision. Some details that might interest an economist are irrelevant to the decision making process and should be excluded from the reported results. Otherwise, the result is likely to be a confused management, distracted by details and, thus, inhibited rather than helped in reaching a decision.

WHAT BUSINESS ECONOMISTS FORECAST

The subject matter of economic forecasts in business is broad, reflecting the varied needs of business managers. In general, these forecasts cover a variety of economic background conditions and often some more focused concept which may be a general economic variable, or a specific measure of the firm's performance. Some feel for the range of economic forecasts can be gained by considering several types of economic forecasts prepared in a business environment.

The narrowest form of forecasting is *indicator* forecasting. Financial markets react to the announcement of a particular economic measure. For instance, the announcement that the unemployment rate for a particular month declined from 7.1% to 6.8% may be interpreted favorably by stock market participants—as a sign that the economy is growing and will lead to growth in corporate sales and profits. On the other hand, bond market participants may react adversely—regarding the decline in the unemployment rate as a sign that wage costs and, in turn, prices will soon rise rapidly. In either case, firms engaged in these markets as brokers or dealers desire a forecast of the impending announcement. This provides them with a basis for positioning themselves in advance of the announcement. The economist must be quite explicit about the underlying rationale for such an indicator and about the degree of confidence that may be attached to it. Nevertheless, the forecast itself may be expressed as a range of values. As Keynes said, it is often "better to be vaguely right than precisely wrong."

Preparation of *a general macroeconomic forecast* which indicates the current and expected state of economic activity is a function of most business economists. There are three purposes for which such an overall view may be required. First, the economist may use the broad forecast to conduct an ongoing process of informing management of the current state of, and expected changes in, business conditions. This flow of updated information permits management to adapt to a changing environment. Second, the firm may wish to publish its view of economic conditions for the benefit of its customers. This is especially true for brokerage houses and many large banks where the internal economic forecast is shared with clients as an added service. In addition, there are economic consulting firms and publications, the main function of which is to publish such output. Finally, even if the results of an overall forecast are not published outside the economics department, it may be a necessary prerequisite to preparing a narrower forecast. In the example above for carpet demand, while it may be true that carpet demand can be forecast on the basis of one measure alone—say housing starts—in order to derive the expected value of that measure, it may be necessary to prepare an overall forecast. The economist need not derive the overall forecast from scratch; it may be possible to use some published macroeconomic forecast either as is, or with only slight modification.

The narrower *firm or industry forecast*, referred to just above, has grown in importance in recent years in business management and planning. The focus of these forecasts is usually restricted to measures of the firm's or industry's performance. In particular, determining the potential demand for the firm's products is crucial to deciding how much to produce and at what price it can be sold. Thus, while the macroeconomic background may be important as a setting, the industry economist is more concerned about microeconomic concepts as the amount and strength of demand, how much should be produced, and at what price.

Long-term forecasts are required for strategic, as opposed to operational, planning. A long-term forecast—covering five to twenty years—is not merely a macroeconomic forecast for which the forecast horizon has been extended. There are fundamental differences between the two approaches. Policy variables may be the most important determinants of a short-term forecast. In the long term, policy-makers, and thus the policies, are likely to change as the horizon is extended. Therefore, the impact of policy will be downplayed in a long-term forecast. On the other hand, many background factors—such as population growth, technology, and the rate of capital accumulation—which are regarded as nearly constant in a shorter-term forecast, are regarded as variables in a long-term forecast, which may influence the outcome. A long-term forecast need not be fixed forever. Its most useful role may well be in tracking the changes in the outlook. As these changes emerge from one version to another it becomes possible for managers to recognize the reasons for these changes and to respond to these factors in their own planning.

HOW BUSINESS ECONOMISTS FORECAST

The exact method by which a forecast is compiled may vary, but the logical sequence which leads to the forecast has several common features. The main concern of this book is with this methodological question. Consequently, a complete answer to the question in the section heading can not be given here, but some of the chief components of forecasting can be described with the detail to be filled in by later chapters.

The first step in any forecast is to start with a theoretical model of the process being forecast. A model may have a quantitative form, but it need not. It is only necessary that the model offer a description in simple terms of the way an economic process works. A quantitative model is usual, however, and it may be either univariate (*time series*) or multivariate (*structural*).

In either case, the model will process data to arrive at a forecast solution. A time series model uses past values of a data series to forecast current and future values. Time series models are most useful when information about the structure of the process is lacking, or a theoretical explanation is inadequate. A structural model uses one or more theoretic relationships—or equations—to determine forecast values for one or more variables. It is not necessary that the forecast method be complex; simple methods are often best. Thus a forecast may be derived by merely extending a straight line of past values for some measure, or, at another extreme, may be the result of a simultaneously-determined set of complex equations. In either case a model is being solved.

Economic forecasts are usually expressed in some quantitative form. Data on economic activity may be used to forecast future levels or growth rates. Thus knowledge of data sources is another important input to an economist's forecast. Most often, data used will be government-compiled; however at times industry sources or a firm's own records are used. This is especially true when the forecast is of sales or some other specific performance measure which is not public reported.

A forecast can be expressed in qualitative terms. The merit in such a course is that it avoids the danger of providing a false sense of precision that a quantitative forecast may suggest. The difficulty is in providing enough real information to permit operational decisions to be made. Forecasts are supposed to reduce uncertainty, not add to it.

The goal of reducing uncertainty should always be kept in mind by the business economist. This end can be achieved by: (1) starting with a model of the economic process being forecast; (2) solving this model in a consistent, logical manner; and (3) expressing the results in the clearest, simplest manner so that management can easily discern the operational implications of the forecast.

Some consideration should be given to the cost-benefit tradeoffs between detailed and "core" forecasts, and between "in-house" forecast models and those available from commercial vendors. Constructing, maintaining, and solving detailed economic forecast models is an expensive operation. This expense should be viewed not only in terms of salaries and computing costs, but also in terms of the resource costs of both the forecasters and management. If these talented people were not involved in economic forecasting, and management's time were not taken up in digesting and implementing the forecasts, it could be allocated more directly to other business operations. Of course, then the benefits of having the forecast results would be lost. Weighing the relative costs and benefits of having an economic forecast is usually a decision of senior management. The economist, however, can help by providing the necessary input for their decision and by providing different plans arranged by detail and cost. The chief benefit of an in-house forecast is that the assumptions are tailored to the needs of the business and can be more easily challenged and changed than if externally prepared. Moreover, commercially-supplied forecasts are expensive. Many firms find it worthwhile to subscribe to a commercial forecast to get an overview and then perform in-house modifications to adapt the forecast to the specific needs of the firm. Once again, this is a question about which management will likely have the final say, but the economist should have a view on it and make this view known.

FOR WHOM BUSINESS ECONOMISTS FORECAST

As has already been stated, most business forecasts are prepared for senior management to use in developing short-term and long-term policies. For this reason, business economists usually report at a fairly high level in the corporate hierarchy. It is quite common for the senior economist to report directly to the chief executive officer. In addition, however, economic forecasts may often be used by line groups in setting group budgets and plans. In some firms—particularly in the banking and brokerage industries—economists may have direct client contact, providing briefings or supplying advice on behalf of the firm.

In all cases the business economist should keep in mind the interests of the audience addressed. Reports should be concise and offer operational suggestions, but they should avoid excessive detail. The detailed analysis should be conducted and can be supplied on request, but it should not clutter the report.

QUESTIONS FOR REVIEW AND RESEARCH

1-1   A forecast, as opposed to a prediction, states a future outcome conditionally, on the basis of certain explicit assumptions. Review the broad economic trends for the past year—year-over-year real GNP growth, inflation, the change in the unemployment rate, and the change in the Federal funds rate. (a) State some of the assumptions about economic policy and conditions which a year earlier an economic forecaster might have included in a correct forecast. (b) Explain how slightly altered assumptions might have led to a different outcome.

1-2   Examine the economic forecast contained in the latest *Budget of the United States Government* (published each year in late January). Identify the key assumptions which underlie the forecast and evaluate the forecast in light of subsequent development.

1-3   Review recent issues of *Business Week, Forbes,* and *Fortune* and identify instances where independent economic forecasts for the coming twelve months have been cited. Try to classify these forecasts on a scale from the most to the least optimistic. In coming weeks, watch for changes, or evaluations of these forecasts.

1-4   Choose an industry that interests you. Now assume you are the chief executive officer (CEO) of a leading firm in that industry. List the economic indicators that you, as CEO, would be most interested in receiving regular forecasts of. (How often, and for what time period?)

This exercise should regularly be conducted by all business economic forecasters for the firms in which they are employed. Are there indicators you might think are more important at one time than another?

SUGGESTED ADDITIONAL READINGS FOR CHAPTER 1

BAILS, DALE G. AND LARRY C. PEPPERS. *Business Fluctuations: Forecasting Techniques and Applications*. Englewood Cliffs, NJ: Prentice-Hall, 1982.

BUTLER, WILLIAM F., ROBERT A. KAVESH, AND ROBERT B. PLATT. *Methods and Techniques of Business Forecasting,* Ch. 1, "Economic Forecasting: Some Introductory Remarks." Englewood Cliffs, NJ: Prentice-Hall, 1974.

ECKSTEIN, OTTO. *The DRI Model of the U.S. Economy*. New York: McGraw-Hill, 1983. Chs. 1 and 2 provide an especially good discussion of the postwar evolution of macroeconomic forecasting models.

WHITMAN, MARINA VON NEUMAN. "Economics from Three Perspectives," *Business Economics* (Jan. 1983), pp. 20–24.

2

THEORETICAL MODELS
The foundation of economic forecasting

INTRODUCTION

The process of economic forecasting starts with the specification of the activity to be forecast. Economic theory is rich in models which explain economic activities in total and in detail. This wealth of theory, in turn, serves as the basis for most economic forecasting.

As a general forecasting rule, every effort should be made to keep a model as simple as is consistent with the need to explain the activity under study. This stress on simplicity differs from the approach followed by an economic theorist. The theorist aims at the most complete possible specification of an economic process and, thus, may use many complex explanatory variables to achieve this end. The forecaster, on the other hand, must remember that all values for explanatory variables in future periods must themselves be forecast. Thus, the forecaster is often faced with the dilemma of a particular measure, likely to provide a good explanation of the activity to be forecast, but which itself is even more difficult to forecast accurately than the activity it is meant to explain. Thus simplicity in forecast model specification is not only desirable; in most cases it is a constraint imposed on the forecaster.

This chapter examines two basic economic models: in section I, the IS-LM and aggregate demand and supply models which are at the core of *macroeconomic* analysis; and in section II, the market demand and supply models which form the core of *price* or *microeconomic* theory. The discussion is purposely kept brief since it is assumed the reader is already familiar with these analyses. Moreover, more detailed and specific statements of these relationships will be developed in Part II of the text.

I. A MACROECONOMIC SYSTEM

The overall, or *macro-,* economy consists of demands and supplies of real goods (the actual volume of commodities and services), money, and of productive factors, and the valuation of these real goods and services in money terms. A macroeconomic model should aim at reducing the complex workings of the economy to the fewest *functional relationships* which remain realistic and yet still solve for the particular variables to be forecast.

A basic mathematical rule is that there must be at least one independent equation for each variable to be solved for (the "unknowns"). Clearly, the fewer the number of "unknowns" in a model, or system of equations, the simpler the model will be; but also, the less fully will such a model reflect the workings of a complex economy. The virtue in keeping the model simple is that it strips away the layers of confusing detail to expose the most basic aspects of the underlying system. It is then possible to re-introduce detail, and in this way examine how a more complicated—and more realistic—system changes the outcomes of the basic model.

The approach illustrated here is to construct a system which solves for the equilibrium values of four variables

$$y = \text{real GNP}$$

$$r = \text{the interest rate}[1]$$

$$P = \text{the price level}$$

$$L = \text{the level of employment}$$

This model is based on the seminal article by Hicks[2] which is the basis for most macroeconomic analysis and Smith's[3] model for determining the aggregate levels of prices and employment. Thus, the model solves for the equilibrium conditions in the goods, money, and labor markets. These variables represent some of the most important measures of macroeconomic activity and, thus, provide an important theoretical model for use in forecasting.

EQUILIBRIUM IN THE GOODS AND MONEY MARKETS: DETERMINANTS OF AGGREGATE DEMAND

The Goods Market

The starting point for a macroeconomic model is the *consumption function*. This states that consumption in real (constant price) terms is a function of real income. Moreover, Keynes' assertion that there is a "fundamental psychological law" that consumption will always change in line with changes in income, but by less than the full change in income,[4] has been widely confirmed and accepted. This relationship is shown in equation 2-1, which shows that real consumer spending (c, lower case letters are used to depict *real* volumes) rises as a function of real income (y, equal to real

---

[1] Clearly, there is no one interest rate. However, r can either be regarded as an average interest rate across some maturity-risk range, or as an indicative interest rate such as the Federal funds rate, the six-month Treasury bill rate, or the prime rate.

[2] John R. Hicks, "Mr. Keynes and the 'Classics': A Suggested Interpretation," *Econometrica*, V (1937), 147–59.

[3] Warren L. Smith, "A Graphical Exposition of the Complete Keynesian System," in Warren L. Smith and Ronald L. Teigen, *Readings in Money, National Income, and Stabilization Policy* (Homewood, IL: Richard D. Irwin, 1970), pp. 74–111.

[4] John Maynard Keynes, *The General Theory of Employment, Interest, and Money* (London: Macmillan, 1936), p. 96.

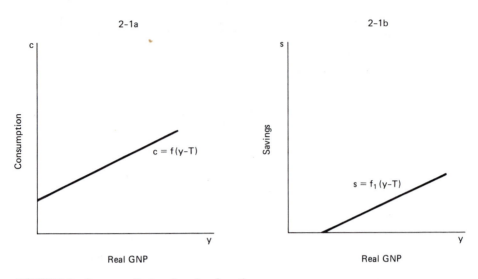

FIGURE 2-1   **Consumption and saving functions**

GNP), but the change in consumption (Δ, or delta, is used to depict change) is less than the change in income.[5]

$$c = f(y) \qquad\qquad (2\text{-}1)$$

where $\qquad\qquad\qquad 0 < \dfrac{\Delta c}{\Delta y} < 1$

Realistically, income can be used for three purposes: to consume goods and services to pay taxes, and to be saved. If taxes (T) are assumed to be a function of income, and recognizing there is no choice in paying taxes, then real consumption must be regarded as a function of after-tax, or disposable, income. Moreover, savings can be regarded as a residual activity. That is, after-tax income that is not spent is saved and thus saving can be viewed as a function of after-tax income. These relationships can be expressed as in equations 2-1a, 2-1b, and 2-1c.

$$c = f(y - T) \qquad\qquad (2\text{-}1a)$$

[5] This is a simple form of the consumption function. More complex theories include: Duesenberry's Relative Income Hypothesis, Friedman's Permanent Income Hypothesis, and Modigliani and Ando's Life Cycle Hypothesis. See James S. Duesenberry, *Income, Saving, and the Theory of Consumer Behavior* (Cambridge, MA: Harvard Univ. Press, 1949); Milton Friedman, *A Theory of the Consumption Function* (New York: National Bureau of Economic Research, Inc., 1955); and Franco Modigliani and Albert Ando, "The Life Cycle Hypothesis of Saving: Aggregate Implications and Tests," *American Economic Review* (1963), pp. 55–84.

where
$$0 < \frac{\Delta c}{\Delta(y - T)} < 1$$

$$s = f_1(y - T) \tag{2-1b}$$

where
$$0 < \frac{\Delta s}{\Delta(y - T)} < 1$$

and
$$T = f_2(Y) \tag{2-1c}$$

where
$$0 < \frac{\Delta T}{\Delta Y} < 1$$

The consumption and saving relationships can also be depicted graphically as in Figure 2-1a and 2-1b.

Equations 2-1a through 2-1c account for one of the two concepts of GNP, *income,* where income is disposed of by consuming, saving, and paying taxes. Recalling that every dollar of income is generated by the production of *output,* the other concept of GNP, an identity showing these two concepts can be stated.

$$c + s + t \equiv y \equiv c + i + g + (x - m)$$

$$\text{Income} \qquad\qquad \text{Output}$$

Output consists of consumption, investment (i), government spending (g), and net exports—exports (x) less imports (m)—all expressed in real terms.

Since consumption appears on both sides of the identity, the relationship can be simplified by excluding it. The identity can be further simplified by rearranging the foreign sector: imports are regarded as a special form of consumption and are also a function of after-tax income ($m = f_3(y - T)$). Exports are determined by demand abroad which is exogenous, or determined outside the model. Thus the goods market equilibrium condition becomes.

$$s + t + m = i + g_0 + x_0. \tag{2-2}$$

Note that all the variables on the left-hand side of the equation are functions of real GNP. It will be assumed that government spending is a policy variable determined outside the model, and thus like real exports is exogenous. (The symbols for both real government spending and real exports are subscripted to indicate that they are exogenous variables.) Thus, of the variables needed to produce equilibrium in the goods market only investment still needs to be explained.

In considering investment there are a number of key points.

(1) Investment in economics refers to the purchase of capital goods in the form of additions to plants, producers' durable equipment, and inventories. Thus, investment represents a change in the real capital stock ($i = \Delta k$).

(2) This addition may merely be to replace worn-out capital, or to effect a net increase in the capital stock.

(3) Because of the durable nature of capital assets, what is really purchased when the asset is acquired is a *flow of capital services over time*. This last point is particularly important in specifying an investment function because it underscores the fact that a current action—the decision to invest—is based on the expectation of a return—the flow of output generated by the capital services—which will accrue over time.

Businesses can rank investment opportunities by their discounted rates of return. That is, a discount rate (d) can be found that, when compounded and divided into the expected stream of returns, causes the present discounted value of the sum of the returns to just equal the cost of the capital asset as in 2-3.

$$C = \frac{R_t}{1 + d} + \frac{R_{t+1}}{(1+d)^2} + \cdots + \frac{R_{t+n}}{(1+d)^n} \qquad (2\text{-}3)$$

where C = cost of the capital asset
    R = expected return per period
    d = rate of discount

When rates of discount are calculated for a range of investment projects, they can be ranked, forming a schedule which Keynes termed the marginal efficiency of capital.[6] Figure 2-2a portrays such a schedule. The business can then contrast these rates of return with a relevant interest rate. It will invest in those projects which yield a discounted rate of return greater than or equal to the prevailing interest rate. Thus investment can be viewed as an inverse function of interest rates as in 2-4. If the interest rate

$$i = h(r) \qquad (2\text{-}4)$$

where $$\frac{\Delta i}{\Delta r} < 0$$

declines, additional projects will become viable and, thus, total investment will increase. Conversely, if the interest rate rises, projects which earlier

[6] John Maynard Keynes, *The General Theory of Employment, Interest, and Money*, Ch. 11, pp. 135–46. For a superb treatment of investment theory, see Gardner Ackley, *Macroeconomic Theory* (New York: Macmillan, 1961), Ch. XVII.

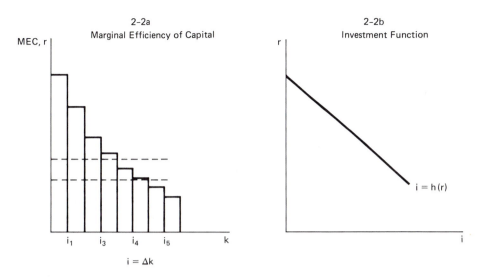

FIGURE 2-2   **Marginal efficiency of capital and investment functions**

were viable cease to be so, and so total investment declines. When this relationship is aggregated for the entire economy, a smooth investment function like that depicted in Figure 2-2b can be derived.

With all the variables in equation 2-2 now identified as either functional relations or exogenously- or policy-determined, the goods market equilibrium can be expressed in functional form as in 2-5.

$$s + m + t = i + g + x \tag{2-2}$$

$$f_1(y - T) + f_3(y - T) + f_2(Y) = h(r) + g_0 + x_0 \tag{2-5}$$

or simplifying,

$$F(y) = h(r) + g_0 + x_0 \tag{2-6}$$

where $F(\ )$ is the reduced form version of the saving, import, and tax functions. Equation 2-6 is expressed in terms of two unknown variables, real GNP and the interest rate. This can be represented by a schedule of GNP and interest rate combinations each of which represents equilibrium in the goods market. This schedule is depicted by the IS curve shown in Figure 2-3.[7]

---

[7] For a more complete graphical exposition of the construction of the IS curve the reader is referred to any standard macroeconomic text, such as Thomas F. Dernburg and Duncan M. McDougall, *Macroeconomics: The Measurement, Analysis, and Control of Aggregate Economic Activity*, 6th ed. (New York: McGraw-Hill, 1980), pp. 140–43.

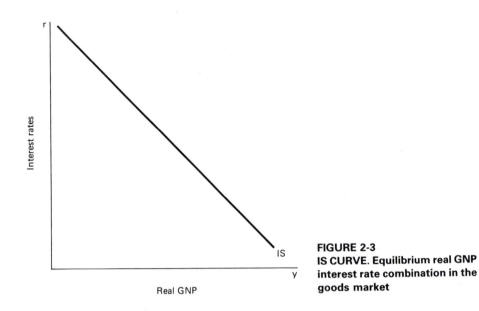

FIGURE 2-3
IS CURVE. Equilibrium real GNP interest rate combination in the goods market

The Money Market

Like any other market, the money market is defined by demand and supply; in this case the demand and supply of money balances.

There are several definitions of the money supply. The one used here is the most basic one, M-1, which defines money as currency plus demand and other checkable deposits. The chief feature of this concept is that currency and checks are perfectly liquid money assets. Other, wider, definitions of the money supply include assets which are less liquid.[8]

In this simple model it will be assumed that the money supply—like government spending and the parameters of the tax function—is determined outside the model by the economic policy makers. It might be argued that reaction functions for fiscal and monetary policy can be estimated, thus making the money supply (and government spending and the tax function) endogenous. While policy functions can be estimated, the evidence of recent years suggests the functions are not stable.[9]

The money supply (M) is expressed in current dollar terms since it represents the amount of current assets supplied. However the demand for money appears more likely to be a real demand. Thus, the money supply-demand identity is expressed as in 2-7.

[8] These other measures are defined in Chapter 3. A more detailed discussion of the actual demand and supply of money is offered in Chapter 9.

[9] This is a topic taken up in Chapter 9. The interested reader may refer to Ronald L. Teigen, "The Demand for and Supply of Money," in Ronald L. Teigen, ed., *Readings in Money, National Income, and Stabilization Policy* (Homewood, IL: Richard D. Irwin, 1978), pp. 54–81.

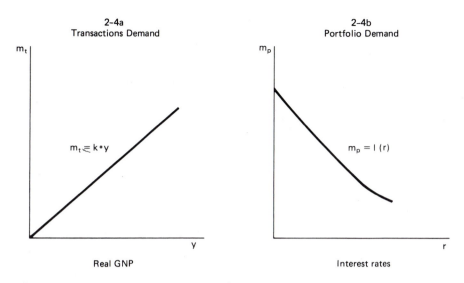

FIGURE 2-4   Demand for money functions

$$\frac{M_0}{P} \equiv m \qquad (2\text{-}7)$$

The demand for money can be divided into two parts: a portion which is proportional to the level of real GNP, called the *transactions demand*; and a portion which is inversely related to the rate of interest, called the *portfolio demand*.

The transactions demand for money (m_t) merely recognizes that since money is used as a medium of exchange, the public will hold money balances in some proportion to their total transactions, which are in this case proxied by real GNP. This relationship is shown in equation 2-8 and figure 2-4a.

$$m_t = k * y \qquad (2\text{-}8)$$

where $\qquad k = \dfrac{\Delta m_t}{\Delta_y} > 0$

The portfolio demand for real money balances is Tobin's[10] term for the concept Keynes originally called the speculative demand.[11] Keynes' concept assumed that wealth holders would hold all their wealth in one of two assets:

[10] James Tobin, "Liquidity Preference as Behavior Towards Risk," *Review of Economic Studies*, Feb. 1958, pp. 65–86.

[11] John Maynard Keynes, *The General Theory of Employment, Interest, and Money*, pp. 170–74.

(1) interest bearing, but risky, bonds; or (2) non-interest bearing, but risk-free, money balances. The reward from high interest rates would lead investors to liquidate their money balances and to hold just bonds. Conversely, when interest rates declined, investors would sell their bonds and hold money balances so as to be poised to buy bonds when interest rates rose again. Tobin's approach is less restrictive. It recognizes the existence of more than just these two forms of wealth assets, and also that wealth holders can maintain a portfolio of assets, including money balances, depending on the risks and rewards of holding wealth in different forms and the liquidity preferences of investors. In Tobin's theory, interest rates represent an opportunity cost of holding assets in the form of money balances. In earlier articles, Tobin and Baumol showed that even the size of transactions balances could be partly related to the opportunity cost represented by interest rates.[12] The key point is that a large number of theoretic and empirical studies have shown the existence of an inverse relationship between the demand for real money balances and interest rates. This relationship is shown in equation 2-9 and depicted in Figure 2-4b. (The existence of a horizontal section of the curve, such as in Keynes' original specification, is more questionable, and then only in an extreme depression case such as existed at the time *The General Theory* was written.)

$$m_p = l(r) \qquad (2\text{-}9)$$

where
$$\frac{\Delta m_p}{\Delta r} < 0$$

The two parts of the demand for real money balances can be substituted in equation 2-7 to form the supply-demand equilibrium condition in the money market.

$$\frac{M_0}{P} = m_t + m_p$$

$$\frac{M_0}{P} = k * y + l(r) \qquad (2\text{-}10)$$

This relationship describes a schedule of real GNP and interest rate combinations that produce equilibrium between supply and demand in the money

[12] William J. Baumol, "The Transactions Demand for Cash: An Inventory Theoretic Approach", *Quarterly Journal of Economics,* November, 1952, pp. 545–56; and James Tobin, "The Interest-Elasticity of Transactions Demand for Cash", *Review of Economics and Statistics* (Aug. 1956), pp. 241–47.

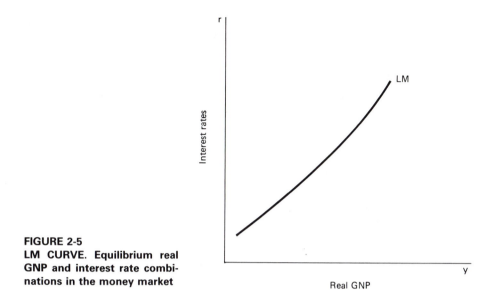

FIGURE 2-5
LM CURVE. Equilibrium real GNP and interest rate combinations in the money market

market. This LM curve is shown in Figure 2-5.[13] The precise shape of the LM curve depends on the value for the policy variable, M_0, the (so far) exogenous variable, P, the proportionality constant, k, and the parameters of equation 2-9, the portfolio demand for money.

Once again, unique equilibrium values for real GNP and the interest rate are not determined because these are both "unknowns" in equation 2-10. However, when the equilibrium condition in the goods market (equation 2-6) is combined with the equilibrium condition in the money market (equation 2-10) it can be seen that these two relationships are specified in terms of the same two unknowns: y and r.

$$\text{IS:} \quad F(y) = h(r) + g_0 + x_0 \qquad\qquad (2\text{-}6)$$

$$\text{LM:} \quad \frac{M_0}{P} = k * y + l(r) \qquad\qquad (2\text{-}10)$$

When these equations are solved simultaneously, a unique real GNP-interest rate combination can be found that will bring about equilibrium in both the goods and money markets. This solution is shown graphically in Figure 2-6. The equations for the IS and LM curve relations, thus, solve for two of the

---

[13] For a more complete graphical exposition see Dernburg and McDougall, *Macroeconomics*, pp. 142–45, or any standard text.

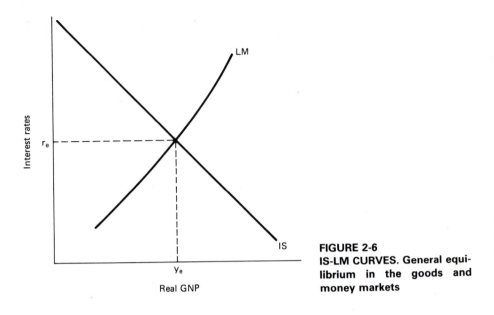

FIGURE 2-6
IS-LM CURVES. General equilibrium in the goods and money markets

four aggregate variables of this basic macroeconomic system. In addition, they provide the medium for deriving an aggregate demand function.

AGGREGATE DEMAND: THE EFFECT OF PRICE CHANGES

This IS function can be solved for the interest rate in terms of real GNP as in equation 2-6a, where h′ represents the transformed parameters of the investment function, $i = h(r)$.[14]

$$r = h'(F(y) - g_0 - x_0) \qquad (2\text{-}6a)$$

Equation 2-6a can then be substituted into 2-10 and solved for real GNP. Because these relationships are expressed in functional form the algebra is

---

[14] For instance, using specific functions, if

$$F(y) = 20 + 0.6 * y$$

$$g_0 = 100, \ x_0 = 40, \text{ and}$$

$$h(r) = 50 - 0.2 * r$$

then

$$\text{IS:} \quad 20 + 0.6 * y = (50 - 0.2 * r) + 100 + 40$$
$$r = 850 - 3 * y.$$

cumbersome. Nevertheless, real GNP can be shown to be a function of: the nominal money supply, the price level, real government spending, real exports, and the proportionality constant k. The function l' is composed of the transformed parameters from the saving, import, tax, investment, and portfolio demand functions. This reduced form function is shown in 2-10a.

$$y = 1'(M_0, P, g_0, x_0, k) \tag{2-10a}$$

If all variables except prices are held constant, it can be shown that the equilibrium level of real GNP will vary inversely with the price level. In other words, a demand curve for total output (y) as a function of the aggregate price level (P) can be derived. Figure 2-7 shows this graphically: a fall in the price level from P_1 to P_2 causes the LM curve to shift, resulting in an increase in the equilibrium level of real GNP from y_1 to y_2. A series of such shifts would produce the aggregate demand curve shown in Figure 2-7b. The decline in prices in this instance results in an increase in the real money supply

$$\left(\frac{M_0}{P_2} > \frac{M_0}{P_1}\right)$$

just as if the nominal money supply had increased. Thus, interest rates decline, investment increases, real GNP increases, leading to further induced increases in consumption, saving, tax payments, and imports.

When combined with an aggregate supply curve, the aggregate demand curve can be used to solve for the aggregate price level.

FIGURE 2-7   Derivation of aggregate demand curve

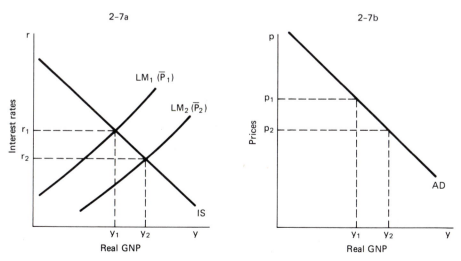

AGGREGATE SUPPLY: EQUILIBRIUM IN THE LABOR MARKET

The supply of total goods produced in the economy depends upon: factor availability, technology, and utilization of the factors of production. In the short run, the level of employment—the utilization of labor services—is the more variable factor of production. This can be seen from the production function shown in equation 2-11 and in Figure 2-8.

$$y = \emptyset(L, \overline{K}) \tag{2-11}$$

In the short run, real output (y) is a function of employment (L) given a fixed capital stock (K). Over longer periods, the capital stock can increase as a result of net investment. Increases in the capital stock will result in the entire production function shifting upwards, as in Figure 2-8 where net investment increases the capital stock from $\overline{K}_1$ to $\overline{K}_2$. As a result the same amount of labor can produce more output since it has more capital to work with—the marginal productivity of labor $\left(\dfrac{\Delta y}{\Delta L}\right)$ has increased. However, in the short run, the level of real output can be chiefly regarded as a function of employment. The amount of labor employed is, in turn, a function of the demand and supply of labor.

The demand and supply of labor services is expressed in hours (that is, the number of workers employed times hours worked per worker). The demand for labor is equal to the marginal revenue product of labor (MRP_L).

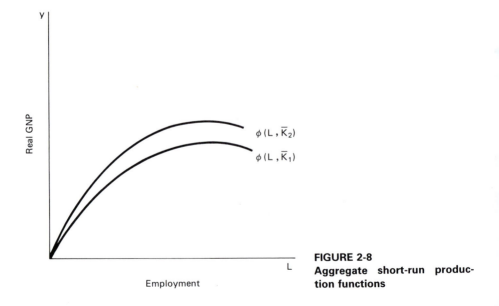

FIGURE 2-8
Aggregate short-run production functions

The marginal revenue product itself consists of two basic components which contribute to a firm's revenue and, ultimately, profits: the marginal productivity of labor $\left(MP_L = \dfrac{\Delta y}{\Delta L}\right)$, and the firm's marginal revenue $\Big($the change in total revenue due to the last unit of output sold, $MR = \dfrac{\Delta TR}{\Delta y}\Big)$, itself a function of the demand curve for the product, and thus a function of price. Thus, the total demand for labor can be shown to be a function of the marginal productivity of labor and prices as in equation 2-12.

$$D_L = MP_L * MR \tag{2-12}$$

$$= f(L) * P$$

Labor is supplied according to workers' utility tradeoff between leisure and income, which Keynes referred to as the disutility of labor.[15] That is, individuals give up leisure in return for income, represented by an hourly wage (W). It is crucial that workers have some "money illusion," that is, that they supply their labor for a money wage, or an imperfectly adjusted real wage. (Since wages are not adjusted every time prices change, this is a reasonable assumption.) Thus the supply of labor is a function of money wages, as in equation 2-13.

$$S_L = f(W) \tag{2-13}$$

Thus, the equilibrium condition for the labor market is described by equation 2-14, where the supply of labor is a function of the money wage, and the demand is a function of employment (the marginal product of labor) and the price level. Importantly, as shown in Figure 2-9, starting from

$$f(W) = f(L) * P \tag{2-14}$$

less than full employment ($L < L_{fe}$), if prices increase the demand for labor will increase without being (fully) matched by a change in the supply of labor. Since increased employment leads to increased output (by means of the production function in Figure 2-8 and equation 2-11), a positive relationship exists between prices and real output that may be termed the aggregate supply curve.

The derivation of the aggregate supply curve can be traced in Figure 2-10. Given a particular price level (P_1), a demand for labor curve can be derived which, when combined with a supply of labor curve, solves for an equilibrium money wage rate and employment level. The equilibrium level of

[15] Keynes, *The General Theory of Employment,* pp. 5–6.

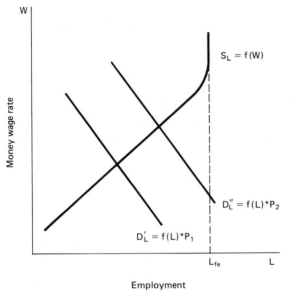

FIGURE 2-9
Demand and supply for labor

employment, in turn, is consistent with a particular level of real output which is also consistent with the price level. The process can be repeated for other price levels to derive an aggregate supply curve. The aggregate supply curve is upward sloping and eventually becomes vertical at full employment, given the capital stock. (If the capital stock increases, the production function shifts upward, the marginal product of labor increases, and the aggregate supply curve will shift outwards.)

The intersection of the aggregate demand and supply curves determines the price level that is consistent with the equilibrium level of real output. In turn, the equilibrium level of real output can be traced back to a particular level of employment through the production function and an average money wage rate through the demand and supply functions for labor.

SUMMARY

These basic IS-LM, aggregate demand-supply models serve as a rich theoretical source of information about the macroeconomy. The IS-LM models together, provide a simultaneous set of equations which solve for the equilibrium levels of real GNP and the interest rate.

$$\text{IS:} \quad F(y) = h(r) + g_0 + x_0 \tag{2-6}$$

$$\text{LM:} \quad \frac{M_0}{P} = k * y + 1(r) \tag{2-10}$$

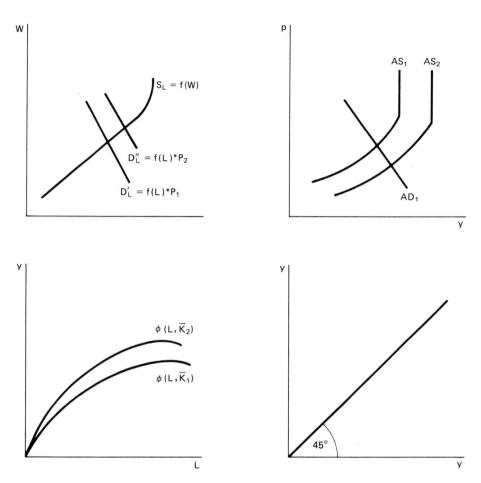

FIGURE 2-10   Aggregate demand and supply. Equilibrium in the labor market.

By varying the price level in equation 2-10 it is possible to effect shifts in the LM curve and, thus, in the equilibrium level of real GNP. Thus an aggregate demand curve can be specified as in 2-15 (based on equation 2-10a).

$$\text{AD:}\quad y = d(P) \tag{2-15}$$

The short-run production function (where the capital stock is assumed constant) provides a relationship between employment and real GNP. Employment itself is determined by the demand and supply of labor services; the former is a function of labor (MP_L) and prices, the latter is a function of the money wage rate. When these relationships are solved together an aggregate supply function can be derived.

$$\text{Demand for Labor:} \quad D_L = f(L) * P \qquad (2\text{-}12)$$

$$\text{Supply of Labor:} \quad S_L = f(W) \qquad (2\text{-}13)$$

$$\text{Production Function:} \quad y = \emptyset(L, \overline{K}) \qquad (2\text{-}11)$$

$$\text{Aggregate Supply:} \quad y = s(P, L, \overline{K}) \qquad (2\text{-}16)$$

Finally, equilibrium between aggregate demand and supply produces the equilibrium levels of employment and prices.

In Parts II and III of the text these theoretical relationships will be used as the core around which empirical forecasts will be structured.

II. THE MICROECONOMICS OF THE FIRM: DEMAND AND SUPPLY

The aggregate measures of economy-wide macroeconomic activity which are the focus of the model in the preceeding section are important inputs to many business forecasts. Of more basic concern to most business forecasters, however, are the demand and supply conditions that characterize the markets in which their firms operate. These market conditions—the total likely demand for the product, the potential supply from all sources, the cost of producing it, and the price at which it can be sold—often depend on macroeconomic inputs, but solution is usually at a less aggregate level. This section reviews the main features of market demand and supply and suggests ways in which models for these processes can be developed.

Market Demand

The market demand for a product is characterized by the market demand curve and function. A typical demand curve is shown in Figure 2-11a and the demand function is presented in equation 2-17. There are three key aspects

$$Q_{dt} = f_d(P_t, \overline{Y}_t, \overline{P}_{ot}, \overline{T}_t, \overline{N}_t) \qquad (2\text{-}17)$$

about the demand relationship.

First, the demand curve usually slopes downward to the right, reflecting the basic relationship between the quantity demanded of the good (Q_d) and the price of the good (P). More will be demanded as the price decreases, all other conditions equal. Less will be demanded as the price rises.

The second aspect concerns the phrase "all other conditions equal." Other variables—including income (Y), prices of other related goods (P_o), consumer tastes and preferences (T), and the number of consumers in the market (N)—

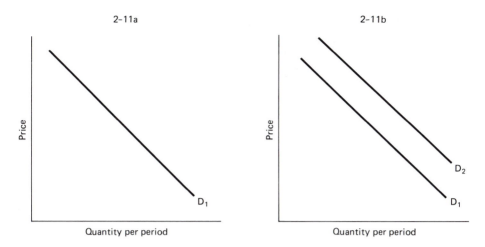

FIGURE 2-11   Market demand curve and demand curve shifts

also affect the demand for the good, but in a secondary way. That is, the main factor affecting the quantity of a good demanded at a *point in time* is the price of the good. The primacy of this relationship is represented in the function's notation by the little bars over income, other prices, taste, and population. The bars, denote these *exogenous* factors are assumed given and fixed. Their values, however, determine the demand curve's position in price-quantity space; if the value of any of the exogenous values changes for any reason, the demand curve may shift, as in Figure 2-11b.

The third key aspect of the demand function is that it is specified for a particular time frame. This is important because as the time frame lengthens, the exogenous variables are more likely to change. Moreover, since forecasters are mainly concerned with determining the value of measures *over time,* particular stress is placed on the changes in these exogenous variables. The time trend of these variables can often be forecast using a macroeconomic model.[16]

Market Supply

The supply of a product to a market is represented by a supply curve and function as shown in Figure 2-12a and equation 2-18, respectively. The key aspects of the

$$Q_{st} = f_s(P_t, \overline{P}_{Lt}, \overline{P}_{Kt}, (\overline{K/L})_t, \overline{Z}_t) \qquad (2\text{-}18)$$

[16] This is already the case with income (Y) in equation 2-17. It is only slightly less clear, but equally true, for the price of other goods (P_o), which usually can be approximated by the general price level (on the principle that the price of the particular good under study is not so important as to distort the general price trend when it is excluded). Population and populaton segments are often included in the output from a macroeconomic forecast. Quantifying tastes is more complicated, and is often done judgmentally. Fortunately, tastes change slowly and can often be ignored in short-term and medium-term forecasts, unless specific assumptions about such changes are made.

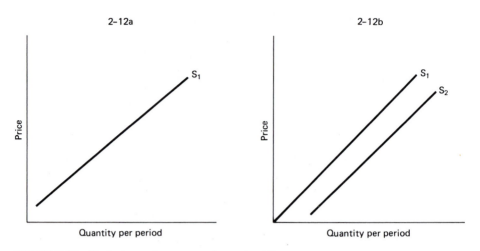

FIGURE 2-12   Market supply curve and supply shift

market supply curve are similar to those for the demand curve.

First, the supply curve usually slopes upward to the right, reflecting a positive relationship between the quantity of a product producers will supply as the price increases, all other conditions equal.

Once again, the other conditions which determine the supply curve's position in price-quantity space are indicated as given and fixed in equation 2-18 by little bars. These other influences are: factor prices—indicated in 2-18 by the price of labor (P_L), or the wage rate, and the price of capital (P_K)[17]—the state of technology (represented here by the capital/labor ratio in production, K/L), and the number of producers in the market (Z).

The supply relationship is also specified at a *point in time,* though it is the nature of forecasting to be concerned with *time trends.* Again, as with demand, the exogenous factors are likely to be changing over time, thus producing supply curve shifts.

Static Equilibrium, and Demand and Supply Curve Shifts

Standard microeconomic analysis focuses on market equilibrium for a particular market period, as is depicted in Figure 2-13. This static analysis does assume that the exogenous variables in equations 2-17 and 2-18 are given and fixed for the market period. Thus, the two equations form a model in two variables, the equilibrium price and quantity that will satisfy both consumers and producers.

---

[17] Of course, other less aggregate inputs to production can be specified. The decision to do so is usually an empirical one depending on the availability of data and the likelihood that an accurate forecast of the factor input prices can be prepared.

FIGURE 2-13
Market equilibrium

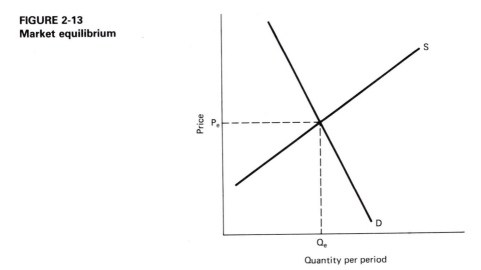

Quantity per period

As mentioned above, however, forecasters are mainly concerned with forecasting prices and quantities over time. This is complicated by the fact that the price and quantity combinations actually observed over time are the equilibrium points of a series of demand and supply curves which are, themselves, shifting over time. Thus, the time trend for price and quantity may well look like the dotted line AB shown in Figure 2-14. This curve is the result of a series of demand and supply curve shifts over time, which reflect

FIGURE 2-14   Demand and supply over time

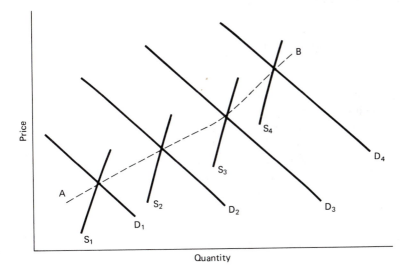

Quantity

changes in some or all of the exogenous variables in equations 2-17 and 2-18. For instance the demand curve will shift due to: (1) changes in income (ΔY), which in a growing economy will produce rightward shifts (increases) in the demand for a normal good; (2) changes in other prices (ΔP_o) can affect the relative affordability of the product;[18] (3) changes in tastes (ΔT) may directly affect the demand for the product; while (4) population growth (ΔN) usually increases demand. The supply curve can shift as a result of: (1) change(s) in factor prices (ΔP_L, ΔP_K), which will affect the cost of producing the product; (2) a change in technology, the ratio in which factors are used in production ($\Delta(K/L)$), which also affects the cost of production; and (3) changes in the number of producers (ΔZ).

Equations 2-17a and 2-18a are more general, time trend, versions of the earlier market demand and supply equations.

$$Q_{dt} = f_d(P_t, Y_t, P_{ot}, T_t, N_t) \qquad (2\text{-}17a)$$

$$Q_{st} = f_s(P_t, P_{Lt}, P_{Kt}, (K/L)_t, Z_t) \qquad (2\text{-}18a)$$

Here, the absence of the bars over the formerly given and fixed variables mean that these variables are now truly variable. As a result, these two equations are no longer sufficient to determine equilibrium—there are now more unknown variables than equations. In general, the variables other than the equilibrium price and quantity can be determined either by judgment or macroeconomic relationships. Then using forecast values for these measures, equations 2-17a and 2-18a can be solved. There will not be one equilibrium price and quantity, but rather an equilibrium price-quantity combination for each time period based on the forecast values for the other determinants in equations 2-17a and 2-18a.

III. THEORY IS THE BASIS FOR FORECASTING

The two basic theoretical systems—macro- and microeconomic—reviewed in this chapter summarize the core of standard economic analysis. More important for the purpose of this text, they will serve as the theoretical basis for the empirical forecasts developed in Parts II, III, and IV. This linkage reflects an important principle in economic forecasting referred to at the outset of this chapter. The economic forecaster is first and most basically an economist. The economist's in-depth knowledge of economic theory serves

---

[18] This is for the case of a general change in the price level. Changes in the prices of specific goods may exert stronger effects on demand if these goods are either substitute or complimentary goods to that under study.

as the basis for the effort to make sense out of often surprising economic developments and to aid in anticipating and forecasting these developments.

The relationships examined in this chapter were, in general, simple, standard ones. They were not the "state of the art" relationships often found in the theoretical literature. There is a simple reason for this. While more complex relationships may more fully explain past trends, the forecaster may be confounded by an inability to forecast the explanatory variables. Thus, a complex specification may require several additional relationships to estimate values for the explanatory variables. In addition to the empirical constraint imposed by data availability, there is a danger that as the forecast model becomes larger and more complex, the forecast errors also become more numerous and complex. In fact, as forecasting models are developed in the text, the relationships will become more complex than those presented here. However, the basic relationships, in general, have their roots in the simple relationships presented in this chapter.

The final message for the would-be forecaster from this chapter is: forecast models should always evolve from a theoretical model. Economic theory is the most powerful tool any economic forecaster has and it should be used.

QUESTIONS FOR REVIEW AND RESEARCH

2-1 Assume there is an economic model explained by 2-i and 2-ii.

$$Y = f(X_1, X_2, X_3) \qquad \text{(2-i)}$$

$$Z = f(X_2, U) \qquad \text{(2-ii)}$$

where X_1, X_2, and X_3 are known (exogenous) variables. Explain why this model can not be solved. Suppose it were known that $U = b^*X_1$. Would this fact alter the situation?

2-2 The IS-LM model is now a standard basis for macroeconomic analysis. It contains, however, a number of simplifying assumptions which have to be relaxed in a forecasting situation. Identify some of the simplifications in the IS-LM model and suggest ways of adapting the model relationships so that the model reflects the "real" world better.

2-3 The accelerator relationship hypothesizes that investment is positively related to the change in real income (Δy) in addition to being inversely related to the interest rate. Show how this more complex relationship can be graphically incorporated into the IS-LM system.

2-4 Consumption and saving were hypothesized in equations 2-1a and 2-1b to be functions of real disposable income alone. It may be argued, however, that consumer spending on high-priced durable goods is inversely related to the level of interest rates and that saving may be partly induced by interest rates. (a) Develop these hypotheses more fully, and (b) integrate your findings into a revised model for goods market equilibrium. You might also consider whether consumption and saving are affected equally by interest rates at all levels, or whether there is a certain threshold level they must reach before they begin to alter the basic spending-income and saving-income relationships.

2-5   The Economic Recovery Tax Act of 1981 (ERTA) was passed and enacted on the basis of ''supply-side'' assumptions that economic activity would be spurred by lower tax rates and, in turn, the increased economic activity would induce higher levels of saving, investment, and tax receipts. These assumptions were detailed in the *Economic Report of the President* for 1982.

   (a) Analyze and discuss the differences between this approach and the macroeconomic model described in this chapter.

   (b) Indicate how, if at all, the model described in this chapter should be modified to reflect this different approach.

   (c) Contrast the actual behavior of the U.S. economy between 1982 and 1984 with the forecast in the 1982 *Economic Report of the President*. Did ERTA achieve its goals?

2-6   The bend in the aggregate demand curve can be cited as an example of a tradeoff between wage inflation and unemployment. This tradeoff is known as the Phillips' Curve. See A. W. Phillips, ''The Relation Between Unemployment and the Rate of Change in Money Wage Rates in the United Kingdom, 1861–1957,'' reprinted in M. G. Mueller, ed., *Readings in Macroeconomics* (New York: Holt, Rinehart & Winston, 1966), pp. 245–56. Using annual data from the statistical section of the latest *Economic Report of The President,* plot the change in wage rates (average hourly earnings) and the unemployment rate for the years since World War II. Do they support Phillips' findings? See George L. Perry, ''Slowing the Wage-Price Spiral: the Macroeconomic View,'' in Arthur M. Okun and George L. Perry, eds., *Curing Chronic Inflation* (Washington, DC: The Brookings Institution, 1978), pp. 23–55.

2-7   Consider the demand for television sets since 1950. (Monthly data on production are contained in the *Survey of Current Business*.) Suggest how changes in income, prices of other goods, tastes, and population have affected this demand. If you were employed by a television manufacturer, what economic variables would you recommend be followed to help forecast demand?

3

ECONOMIC DATA
*The raw material
of forecasting*

When business economists prepare a forecast—whether of aggregate economic activity or of some variable or set of variables specific to their own firms—they use current and past economic data to support their forecasts. Often these data are derived from relevant sales or other market records compiled by the firm or some industry source. Usually, however, economic measures compiled by agencies of the Federal government are used to compliment these other data. Indeed, when a forecast of aggregate economic activity is the goal, government data are the principal, if not the only, inputs.

Data inputs are truly the raw material of forecasting. Thus, a thorough familiarity with the main economic series that the government compiles is vital to the forecaster. This chapter looks at three aspects of the most widely used U.S. government data series. First, the data series itself is described in terms of the economic concept it is intended to measure. Second, the characteristics of the series are described: the history of its compilation, how it is compiled, the main sources, its frequency (usually monthly, quarterly, or annually), and its reliability. Third, relationships with other data series—either as components or in a causal sense—are described.

The first topic in this chapter (section I) is a conceptual discussion of the National Income and Product Accounts (NIPA). These accounts represent the broadest and most often used measures of economic activity. Thus, a thorough knowledge of the concepts they express is a necessary attribute of the well-equipped business economist. The second section (II) discusses a variety of measures—most of which are reported monthly—of a less aggregate nature related to specific economic activities. Some of these measures are, in turn, used to construct the National Income and Product Accounts. Others serve important roles as proxies or inputs for forecasting total, and/ or some aspect of, economic activity. Section III examines the way in which the Bureau of Economic Analysis (BEA) of the Department of Commerce constructs the National Income and Product Accounts. Knowledge of this methodology can be helpful to the business economist in making "current quarter" estimates of the accounts, particularly GNP. Section IV discusses a number of data series less closely related to the National Income and Product Accounts, including: the monetary aggregates, interest rates, financial flows, foreign trade statistics, and foreign exchange rates.

I. NATIONAL INCOME AND PRODUCT ACCOUNTS: CONCEPTS

The National Income and Product Accounts comprise the principal measures of economic activity for the U.S. They are presented quarterly (at annual rates) by the Bureau of Economic Analysis, U.S. Department of Commerce. The basic concept in the accounts is that of Gross National Product (GNP).

GNP is the most widely used measure of economic activity by business economists; it purports to measure the nation's annual output of final goods and services. Indeed, the concept of GNP has become so familiar to even first-year economics students that it has acquired an aura of age-old permanence. In fact, the estimation of the gross national product is a rather recent development in economic analysis, and the development and improvement of the estimates and coverage of the National Income and Product Accounts is a dynamic process, still evolving. It is important for the business economist to recognize this fact, so as to be constantly alert to new developments and improvements in the presentation of the data. Thus, a brief history of the development of the National Income and Product Accounts in the U.S. is useful.[1]

The National Bureau of Economic Research, a private, nonprofit organization, began attempts to measure GNP shortly after its founding in 1922. In 1934, Simon Kuznets, who had been working under National Bureau auspices, prepared an annual estimate for the Department of Commerce. The estimates were continued on an annual basis through 1941. The approach of World War II and the theoretical impetus provided by John Maynard Keynes' *The General Theory of Employment, Interest, and Money* supplied further spurs to the development of the accounts. (The goal of economic preparedness just before and during World War II as a purpose for the accounts is less well understood today than it should be. It was necessary to transfer enormous amounts of resources from peacetime employment to the production of military material. The existence of these data in the U.S. and Great Britain was an important weapon in the effective use of economic resources in the conduct of the war.) The National Income Division of the Department of Commerce published the first quarterly estimates of GNP in the March 1942 issue of the *Survey of Current Business*. The *Survey* has been the official source of the quarterly and annual estimates of GNP ever since. The accounts have undergone periodic revision and development in the years since. The most recent such "benchmarking" was released at the end of 1980, and has been described in the monthly issues of the *Survey of Current Business* for 1981. Regular three-year revisions incorporating Internal Revenue Service (IRS) data are made and reported each July in the *Survey of Current Business*.

GNP is not just one concept but several. For instance, the annual output of all final goods and services can be viewed as the sum of all final goods and services *produced*—the national product accounts. Alternatively, GNP can be viewed as the sum of the *income* payments made to the owners of the factors of production used to produce the final output (with some modifications for depreciation, inventory valuation, and transfer payments)—the national income accounts. In addition, GNP can be compiled in both current dollar (market price) terms and constant dollar (real) terms.

---

[1] For a more detailed description and references to other source material, see John W. Kendrick, *Economic Accounts and Their Uses* (New York: McGraw-Hill, 1972).

Finally, economists often make the fine distinction between total output *produced* (*ex ante* GNP) and total *expenditures* for this output (*ex post* GNP).

A useful way to recognize these different concepts is to recall the circular flow diagram used in the basic economics course.

The top half of the diagram in Figure 3-1 depicts the flow of factor services from the household sector to the sector which employs these services. In a true sense this flow represents the real cost to society of the nation's final output. In return the household sector receives payment for the labor, capital, and natural resource services supplied, which represent national income—one concept of GNP. In the bottom half of the diagram we see the flow of final goods and services produced to the household sector—gross national product—and the payments by the household sector—gross national expenditure—for these goods and services.

All of these concepts measure the same thing: the total final output of goods and services produced in the nation. They do so in different ways, however, for two important reasons. First, the different concepts of GNP have important, but distinct, economic significance. Second, the word "estimates" has already been used several times in referring to the National Income and Product Accounts. BEA does not, and can not, have an entirely accurate measure of the output of all final goods and services produced. One way in which BEA tries to improve the accuracy of the estimation process is to use these different conceptual approaches.

The rest of this section offers brief descriptions of the main components and methods associated with these concepts.

GNP as Product and Expenditure

The presentation of GNP as product and expenditure is broadly the same, and the concepts are equal when all that is produced is sold. This is often not the case, however. Producers may misjudge the economy's effective demand, so that more (or less) may be produced than the various spending units in the economy demand. When this happens, the change in business inventories will also differ from what the business sector had intended. The

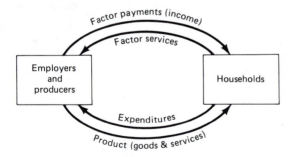

FIGURE 3-1
The circular flow of economic activity

subtle difference between a planned and an unplanned change in inventory levels—often difficult to assess—is the basic difference between GNP viewed as product and viewed as expenditure. In either case there are four main categories of goods and services which make up GNP:

(1) Personal Consumption Expenditures
(2) Gross Private Domestic Investment
(3) Net Exports of Goods and Services
(4) Government Purchases of Goods and Services

These categories of output conform closely to the four spending sectors commonly analyzed: households, businesses, government entities, and foreigners. (The major area of nonconformity, discussed below, is the inclusion of residential construction—largely an expenditure by the household sector—in gross private domestic investment rather than in personal consumption expenditures. This reflects an assessment that housing is not "consumed" over a short period, but rather is an "investment" in an asset which returns a flow of services over an extended period.)

Personal Consumption Expenditures comprise the largest share of GNP, equalling just over 65% of the total in 1982. These are expenditures by households on goods and services. In one sense, consumption represents the purpose of all economic activity. Investment and government activities are, in the end, performed to produce future flows of consumer goods and to create or maintain an environment within which consumption can take place.

Personal consumption expenditures are divided into three main groups in the accounts: durable, and nondurable goods, and services. *Durable goods* are commodities, the useful life of which is assumed to be longer than three years. The chief categories of durable goods are: motor vehicles and parts, furniture and household equipment. Because these are long-lived assets their acquisition can be postponed. For this reason, durables are subject to considerable volatility: in times of weak economic activity, consumer spending for durables—which also happen to be high-priced—often weakens more than does the overall economy. Conversely, in times of strong economic growth, consumer spending on durables is often an important source of overall economic strength.

Nondurable goods are commodities which are generally "consumed"—their usefulness is exhausted—in three years or less. Among the chief types of nondurable goods are: food, clothing and shoes, gasoline and motor oil, fuel oil and coal. These goods are largely necessities and, hence, show little cyclical volatility, but rather respond slowly to changes in population, tastes, and social conditions.

Services are personal services for which actual or imputed payments are made. The chief types of services are: housing—an imputed rent is estimated for households in owner-occupied dwellings, actual rents for households in rented dwellings; electricity and gas; other services for household operation; and transportation services. Services are also unrelated to the state of economic activity since they also largely consist of necessities. There has been a noticeable shift in the structure of the U.S. economy toward the service sector in the last thirty years. In 1950, 39.4% of personal consumption expenditures were in the form of services; in 1982 48.1% was accounted for by services. Over the same period, spending on nondurables went from 48.0% in 1950 to 37.5% in 1982.

The concept of *gross private domestic investment* is well defined by its name. Investment refers to the notion that the goods included in this sector are used to produce other goods, or satisfactions, and typically are not used up in one accounting period. Only goods acquired by private (non-governmental), domestic (excluding foreign investment by U.S. firms) entities are included. Lastly, gross investment is considered; that is, net new investment plus the replacement of fully depreciated (worn-out) capital assets. There are three main components of gross private domestic investment: residential fixed investment, nonresidential fixed investment, and the change in business inventories.

Residential fixed investment consists chiefly of the construction of new residential units. This construction is split between farm and nonfarm components, although in recent years construction of nonfarm dwelling units has been fifty times as great as construction of dwelling units on farms (construction of other farm structures is included in nonresidential fixed investment). Investment in producers' durable equipment in residential structures—chiefly appliances installed by landlords—is also included in this category.

Residential fixed investment, particularly the nonfarm portion, is one of the most cyclical components of GNP. This is true for a number of reasons. First, like consumer durable goods, new homes are high-priced, long-lived assets which can be postponed in times of economic weakness. Second, most new home purchases are financed with the use of long-term mortgage credit. The supply of mortgage funds is itself quite cyclical: ample in the early post-recession phase of the business cycle, when there are fewer competing borrowers; scarcer near the peak in economic activity when competition from business borrowers, who can foresee a higher return on borrowed funds, may bid away mortgage funds. Third, the confidence and willingness of households to take on mortgages is cyclical—low in periods of economic weakness, stronger in periods of growth.

Nonresidential fixed investment, or business spending for plant and equipment, is perhaps the most standard form of investment. It takes two major forms: investment in structures, and in producers' durable equipment (spending on the latter is roughly twice that on structures).

Included in investment on nonresidential structures are: the construction and maintenance of buildings (plants, and office, store, and utility structures); farm buildings other than dwellings; and oil and gas wells and mines. Producers' durable equipment includes, in addition to tools and machinery, business purchases of autos, trucks, aircraft, and other transportation equipment.

Nonresidential fixed investment (also called business fixed investment) is responsive to cyclical developments in the overall economy, but often with a lag. In essence, investment represents an addition (a flow) to existing capital (a stock), which must be adjusted for two reasons: (1) to replenish the portion which wears out or becomes technically obsolete in any period; and (2) to maintain the necessary relationship to the level of output (the capital/ outlay ratio), which must constantly adjust to changing levels of economic activity. There is, unfortunately, an information lag which may slow the response of business to changes in economic activity, which is compounded by the lag in actually installing the new capital. If output is growing more than expected, there will be some period before business expectations adapt to the new realities, and usually a further lag between the time the decision to add to capital is made and the time when it becomes productive. Conversely, if activity is weakening, the information lag may be shorter, but because of the difficulty of adjusting investment downward—mainly, through not replacing worn out capital—the adjustment may take longer. One role of the business economist is to shorten the information lag by means of prescient forecasts.

The *change in business inventories* represents the investment in goods, principally by manufacturers, wholesalers, and retailers, which they expect to sell in the future. Just as fixed investment represents the flow adjustment to the stock of fixed capital, the change in inventories represents a flow adjustment to the inventory stock—sometimes referred to as working capital. Moreover, just as businesses attempt to maintain some (relatively) fixed relationship between the stock of capital and the level of output (the capital-output ratio) they also attempt to maintain a (relatively) constant relationship between the level of inventories and sales (the inventory/sales ratio).

There are three special features to the treatment of the change in business inventories in the National Product Accounts: one of which is obvious; the other two are less so. The obvious problem is, that since a change in a stock is being measured, the change will be negative at times. If businesses expect a decline in sales they may permit the stock of inventories to be run down, that is, the lower level of sales will be met out of existing stocks and not replaced by current production. This fact results in the change in inventories being one of the most volatile components of GNP—it will reflect fully the variability in overall economic activity.

A related, less obvious, problem arises because the expectations of businesses are often less than perfect. This results in unintended fluctuations in the inventory/sales ratio. For instance, if a downturn in final demand occurs suddenly, the level of sales will decline but businesses may, for a time, continue adding to inventories as if their earlier, more hopeful expectations about sales were being realized. This will result in a higher than intended inventory/sales ratio, and require a downward adjustment to inventories in future periods even greater than warranted by the level of sales had the inventory/sales ratio remained at the desired level. (Clearly, the opposite is also possible. A greater than expected increase in sales will be met by drawing down inventories at first, depressing the inventory/sales ratio below desired levels, and requiring a greater than normal addition to inventories in future periods. Production will be increased to meet the new, higher level of demand only with a lag.) Thus, the change in business inventories is highly cyclical, and the response may, at first, be perverse. This feature not only underscores the role of business expectations and the importance of accurate forecasts, but also indicates a difference between the concepts of GNP viewed as expenditure—where only intended changes in inventories would be counted—and as product—where all changes in inventories, both intended and unintended, are counted.

The third special problem the change in inventories poses is the valuation problem. While only the *change* in inventories is included in GNP, the Bureau of Economic Analysis does maintain and publish data on the level of the inventory stock (see section II). In essence, the change in business inventories component of GNP measures the change in the level of business inventories from the *end* of the prior quarter (the last month in the quarter) to the *end* of the current quarter at an annual rate.[2] A complication arises, however, from the fact that a *net* flow is being measured. That is, during the quarter, goods are being added to and drawn out of the inventory stock at the same time. The problem is a compound one: (1) because prices are apt to be changing during the quarter, the value of the goods added is likely to differ from the value of the goods drawn out; and (2) because businesses value their inventories by different accounting methods (first-in-first-out, or FIFO; last-in-last-out, or LIFO, etc.). In an attempt to deal with these problems, BEA computes an Inventory Valuation Adjustment (IVA) which reflects the mix of accounting methods used by business derived from data compiled by the Bureau of the Census.[3] The IVA is deducted from the book value change in inventories to eliminate the effects of changes in the valuation of inventories—which are unintended—from the GNP concept of the change in inventories as a change in working capital.

The change in business inventories is presented in the National Product Accounts in total, for farms, and for nonfarm businesses. Some feel for the volatility of inventories can be gained by examining the extremes in the

---

[2] All other GNP components measure the *average level during the quarter*. For instance, residential fixed investment measures the average level of new residential construction that occurs in each of the three months of the quarter.

[3] The IVA is not a deflation method; it merely removes the biases that would otherwise occur due to the different valuation methods for book value inventories.

quarterly series on the change in business inventories. The largest one-quarter increase in real business inventories was $30.6 billion in the third quarter of 1984, although the $22.1 billion increase in the fourth quarter of 1950 (during the Korean War) was the largest increase measured as a share of real GNP (4.0% versus 1.9% in 1984). The largest one-quarter decline was the $22.7 billion fall off in the fourth quarter of 1982.

Net exports of goods and services are equal to exports of merchandise and services, plus net capital grants received by the U.S., less imports of merchandise and services, net official and private transfers, interest paid by the U.S. government to foreigners, and net foreign investment in the U.S. These international flows of goods and services are viewed on a net basis in computing GNP for two reasons. When viewed as product, the net flow represents the product of domestic resources less the product of foreign resources which enter the U.S. economy. Viewed as expenditure, net exports represents receipts from foreigners by entities in the U.S. less payments by U.S. entities to foreigners. In fact, then, net exports reflect the net benefits—in terms of both resource utilization and income—that accrue to the U.S. economy from international commerce.

The largest portion of receipts from foreigners (60% in 1982) is accounted for by merchandise exports of durable and nondurable goods. Most of the remainder (39.8% in 1982) consists of service receipts, including: interest, insurance, freight and passenger fares, tourist receipts, and profits earned by U.S. corporations abroad. Finally, a small portion (less than 1% in 1982) consists of capital grants paid to the U.S. less capital grants paid by the U.S. to foreigners.

The largest portion of payments to foreigners (70.3% in 1982) is comprised of merchandise imports. Payments for services is the next largest, though much smaller (24.7% in 1982), payment to foreigners. Transfer payments, for which no economic resource is purchased, from both persons (usually in the form of cash gifts to relatives of U.S. residents living abroad) and the government (foreign aid) are included on a net basis, but usually are an outflow from the U.S. (2.2% in 1982). Interest payments to foreigners by the U.S. are also included in imports. Finally, net foreign investment in the U.S. is included in imports, although if foreigners invest more in the U.S. than U.S. residents invest abroad this item is a negative. In general the rule is, if an inflow of money (receipts) occurs, the item is regarded as an export; if an outflow (payment) occurs the item is treated as an import.

Because they are the difference between two separate activities, each of which has its own cyclical characteristics, there is no consistent cyclical pattern for net exports. Imports are more directly related to U.S. cyclical conditions than exports. In times of strong economic growth, when productive resources are nearly fully employed, imports are strong. This is because of a high degree of domestic absorption as high income pulls in imports, and as a result of efforts to economize on the use of domestic resources. Exports are less responsive to U.S. business cycle developments because their demand is determined by economic conditions in the importing country (our exports are another country's imports). There are two caveats to this, however. First, in boom periods, resources may be bid away from export production to the production of goods for domestic absorption. Second, because of the important role the U.S. plays in world trade, cyclical weakness (and strength) has been transferred increasingly in recent years to other countries. This occurs because as economic growth slows (picks up) in the U.S., import demand lessens (rises), which means the share of foreigners' exports to the U.S. decreases (increases); this in turn results in weaker (stronger) GNP in those countries with an accompanying result on U.S. exports. Unfortunately, no general statement can be made about the cyclical behavior of net exports. This will depend on whether the forces affecting imports—which exert a counter-cyclical impact on GNP—or the forces affecting exports—which may have a pro-cyclical effect on GNP—are stronger.

Government purchases of goods and services is the final component of GNP in the product (expenditure) account. These purchases include all durable and nondurable goods purchased, and payments for factor services by Federal, state, and local government units. They do not include transfer payments—such as unemployment compensation, and welfare benefits—Federal grants and aid to state and local governments, net interest payments, or subsidies. While these outlays are important from a budgetary standpoint, they do not reflect payment for final product and, thus, are not included in GNP.

Government purchases are deemed necessary for maintaining stable economic and social conditions. Thus, they generally do not possess cyclical characteristics. (This, of course, is only true in terms of the final product; budget outlays—especially transfers—do display definite cyclical characteristics, hence the concept of the "full employment" budget.)

GNP as Income

The National Income Account depicts the payments to the owners of the factors of production used to produce the output which comprises the National Product Account. These payments also constitute the income out of which expenditures are made. It represents the uppermost flow of the circular flow diagram of Figure 3-1. When the two sets of accounts are compared it can easily be seen that they each sum to the same GNP. In a vivid way such a comparison underscores the axiom, "for every dollar of output produced, a dollar of income is earned."

The National Income Account, taken as a whole, appears more complicated than the product account. For this reason it will be examined in three parts: (1) personal income, which is the core of the account; (2) the summation up from personal income to GNP; and (3) the breakdown of personal income into taxes, outlays, and savings.

Personal income is mainly composed of the payments actually made to the household sector for the factor services they supply. (As will be seen below, some of the rewards of production are either retained by businesses or taxed before disbursement.) In addition, personal income is supplemented by transfer payments—such as: social security, veterans', and government retirement benefits, unemployment insurance benefits, and welfare payments—for which no current productive services are performed. Personal income data are reported annually, quarterly and monthly (see section II-A, below) at seasonally adjusted annual rates.

Table 3-1 shows the principal personal income components for 1982. Wage and salary disbursements comprise the largest component by far, accounting for just under 61% of the total. Details for major industry sectors—manufacturing, distributive industries, services, and government—are also provided. These represent the bulk of payments for labor services. Other labor income—including non-wage benefits, (such as for health and pensions)—comprised a further 6.1% of personal income in 1982. Proprietors' income, including inventory and capital gain profits, are complex because they include returns for the proprietors' total income: returns for both the proprietors' managerial services (profit) and for labor services. These payments accounted for a little over 4% of personal income in 1982. Rental income of persons are the rents received by individual landlords, excluding rents paid to corporations, and accounted for 1.9% of personal income in 1980. Dividend income represents the return to capital which is actually paid out to the owners (shareholders) of corporations (as opposed to the portion that is retained by the corporations), while interest payments reflect the returns to savers. Together these two components accounted for nearly

TABLE 3-1   Personal Income Components*

	1982 (billions)	SHARE OF TOTAL*	SHARE OF GNP*
Wage and Salary Disbursements	$1568.1	60.8%	51.0%
Other Labor Income	156.6	6.1	5.1
Proprietor's Income with IVA and CCAdj	109.0	4.2	3.5
Rental Income of Persons with CCAdj	49.9	1.9	1.6
Personal Dividend Income	66.4	2.6	2.2
Personal Interest Income	366.2	14.2	11.9
Transfer Payments	374.5	14.5	12.2
Less: Personal Contributions for Social Insurance	112.0	4.3	3.6
Equals: Personal Income	2578.6	100.0	83.9

* Total may not add up due to rounding.

Source: *Survey of Current Business,* December 1983.

17% of personal income in 1982. Finally, transfers—which are not payments for factor services—are included, while personal contributions for social (security) insurance are deducted since this is a portion of personal income which is withheld, not paid. These two components netted to a 10.2% addition to personal income in 1982.

As can be seen from the third column in the Table, the share of GNP, total personal income accounts for less than total GNP (83.9% in 1982). This highlights the difference between the value of output produced (GNP) and the factor payments actually made (personal income). Table 3-2 presents the detail for 1982 which adjusted personal income up to national income, net national product, and gross national product.

National income is equal to: personal income, less transfers, interest income, and dividends; plus corporate profits (including inventory profits and capital gains), net interest payments, and total contributions (by both employers and employees) for social insurance. The effect of these additions and subtractions is to strip personal income down to just that portion which is payment for current factor services (i.e., income less transfers), and then add to this that portion of income that is not paid out—mainly the retained

TABLE 3-2   Relation of Gross National Product, Net National Product, National Income, and Personal Income

		1982 (billions)	SHARE OF GNP
Personal Income		$2578.6	83.9%
Less:	Government Transfer Payments to persons	360.4	11.7
	Personal Interest Income	366.2	11.9
	Personal Dividend Income	66.4	2.2
	Business Transfer Payments	14.1	0.5
Plus:	Corporate Profits with IVA and CCAdj	164.8	5.4
	Net Interest	261.1	8.5
	Contributions for Social Insurance	253.0	8.2
	Wage Accruals less Disbursements	0	
Equals:	National Income	2450.4	79.7
Less:	Subsidies less current Surplus of Government enterprises	9.5	0.3
Plus:	Indirect Business Taxes	258.3	8.4
	Business Transfer Payments	14.1	0.5
	Statistical Discrepancy	0.5	0.02
Equals:	Net National Product	2713.8	88.3
Plus:	Capital Consumption Allowances with CCAdj	359.2	11.7
	Capital Consumption Allowances without CCAdj	312.6	10.2
	CCAdj	46.6	1.5
Gross National Product		3073.0	100.0

Source: *Survey of Current Business,* December 1983.

earnings kept by corporations. Thus, dividends are deducted from personal income so that total (distributed plus undistributed) corporate profits can be added. Likewise, personal interest income is deducted so that net interest (for households, corporations, government, and foreigners) can be added.

Net national product is national income with indirect business taxes (largely sales, property, and excise taxes) and business transfers added, and government subsidies deducted. The item, statistical discrepancy, is the difference between the product and income accounts which BEA is unable to reconcile. As can be seen from Table 3-2, this amount was quite small in 1982. This is usually the case for a year as a whole, although the quarterly accounts often show a larger discrepancy.

Finally, capital consumption allowances (depreciation) with an adjustment for valuation changes (capital gains or losses), is added to *net* national product to arrive at *gross* national product. This adjustment recognizes the fact that a portion of the capital stock is used up in creating final output.

Table 3-3 shows the ways in which households allocate their income. This breakdown confirms personal income as the source of personal consumption spending in the National Product Account. Personal income also constitutes a major source of government revenue which, in turn, serves as a basis for government spending.

Personal income is reduced by personal tax and nontax payments to governments to derive *disposable personal income,* or the amount households actually have available to spend. The bulk of these payments ($348.5 billion out of a total of $402.1 billion in 1982) are in the form of personal

TABLE 3-3   Disposition of Personal Income

		1982 (billions)	SHARE OF PERSONAL INCOME	SHARE OF GNP
Personal Income		$2578.6	100.0%	83.9%
Less:	Personal Tax and Non-Tax Payments	402.1	15.6	13.1
Equals:	Disposable Personal Income	2176.5	84.4	70.8
Less:	Personal Outlays	2051.1	79.5	66.7
	Personal Consumption Expenditures	1991.9	77.2	64.8
	Interest Paid by consumers to Business	58.1	2.3	1.9
	Personal Transfer Payments to Foreigners	1.1	*	*
Equals:	Personal saving	125.4	4.9	4.1

* Less than 0.05%

Source: *Survey of Current Business,* December 1983.

income tax payments to Federal, state, and local governments. The rest consists mainly of estate and gift taxes, user fees to the Federal government, and property taxes to state and local governments. Disposable personal income can either be spent, in the form of personal outlays, or saved. Personal outlays mainly consist of personal consumption expenditures, but also include net interest payments by households to businesses and personal transfer payments abroad. Personal saving—disposal personal income less outlays—accounts for the remainder. It is appropriate that saving should thus be shown as a residual, for theory suggests that consumption is the active role of households and saving a passive one—what is not spent is saved, not what is not saved is spent, except in a tautological sense. An important implication of this fact for the forecaster is that the level of saving is not forecast directly, but rather results from forecasts for disposable personal income and consumption.

GNP Measured in Current (Market) and Constant Prices

GNP is intended to measure the final *value* of all goods and services produced in order to indicate the level of economic activity. Unfortunately, in a world in which both general and relative prices are changing, attempting to assess the real level of economic activity from GNP valued at current (market) prices is like trying to watch a football game in a blizzard. Just as the blizzard obscures the action taking place on the football field, so also a general change in prices—inflation—obscures the true relationships between the different sectors of the economy. Thus, some method for removing the effects of price changes—a *de*flation method—must be found so that the *real* change in the quantity of output can be isolated from the change due solely to price. The result is to present GNP in three ways as in Table 3-4, which shows: (1) output in total and by sector in current (market) dollars, (2) output in total and by sector in constant (real) dollars, and (3) the deflators (price index levels) for total output and for each sector.

The value of output is equal to the product price times output: $V = P \times Q$. The object of deflating current dollar GNP is to separate these two components of value. The method by which this is done is unique. There are in general two types of price indices: the widely used *Laspeyres* index and the *Paasche* index.

The Laspeyres index uses a constant "market basket" of goods and services for some base year to represent the quantity portion of value (Q_o), so that only prices are allowed to change.

$$L = \frac{\Sigma P_n Q_o}{\Sigma P_o Q_o} \times 100$$

TABLE 3-4   GNP in Current and Constant Dollars, and Implicit Price Deflators*

	BILLIONS OF DOLLARS	BILLIONS OF 1972 DOLLARS	1972 = 100
Gross National Product	3073.0	1485.4	206.88
Personal Consumption	1991.9	970.2	205.3
Durable Goods	244.5	139.8	174.8
Nondurable Goods	761.0	364.2	209.0
Services	986.4	466.2	211.6
Residential Construction	90.8	37.8	240.2
Business Fixed Investment	384.3	166.1	209.7
Structures	141.9	53.4	265.8
Producers Durable Equipment	206.4	112.7	183.1
Change in Business Inventories	−24.5	−9.4	
Net Exports	17.4	28.9	
Exports	347.6	147.3	236.0
Imports	330.2	118.4	278.9
Government Purchases	649.2	291.8	222.5
Federal	258.7	116.6	222.0
State & Local	390.5	175.2	222.9

* All figures are for 1982.

Source: *Survey of Current Business,* December 1983.

This is the most widely used method for constructing price indexes. It has the disadvantage, however, of not reflecting the substitution of goods, the prices of which are rising less rapidly, for goods with rapidly rising prices. (For instance, consumers may switch to chicken when beef prices are rising more rapidly.) This method is used for compiling the Consumer and Producer Price Indexes in the U.S. (See section II, below.)

To avoid this problem, the Paasche index can be used. This index uses changing weights, based on the current period, so that both prices and quantities are changing each period.

$$P = \frac{\Sigma P_n Q_n}{\Sigma P_o Q_n} \times 100$$

This method permits price changes and substitutions to be tracked. Its disadvantage is that it is usually an expensive method to compile.

GNP deflation is carried out by a combination of the two methods. Individual output sectors, and components of those sectors, are first deflated by available price measures: price indexes compiled by the Bureau of Labor Statistics (BLS), and quantity measures compiled by BEA and other, often industry, sources. In many cases components of the Consumer Price Index and the Producer Price Index are used. This results in quantity estimates

(Q_n) of the various GNP components which can then be used in a Paasche index. The implicit GNP deflator is the derived by multiplying current dollar GNP (Q_nP_n) by this index. Thus, the implicit deflator is derived such that

$$P_n = \frac{\Sigma Q_nP_n \times \Sigma P_nQ_n}{\Sigma P_oQ_n}$$

For this reason the Implicit GNP Price Deflator is often regarded as a better measure of the "cost of living" than the Consumer Price Index—it allows for substitution. It should be noted that the steps to this method are: (1) to derive quantities for the GNP components (real GNP components) using available price measures, from current dollar amounts; and then (2) to compile the price index. Thus, when revisions are made to the current dollar estimates (prices times quantities) both the constant dollar GNP estimates (real quantities) and the price deflators (prices) will be revised, not because the price (or quantity) estimates alone were wrong, but because the compound estimate of value $(P \times Q)$ was wrong.

These subjects will be addressed again in section III after examining some of the principal, less aggregate measures of economic activity which are used to construct the National Income and Product Accounts.

II. LESS AGGREGATE MEASURES OF ECONOMIC ACTIVITY

The National Income and Product Accounts are not the only data series compiled by the government. A large number of series are compiled which measure specific economic activities in detail. Indeed, many of these series are in turn used to construct the estimates which form the National Income and Product Accounts (a process which will be examined in detail in section III). Ironically, many of these less aggregate series have been compiled longer than GNP.

These series measure aspects of economic activity which are important in themselves—such as, employment, production, sales, and price changes—and which often have greater relevance to a business's operations than does GNP. In addition, because most of the series examined measure and report on activity monthly, they offer more timely information than the quarterly estimates of GNP.

This section describes the principal, mainly government-compiled, measures of domestic, nonfinancial business activity. (Financial and international data will be examined in section IV.)

There are four main sources of government-compiled economic data. These are: (1) the Bureau of the Census, U S. Department of Commerce (Census); (2) the Bureau of Economic Analysis, U.S. Department of Commerce (BEA); (3) the Bureau of Labor Statistics, U.S. Department of Labor (BLS); and (4) the Federal Reserve Board (FRB). These four account for most of the regularly published data on economic activity, but they are not the only sources of such information within the Federal government. Others include: the Department of Agriculture, the Department of the Treasury, the Federal Trade Commission, the Securities and Exchange Commission, and the Office of Management and the Budget.

To provide some order to this mass of data, this section is arranged into five categories of economic activity. These are: (1) employment, income, and consumer spending measures; (2) orders, production, and sales; (3) capital spending measures; (4) prices and costs; and (5) cyclical indicators.

Employment, Income, and Consumer Spending

In Chapter 2, it was stated that the consumption function is the starting point for analyzing the macroeconomic system, while in section I, it was shown that personal consumption expenditures account for the largest portion of GNP on the product side. Thus it is appropriate to look first at the data which are inputs into the consumption function.

In tracing the causal factors that result in consumption, there is a retrogressive sequence from consumption back to its determinants. Consumer spending is usually depicted as a function of personal income. It was shown in Chapter 2 that income is in turn a function of employment. The supply of labor available for employment is determined by the size of the working-age population and the utility trade off between work and leisure. All of these concepts, except the work-leisure trade off, are represented by series compiled by government offices.

The Bureau of the Census is best known for the decennial Census of Population it conducts. This is the oldest data gathering activity carried out by the government. Indeed, a decennial census is mandated by the Constitution, and one has been done every decade since 1790. A "census" enumerates each individual or item in a particular population.[4] Most data series compiled by the government, on the other hand, are based on "surveys" designed to reflect the entire population. The reasons for this are: censuses are far more expensive to conduct than surveys, it takes a long time to compile the data in a census, and so long as a survey is conducted frequently, it should be nearly as reliable as a census.

The Bureau of the Census conducts a monthly survey of 60,000 households in which, in addition to data on population characteristics, "statistics on the employment status of the population; the personal, occupational, and other characteristics of the employed, the unemployed, and persons not in

---

[4] In addition to the Census of Population, the Bureau also compiles censuses of housing, manufactures, and trade.

the labor force are compiled for BLS".[5] The survey garners information on all household members 16 years of age and older. (Separate statistics are collected and published for 14 and 15 year olds.) Inmates of institutions, members of the Armed Forces, and persons under 14 years of age are excluded from the survey results. The data for certain months are actually collected for, and relate to, the calendar week containing the twelfth day of the month. Of course, whenever data from a complete census become available, these "Current Population Survey" data are adjusted to conform with the more complete results. The Bureau of the Census publishes extensive results in its "Current Population Survey" series of reports. BLS publishes the principal employment-related series in its monthly bulletin *The Employment Situation*—available from BLS—and in greater detail in *Employment and Earnings* (available for $2.75 per issue or $22.00 per year from the U.S. Government Printing Office, Washington, DC 20204).

The basic labor series from which all others are derived are: the total noninstitutional population (16 years of age and over) and, after excluding members of the Armed Forces, the *civilian noninstitutional population*. This last group forms the basis from which the *civilian labor force* is estimated. Those respondents who are *employed* are counted as such and included in the labor force. Each employed person is counted only once—on the basis of the job in which the greatest number of hours were worked if more than one job was held. Those respondents who were not employed are counted as *unemployed* if: (a) they left or lost their job in the past four weeks; and/or (b) they actively sought employment in the prior four weeks. There are four groups of unemployed persons. First, job losers are persons who lost their jobs or were laid off. Second, job leavers are persons who quit their jobs voluntarily and immediately began looking for work. Third, reentrants are persons who previously worked full time, but who were out of the labor force prior to beginning to look for work. Fourth, new entrants are persons who never worked at a full-time job for two weeks or longer. The unemployed are also included in the civilian labor force; all other respondents are classified as "not in the labor force."

The *unemployment rate* is equal to the percentage of unemployed in the labor force (employed plus unemployed). These data are available in both "not seasonally adjusted" (nsa) and "seasonally adjusted" (sa) forms except for the total noninstitutional population, the number in the Armed Forces, and the civilian noninstitutional population, for which no stable seasonal patterns exist. Table 3-5, depicts these data for December 1983 on both bases. Similar data are also available by age, sex, and racial characteristics.

[5] U.S. Department of Labor, Bureau of Labor Statistics, *Handbook of Labor Statistics: 1978* (Washington, DC: U.S. Government Printing Office, 1979), p. 1.

TABLE 3-5 Employment Status of the Working Age Population—December 1983 (number in thousands)

	nsa*	sa*
Total noninstitutional population	176,809	—
Resident Armed Forces	1,688	—
Civilian noninstitutional population	175,121	—
Civilian labor force	111,795	112,136
Employed	102,803	102,941
Unemployed	8,992	9,195
Unemployment Rate (%)		8.2
Not in labor force	63,326	62,985

* nsa = not seasonally adjusted
* sa = seasonally adjusted

The population and armed forces figures are not adjusted for seasonal variation.

Source: *The Employment Situation,* December 1983.

In addition to the Household Survey, on which the above employment characteristics are based, BLS also conducts an Establishment, or Payroll, Survey. This latter survey covers roughly 116,000 workplaces and provides data on employment, hours, and earnings for workers on nonagricultural payrolls. The survey week for establishments is the pay period including the twelfth of the month, which may or may not be the calendar week in which the household survey is taken.

Unlike the household survey, the establishment survey only counts wage and salary employees of nonagricultural establishments. This highlights one of several differences in coverage: (1) agricultural workers are not included; (2) strikers and others affected by unpaid work stoppages are not included among the employed in the establishment survey, but they are in the household survey; (3) workers employed at two places are counted twice in the establishment survey, but only once in the household survey; and (4) the household survey only includes employees 16 years and older, while the establishment survey includes all workers, regardless of age.

Because the establishment survey categorizes employment, hours worked, and earnings (hourly and weekly) by industry, it is a valuable input for official and private estimates of personal income. These data are also available on not seasonally adjusted and seasonally adjusted bases. Table 3-6 shows seasonally adjusted data for major industry groups for December 1983.

These data are detailed in *The Employment Situation,* released by BLS usually in the first calendar week following the end of the month covered.

TABLE 3-6   Establishment Survey Data on Employment, Average Weekly Hours, and Average Hourly Earnings (December 1983)

	EMPLOYMENT	AVERAGE WEEKLY HOURS[1]	AVERAGE HOURLY EARNINGS[1]
	(THOUSANDS)	(HOURS)	(DOLLARS)
Total[2]	91,644	35.2	8.17
Manufacturing	19,271	40.5	9.05
Mining	1,053	n.a.*	11.42
Construction	4,110	n.a.	12.02
Transportation and public utilities	5,024	39.6	11.04
Wholesale trade	5,304	38.7	8.57
Retail trade	15,428	30.0	5.78
Finance, insurance, and real estate	5,537	n.a.	7.42
Services	20,122	32.7	7.43
Government	15,795	n.a.	n.a.

(1) Hours and earnings are for production and nonsupervisory workers only. These groups account for roughly four-fifths of total nonagricultural employment.

(2) Total earnings and hours are for private production and supervisory workers only. Data on government workers are not available.

* n.a. = Data not available.

Source: *The Employment Situation,* December 1983.

(For instance, *The Employment Situation* covering December 1983 was released on Friday, January 6, 1984.) The timeliness of these data—possible because the survey week is that of the twelfth of the month—is one of its more useful features. These data are often the first official measures of economic activity available for a particular month. More detailed information is released, with a slightly longer lag, in *Employment and Earnings.* Finally, historical data and more detailed descriptions can be found in the annual publication, *Handbook of Labor Statistics.*

Personal income is perhaps the broadest measure of monthly economic activity. These data are compiled by BEA and released roughly three weeks after the end of the month measured in the same detail as contained in the quarterly National Income and Product Accounts. Both the monthly and quarterly data are presented at seasonally adjusted annual rates; in other words, after seasonal adjustment, the monthly income level is multiplied by twelve, the quarterly level by four. Thus, the quarterly personal income level equals the average of the three monthly levels in that quarter, and the annual total equals the average of both the four quarterly and twelve monthly levels for the year.

The data are compiled by BEA from a number of sources. Estimates for *wage and salary payments*—which account for over 60% of the total—are derived from employment, hours worked, and earnings data compiled by

BLS and other government sources. The other components are based on government source data where available: for instance, transfer payments are based on reports by government agencies such as the Social Security Administration and the Veterans Administration; farm proprietors' income is based on data supplied by the U.S. Department of Agriculture, Statistical Reporting Service. Some components are estimated in other ways, however: dividend income is estimated from a sample of corporate dividend payments; nonfarm proprietors' income and other labor income are estimated by regressions on past annual data and then updated when data become available from the Internal Revenue Service.

Besides monitoring the monthly flow of personal income—thus, supplying a measure of overall economic activity between GNP reports—the personal income data are useful to the business forecaster for estimating the level of overall economic activity. For one thing, recognizing that personal income is a large component of total GNP, these monthly estimates can be used to track the current quarter's GNP from the income side. In addition, since the monthly release provides data on *personal consumption expenditures,* this component of GNP—from the product side—can also be tracked monthly. Each monthly release contains an estimate of personal consumption spending in current dollar terms, and in constant dollar terms with a one month lag (i.e. the December 1983 release included estimates of current dollar consumption for December and constant dollar consumer spending for November). These data are largely based on retail sales data compiled by the Census Bureau, discussed below.

Personal income estimates are first released in a monthly news release, *Personal Income and Outlays.* More detailed data are contained in the *Survey of Current Business.* Detailed descriptions and historical data are contained in the biennial (odd years) supplement to the *Survey* entitled *Business Statistics,* published by BEA.

The basic source of data on consumer spending is the *Monthly Retail Trade* report published by the Bureau of the Census. Sales of all establishments primarily engaged in retail trade are reported in millions of dollars, in total, by major types of retail establishment, and by geographic regions. The sales data are adjusted for seasonal, holiday, and trading day differences, but not for price changes. The data do not include sales by manufacturers, wholesalers, or service establishments, although businesses primarily engaged in retail trade but which also sell to non-household customers—for instance, gasoline stations—are counted as solely retail.

The monthly data are released roughly ten days after the end of the month covered. The estimates are based on two samples. First, there is a sample of all establishments with eleven or more employees which also meet a minimum sales volume test (varying from $2 million to $25 million annually, depending on the type of business). This sample is designed to have a 95% coverage. Second, a sample based on geographic regions is used to capture smaller establishments. The total sample of establishments is further divided into three subsamples and reports are filed on a rotating basis for the current and two prior months. For example, the first subsample would report sales for January, February, and March; the second subsample for February, March, and April; and the third for March, April, and May. Thus, the first report for March is termed "advance," the second "preliminary," and the third "final." Sales include all cash and credit transactions, though carrying and other credit charges are excluded. Sales and excise taxes are also excluded.

There are eleven major establishment groups and many subgroups. Three durable goods groups account for roughly one-third of the total. These are: (1) building materials, hardware, garden supplies, and mobile home dealers; (2) automotive dealers; and (3) furniture, home furnishing, and equipment stores. There are eight major nondurable goods groups. These are: (1) general merchandise stores (including department and variety stores), (2) food stores, (3) gasoline service stations, (4) apparel and accessory stores, (5) eating and drinking places, (6) drug and proprietary stores, (7) liquor stores and (8) all others. These data are presented at monthly, *not* annual rates. More detailed descriptions of the data and estimation methods can be found in the *Monthly Retail Trade* reports, available from the Superintendent of Documents, U.S. Government Printing Office, and in less detail in *Business Statistics*.

Another useful source of consumer spending data are the ten-day auto sales reports made by the major U.S. auto producers three to five days after the end of the three "ten-day" periods each month. Because these figures are compiled by the auto producers, and reported in units, rather than from dealer sales, they often differ from the movements shown by the dollar sales data reported as part of the retail sales data. Nevertheless, the unit sales data are useful because: (1) they are available on a timely basis, and (2) they are used as inputs in computing the auto consumption portion of GNP (see section III, below).

Orders, Production, and Sales

The series discussed above largely relate to household demand and its determinants. In this section, we examine some of the main monthly measures which show the response to this demand by the goods-producing sectors of the economy. These data are largely represented by three series which portray the sequence by which changes in demand are met by changes in supply. Namely: changes in new orders received by manufacturers, which lead to changes in production, which, in turn, result in changes in manufacturers' shipments, or sales.

New orders, net of cancellations received by manufacturers, are compiled and released each month by the Bureau of the Census. These data are based on a sample of some 3,800 manufacturers that includes nearly all companies with 1,000 or more employees, strengthened by a small company sample to insure coverage of all major industry segments. The data are adjusted for seasonal, holiday, and trading day variations, but not for price changes, and are reported in millions of dollars at monthly rates, usually 30 to 35 days after the end of the month covered. (Advance data on orders received by durable manufacturers only, based on a subsample of durable goods producers, are reported about ten days prior to the more comprehensive manufacturers report.) Data are reported for major durable and nondurable industry groups. In addition, data are reported for two major market groups: (1) household durable goods industries, such as manufacturers of furniture and appliances; and (2) capital goods industries, including separate breakdowns for defense and nondefense capital goods producing industries.

The data are first released in the *Manufacturers' Orders, Shipments and Inventories* report, and subsequently in the *Survey of Current Business*. Historical data can be found in *Business Statistics*.

Orders are the basis for future production. Monthly data on production by manufacturers, as well as by mines and utilities, are presented in the Federal Reserve Board's report *Industrial Production,* released around the middle of the month following that being reported on. (For example, the *Industrial Production* report for December 1983 was released on January 13, 1984.) The index of industrial production is a measure of the physical (real) output of the nation's factories, mines, and utilities. Thus, it is nearly as broad a measure of economic activity from the output side as personal income is from the income side. In addition, it measures output in seasonally adjusted real terms, making it a powerful monthly measure of overall activity.

In addition to the overall index—where the level of output in 1967 is equal to 100 and all other periods are indexed to this—there are component indexes for some 235 industry groups. These indexes are aggregated into: (1) market groups, such as consumer goods, business equipment, intermediate goods, and materials; and (2) industry groups, such as manufacturing, mining, and utilities.

Roughly half of the data are derived from actual statistics on the volume of output for the first and subsequent releases. The remainder are derived from industry employment and industrial electricity demand data for the first monthly estimate and updated with output volume data over the subsequent two months. Thus, after three months the data are final and only revised again when annual benchmarking is done, usually for the January release.

The first release of the detailed data is in the Federal Reserve's *Industrial Production* report. The monthly data are also included in summary detail in the *Federal Reserve Bulletin* and the *Survey of Current Business*.

Manufacturers' shipments, or sales, are reported in the Census Bureau's *Manufacturers' Orders, Shipments, and Inventories* report. The methods for compilation and reporting are broadly the same as for new orders. "Shipments" refer to manufacturers' receipts or the value of products shipped, less discounts, returns, and allowances and excluding freight charges and excise taxes.

Capital Spending Measures

The various components of gross private domestic investment—residential fixed investment, nonresidential fixed investment, and the change in business inventories—can also be tracked on a monthly basis by a number of data series. Indeed, as will be seen in section III below, the quarterly GNP components are constructed, at least initially, on the basis of these monthly measures.

The most basic measure of residential activity is the monthly series on *housing starts*. That is, the start of construction on a new housing unit, either single-family or multi-family buildings (apartment houses) which are intended for nontransient occupancy. (Group quarters, such as dormitories, and transient accommodations, such as hotels, are excluded.) A housing "start" for private housing units is defined as the beginning of excavation for the building's foundation; all units in multi-family buildings are regarded as "started" when excavation of the building's foundation is begun. (Thus, when the foundation of a twenty-unit apartment building is excavated, twenty housing starts are recorded.) For public housing, the "start" is counted when the contract is awarded.

Monthly data for private housing starts[6] are presented at seasonally adjusted annual rates for single-family homes, 2–4 unit residences, and residences of 5 units or more. Housing start data are also presented by four major regional groupings: Northeast, North Central, South, and West. A further breakdown between units started in metropolitan and nonmetropolitan areas is presented with a longer lag.

Data on privately owned housing units authorized by building permits in 17,000 permit-issuing places[7] are also included in the same report. *Housing permits* are also presented at seasonally adjusted annual rates for the same groupings as housing starts. There is at best a loose correspondence between the issuing of permits and actual housing starts. Roughly 2% of all housing permits issued are never used. Moreover, of those permits that do result in starts, some units are started in the same month in which the permit

---

[6] Data on publicly owned housing starts are released in a fuller report roughly one month after the initial report. In the 1960s and early 1970s, publicly owned starts accounted for about $1\frac{1}{2}$% of total starts. Since 1976, however, the portion of total starts accounted for by publicly owned units has fallen to $\frac{1}{2}$% or less.

[7] There are still places in the U.S. which do not require permits for a housing unit to be built. Nearly 90% of all housing units started occur in places requiring permits.

is issued; for others, construction may not start for several months. Permits do, however, provide some indication of future construction.

Special care must be used in interpreting housing start data because of the strong seasonal effects on housing construction. Seasonal factors are constructed and revised using the X-11 version of the Census Method II.[8] Simply, this recognizes that construction activity is susceptible to weather-related disruption in the winter months, and is strongest in the spring and summer months. Raw monthly data are adjusted by a seasonal factor to arrive at a seasonally adjusted monthly start number, and then multiplied by twelve to arrive at a seasonally adjusted annual rate. This method raises the prospect of greater than normal monthly changes whenever weather conditions depart from "normal." For instance, especially severe winter weather may disrupt construction and thus depress starts more than the seasonal factor adjusts for; or, conversely, mild winter weather may permit a greater amount of construction to be started in a particular month than is normal, boosting the seasonally adjusted annual rate reported. For these reasons, the Census Bureau suggests it may take three months to establish an underlying trend for starts and two months for permits. A moving average of the monthly statistics may, therefore, be a useful way of viewing these data.

The data on housing starts and permits are usually released in the third week following the end of the month under review. The data are subject to two revisions in subsequent months. The Census Bureau estimates that the revisions average roughly 1%. Roughly 40–45 days after the end of the month under review the Census Bureau and the U.S. Department of Housing and Urban Development release a joint report on *New Privately Owned Housing Units Completed and Under Construction*. These data are also reported at seasonally adjusted annual rates and are thus compatible with data on starts and permits, but have only been compiled since 1968, whereas data on housing starts are available back to 1889. All of these data are released in detailed reports by the Census Bureau and are also contained in the *Survey of Current Business* with historical data published in *Business Statistics*. Thus, it is possible to track new home construction quite closely from when the permit authorizing construction is issued through completion.

More extensive data on construction are included in the Census Bureau's report on the *Value of New Construction Put-in-Place*. This series reports on the value of all new construction—private and public, residential and nonresidential—in billions of dollars at seasonally adjusted annual rates. All construction underway during the month, whether started or completed during the month, is included. Private construction includes: residential, nonresidential buildings (except farm and public utilities), and public utilities. The estimates for private, nonfarm, nonresidential buildings include

---

[8] Described in Bureau of Census Technical Paper No. 15, "The X-11 Variant of the Census Method II Seasonal Adjustment Program," available from Census on request.

details on the construction of commercial and industrial buildings. Public construction includes details on nonmilitary buildings—with separate estimates on housing and redevelopment, and industrial buildings—military facilities, and construction of highways and streets. Data on construction put in place include estimates for new construction and for additions and alterations, but not for repair. These data are first released in the Census Bureau's *Construction Report,* roughly three weeks after the end of the month under review. These data are also included in the *Survey of Current Business* and *Business Statistics.*

Data on investment in producers' durable equipment are available in less detail than on structural investment on a monthly basis. The principal source of data on monthly flows of producers' durable goods is the Census Bureau's report on *Manufacturers' Orders, Shipment, and Inventories.* This report (discussed above) provides data on shipments for a supplementary group—nondefense capital goods industries. This series comprises shipments of: nonelectrical machinery (including farm machinery and equipment and machinery shops), electrical machinery (including household appliances and components), the nondefense portions of shipbuilding and repairing, railroad equipment, communications equipment, aircraft and aircraft parts, and ordinance. In addition, monthly estimates of the value, in millions of dollars, of each of these categories are reported separately. One feature of these data is they provide an indication of the form business equipment spending is taking, whether on machinery or vehicles for instance. They do not, however, indicate which industries are doing the capital spending.

More comprehensive data on recent and planned capital spending are supplied in BEA's quarterly *Survey of Plant and Equipment Spending.* This report gives actual outlays for the prior quarter, planned outlays for the next two quarters, and planned outlays for the current year. New plant and equipment expenditures refer to all costs of gross investment charged to capital accounts. (Repairs and expenditures charged to current accounts are excluded). Coverage includes all nonfarm businesses with the exception of spending by institutions, professionals, and real estate firms.

The estimates are released in the final months of each quarter (March, June, September, and December) based on a survey covering about 75% of estimated spending taken in the middle of the quarter. (For instance, the survey for the December estimate is taken in late October-early November.) The data are presented in billions of dollars at seasonally adjusted annual rates. The March survey is always of special importance because it is the first release to provide a full estimate for the year's planned spending.

The spending data are detailed separately for manufacturing—durable and nondurable—and for nonmanufacturing, including the separate nonmanufacturing categories of mining, transportation, public utilities, trade and services, communications, and others. In addition, total plant and equipment spending estimates are available for some thirty industry groups and subgroups. The data are presented in the *Survey of Current Business* in an article on first release, and in summary tables in intervening months. Estimates are only made quarterly, however.

Monthly estimates on the stock of business inventories are presented by the Bureau of the Census in three reports. The first, released roughly thirty days after the end of the month under review, is the *Manufacturers' Orders, Shipments, and Inventories* report, discussed above. These are seasonally adjusted, end of month estimates of the book value of the stock of inventories on hand, reported in the same detail as the orders and shipment data. Roughly, ten days later, a report on *Sales and Inventories by Merchant Wholesalers* is released with comparable data on inventories held by merchant wholesalers. Finally, roughly 45 days after the end of the month under review, a report on *Manufacturing and Trade Sales and Inventories* is released. This report includes end-of-month book value, seasonally adjusted estimates of retailers' inventories, and the previously reported estimates for manufacturers' and wholesalers' inventories. Included are estimates of total, durable, and nondurable sales and inventories. Excluded from manufacturing and trade inventories, but included in the stock of total business inventories used to determine the change component in the National Income and Product Accounts, are stocks held by nonmerchant wholesalers and jobbers.

Prices and Costs

There are a number of indexes compiled to monitor changes in prices. These indexes can be used in the aggregate to track inflation, while component series can be used to deflate measures such as sales or orders—or portions of such measures—expressed in current dollar terms. The various price indexes differ mainly in that they measure prices at different stages of processing, or marketing. This fact is useful because: (1) it permits forecasters to use price indexes at early stages to forecast the change in price measures at more advanced stages of processing; and (2) it may help to identify at what stage inflationary pressures are most intense.

The most basic price data are the daily cash prices quoted on the major commodity exchanges. These prices are no longer compiled by the Government but are presented in the financial pages of major newspapers for most raw agricultural and industrial commodities.[9] This is a readily available source of information on basic price pressures.

The Crop Reporting Board, U.S. Department of Agriculture, publishes a monthly *index of prices received by farmers* based on the prices received

---

[9] Futures prices—prices for delivery of a commodity at some future date—are also often used. In general, futures prices correlate closely with "spot" or "cash" prices. At times, however, further information about expected demand or supply conditions can be derived by comparing cash and futures prices—that is, by looking at the spread between them.

by farmers for their products at first point of sale—either at the farm, local markets, or point of delivery. There are about forty-five commodities included in the index, weighted on the basis of average cash receipts in the 1971–73 marketing years. The index is published on a 1977=100 basis. (An index based on 1910-14=100 is also published for use in computing parity— the ratio of prices paid to prices received by farmers.) The data are *not* seasonally adjusted: no stable seasonal pattern can be determined, partly because of variations in crop conditions. The first estimate is based on prices at mid month; later revisions reflect prices throughout the month. This fact explains the timeliness of the release: data are usually released on the last day of the month under review. Data are presented in the report *Agricultural Prices,* available from the Crop Reporting Board, Statistics and Cooperative Service, U.S. Department of Agriculture, Washington, DC 20250.

Producer price indexes (PPI) measure average changes in prices received in primary U.S. markets by producers of commodities at all stages of processing compiled by BLS. These indexes were formerly known as the "wholesale price index," a name which led to some confusion because it suggested these were prices charged by wholesalers. There are currently some 2,800 commodities covered by these indexes representing all commodities produced or imported in the U.S. economy. The price indexes are computed using the Laspeyres method using weights based on the relative importance of each item in 1972 (relative importances are updated in December of each year) and expressed on a 1967=100 basis. Prices are actual transaction prices where available (where unavailable, list or book prices are used) on the Tuesday of the week containing the thirteenth of the month.

The indexes are presented by commodity groups and by stage of processing. The commodity structure presents prices by similarity of end use of material composition. The two major commodity groups are: (1) farm products and processed food and feed, and (2) industrial commodities.

There are three major stages of processing: (1) crude materials; (2) intermediate materials, supplies, and components; and (3) finished goods. The stages of processing data are often more useful than the all commodity data because they avoid multiple counting. For instance, wheat is in the crude index, flour in the intermediate index, and bread in the finished goods index. If wheat prices rise, this change will first show up in the crude index, and only in the other two indexes as and when the increase is passed on. The all-commodities index and the farm products and processed foods and feeds component would reflect the same price change three times because the weighting structure uses the total shipment values for all commodities at all stages of processing. Finished goods are commodities that will not undergo further processing and are ready for sale to a final user, either a consumer or business firm. Intermediate materials, supplies, and components are commodities that have been processed but require further processing and are commodities that will not undergo further processing before they become finished goods. Crude materials include products entering the market for the first time which have not been manufactured or fabricated but which will be processed before becoming finished goods.

The producer price indexes are presented by BLS in *not* seasonally adjusted terms, but the month-to-month percent changes are seasonally adjusted. Thus, it is possible to construct seasonally adjusted indexes by linking seasonally adjusted percent changes. Moreover, seasonally adjusted index levels are presented in the *Survey of Current Business*. The data are released in a report titled *Producer Price Indexes* (available from the Bureau of Labor Statistics, U.S. Department of Labor, Washington, DC 20212) at the end of the first full week following the month under review.

The *consumer price index* (CPI) measures the average change in price of a fixed market basket of goods and services. Since January 1978, two CPI series have been published by BLS to cover two population groups. First, the former concept, which is based on expenditure patterns by "urban wage earners and clerical workers," represents about 40% of the population (CPI-W). This series is still published, primarily to satisfy cost of living adjustments in wage contracts which are based on it. The more widely used concept is the more comprehensive "all urban consumers" series (CPI-U) which covers roughly 80% of the population.

The consumer price indexes are estimated on the basis of some 400 goods and services which are priced each month in 85 urban areas across the country. All taxes directly associated with the purchase and use of these items are included in the indexes. Among the principal categories in the indexes are: food and beverages; energy commodities and services (natural gas and electricity are considered services); nonfood, nonenergy commodities and services including: housing (rent—both actual and imputed for homeowners—home repair and maintenance), apparel and shoes, transportation (including prices of new and used vehicles), entertainment, and medical costs.

The indexes are currently presented on a 1967=100 basis, with relative importances determined each December. As with the producer price indexes, the CPI levels are presented by BLS in not seasonally adjusted terms, but percent changes are seasonally adjusted. Seasonally adjusted levels can be computed, or found in the *Survey of Current Business*. The indexes are released roughly three weeks after the end of the month under review in a report titled *The Consumer Price Index* (available from BLS).

A final set of more complex price measures are the quarterly data on *productivity and costs* compiled by BLS. Whereas the above price measures mainly look at the average change in prices as a result of price changes in individual commodities, these measures look at output price changes as a result of the change in factor input costs. Moreover, the main emphasis tends to be on labor costs. Briefly, this approach derives an index of unit labor costs by dividing an index of hourly labor compensation by an index of productivity (output/employee-hour).[10] Unit labor costs and unit nonlabor payments are then combined on a weighted average basis to derive an implicit deflator reflecting the costs of production and distribution. These measures provide an insight into the cost trends which underlie and shape output prices. The data are compiled at several levels of aggregation: (1) all private businesses; (2) nonfarm businesses; (3) nonfinancial corporations; and (4) manufacturing, with separate detail for durable and nondurable manufacturers. Seasonally adjusted indexes, 1977=100, and percent changes on both year-over-year and seasonally adjusted annual rate bases are released roughly thirty days after the end of the quarter under review (data on nonfinancial corporations are released one month later than the other data). The report, *Productivity and Costs,* is available from BLS.

Cyclical Indicators

The U.S. economy, when viewed over long periods, has exhibited cycles of expansions, contractions (recession, or more serious downturn, depression), and recoveries within its overall long-term growth trend. Indepth study of these cycles began under the direction of Wesley C. Mitchell and Arthur F. Burns at the National Bureau of Economic Research (NBER) in the late 1930s.[11] This work has since been carried on by the NBER and the Statistical Indicators Division, Bureau of Economic Analysis.

One result has been the classification of some 300 statistical series by cyclical response. These series are classified as either leading, coincident, or lagging cyclical indicators based on analysis of their historical performance around business cycles. In addition, BEA constructs three composite indexes: an index of leading indicators; an index of coincident incidators; and an index of lagging indicators.

All of the individual series and the composite indexes are presented in graphic and tabular form each month in the BEA's publication, *Business Conditions Digest* (available from the Superintendent of Documents, U.S. Government Printing Office, Washington, DC 20402). A detailed description of the series and methodology of compilation and construction is contained in the BEA's supplement, *Handbook of Cyclical Indicators,* published in May 1977. The most recent revisions are described in the February 1983 issue of *Business Conditions Digest.* This section contains brief descriptions of the composite indexes.

Cyclical indicators are classified on the basis of six criteria: (1) the economic significance of the indicator; (2) the statistical adequacy of the data; (3) the timing of the series—whether it leads, coincides with, or lags

---

[10] This productivity index does not measure the specific contribution to output of labor input alone, but rather the combined output resulting from all factors and influences.

[11] W.C. Mitchell and A.F. Burns, *Statistical Indicators of Cyclical Revivals* (New York: NBER Bulletin 69, 1938).

turning points in overall economic activity; (4) conformity of the series to overall business cycles; a series conforms positively if it rises in expansions and declines in downturns; it conforms inversely if it declines in expansions and rises in downturns; a high conformity score indicates the series consistently followed the same pattern; (5) the smoothness of the series' movement over time; and (6) timeliness the frequency of release—monthly or quarterly—and the lag in release following the activity measured. The series included in *Business Conditions Digest* are classified according to seven economic processes measured. These are: (1) employment and unemployment; (2) production and income; (3) consumption, trade, orders, and deliveries; (4) fixed capital investment; (5) inventories and inventory investment; (6) prices, costs, and profits; and (7) money and credit.

The twelve components of the composite leading indicator index, the four components of the coincident index, and the six components of the lagging index are all data series that are published elsewhere, and that, on the basis of the six criteria listed above, have been elected for inclusion in these cyclical indexes. It is often possible to estimate changes in the composite indexes quite closely in advance of their release because most of the component series are already known and the method of construction is quite simple. Two caveats should be borne in mind, however. First, because many of the component series are subject to revision, the composite indexes are revised to a considerable extent. Second, these indexes are meant to be analytical measures of the cyclical behavior of the overall economy over prolonged periods. Thus, the indexes are primarily intended for use by business cycle analysts, and only secondarily for forecasting turning points in economic activity. Thus, despite the considerable effort spent by business economists in forecasting and analyzing the monthly wiggles in these indexes—especially the index of leading indicators—the short-term predictive value of the indexes is not great.

There are five steps in constructing the monthly composite indexes. First, month-to-month changes are calculated for each component series. In most cases there are percent changes, but in a few cases first differences are taken. Second, to prevent the more volatile series from dominating the index, the percent changes (or first differences) are standardized to make the average of the absolute values equal to one. Third, the standardized changes are then weighted. The weights used reflect the overall performance scores of the series as cyclical indicators. Fourth, a weighted average of the standardized changes for all available components is compiled for each month. Finally, the weighted average monthly changes for the leading and lagging indexes are each standardized once again to conform to the coincident indicator index. In this way, the movements of all three indexes are of similar magnitudes. The component series, standard factors, and weights for the leading, coincident, and lagging indicators are presented, respectively, in Tables 3-7, 3-8, and 3-9 below.

TABLE 3-7   Index of Leading Indicators

	STANDARDIZATION FACTORS	WEIGHTS
Components		
1. Average workweek of production workers, manufacturing	0.467	1.014
2. Average weekly initial claims, State unemployment insurance[1]	5.374	1.041
3. *Vendor performance	3.840	1.081
4. Change in credit outstanding	2.626	.959
5. *Percent change in sensitive prices, smoothed[2]	.324	.892
6. Contracts and orders, plant and equipment, 1972 dollars	6.194	.946
7. Index of net business formation	.996	.973
8. Index of stock prices	2.633	1.149
9. Money supply (M–2), 1972 dollars	.417	.932
10. New orders, consumer goods and materials, 1972 dollars	2.818	.973
11. Building permits, private housing	5.064	1.054
12. *Change in inventories on hand and on order, 1972 dollars, smoothed[2]	2.530	.986
Index Standardization Factor	.582	

* First differences are computed for these series rather than symmetrical percent changes.

(1) The changes for this series are inverted, i.e., multiplied by −1.

(2) Series is a weighted 4-term moving average (with weights 1, 2, 2, 1,) placed at the terminal month of the span.

Source: *Business Conditions Digest,* February 1983.

TABLE 3-8   Index of Coincident Indicators

	STANDARDIZATION FACTORS	WEIGHTS
Component		
1. Employees on nonagricultural payrolls	.321	1.064
2. Index of industrial production, total	.924	1.028
3. Personal income, less transfer payments 1972 dollars	.502	1.003
4. Manufacturing and trade sales, 1972 dollars	1.021	.905

TABLE 3-9   Index of Lagging Indicators

	STANDARDIZATION FACTORS	WEIGHTS
Component		
1. Average duration of unemployment[1]	3.587	1.098
2. Labor cost per unit of output, manufacturing	.557	.868
3. Ratio constant-dollar inventories to sales, manufacturing and sales	.016	.894
4. Commercial and industrial loans outstanding in 1972 dollars	.901	1.009
5. *Average prime rate charged by banks	.376	1.123
6. *Ratio, consumer installment debt to personal income	.062	1.009
Index Standardization factor	.707	

* First differences are computed for these series rather than symmetrical percent changes.

(1) The changes for this series are inverted, i.e. multiplied by −1.

Source: *Business Conditions Digest,* February 1983.

III. THE CONSTRUCTION OF GROSS NATIONAL PRODUCT

The concepts which underline the National Income and Product Accounts were discussed in the first section of this chapter. Section II described some of the less aggregate measures of economic activity. This section outlines the way in which the economists at the Bureau of Economic Analysis construct the quarterly GNP estimates from these other data series. This examination serves two purposes. First, the economic processes these indicators measure are exposed more clearly. Second, the business forecaster's ability to estimate GNP is enhanced by looking more closely at the relationships between monthly data series and the quarterly GNP data.

The focus here will be restricted to estimation of GNP from the product side (the monthly estimates of personal income form the basis of the estimation of GNP from the income side). There are three basic steps in BEA's initial estimate of GNP each quarter: (1) current dollar estimates of the major sectors are made; (2) deflators for each of the spending sectors are then constructed; and (3) using the constructed deflators, the current dollar estimates are deflated in order to arrive at constant dollar spending estimates. In general, monthly measures which closely approximate the spending activities being measured are used to construct the quarterly GNP components. In many cases the monthly data for the quarter may be incomplete, so projections for the missing data must be made by BEA. Nevertheless, to the extent possible, BEA attempts to match the GNP components with direct measures of the specific activity.

The estimation processes examined below are those followed by BEA for its first, preliminary, estimate of GNP, prepared roughly two weeks after the end of the quarter under review. Despite the partial nature of the data actually available, and the extent to which estimates are based on extrapolation, interpolation, and other statistical methods, the preliminary estimate of GNP is usually fairly accurate. Later, revised estimates using more complete data are made which fill in many of the gaps in the preliminary estimates.

Personal Consumption Expenditures

Spending estimates are made for nine consumption categories: three commodity and six service groups:

(1)   *Motor vehicles and parts* are somewhat unusual in that this is one of several categories for which the basic data are available in real terms, which are then inflated by a price measure to arrive at current dollar estimates. Monthly data on unit sales of domestic and imported autos and trucks, expressed in millions of units at seasonally adjusted annual rates—reported by the Motor Vehicle Manufacturers Association and Wards' Automotive Reports—are multiplied by separate BEA estimates of their average unit value. The resulting total value of motor vehicle sales is then multiplied by the shares of new auto and new truck purchases made by consumers—derived from market data supplied by R.L. Polk & Co.—resulting in a current dollar estimate of consumer expenditures on new motor vehicles. The remaining new motor vehicle sales are included in spending for producers' durable equipment.

(2)   Spending on *gasoline and oil* is estimated from trade source data on automotive gasoline sales, in billions of gallons, and BLS estimates of the average price per gallon.

(3)   Consumption of *all other commodities* is estimated from the Census Bureau's series on total monthly retail sales, excluding sales by: the building materials groups, motor vehicles dealers, and gasoline service stations. These retail sales data are expressed in millions of dollars.

(4)   Spending on *housing services* is estimated using BEA's estimate of the housing stock and the BLS consumer price index component for residential rent.

(5)   Consumer spending on *electricity* is estimated using data on revenue from sales to ultimate residential customers in millions of dollars compiled by the Edison Electric Institute and the CPI component for electricity.

(6)   Spending on *natural gas* is estimated from data compiled by the American Gas Association on sales of gas to ultimate residential customers in trillions of BTUs and the CPI component for piped gas.

(7)   *Telephone* expenditures are based on millions of dollars of local telephone revenues recorded by the Federal Communications Commission.

(8)   *Spending at privately controlled hospitals and sanatoriums* is estimated from data on the total expenses of community hospitals, expressed in millions of dollars, as reported by the American Hospital Association.

(9) Spending for *other services* is estimated statistically, based on past actual trends.

It can be noted that nearly two-thirds of consumer spending is accounted for by categories (3) and (9), for which there is less detailed data than for the other seven groups. Nevertheless, as noted above, the statistical methods used by BEA to supplement the specific spending measures produce quite good estimates of total consumer spending. Indeed, BEA estimates spending for all major components of consumer spending, not merely for those detailed above, and CPI components are used to derive deflators for twelve consumption categories. These are:

(1) Motor vehicles and parts
(2) Furniture and household equipment
(3) Other durable goods
(4) Food
(5) Clothing and shoes
(6) Gasoline and oil
(7) Fuel oil and coal
(8) Other nondurable goods
(9) Housing services
(10) Household operations
(11) Transportation services
(12) Other services

Gross Private Domestic Investment

Spending estimates are made for six categories of nonresidential fixed investment, residential fixed investment, and the change in business inventories.

Estimates of investment spending on nonresidential structures are made for three categories.

(1) *Building, utilities, and farm structures* are estimated on the basis of the Census Bureau's report on the value of new nonresidential construction put in place, expressed in billions of dollars at annual rates.
(2) *Oil and gas well drilling and exploration* are estimated by multiplying the American Petroleum Institute's reported total for oil and gas drilling footage, by BEA's estimate of the cost per foot.
(3) *Other* nonresidential structures are estimated using statistical methods.

Estimates for *producers' durable equipment* are made for three categories.

(1) Spending on *motor vehicles* is based on the remainder of the estimate of new auto and new truck purchases made for consumer spending, above.

(2)   Spending on *aircraft* is estimated based on the Census Bureau's report on manufacturers' shipments of complete civilian aircraft, expressed in millions of dollars.

(3)   *Other* producers' durable expenditures are estimated from three sources: (1) the Census Bureau's report on shipments of nondefense capital goods, expressed in millions of dollars; (2) an estimate of capital goods purchased by businesses, expressed in billions of dollars at an annual rate, prepared jointly by the Census Bureau and BEA; and (3) BEA's survey of planned new equipment expenditures, expressed in billions of dollars at an annual rate.

Residential fixed investment spending is estimated from three data sources: (1) the value of new residential construction put in place, expressed in billions of dollars at an annual rate, reported by the Census Bureau; (2) new single family housing units started, expressed in thousands of units at an annual rate, also reported by the Census Bureau; and (3) manufacturers' shipments of new mobile homes, in thousands of units at an annual rate, from data compiled by the National Conference of States on Building Codes and Standards.

The *change in business inventories* is estimated using the Census Bureau's reports on inventories of manufacturers, merchant wholesalers, and retail trade, expressed in millions of dollars; the producer price index components for farm products and processed foods and feeds, and for industrial commodities, both on a 1967 = 100 basis, as well as inventory book value price indexes are prepared jointly by BEA and BLS, on a 1972 = 100 basis.

Deflation for gross private domestic investment components is done using a number of special price measures in addition to those already referred to.

(1)   Nonresidential structures are deflated by using the Federal Highway Administration cost index for highway structures, 1972 = 100, and the Turner Construction Company construction cost index, 1972 = 100.

(2)   Expenditures on producers' durable equipment are deflated using the producer price index for finished capital equipment, 1967 = 100 basis, as well as inventory book value price indexes prepared jointly by BEA and BLS, on a 1972 = 100 basis.

(3)   Expenditures on residential structures are deflated using the Bureau of the Census index of new one family houses, 1972 = 100.

(4)   The change in business inventories is deflated by the nonfarm inventory change price indexes for food and farm products and other goods, prepared jointly by BLS and BEA, 1972 = 100.

Net exports of goods and services are estimated using the joint Census Bureau-BEA data on U.S. exports and imports of merchandise, expressed in billions of dollars. Deflation is done by using the unit value indexes of U.S. exports and imports, 1972 = 100, prepared by the Census Bureau.

Estimates of Federal *government purchases of goods and services* are based on Treasury Department reports on a cash basis. There is no data basis for deflation.

Estimates of *state and local government spending* are based on three data sources: (1) state and local government employment as reported by BLS in thousands; (2) the values of new construction put in place by state and local governments, reported by the Census Bureau in billions of dollars at annual rates; and (3) medical vendor payments under federally assisted and other state programs, reported in billions of dollars at an annual rate by the Department of Health and Human Services. There is again no data basis for deflation.

Table 3-10 below, presents the preliminary estimates for GNP components used by BEA for constructing GNP for the fourth quarter of 1983 (IV 83), and the data sources on which these current dollar estimates were based. The data series for each month during the fourth quarter and the fourth quarter totals are presented in detail. This table offers three insights to the construction of the GNP estimates. First, the relationship of each of the estimated components to the total GNP can be seen. Second, the relationships between the monthly and quarterly source data can be seen: in some cases (such as retail sales of autos) the monthly data are expressed at monthly rates, so that the quarterly total equals the sum of the three monthly observations and is itself expressed at a quarterly rather than at an annual rate. Finally, a feel can be derived for the relationships that underlie the construction of the GNP components from the diverse data sources these estimates are based on.

IV. FINANCIAL AND FOREIGN EXCHANGE MARKET MEASURES

The measures examined so far in this chapter have been mainly related to the goods market, or "real side" of the economy. This section discusses some of the principal measures of financial activity—the money market—grouped under four headings: (1) monetary aggregates and their components, (2) financial instruments and interest rates, (3) the flow of funds, and (4) foreign trade and finance. The basic source of most of this material is the *Federal Reserve Bulletin,* published monthly and available by subscription from the Board of Governors of the Federal Reserve System, Washington, DC 20051. Many measures are also released in separate reports, issued on a more timely basis by either the Board of Governors or individual Federal Reserve Banks.

Monetary Aggregates and Their Components

In practice, the concept of "money" is more complicated than the single "money supply" discussed in Chapter 2. As the U.S. economy has become more complex the types of financial assets which the public views

TABLE 3-10 Current Dollar GNP Estimates and Source Data—Fourth Quarter 1983

Estimated GNP and Components

			Source Data			
			OCT.	NOV.	DEC.	IV.
Billions of dollars seasonally adjusted annual rates						
Gross National Product	3,432.0					
Personal Consumption Expenditures	2,233.1					
1) Motor Vehicles and Parts	143.2	1) New Motor Vehicles:				
		Domestic autos:				
		Retail sales (mil. a.r.)	7.0	6.9	7.8	7.2
		Average unit value ($)	10,554	10,574	10,473	10,534
		Imported autos:				
		Retail sales (mil. a.r.)	2.8	2.6	2.7	2.7
		Average unit value ($)	10,926	11,391	11,292	11,203
		Consumer share of new auto purchases (%)	65.7	67.3	68.1	67.0
		Trucks				
		Retail sales (thous.)	237.1	243.9	257.8	738.8
		Average unit value ($)	16,402	16,859	16,296	16,516
		Consumer share of new truck purchases (%)	39.8	38.2	39.6	39.6
2) Gasoline and oil	91.6	2) Automotive gasoline:				
		Sales (bil. gal)	8.7	9.0	8.0	26.5
3) Other commodities	886.4	3) Sales of all retail stores less building materials group, motor vehicle dealers and gasoline service stations (mil. $)	69,742	70,052	69,890	209,684
4) Housing services	375.2	4) Housing stock (mil.)	81.7	81.8	81.9	81.8
		CPI, rent, residential (1967 = 100)	240.4	241.3	242.3	241.3

5) Electricity	56.1	5)	Kilowatt hour sales to ultimate residential customers (mil. $)	62,742	70,052	69,890	209,684
			CPI, electricity (1967 = 100)	337.1	341.8	341.5	340.1
6) Natural gas	31.5	6)	Sales of gas to utimate residential customers (tril. Btu.)	363.1	391.5	465.2	1,219.8
			CPI, utility (piped) gas (1967 = 100)	572.6	576.8	579.1	576.2
7) Telephone	37.5	7)	Local telephone revenues (mil. $)	2,640.7	2,679.1	2,713.4	8,033.2
8) Privately controlled hospitals and sanatoriums	109.6	8)	Total expenses of community hospitals (mil. $)	10,257.3	10,270.1	10,354.8	30,882.2
9) Other services	502.0	9)		—	—	—	—
Gross private domestic investment							
Fixed investment	512.1						
Nonresidential	371.2						
Structures	134.5						
1) Buildings, utilities and farm	102.6	1)	Value of new nonresidential construction put in place (a.r.)	101.3	105.0	105.5	103.9
2) Oil and gas well drilling and exploration	30.5	2)	Oil and gas drilling footage (mil. ft.)	25.7	26.8	27.0	79.5
			Cost per foot ($)	—	—	—	93.1
3) Other	1.4	3)		—	—	—	—
Producers' durable equipment	236.8						
1) Motor Vehicles	36.8	1)	See personal consumption expenditures for sales and prices of autos and trucks:				
			Business share of new motor vehicle purchases (%):				
			Trucks	48.1	50.1	48.8	49.1
			Autos	33.3	31.7	30.9	32.0
2) Aircraft	6.0	2)	Manufacturers' shipments of complete civilian aircraft (mil. $)	48.1	50.1	48.8	49.1

TABLE 3-10 Current Dollar GNP Estimates and Source Data—Fourth Quarter 1983

Estimated GNP and Components				Source Data			
				OCT.	NOV.	DEC.	IV.
3) Other	194.0	3)	Manufacturers' shipments of nondefense capital goods (mil. $)	23,077	24,411	24,500	71,988
			Capital goods purchased by business (a.r.)	221.0	230.7	233.6	228.4
			New equipment expenditures	—	—	—	208.7
Residential	140.8		Value of new residential construction put in place (a.r.)	121.7	118.3	118.1	119.4
			New single family housing units started (thous. a.r.)	1010	1065	1040	1038
			Manufacturers' shipments of mobile homes (thous. a.r.)	279	319	311	303
Change in business inventories	+17.7						
Nonfarm	+26.0						
1) Manufacturing and trade	+24.7	1)	Change in book value of inventories:				
			Manufacturing (mil. $)	795	−119	853	1,529
			Merchant wholesalers (mil. $)	1,472	−327	1,501	2,646
			Retail trade (mil. $)	−151	2,447	1,900	4,196
			PPI (1967 = 100)				
			Farm products and processed foods and feeds	262.9	261.8	261.5	262.1
			Industrial commodities	318.0	318.9	319.7	318.9
			Inventory book value price indexes (1972 = 100) Food	198.7	198.5	199.1	199.1

			198.1	198.3	198.8	198.8
2) Other	+1.3					
Farm	−8.3					
Net exports of goods and services	−32.6					
Exports	348.1					
Merchandise	115.9	U.S. exports of merchandise	16.7	17.1	17.2	51.0
Other	145.1					
Imports	380.7					
Merchandise	288.6	U.S. imports of merchandise	24.9	23.4	24.2	72.5
Government purchases of goods and services	701.7					
Federal	275.6	Federal purchases (cash basis, not seasonally adjusted)	22.3	23.4	23.5	69.2
State and local	426.1					
1) Compensation of employees	246.9	State and local government employment (thous.)	13,001	13,003	13,006	13,003
2) Structures	40.5	New construction put in place (a.r.)	38.9	40.5	42.2	40.5
3) Other	138.6					

Source: *Key Source Data and Projections for National Income and Product Estimates*, U.S. Department of Commerce, Bureau of Economic Analysis, January 1984.

and uses as "money" have multiplied. The Federal Reserve has responded to these changes in public usage by refining the concepts measured to track the role of money in the economy. Just as the National Income and Product Accounts have steadily evolved in the postwar period, so also have the monetary aggregates. The latest revision and redefinition of these aggregates began in early 1980.[12] As a result, there are four money measures ranging from the narrowest, which is closest to a measure of the transaction demand, to the broadest, which includes assets much less suitable for transactions purposes, but which yield a return in the form of interest and still possess some liquidity.

It should be recognized that these aggregates, often referred to as the money "supply," measure neither supply nor demand in the strict microeconomic sense. Rather, the measured money "supply" tracks the intersections of the demand and supply functions for money over time.

The narrowest money measure is *M–1*, which includes the nonbanking public's holdings of currency and checkable deposits. Checkable deposits consist of: demand deposits (checking accounts) at commercial banks; travelers checks of nonbank issuers; and interest-earning checkable deposits at all depository institutions—namely negotiable orders of withdrawal (NOW) accounts, automatic transfer from savings (ATS) accounts, and credit union share draft balances. The nationwide introduction of interest-bearing checkable accounts beginning in 1981 raised problems of compatibility with past data.

Thus, for a transition period in 1981 there were three different M–1 measures; (1) *M–1A* consisted only of currency and demand deposits at commercial banks; (2) *M–1B* included M–1A and other checkable deposits; while (3) *M–1B shift-adjusted* removed from M–1B inflows to other checkable deposits deemed to have originated in sources other than demand deposits (mainly savings deposits). As the transition to nationwide, other checkable deposits progressed in 1981 it was possible to return to one measure of M–1, essentially equal to M–1B, in 1982.

M–1 represents highly liquid assets which are chiefly used for transactions purposes. These data are released each Thursday, except when holidays delay release, ten days after the reporting week (ending Monday) covered. The data are also reported on a monthly and quarterly average basis in the *Federal Reserve Bulletin*. Monthly data for M–1, the other main money stock measures, and their main components for June 1983 are presented in Table 3-11.

M–2 is roughly four times as large as M–1, which it includes, as well as five other classes of less liquid assets. The largest such class of assets as of June 1983 were small-denomination time deposits at commercial banks and

---

[12] See "The Redefined Monetary Aggregates," *Federal Reserve Bulletin* (Feb. 1980), for a detailed account.

TABLE 3-11   Money Stock Measures and Main Components: June 1983 (billions of dollars)

M-1	511.7
Currency	140.3
Demand deposits	244.0
Travelers checks	4.7
Other checkable deposits	122.7
M-2	2114.4
M-1	511.7
Money market deposit accounts	367.3
Savings deposits	325.0
Small-denomination time deposits	722.1
Overnight RPs and Eurodollars	56.0*
Money market mutual funds	
(general purpose and broker/dealer)	132.9*
M-3	2498.8
M-2	2114.4
Large-denomination time deposits	304.1
Money market mutual funds	
(institution only)	34.7*
Other (mainly term RPs)	45.6
L	3059.9
M-3	2498.8
Other liquid assets	561.1

* These items are not seasonally adjusted.
Source: *Federal Reserve Bulletin,* December 1983.

thrift institutions. These are deposits of less than $100,000 that earn higher interest rates than savings accounts, but which must be left on deposit for some specified term or else the interest premium is forfeited. The second largest and newest (introduced in December 1982) type of deposits in M–2 are high-yielding Money Market Deposit Accounts. These accounts require a minimum deposit and offer check writing privileges, but only in excess of some minimum amount (usually $500). The next largest class of assets included in M–2 are savings deposits at commercial and thrift institutions. The liquidity of these deposits is greater than for time deposits, but their usefulness as transaction balances is less than that of checkable deposits. The fourth largest component of M–2 consists of money market mutual fund shares. These funds require a minimum initial investment and often offer their customers check writing privileges, subject to a minimum amount per check (typically $500). The remaining asset classes are overnight repurchase agreements (RPs) issued by commercial banks and overnight Eurodollar deposits held by U.S. nonbank residents at Caribbean branches of U.S.

banks. Repurchase agreements are transactions in which one party "sells" a U.S. government security with an explicit agreement to buy it back—in this case the next day—at the same price plus an agreed upon interest payment. Thus, an overnight RP is a one-day collateralized loan. RPs are usually executed for amounts of $500,000 or more, and interest is calculated on a 360 day year. Eurodollar deposits are either time deposits or negotiable certificates of deposit denominated in U.S. dollars on the books of banks or branches outside the U.S. Finally, there is a small consolidation amount subtracted from M–2 reflecting the demand deposits owned by thrift institutions (included in M–1) to avoid double counting.

The next broadest monetary aggregate, M–3, differs from M–2 mainly by including large (over $100,000) time deposits, or certificates of deposit (CDs), at commercial banks and thrift institutions. Money market mutual fund shares owned by institutions are also included (accounting for just over 1% of M–3 in June 1983). In addition, term RPs—repurchase agreements for longer than one day—issued by commercial banks and savings and loan associations are included. These latter are a small portion of M–3 but quite like CDs in terms of their role in portfolios.

The broadest measure of money, *L*, contains M–3 and all other liquid assets. These include: liquid Treasury obligations, U.S. savings bonds, commercial paper, banker's acceptances, and other Eurodollar deposits of nonbank U.S. residents. Commercial paper refers to short-term (from one to 270 days), unsecured promissory notes sold by large businesses at a discount. A banker's acceptance is a time draft—issued by a person or corporation, for which the responsibility of payment has been "accepted" by a commercial bank.

Financial Instruments and Interest Rates

This section identifies some of the main deposit and credit instruments used in U.S. financial markets and the interest rates associated with them. These instruments can be grouped into three classes: (1) loans that affect bank reserves, (2) short- and long-term money market instruments, and (3) bank loans and deposits. Data on outstanding amounts and interest rates offered on all these instruments are reported in the *Federal Reserve Bulletin*.

Before turning to specifics it is necessary to describe how interest rates are computed. In general, there are two methods. Interest rates for many short-term instruments—including U.S. Treasury bills, commercial paper, directly placed finance paper, and banker's acceptances—are computed on a bank *discount* basis. Most other interest rates are computed on an investment *yield* basis.

For instance, U.S. Treasury bills—obligations of the U.S. Treasury with a maturity of a year or less—are sold at auction. The rate of return is calculated by dividing the difference between the par price (100) and the average auction price—this difference is the discount—by the par price and multiplying this amount by the portion of a 360-day year the bill is for. Thus, a 91-day bill sold at 97 ($970 per $1,000 of face value) would return

$$\frac{100 - 97}{100} \times \frac{360}{91} = 11.87\%$$

These highly liquid securities can be resold in the secondary market with either capital gain or loss accruing to the buyer, depending on then current conditions.

An investment *yield* is computed on a 365-day year. For long-dated securities, a particular yield is quoted when the securities are first sold, say 10% on a 10-year bond (interest of $100 per $1,000 of face amount) payable at stated times. The market yield to maturity is computed using the purchase price as the divisor. Thus, the yield on a 10%, 10-year bond selling for 99 ($990) is equal to

$$\frac{100}{99} = 10.10\%$$

Interest rates on most other forms of bank and money market instruments are quoted at annual rates (365-day basis) even if the term is for a portion of a year.

Interest rates on monthly and quarterly average bases for the instruments described below are published in the *Federal Reserve Bulletin*. Daily quotes are reported in the financial pages of major newspapers, particularly the *Wall Street Journal*.

Federal Funds and the Discount Window

Interbank loans in the Federal funds market and bank borrowings through the discount window of Federal Reserve Banks are among the shortest-term loans made. They also possess a special importance because these loans affect the amount of reserves in the banking system, the growth of deposits, and ultimately the growth of the monetary aggregates. Thus, the *Federal funds* rate and the *discount* rate are affected by Federal Reserve policy.

The need for member banks to maintain a required level of reserves against deposits—the reserve requirements set by the Federal Reserve— comprise one side of the market for reserves. The other key factor stems from the fact that deposit and loan flows vary, leaving some banks with temporary excess reserves and others with a shortfall. Federal funds loans are made by banks with idle reserves in excess of their own level of required reserves to banks with a reserve shortfall. The loans are usually one-day (overnight) loans, though the interest rate—the Federal funds rate—is quoted at an annual (365-day) rate. (An overnight loan is thus made at an interest rate equal to 1/365th of the annual rate, an over-the-weekend loan at 3/365th of the annual rate.) The Federal funds rate level, thus, serves as a barometer of the ease or tightness of reserves in the banking system. The Federal Reserve, in turn, monitors the Federal funds market to gain a "feel" for the availability of reserves and the likely implications of this demand/supply for monetary growth. Through its open market operations the Federal Reserve may offer to buy Treasury securities from dealers, thus injecting reserves into the banking system; or it may offer to sell securities, thereby absorbing (draining) reserves. Consequently, the Federal funds rate is important both as a measure of deposit creation in the banking system, and as a measure of the Federal Reserve's response to reserve flows and monetary growth.

Another source of bank reserves is direct borrowing from the Federal Reserve through the discount window at the discount rate. This is intended to be a source of "last resort" for occasional use by the banking system. As such, the discount rate is usually set close to the Federal funds rate, and at times a surcharge has been leveled against borrowers who make too frequent use of this option. Loans through the discount window represent direct additions to the level of reserves. Thus, both the discount rate and the ease with which these loans are made reflect the posture of Federal Reserve policy.

Short- and Long-term Money Market Instruments

Certificates of deposit (CDs) are funds placed on deposit with a bank at an agreed upon rate for an agreed term. CDs are another instrument banks use to obtain reserves, especially when the bank wishes to "lock in" the funds for a longer period than the usual overnight term in the Federal funds market. CDs may be in nonnegotiable form, in which case the interest rate is computed on a yield basis, or in negotiable form in which case the interest rate is computed on a discount basis.

Eurodollar deposits and *Eurodollar certificates of deposit* are deposits at, or CDs issued by, foreign branches of U.S. banks. Interest rates are computed on a yield basis for deposits and on a discount basis for CDs.

Securities—bills, notes, and bonds—are credit instruments issued directly to lenders which can be resold in secondary markets and reflect the creditworthiness of the issuer. The major issuers of these instruments, ranked from lowest risk to highest risk are: the U.S. Treasury, Federal agencies, state and local governments and their agencies, utilities, and corporations.[13] In general, interest rates for issues of similar maturities reflect this

---

[13] Banks, brokerage houses, and other institutions may act as dealers, however, and so do fulfill the role of a financial intermediary. Indeed, banks may, at times, act directly as either a borrower or a lender in these markets.

risk spectrum: rates on Treasuries are lowest,[14] while those on corporate bonds are highest. Interest rates vary within each class of security depending on a number of factors including: the term to maturity, the relative supply-demand in each issuer-maturity class, and the assessed credit rating of the issuer.

Bills are securities with a maturity of a year or less and the interest is computed on a discount basis. Notes usually have maturities between one and ten years, while bonds have maturities beyond ten years of the issue date. Interest rates for both notes and bonds are computed on a yield basis.

Bank Loans and Deposits

Most of the remaining credit raised in the U.S. by the private nonbanking sector is raised through bank loans. These comprise a variety of forms, including: commercial and industrial loans, real estate loans, consumer loans, loans for the purchase of securities, agricultural loans, and leasing finance loans. Most of these loans are typically made for varying maturities at a floating rate based on the *prime rate*. The prime rate is a notional rate commercial banks quote as a guide to their best customers.

The basic forms of bank deposits are: demand deposits, other checkable deposits, time deposits, and "small" (under $100,000) term deposits. No interest is paid on demand deposits. Maximum interest rates paid on other deposits are set by bank regulatory authorities, but generally increase as the term to maturity lengthens.

The Flow of Funds

The credit instruments and interest rates described above are but a sample of the complex flow of credit that takes place in the U.S. economy. Indeed, the *Federal Reserve Bulletin* is just one source of data, and it provides far more detail than can be described here. One place in which the flows of borrowings and loans come together is in the Flow of Funds accounts constructed by the Federal Reserve. The Flow of Funds accounts attempt to summarize the relationships for the financial side of the economy similar to the way the National Income and Product Accounts treat the market for goods and services.

The Flow of Funds accounts portray the total amount of borrowed funds raised, the sources of these funds by both sector and debt instrument, and the principal uses to which these funds are put. The *Federal Reserve Bulletin* presents two summary tables which show flows on an annual and

---

[14] State and local government-issued securities—referred to as municipals—usually have lower yields than for Treasury securities. This reflects the exemptions from Federal income tax of interest earned on municipals. When this difference is adjusted for, however, Treasury yields are usually lower, reflecting their low risk.

semi-annual basis for recent years. The first shows funds raised by sector and debt instruments in U.S. credit markets. The second shows direct and indirect sources of funds to credit markets. In addition, the Federal Reserve compiles and reports quarterly Flow of Funds data, providing more detail about each borrowing and supplying (lending) sector. This report is released about eight weeks after the end of the quarter covered.

Foreign Trade and Finance

In addition, to the measures of exports and imports of goods and services used in the National Income and Product Accounts, the Department of Commerce compiles extensive data on the flows of goods, services, and payments between the U.S. and the rest of the world. In general, there are three levels of aggregation on which data on foreign trade and commerce are kept.

(1)   The *merchandise trade account* reports exports and imports of goods for the U.S. These reports are made monthly roughly four to six weeks after the end of the month covered. These data are in turn used as inputs to the current account and the National Income and Product Accounts.

(2)   The *current account* measures the exports and imports of goods and services for the U.S. In addition to the flows of goods measured by the merchandise trade account, services such as interest payments and receipts, freight charges, transportation fares, and tourist flows are included. In addition to the components which are included in the GNP, the current account includes private transfers and U.S. government grants.

(3)   The *balance of payments* includes, in addition to the current account, a capital account which measures private and official flows of short- and long-term capital. In one sense—when all of the components are regarded—the balance of payments must always balance. However, since some of the items—official reserves and official capital flows, for instance—may be regarded as compensating movements, a balance is usually struck at some point to determine the health of the economy's external account. There are three methods by which this is done in the U.S.: the *basic balance* is derived by adding the balance on long-term capital to the current account balance; the *net liquidity balance* adds the short-term private nonliquid balance, the allocation of Special Drawing Rights, and errors and omissions to the basic balance; and the *official settlements balance* comprises the net liquidity balance plus the short-term private liquid capital balance.

The data on the current account and the balance of payments are reported quarterly, though with a long lag. Generally, these detailed accounts are reported nearly three months after the end of the quarter covered.

Data on foreign exchange rates and interest rates are reported in the *Federal Reserve Bulletin*. A more comprehensive source of data on exchange rates and foreign interest rates is *International Financial Statistics* published by the International Monetary Fund.

QUESTIONS FOR REVIEW AND RESEARCH

3-1 Gross National Product is a "flow" concept, whereas wealth is a "stock" concept. Viewing the main components of the product account of GNP, indicate which reflect a change in the stock of wealth and identify these stocks.

3-2 Plot the annual shares of total real consumer spending accounted for by real consumption of durable goods, nondurable goods, and services for the years of the post-war period. (These data can be found in the statistical section of *The Economic Report of the President* for the most recent year.) What conclusions can you draw about the evolving consumption habits of U.S. households? Contrast the behavior of these trends in business cycle downturns, recoveries, and expansions.

3-3 Contrast the cyclical behavior of personal income and after-tax corporate profits in a similar manner to that done for the consumption components in question 3-2.

3-4 Every July, the U.S. Commerce department publishes revised estimates of GNP and its components for the prior three years in the July issue of the *Survey of Current Business*. Using the July issues of the *Survey* for 1976–78, trace the revisions to the main product components of GNP for the 1974-75 recession (the four quarters of 1974 and the first quarter of 1975). In December 1980, BEA released an extensive revision of NIPA estimates back through the 1960s in a special supplement to the December 1980 *Survey of Current Business*. Contrast these revisions with the original data and the 1976–78 revisions for the 1974–75 recession. How do the revised data change your impression of this recession?

3-5 Contrast annual employment data as measured by the Bureau of Labor Statistics' household and payroll surveys for the post-war period. Suggest reasons for the differences.

3-6 Compare the inflation rates measured by the implicit price deflator for personal consumption expenditures and the Consumer Price Index in 1973–74 and 1979–80. Suggest reasons for the differences that emerge.

3-7 Using monthly data for the latest complete quarter, perform a reconstruction of the current dollar GNP estimate of the quarter.

3-8 Contrast the revised definition of the narrowly defined monetary aggregate (M–1) with the concept of money used in developing the LM curve in Chapter 2. Identify those components which are: mainly transactions components, mainly portfolio components, and mixed components. What modifications does the Federal Reserve's definition of narrow money suggest are needed in a money demand-supply forecast?

4

STATISTICAL METHODS
The tools
of forecasting

An economic forecast is much more than a set of quantitative measures of future events. As described in Chapter 1, a forecast prepared by a business economist should be an important input to the decision making process of business managers. This requires that a clear, operational picture of the future business climate be presented so that managers can make equally clear decisions about the future conduct of their operations. Thus, the *qualitative* findings are essential if the forecast is to be a useful management tool.

Still, at the core of an economic forecast are quantitative results. Economic activity is measured in quantities—as described in Chapter 3—and forecasts are presented in quantitative terms for two reasons. The first reason is to extend the quantitative measurement of past economic activity into the future. At the most aggregate level, economic activity is expressed in terms of the billions of dollars of the Gross National Product; one way to evaluate future economic performance is to compare the value of GNP in future periods to past values. The second role of quantitative measures in a forecast is to provide the business manager—the ultimate "customer" of the business economist—with a means of applying the results to future operations.

This chapter discusses some of the main statistical methods the business economist uses to analyze data and construct economic forecasts. Such a one-chapter treatment must be cursory. A thorough treatment would require a book of its own, and still only scratch the surface. The reader can, and should consult other works which provide thorough treatment of this subject.[1] The brief discussion in this chapter is intended to provide the reader with an overview of the basic quantitative approaches to forecast, and to prepare the reader for the forecast examples in Part II.

It is likely that, in practice, a computer will be used to relieve the forecaster of tedious calculations. Nevertheless, the novice forecaster in particular should be familiar with the basics of statistical and econometric analysis. Unless a forecaster has a thorough knowledge of the computations a computer performs rapidly, there is a danger that results which violate one or more of the basic assumptions of statistics and econometrics will be accepted as valid simply because they have the "authority" of being computer generated. The computer, which should be a tool of the forecaster, thus has the potential of becoming a dangerous weapon that can mislead the forecaster if the procedures performed are not fully understood.

The first section of this chapter (section I) discusses simple methods of looking at quantitative data, and preparing it to be used in forecasting. Some of these methods—plotting the data on a graph and making simple transfor-

---

[1] There is a vast literature on statistics and econometrics. Two works which provide accessible treatments for the novice forecaster are: Robert S. Pindyck and Daniel L. Rubinfeld, *Econometric Models and Economic Forecasts* (New York: McGraw-Hill, 1976); and Dominick Salvatore, *Theory and Problems of Statistics and Econometrics* (New York: McGraw-Hill, 1982). A more advanced treatment, directly geared to forecasting, is Michael D. Intriligator, *Econometric Models, Techniques and Applications* (Englewood Cliffs, NJ: Prentice-Hall, 1978). A classic, but advanced, treatment is J. Johnston, *Econometric Methods* (New York: McGraw-Hill, 1972).

mations—may seem self-evident, but are stressed because, as with most complex processes, a thorough preparation yields great results. Moreover, many times simple arithmetic transformations reveal useful insights to the forecasting process. In any case, the greater the analyst's knowledge of the behavior of a data series over time, the greater is the confidence with which it can be forecast. The section concludes with a discussion of "time series forecasting." This approach includes techniques from the simple to the complex. They share a reliance on past values of a data series to forecast future values.

Section II deals with the technique of regression analysis, the most common approach used by economists for quantifying the relationships among economic variables. The first detailed illustration of this process is a simple regression of the consumption function, described in Chapter 2. This example serves to highlight the main properties as well as some of the major pitfalls of regression analysis. Some of the main differences encountered in a multiple regression analysis are examined in an example estimating a somewhat more complex consumption function.

The chapter concludes with a discussion of *ex post,* out-of-sample forecasting and forecast error analysis (section III). These techniques are important methods by which forecasters can evaluate the accuracy of the forecast models, judgmentally adjust the results, and offer guidance to the users of a forecast on its reliability.

I. LOOKING AT DATA OVER TIME

Economists rarely forecast discrete events, such as the outcome of an election, or whether there will be a major war in the next year. Even a forecast of the next year's GNP is seldom restricted to the either/or choice of whether it will be up or down from the current level. Instead, these forecasts are concerned with the value of the next observation, or the next several observations in a sequence.[2] This reflects the fact that economic forecasts most often attempt to extend a series of past observations into the future; in other words, forecasts deal with time series data.

Chapters 2 and 3 discussed two needs of the economic forecaster: (1) a theoretical model, or hypothesis, as a basis; and (2) a thorough knowledge of the concepts used to measure economic activities. It is equally important for a forecaster to know how a measure has performed in the past. This does not mean that the future will merely repeat the past. Nevertheless, the

---

[2] The forecast need not be explicitly expressed in levels for this to be true. It may be expressed in terms of the change, or growth rate, between levels. Implicitly, the next level is still being forecast. For instance, if a GNP forecast is for 3% growth over the next year, then, given the current level of GNP, next year's level can be forecast.

behavior of a particular economic measure is more likely to reflect its past behavior than to differ completely from it. Moreover, careful analysis of past behavior provides the forecaster with a "feel" for the data as more than mere random observations. Rather they are seen as a set of related information about an economic process. Such analysis should reveal: whether there is a strong consistent trend to the series; whether seasonal forces are important; the degrees of variation around the trend in different phases of the business cycle; and whether variations in the series are related to changes in other series.

Analysis of time series data should always include two basic steps: (1) simple transformation of the series, such as computing first differences and growth rates; and (2) plotting past values, either in original or transformed form, on a graph. These steps help to highlight both the trend over time and its stability. It is especially helpful if, by transforming the data, a near-constant trend—or one with much less variation than the original series—can be found. If this can be achieved—and it is more likely to be true of transformed than raw data—the task of forecasting becomes much easier. Often looking at transformed data may suggest a forecasting approach. Examples of these two steps in forecast preparation will be examined using a number of labor market indicators for 1982 and 1983. The five series used are: the noninstitutional civilian population aged sixteen and over (Population); the civilian labor force (Labor Force); the number of civilians employed based on the Bureau of Labor Statistics' Household Survey (Employment); the number of unemployed for the BLS Household Survey (Unemployment); and the unemployment rate that results (Unemployment Rate, equal to unemployment divided by the labor force). Monthly values for each of these series for 1982 and 1983 are shown in Table 4-1.

The data in Table 4-1 are graphed in Figures 4-1a and 4-1b. The table and graphs by themselves supply some useful information about the *relative size* and *variability* of the data.

> It can be readily seen that the first four series—population, labor force, employment and unemployment—range from the most aggregate, population—of which, the other three are components—to the least comprehensive measure, unemployment.
>
> Minimum inspection confirms the composition of the labor force by its two components: employment and unemployment. It can also be easily confirmed that the unemployment rate is equal to unemployment divided by the labor force, expressed in percent.
>
> It is apparent from the graphs that the more aggregate the series, the more stable the trend.

This last observation has to be made carefully. Comparing Figure 4-1a with Figure 4-1b, it can be seen that the trends for the series in the former are far more stable than those in the latter. Part of this difference, however, is

TABLE 4-1   Labor Market Conditions (seasonally adjusted levels)

	POPU-LATION	LABOR FORCE	EMPLOYMENT	UNEMPLOYMENT	UNEMPLOYMENT RATE
			(IN MILLIONS)		(%)
Jan. '82	171.335	109.075	99.682	9.393	8.6
Feb.	171.409	109.503	99.810	9.693	8.9
Mar.	171.667	109.664	99.754	9.910	9.0
Apr.	171.844	109.901	99.598	10.303	9.4
May	172.026	110.542	100.179	10.363	9.4
June	172.190	110.133	99.653	10.480	9.5
July	172.364	110.399	99.503	10.896	9.9
Aug.	172.511	110.473	99.563	10.910	9.9
Sept.	172.690	110.679	99.412	11.267	10.2
Oct.	172.881	110.690	99.146	11.544	10.4
Nov.	173.058	110.923	99.036	11.887	10.7
Dec.	173.199	110.873	98.979	11.894	10.7
Jan. '83	173.354	110.677	99.154	11.523	10.4
Feb.	173.505	110.688	99.172	11.516	10.4
Mar.	173.656	110.735	99.316	11.419	10.3
Apr.	173.794	110.975	99.606	11.369	10.2
May	173.953	110.950	99.762	11.188	10.1
June	174.125	111.905	100.743	11.162	10.0
July	174.306	111.825	101.225	10.600	9.5
Aug.	174.440	112.117	101.484	10.633	9.5
Sept.	174.602	112.229	101.876	10.353	9.2
Oct.	174.779	111.866	101.970	9.896	8.8
Nov.	174.951	112.035	102.606	9.429	8.4
Dec.	175.121	112.136	102.941	9.195	8.2

Source: Bureau of Labor Statistics, U.S. Department of Labor.

due to the different scales used on the vertical axes. The graph in Figure 4-1a plots those three series against a vertical scale with increments of 20 million, while the scale for unemployment in Figure 4-1b has increments of 500,000. In other words, the vertical scale in Figure 4-1b is forty times more sensitive to changes than the scale in Figure 4-1a. When employment is plotted on a graph where the vertical scale has increments of 500,000 as in Figure 4-2, much more variation is revealed. Where one might have been tempted to disregard the seemingly slight variations from trend for employment in Figure 4-1a and treat the trend as a straight line, Figure 4-2 shows that this is inappropriate. Thus, graphing a series is a useful aid, but it must be done with care and it is rarely a sufficient analysis.

Indeed, it is the variation in the series—absence of a fixed stable trend—which seems most important in terms of the recent past and future paths. In order to focus on this variation the series is transformed in Tables

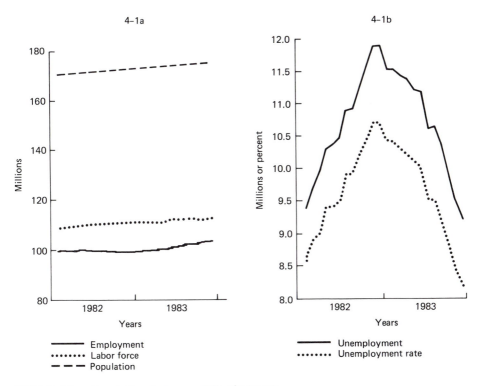

FIGURE 4-1a   **Population, Labor, and Employment**
FIGURE 4-1b   **Unemployment and Unemployment Rate**

4-2 through 4-5 into first differences and growth rates. These transformations have the desired effect of emphasizing the variation within each series. Each transformation will be discussed in detail.

Table 4-2 shows the first differences—that is, the change in value from one period to the next—in the levels for the five series shown in Table 4-1. The month-to-month changes listed in Table 4-2 are shown in millions for the first four series and in percentage points for unemployment. For instance, the value of .074 for population in February 1982 is derived from the data in Table 4-1: it is the difference between the 171.409 million for February 1982 and the 171.335 million for January 1982. This most basic of all transformations is a useful method for distinguishing data which have regular changes (like population) from those which have volatile changes (employment or unemployment).

Period-to-period simple growth rates, or percent changes, are another, slightly more complex, but very useful, data transformation. Monthly percent changes for the series in Table 4-1 are shown in Table 4-3. For instance,

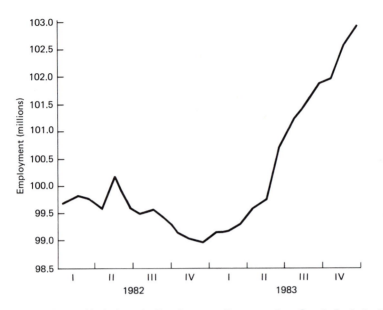

FIGURE 4-2   **Variations in Employment Emerge when Graph Scale is Changed**

focusing again on the value for population in February 1982, the value is found by dividing the change from January to February by the level in January (the base month) and then multiplying by 100 to express the result as a percent.

$$\%\Delta \text{ in Population} = \left(\frac{(\text{Pop}_{t=1} - \text{Pop}_{t=0})}{\text{Pop}_{t=0}}\right) * 100$$

$$= \left(\frac{(171.409 - 171.335)}{171.335)}\right) * 100$$

$$= 0.04\%$$

This is an often used transformation for looking at time series data. It is like first differences in showing regularity or variability within a data series. A further advantage is that, since it puts all series on a similar base—percentage changes—unlike first differences, which show varied sized changes depending on the units the original series is measured in, it is easier to compare series for relative variability. For instance, it is evident that unemployment shows more variability than employment, and both undergo larger changes than the labor force. It is no longer as clear as it was with the first differences, however, that changes in employment and unemployment when added equal changes in the labor force. Knowing this relationship, however,

TABLE 4-2   First Differences

	POPU-LATION	LABOR FORCE	EMPLOYMENT	UNEMPLOYMENT	UNEMPLOYMENT RATE
			(IN MILLIONS)		(%)
Jan. '82					
Feb.	0.074	0.428	0.128	0.300	0.2
Mar.	0.258	0.161	−0.056	0.217	0.2
Apr.	0.177	0.237	−0.156	0.393	0.3
May	0.182	0.641	0.581	0.060	−0.0
June	0.164	−0.409	−0.526	0.117	0.1
July	0.174	0.266	−0.150	0.416	0.4
Aug.	0.147	0.074	0.060	0.014	0.0
Sept.	0.179	0.206	−0.151	0.357	0.3
Oct.	0.191	0.011	−0.266	0.277	0.2
Nov.	0.177	0.233	−0.110	0.343	0.3
Dec.	0.141	−0.050	−0.057	0.007	0.0
Jan. '83	0.155	−0.196	0.175	−0.371	−0.3
Feb.	0.151	0.011	0.018	−0.007	−0.0
Mar.	0.151	0.047	0.144	−0.097	−0.1
Apr.	0.138	0.240	0.290	−0.050	−0.1
May	0.159	−0.025	0.156	−0.181	−0.2
June	0.172	0.955	0.981	−0.026	−0.1
July	0.181	−0.080	0.482	−0.562	−0.5
Aug.	0.134	0.292	0.259	0.033	0.0
Sept.	0.162	0.112	0.392	−0.280	−0.3
Oct.	0.177	−0.363	0.094	−0.457	−0.4
Nov.	0.172	0.169	0.636	−0.467	−0.4
Dec.	0.170	0.101	0.335	−0.234	−0.2

and knowing that changes in unemployment are more variable than changes in either employment or the labor force, the insightful forecaster will recognize the value of forecasting the relatively more stable trends for the labor force and employment, treating the level of unemployment (and, thus, the unemployment rate) as a residual.

Another approach, which stresses the volatility of the period-to-period changes (or their stability), is to look at the percent changes at compound annual rates. This method takes a monthly (or weekly, or quarterly) percent change and compounds it, treating the change as if it persisted for a year.[3] This can be done simply for the change in population in February 1982. The population in February 1982 is divided by the value of the population in

[3] To convert a monthly percent change to an annual rate it is necessary to raise it to the twelfth power—the number of periods (months) over which it must be compounded. Thus, a quarterly percent change would be raised to the fourth power, a weekly change to the 52nd power.

TABLE 4-3   Monthly Percent Changes

		POPU-LATION	LABOR FORCE	EMPLOYMENT	UNEMPLOYMENT	UNEMPLOYMENT RATE
Jan.						
Feb.	'82	0.0	0.4	0.1	3.2	2.8
Mar.		0.2	0.1	−0.1	2.2	2.1
Apr.		0.1	0.2	−0.2	4.0	3.7
May		0.1	0.6	0.6	0.6	−0.0
June		0.1	−0.4	−0.5	1.1	1.5
July		0.1	0.2	−0.2	4.0	3.7
Aug.		0.1	0.1	0.1	0.1	0.1
Sept.		0.1	0.2	−0.2	3.3	3.1
Oct.		0.1	0.0	−0.3	2.5	2.4
Nov.		0.1	0.2	−0.1	3.0	2.8
Dec.		0.1	−0.0	−0.1	0.1	0.1
Jan.	'83	0.1	−0.2	0.2	−3.1	−2.9
Feb.		0.1	0.0	0.0	−0.1	−0.1
Mar.		0.1	0.0	0.1	−0.8	−0.9
Apr.		0.1	0.2	0.3	−0.4	−0.7
May		0.1	−0.0	0.2	−1.6	−1.6
June		0.1	0.9	1.0	−0.2	−1.1
July		0.1	−0.1	0.5	−5.0	−5.0
Aug.		0.1	0.3	0.3	0.3	0.1
Sept.		0.1	0.1	0.4	−2.6	−2.7
Oct.		0.1	−0.3	0.1	−4.4	−4.1
Nov.		0.1	0.2	0.6	−4.7	−4.9
Dec.		0.1	0.1	0.3	−2.5	−2.6

January 1982 and the result is then raised to the twelfth power and converted to a percent change.[4]

---

[4] Alternatively, this can be done using logarithms. In the above example:
(a)   population in February 1982 is divided by its value in January 1982:
(b)   the natural logarithm is then taken

$$\ln(1.004) = 0.0004$$

(c)   and multiplied by twelve—the periods over which it is compounded;

$$12 * \ln(1.0004) = 0.0052$$

(d)   this value is then exponentiated

$$\exp(12 * \ln(1.0004)) = 1.0052$$

(e)   and converted to a percentage in the normal way.

$$(1.0052 - 1) * 100 = 0.52\%$$

TABLE 4-4 Monthly Percent Changes—Annual Rates

	POPULATION	LABOR FORCE	EMPLOYMENT	UNEMPLOYMENT
Jan. '82				
Feb.	0.520	4.812	1.552	45.830
Mar.	1.821	1.779	−0.671	30.432
Apr.	1.244	2.624	−1.861	59.471
May	1.278	7.228	7.229	7.216
June	1.150	−4.351	−6.122	14.422
July	1.219	2.937	−1.791	59.540
Aug.	1.028	0.807	0.726	1.553
Sept.	1.252	2.261	−1.805	47.164
Oct.	1.335	0.119	−3.164	33.837
Nov.	1.236	2.555	−1.323	42.099
Dec.	0.982	−0.540	−0.688	0.709
Jan. '83	1.079	−2.101	2.142	−31.632
Feb.	1.050	0.119	0.218	−0.727
Mar.	1.049	0.511	1.756	−9.652
Apr.	0.958	2.632	3.561	−5.130
May	1.103	−0.270	1.896	−17.517
June	1.193	10.832	12.460	−2.753
July	1.255	−0.855	5.895	−46.202
Aug.	0.926	3.179	3.114	3.800
Sept.	1.120	1.205	4.735	−27.402
Oct.	1.223	−3.813	1.113	−41.827
Nov.	1.187	1.828	7.747	−44.015
Dec.	1.172	1.087	3.989	−26.034

$$\text{Compound Annual } \%\Delta \text{ in Population} = \left(\left(\frac{\text{Pop}_{t=1}}{\text{Pop}_{t=0}}\right)^{12} - 1\right) * 100$$

$$= \left(\left(\frac{171.409}{171.335}\right)^{12} - 1\right) * 100$$

$$= ((1.0004)^{12} - 1) * 100$$

$$= (1.0052 - 1) * 100$$

$$= 0.52\%$$

As can be seen from Table 4-4, this process results in more dramatic differences in the percent changes, thus providing the analyst with an even better method of distinguishing stable from variable series. Moreover, since changes in economic activity—such as those measured by the National Income and Product Accounts—are often expressed at annual rates, it is useful to express other series at annual rates. There is also a danger, however; the annualized changes in unemployment—particularly for April 1982, and

TABLE 4-5   Year-Over-Year Percent Changes

	POPULATION	LABOR FORCE	EMPLOYMENT	UNEMPLOYMENT
Jan. '83	1.178	1.469	−0.530	22.676
Feb.	1.223	1.082	−0.639	18.807
Mar.	1.159	0.977	−0.439	15.227
Apr.	1.135	0.977	0.008	10.347
May	1.120	0.369	−0.416	7.961
June	1.124	1.609	1.094	6.508
July	1.127	1.292	1.731	−2.717
Aug.	1.118	1.488	1.929	−2.539
Sept.	1.107	1.400	2.479	−8.112
Oct.	1.098	1.062	2.848	−14.276
Nov.	1.094	1.002	3.605	−20.678
Dec.	1.110	1.139	4.003	−22.692

July 1982 and 1983—are far larger than would actually be expected in a year. In fact, annualized growth rates over short periods often exaggerate changes beyond what is likely. (The prime example is that favored by newspaper headline writers: taking a large monthly change in price levels—which often reflect some special influence—and annualizing it in order to attract readers by scaring them.)

A fourth transformation, often useful in forecasting, is to look at year-over-year percent changes. This is useful for highlighting series which change only slowly over long periods—series for which simple extrapolation of growth trends may be a valid forecasting method. Using the value for the population in January 1983 as an example, this process can be easily described. The January 1983 value is divided by the January 1982 value and the quotient is converted to a percent change in the, by now, familiar manner.

$$\text{Year-over-year } \%\Delta \text{ in Population} = \left(\left(\frac{Pop_{t=12}}{Pop_{t=0}}\right) - 1\right) * 100$$

$$= \left(\left(\frac{173.354}{171.335}\right) - 1\right) * 100$$

$$= (1.0118 - 1) * 100$$

$$\text{Year-over-year } \%\Delta \text{ in Population} = 1.18\%$$

The year-over-year percent changes for the first four series in Table 4-1 are shown in Table 4-5. (Neither the annualized monthly growth rates nor the year-over-year growth rates for the unemployment rate are shown. Such changes are usually not shown for derived series like the unemployment rate.) The percent changes are also portrayed, using bar charts in Figures 4-3a and 4-3b. The stability of population and, to a lesser extent, the labor force emerge vividly. Figure 4-4 contrasts year-over-year growth rates for employment with annualized monthly growth rates. This type of comparison is especially useful as it shows how short-period changes affect the long-term growth.

The transformations described above are helpful in isolating the underlying trend over time of a data series. If the series is affected by either *seasonal* and/or *cyclical* disturbances, however, the underlying trend may remain elusive. Moreover, such disturbances may continue to exert impacts in the forecast period which must be taken into account. Thus, a series must be examined for seasonal and cyclical disturbances prior to constructing a forecast. *Seasonal* disturbances refer to forces which affect a data series with periodic rather than constant regularity. As a result, the series may

FIGURE 4-3a   Year over year percentage changes: Population, labor force, and employment

FIGURE 4-3b   Year over year percentage change: Unemployed

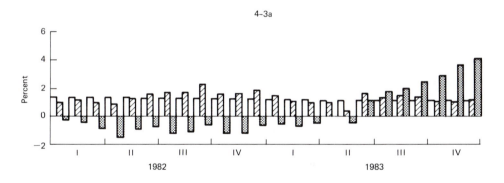

4-3a

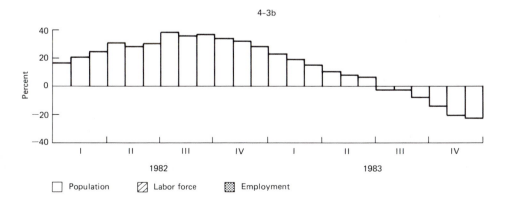

4-3b

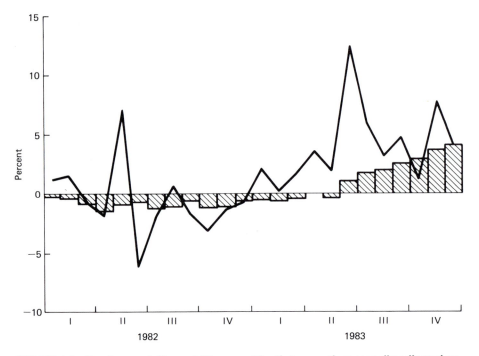

FIGURE 4-4   Employment: Percent Changes. Month to month seasonally adjusted annual rates (line) year over year (bar)

exhibit movements which are greater or less than trend at certain times in a year. A few obvious examples can be cited.

> Retail sales are seasonally strong in November and December when roughly 20% of the full year's sales take place, reflecting holiday shopping. (If there were no seasonal disturbances, one would expect that two-twelfths, or roughly 16.7%, of the year's sales would occur in those two months.) The proportion of sales for department stores in these two months is even higher—more than 25% of the yearly total.
>
> Housing start activity is less in the winter months because of weather disruptions than in the spring and summer months.
>
> The labor force swells in the summer months as students search for summer jobs.

Clearly, such purely seasonal variations must be recognized and adjusted for if such a series is to be forecast. The difficulty, however, is to remove just that variation due to the seasonal disturbance, while leaving the variation due to other forces. A simple four-step process for doing this can be de-

TABLE 4-6   Labor Force (*worksheet for computing moving average index*)

QUARTER	ORIGINAL DATA	FOUR QUARTER MOVING AVERAGE	INDEX OF MOVING AVERAGE
		(IN MILLIONS)	
1978 I	99.824		
II	101.904		
III	103.735		
IV	103.542	102.2512	1.0126
1979 I	103.198	103.0947	1.0010
II	104.295	103.6923	1.0058
III	106.365	104.3498	1.0193
IV	105.998	104.9639	1.0099
1980 I	105.422	105.5200	0.9991
II	106.712	106.1243	1.0055
III	108.220	106.5882	1.0153
IV	107.405	106.9397	1.0043
1981 I	107.178	107.3787	0.9981
II	108.799	107.9004	1.0083
III	109.705	108.2715	1.0132
IV	108.999	108.6701	1.0030
1982 I	108.366	108.9672	0.9945
II	110.099	109.2922	1.0074
III	111.653	109.7793	1.0171
IV	110.700	110.2045	1.0045
1983 I	109.766	110.5545	0.9929
II	111.189	110.8269	1.0033
III	113.252	111.2266	1.0182
IV	111.995	111.5503	1.0040

(handwritten annotation near 1978 IV index: $\dfrac{103.542}{102.2512}$)

Source: Bureau of Labor Statistics, U.S. Department of Labor.

scribed using as an example quarterly labor force data.[5] Fortunately, in practice, most government-compiled data series are adjusted for seasonal variation by the source agency and available in both seasonally adjusted (s.a.) and not seasonally adjusted (n.s.a.) forms. The government agencies use a more complex form of the method described below. The simpler method described below, however, offers an easy-to-follow example of the seasonal adjustment process, which can also be used when a forecaster is confronted with data which are not already adjusted.

Not seasonally adjusted data for the labor force from first quarter 1978 through fourth quarter 1983 are listed in the first column of Table 4-6 and

[5] In practice, seasonal adjustment should be done at the highest frequency for which the data are available, which for the labor force is monthly. Quarterly data are used here because the number of computations is reduced. The labor market data used previously were seasonally adjusted by BLS.

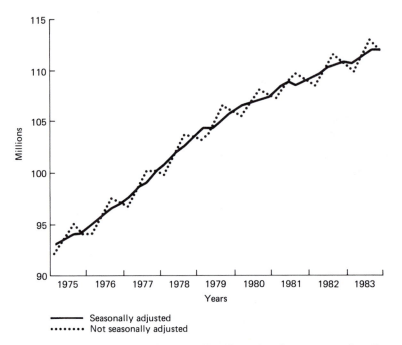

FIGURE 4-5   Comparison of seasonally adjusted and not seasonally adjusted labor force data. (Quarterly data from Table 4-6)

plotted in Figure 4-5. The seasonal pattern of these data is apparent in Figure 4-5. The labor force increases sharply in the third quarter of each year and then declines in the fourth quarter and first quarter of the next year (though the level in each successive fourth quarter is above the level in the year-earlier quarter).

The first step is to take a four-quarter moving average as in the second column of Table 4-6. Because a moving average gives equal weight to all four quarters, it removes the seasonal effect. Unfortunately, it also understates the growth in the series. It can also be seen that the moving average "wastes" data: the first three observations are lost in creating the first moving average. As will be seen, this loss is more apparent than real.[6]

The second step is to relate the actual observed data in column 1 to the moving averages in column 2. This results in the index values in column 3. The purpose of this procedure is to remove the trend effects from the data. The moving average indexes can then be arranged as in Table 4-7, so that each row contains index levels for one quarter across years. These levels are

[6] Moreover, usually more years of data would be desired. The Census Bureau's X-11 seasonal adjustment program uses ten years. For illustrative purposes fewer years were used in Table 4-6.

TABLE 4-7 Worksheet for Computing Quarterly Seasonal Factors for the Labor Force from Moving Average Indexes

	1978	1979	1980	1981	1982	1983	TOTAL	AVERAGE	ADJUSTED SEASONAL FACTORS
I		1.0010	0.9991	0.9981	0.9945	0.9929	3.9927	0.9982	0.9916
II		1.0058	1.0055	1.0083	1.0074	1.0033	4.0270	1.0068	1.0001
III		1.0193	1.0153	1.0132	1.0171	1.0182	4.0649	1.0162	1.0095
IV	1.0126	1.0099	1.0043	1.0030	1.0045	1.0040	4.0217	1.0054	0.9988
							4.0266		4.0000

(handwritten annotations) 79-82 ; 3.9927/4 ; 0.9916 = .9982 × .9934

Adjustment Factor = 4.000/4.0266

= .9934

similar in value. For instance, the moving average index values for the first quarter are all close to 1.000. When these values are totaled across rows and averaged we get the values shown in the second column from the right. When the values in the column are totaled, the sum exceeds the expected value for 4.0000. This reflects the imbalances introduced by taking averages of averages. To correct this distortion, an adjustment factor is calculated as shown and multiplied by each of the averages to compute the adjusted seasonal factors shown in the right-hand column.

Finally, the appropriate seasonal factor is divided into the not seasonally adjusted data to compute seasonally adjusted values for the labor force. These computed values are listed in column 2 of Table 4-8 and plotted in Figure 4-5.

TABLE 4-8   Labor Force: Comparison of Seasonally Adjusted and Not Seasonally Adjusted Data

QUARTER	N.S.A.	S.A. USING SEASONAL FACTORS IN TABLE 4-7	S.A. USING SEASONALS COMPUTED BY BLS	DIFFERENCE
		(IN MILLIONS)		
1978 I	99.824	100.670 _99524_ / _.9916_	100.934	0.264
II	101.904	101.894	101.947	0.053
III	103.735	102.759	102.568	−0.191
IV	103.542	103.666	103.484	−0.182
1979 I	103.198	104.072	104.383	0.311
II	104.295	104.285	104.327	0.042
III	106.365	105.364	105.209	−0.155
IV	105.998	106.125	105.923	−0.202
1980 I	105.422	106.315	106.564	0.249
II	106.712	106.701	106.788	0.087
III	108.220	107.202	107.115	−0.087
IV	107.405	107.534	107.425	−0.109
1981 I	107.178	108.086	108.296	0.210
II	108.799	108.788	108.869	0.081
III	109.705	108.673	108.509	−0.164
IV	108.999	109.130	109.009	−0.021
1982 I	108.366	109.284	109.414	0.130
II	110.099	110.088	110.192	0.104
III	111.653	110.602	110.517	−0.085
IV	110.700	110.833	110.829	−0.004
1983 I	109.766	110.696	110.700	0.004
II	111.189	111.178	111.277	0.099
III	113.252	112.186	112.057	−0.129
IV	111.995	112.130	112.012	−0.118

Source: Bureau of Labor Statistics, U.S. Department of Labor; and the Author's Calculations.

For comparison, the seasonally adjusted labor force data, compiled and published by BLS, are shown in column 3 of Table 4-8. As can be seen from column 4, the differences in level between the simple method described above and the more complex method used by BLS are in most cases small. (For the twenty-four observations shown the average difference is 0.)

As stated above, seasonal disturbances are forces which affect a series with periodic rather than constant regularity. Many economic series are also subject to *cyclical* disturbances which are not periodic, but are recurrent. (In other words, cycles are not of uniform, or even of easily predictable, length.) Because these cyclical forces are often of great importance in determining the pattern a series will follow, it is important for a forecaster to be aware of the cyclical properties of a particular series. Indeed, at certain times the cyclical nature of a series may be the overwhelming factor determining its pattern in a forecast period.

If economic activity grew at a steady rate, period after period, there would be no cycles. For a number of reasons, however, this is not the case. Figure 4-6 shows the quarterly pattern for U.S. GNP, measured in constant (1972) dollars, from 1950 through 1983. As can be seen, far from being steady, economic growth has occurred in a series of fits and starts.

These fits and starts have been analyzed and classified into cycles by

FIGURE 4-6   Gross National Product 1950–83 Constant (1972) dollars. Shaded areas represent recession periods

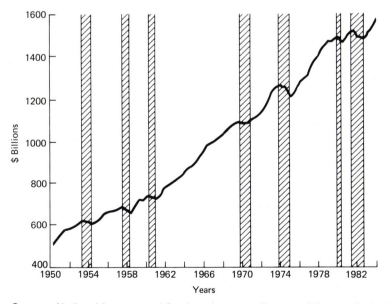

Source: *National Income and Product Accounts,* Bureau of Economic Analysis, U.S. Department of Commerce.

TABLE 4-9   Post-World War II Business Cycle Peaks and Troughs

PEAK	TROUGH
November 1948	October 1949
July 1953	May 1954
August 1957	April 1958
April 1960	February 1961
December 1969	November 1970
November 1973	March 1975
January 1980	July 1980
July 1981	November 1982

Source: *Business Conditions Digest,* December 1983.

the National Bureau of Economic Research (NBER).[7] A business cycle can be viewed as having five phases: (1) the *peak* in economic activity (expressed as a particular month); (2) a period of *downturn* or recession; (3) the *trough* or lowpoint in economic activity (also expressed as a specific month); (4) *recovery,* the period from the trough until the past peak in economic activity is reached again; and (5) *expansion,* the period which extends from the point where the past peak in activity is reattained until a new peak occurs. (Of course a cycle can be described from trough-to-trough as well as from peak-to-peak.) The NBER has identified 30 cycles since 1854. Since the end of World War II, eight cycles have been identified. The dates of the peaks and troughs of these cycles are listed in Table 4-9.[8]

It must be stressed that each cycle is, to a great extent, unique as to cause, duration, and to the responses of both private and government entities to its occurrences. Nevertheless, there is enough similarity in the cyclical behavior of many economic variables to make cyclical analysis of great value to a forecaster. This is especially true when the forecast is prepared at a time which is believed to be close to a cyclical peak or trough. At such times a useful aid in forecasting is to prepare a cyclical index. Such an index can be compared to similar indexes for prior cycles. This contrast may, in turn, suggest how the indexed series will behave in the present cycle.

This approach can be shown using data on employment (household series) for the 1981–82 cycle as the data to be analyzed, in contrast with its

---

[7] The NBER has also classified much of the economic data described in Chapter 3 by cyclical characteristics: distinguishing those series which lead, lag, or are roughly coincident with broad cyclical patterns; and those series which are pro-cyclical (that is, which move in the same direction as overall economic activity) and those which are counter-cyclical.

[8] Dates for all 30 cycles since 1854 can be found in *Business Conditions Digest,* published by the Bureau of Economic Analysis.

behavior in the five previous cycles. The choice of how many and which cycles to contrast current data with is somewhat arbitrary. Enough cycles should be used to insure general cyclical patterns. At the same time, cycles which are far distant in time may reflect forces which now have little relevance to present circumstances.

Table 4-10 shows employment levels for the seven complete cycles from 1953 through 1983. The data are shown for three periods for each cycle: the twelve months prior to the peak in economic activity; the period from peak to trough,[9] and the twelve months following the trough.

In Table 4-11, the data are indexed to the employment level in the peak month (employment in peak month = 100) for each cycle. The last column shows the average index values for the first six cycles. If the analysis were performed shortly after the July 1981 peak was identified, one approach the forecaster might use would be to assume subsequent values would follow the pattern of the average cycle. Comparison with the actual index values for the twelve months following the July 1981 peak show that the differences would, in most cases, be small. This fact illustrates the degree of similarity that exists for most post-war cycles. To the extent that there are differences between the specific and average cycles, some of these may be explained by conditions particular to the cycle under analysis. For instance, since employment did not undergo such volatile changes in the short 1980 cycle as in the five prior cycles, it might have appeared likely that a more severe correction would occur once the 1981 downturn commenced.

A similar analysis is performed in Table 4-12, showing employment data indexed on the trough month. Figure 4-7 depicts the 1981–83 peak and trough indexes plotted against the average peak and trough indexes, respectively. The similarity of the patterns suggests cyclical analysis is useful in preparing a forecast, especially near cyclical turning points.

This section has discussed three steps forecasters can, and should, take in analyzing time series before attempting to forecast future values.

(1)   The data can be transformed by calculating first differences or percent changes. These simple procedures may reveal something about the inherent trend of the series. Plotting the data, either in raw or transformed form, may also prove useful.

(2)   The presence of a seasonal pattern should also be looked for. Even when data are in seasonally adjusted form, it may be useful to know whether present conditions are in line with past seasonal patterns. For instance, the winters of 1980 and 1981 were milder than normal. As a result, housing start activity—

---

[9] The peaks and troughs used are the officially specified *reference* cycle peaks and troughs for overall economic activity. As can be seen, the *specific* peak and trough date for a particular indicator series may differ. Analyzing the difference between reference and specific peaks and troughs is one way to determine whether the indicator leads, lags, or is roughly coincident with overall economic activity. As confirmed by Table 4-10, employment is a roughly coincident indicator.

TABLE 4-10 Employment—Household Survey (reference cycle turning points)

	JULY 1952–MAY 1955		AUG. 1956–APR. 1959		APR. 1959–FEB. 1962		DEC. 1968–NOV. 1971		NOV. 1972–MAR. 1976		JAN. 1979–JUL. 1981		JUL. 1980–NOV. 1983
						(IN MILLIONS)							
	59.971		63.972		64.768		76.778		82.990		97.948		98.799
	59.790		64.079		64.699		76.805		83.400		98.329		98.792
	60.521		63.975		64.849		77.327		83.161		98.480		99.052
	60.132		63.796		65.011		77.367		83.912		98.103		99.300
	60.748		63.910		64.844		77.523		84.452		98.331		99.525
	60.954		63.632		64.770		77.412		84.559		98.679		99.590
	61.600		64.257		64.911		77.880		84.648		99.006		99.951
	61.884		64.404		64.530		77.959		85.185		98.776		100.217
	62.010		64.047		65.341		78.250		85.299		99.340		100.609
	61.444		63.985		65.347		78.250		85.204		99.404		101.074
	61.019		64.196		65.620		78.445		85.488		99.574		101.096
	61.456		64.540		64.673		78.541		85.987		99.933		100.379
Peak 61.397		Peak 63.959		Peak 65.959		Peak 78.740		Peak 86.320		Peak 99.860		Peak 100.705
	61.151		64.121		66.057		78.780		86.401		100.007		100.638
	60.906		64.046		66.168		78.698		86.555		99.728		100.013
	60.893		63.669		65.909		78.863		86.754		99.234		100.324
	60.738		63.922		65.895		78.930		86.819		98.987		100.155
	59.977		63.220		66.267		78.564		86.669		98.762		99.585

					Trough	
60.024	62.898	65.632	78.413	86.891	98.799	99.682
60.663	62.731	66.109	78.726	86.941	98.792	99.810
60.186	Trough 62.631	65.778	78.624	87.149	99.052	99.754
60.185	62.874	65.776	78.498	87.037	99.300	99.598
Trough 59.908	62.730	Trough 65.588	78.685	87.051	99.525	100.179
59.792	62.745	65.850	Trough 78.650	86.995	99.590	99.653
59.643	63.012	65.374	78.594	86.626	99.951	99.503
59.853	63.181	65.449	78.864	86.144	100.217	99.563
60.282	63.475	65.993	78.700	85.627	100.609	99.412
60.270	63.470	65.608	78.588	85.256	101.074	99.146
60.357	63.549	65.852	78.987	Trough 85.187	101.096	Trough 99.036
60.116	63.868	65.541	79.139	85.189	100.379	98.979
60.753	63.684	65.919	78.757	85.451	100.705	99.154
60.727	64.267	66.081	79.305	85.355		99.172
60.964	64.768	65.900	79.539	85.894		99.316
61.515		66.108	79.689	86.234		99.606
61.634			79.918	86.279		99.762
			80.297	86.370		100.743
				86.456		101.225
				86.665		101.484
				87.400		101.876
				87.672		101.970
				87.985		102.606

Source: Bureau of Labor Statistics, U.S. Department of Labor.

which usually falls off in the winter months due to weather disruptions—was stronger than usual.

(3)   Analyzing the cyclical pattern of a series may be specially useful in forecasting the series around peaks and troughs in economic activity.

These procedures are useful preparations for any forecast using data series over time. They provide the forecaster with a "feel" for the data and, perhaps more important, for the economic activity being measured. By carefully examining the past behavior of the data, the forecaster is forced to confront "irregularities" that do not neatly fit expectations based on theory and question whether such "irregularities" will recur in the forecast period.

Time Series Forecasting

Time series forecasting is an approach which has gained increased use in forecasting since the late 1960s. The basic premise underlying time series

TABLE 4-11   Civilian Employment-Household Survey (cyclical indexes, level in peak month equals 100)

		'53'	'57'	'60'	'69'	'73'	'80'	'81'	6 Cycle AVG
	−12	97.677	100.020	98.194	97.508	96.142	98.085	98.107	97.9
	−11	97.383	100.188	98.090	97.543	96.617	98.467	98.100	98.0
	−10	98.573	100.025	98.317	98.205	96.340	98.618	98.359	98.3
	−9	97.940	99.745	98.563	98.256	97.210	98.241	98.605	98.3
	−8	98.943	99.923	98.310	98.454	97.836	98.469	98.828	98.7
	−7	99.278	99.489	98.197	98.313	97.960	98.817	98.893	98.7
	−6	100.331	100.466	98.411	98.908	98.063	99.145	99.251	99.2
	−5	100.793	100.696	97.834	99.008	98.685	98.914	99.515	99.3
	−4	100.998	100.138	99.063	99.378	98.817	99.479	99.905	99.6
	−3	100.077	100.041	99.072	99.378	98.707	99.543	100.366	99.5
	−2	99.384	100.371	99.486	99.625	99.036	99.714	100.388	99.6
	−1	100.096	100.908	98.050	99.747	99.614	100.073	99.676	99.7
Peak	0	100.000	100.000	100.000	100.000	100.000	100.000	100.000	100.0
	1	99.599	100.253	100.149	100.051	100.094	100.147	99.933	100.0
	2	99.200	100.136	100.317	99.947	100.272	99.868	99.313	100.0
	3	99.179	99.547	99.924	100.156	100.503	99.373	99.622	99.8
	4	98.927	99.942	99.903	100.241	100.578	99.126	99.454	99.8
	5	97.687	98.845	100.467	99.776	100.404	98.900	98.888	99.3
	6	97.764	98.341	99.504	99.585	100.661	98.938	98.984	99.1
	7	98.805	98.080	100.227	99.982	100.719	98.931	99.111	99.5
	8	98.028	97.924	99.726	99.853	100.960	99.191	99.056	99.3
	9	98.026	98.304	99.723	99.693	100.831	99.439	98.901	99.3
	10	97.575	98.078	99.438	99.930	100.847	99.665	99.478	99.3
	11	97.386	98.102	99.835	99.886	100.782	99.730	98.955	99.3
	12	97.143	98.519	99.113	99.815	100.354	100.091	98.806	99.2

TABLE 4-12   Civilian Employment-Household Survey (cyclical indexes, level in trough month equals 100)

		'54'	'58'	'61'	'70'	'75'	'80'	'82'	6 Cycle AVG
	-12	101.9	102.3	100.0	99.9	101.9	100.2	101.1	101.0
	-11	102.6	102.2	98.6	100.1	101.7	100.0	100.6	100.9
	-10	102.5	102.5	100.6	100.2	102.0	100.5	100.7	101.4
	-9	102.1	103.0	100.7	100.1	102.1	100.6	100.8	101.4
	-8	101.7	102.1	100.9	100.3	102.3	100.8	100.7	101.3
	-7	101.6	102.4	100.5	100.4	102.2	101.1	100.6	101.4
	-6	101.4	102.3	100.5	99.9	102.2	101.1	101.2	101.2
	-5	100.1	101.7	101.0	99.7	102.1	101.2	100.6	101.0
	-4	100.2	102.1	100.1	100.1	101.7	100.9	100.5	100.8
	-3	101.3	100.9	100.8	100.0	101.1	100.4	100.5	100.8
	-2	100.5	100.4	100.3	99.8	100.5	100.2	100.4	100.3
	-1	100.5	100.2	100.3	100.0	100.1	100.0	100.1	100.2
Trough	0	100.0	100.0	100.0	100.0	100.0	100.0	100.0	100.0
	1	99.8	100.4	100.4	99.9	100.0	100.0	99.9	100.1
	2	99.6	100.2	99.7	100.3	100.3	100.3	100.1	100.0
	3	99.9	100.2	98.8	100.1	100.2	100.5	100.1	100.1
	4	100.6	100.6	100.6	99.9	100.8	100.7	100.3	100.6
	5	100.6	100.9	100.0	100.4	101.2	100.8	100.6	100.7
	6	100.7	101.3	100.4	100.6	101.3	101.2	100.7	100.9
	7	100.3	101.3	99.9	100.1	101.4	101.4	101.7	100.8
	8	101.4	101.5	100.5	100.8	101.5	101.8	102.2	101.3
	9	101.4	102.0	100.8	101.1	101.7	102.3	102.5	101.5
	10	101.8	101.7	100.5	101.3	102.6	102.3	102.9	101.7
	11	102.7	102.6	100.8	101.6	102.9	101.6	103.0	102.0
	12	102.9	103.4	101.4	102.1	103.3	101.9	103.6	102.5

methods is that the best predictors of the future values of a data series are the past values of the series itself. An attractive feature of these methods is that they are often—though not always—cheaper than econometric approaches. Most time series methods also require less data than econometric methods, although time series methods are most useful when a long data series is to be extended over a much shorter forecast period. Finally, time series methods can be used to supplement other forecast methods.[10]

The most widely used time series methods include simple techniques, such as trend lines and moving averages; more complex approaches, such as exponential smoothing; and very complex methods, such as the AutoRegressive Integrated Moving Average (ARIMA) method. Each of these methods will be briefly described, although only the first three are used in the text.

[10] For instance, as will be seen in Chapter 5, roughly 85% of personal income can be forecast using "behavioral" estimated equations. The remaining 15% can be estimated using a time series method.

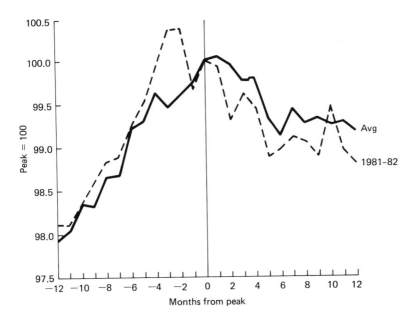

FIGURE 4-7a   Civilian employment cyclical indexes: Comparison of 1981–82 cycle to average of six prior cycles

FIGURE 4-7b   Civilian employment cyclical indexes: Comparison of 1981–82 cycle to average of six prior cycles

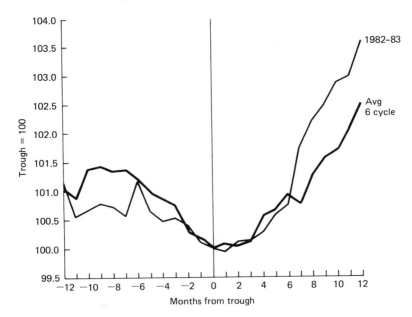

The *trend line* method is the most "naive" time series technique, but is useful in some forecasting situations. It involves fitting a line—either visually or as a simple regression (see section II, below) on time—to actual or transformed data points. If the observations are sufficiently close to the fitted trend line, future values can be forecast by extrapolating (extending) the line over the forecast period. This approach is most useful if: (1) there is a great deal of past data, (2) the data follow a regular pattern with little seasonal or cyclical variation, and (3) the forecast period is short relative to the history on which the trend line is based. A forecast of population for the next twelve months would be a case where trend line forecasting might apply.

Moving averages are used like trend lines, when a data series' behavior over time is quite stable, but subject to random movements around the stable pattern. The stability may be in the series itself, but more likely it is in some transformed version, such as a growth rate. For instance the first two columns of Table 4-13 present the levels and monthly percent changes,

TABLE 4-13 Moving Average of Population Growth

	ACTUAL POPULATION	MONTHLY CHANGE	MOVING AVERAGE MONTHLY CHANGE	ERROR
	(IN MILLIONS)		%	
Jan. '82	171.335	0.10		
Feb.	171.489	0.09		
Mar.	171.667	0.10		
Apr.	171.844	0.10		
May	172.026	0.11		
June	172.190	0.10		
July	172.364	0.10		
Aug.	172.511	0.09		
Sept.	172.690	0.10		
Oct.	172.881	0.11		
Nov.	173.058	0.10		
Dec.	173.199	0.08		
Jan. '83	173.354	0.09	0.10	−0.01
Feb.	173.505	0.09	0.10	−0.01
Mar.	173.656	0.09	0.10	−0.01
Apr.	173.794	0.08	0.10	−0.02
May	173.953	0.09	0.10	−0.01
June	174.125	0.10	0.09	0.01
July	174.306	0.10	0.09	0.01
Aug.	174.440	0.08	0.09	0.01
Sept.	174.602	0.09	0.09	0.00
Oct.	174.779	0.10	0.09	0.01
Nov.	174.951	0.10	0.09	0.01
Dec.	175.121	0.10	0.09	0.01

Source: Bureau of Labor Statistics, U.S. Department of Labor.

respectively, for the civilian noninstitutional population 16 years old and over for 1982 and 1983. The third column presents a moving average of the percent changes for the prior twelve months. (For instance, the value of 0.10 shown for January 1983 is the average of the January–December 1982 percent changes.) The last column shows the errors (actual minus the moving average). In this case, the moving averages provide a useful and quite accurate forecast of the actual monthly percent changes in population. The moving average-based monthly percent changes can then be applied to the most recent known level to derive a forecast of population levels. Experimentation with moving averages of different lengths (three- or six-months, for instance) might provide even smaller errors. Clearly, moving averages are a simple method for forecasting a data series. In this case, however, it proved a useful method because the monthly percent changes displayed a quite stable pattern. The criteria under which moving average methods are most useful are similar to those for trend line forecasting. There should be a great deal of historical data, a stable pattern in either the original or the transformed series should be evident, and the forecast period should be short relative to history.

Exponential smoothing methods are also fairly simple, despite their high-powered title. Like moving averages, exponential smoothing weights past observations to derive forecast values. In addition, however, exponential smoothing weights past forecast values in order to adapt the error pattern of past forecast estimates. As a result, exponential smoothing is better than a moving average at capturing changing trends in a time series. The first step in using exponential smoothing is to compute the single exponential smoothing statistic (S_t^1). This is equal to a weighted average of the current observation and the prior smoothing statistic, as in 4-1.

$$S_t^1 = \alpha * X_t + (1 - \alpha) * S_{t-1}^1 \qquad (4\text{-}1)$$

where S_t^1 = the single exponential smoothing coefficient for the current period,

X_t = the actual value for the series in the current period, and

S_{t-1}^1 = the single exponential smoothing statistic estimated for the prior period.

Two decisions are required of the forecaster in performing a single exponential smoothing analysis. First, it is necessary to derive an initial value for the lagged smoothing statistic (S_{t-1}^1) which precedes the start of the analysis. There are at least two "initializing" procedures that can be followed: (1) the first actual observation can also be regarded as the first lagged statistic ($S_1^1 = X_1$); or (2) the first smoothing statistic can be computed as the average of the first two actuals ($S_1^1 = (X_2 + X_1)/2$), thus "wasting" the first two observations. In either case, some data are "wasted"—one observation in the first procedure, two observations in the second. This is a reasonable price to pay when it is remembered that a twelve-month moving average method "wastes" twelve observations. Moreover, it is recommended that a number of estimates be derived based on known observations to allow the process to become established before making an "out of sample" forecast. On balance, the second initializing alternative seems the more appealing. The second decision the forecaster has to make is on the value of alpha (α), the weight to be applied to the actual value (X_t). Alpha must take a value between 0 and 1, with the residual (1 minus alpha) constituting the weight on the lagged smoothing statistic. The relative weight given to α and $1 - \alpha$ depends on the weight the forecaster wishes to apply to the latest value versus the past forecast value (which captures the forecast error).

Single exponential smoothing is most useful in forecasting a series which shows little trend. For most economic series, therefore, the approach, by itself, is of only limited use. Of greater use is the method known as Brown's Linear Exponential Smoothing,[11] or double exponential smoothing. This method uses the single exponential smoothing statistic to compute a double exponential smoothing statistic (S_t^2).

$$S_t^2 = \alpha * S_t^1 + (1 - \alpha) * S_{t-1}^2 \qquad (4\text{-}2)$$

where S_{t-1}^2 = the lagged double exponential smoothing statistic. With the two exponential smoothing statistics, a forecast of the actual series (FX_{t+m}) can be computed in two further steps. A linear estimating equation is derived in the form

$$FX_{t+m} = a_t + b_t * T \qquad (4\text{-}3)$$

where T = the number of future periods forecast.

The constant term (a_t) is determined as in 4-4.

$$a_t = 2 * S_t^1 - S_t^2 \qquad (4\text{-}4)$$

while the coefficient on time (b_t) is computed as in 4-5.

$$b_t = \frac{\alpha}{1 - \alpha} * (S_t^1 - S_t^2) \qquad (4\text{-}5)$$

[11] R.G. Brown, *Smoothing, Forecasting, and Predicting of Discrete Time Series* (Englewood Cliffs, NJ: Prentice-Hall, 1962). See also Steven C. Wheelwright and Spyros Makridakis, *Interactive Forecasting: Univariate and Multivariate Methods* (San Francisco: Holden-Day, Inc., 1978), pp. 79–84. For an example similar to that used here, see Dale G. Bails and Larry C. Peppers, *Business Fluctuations: Forecasting, Techniques and Applications* (Englewood Cliffs, NJ: Prentice-Hall, 1982), pp. 345–51.

TABLE 4-14   A Double Exponential Smoothing Forecast of the Civilian Labor Force (in millions)

	PERIOD	LABOR FORCE	S_t^1	S_t^2	a	b	FX	ERROR	% ERROR
		(1)	(2)	(3)	(4)	(5)	(6)	(7)	(8)
Jan. '82	1	109.075	109.289	109.289					
Feb.	2	109.503	109.35	109.31	109.40	0.02			
Mar.	3	109.664	109.45	109.35	109.54	0.04	109.42	0.25	0.22
Apr.	4	109.901	109.58	109.42	109.75	0.07	109.58	0.32	0.29
May	5	110.542	109.87	109.55	110.19	0.14	109.82	0.73	0.66
June	6	110.133	109.95	109.67	110.23	0.12	110.32	−0.19	−0.17
July	7	110.399	110.08	109.80	110.37	0.12	110.34	0.06	0.05
Aug.	8	110.473	110.20	109.92	110.48	0.12	110.50	−0.02	−0.02
Sept.	9	110.679	110.34	110.05	110.64	0.13	110.61	0.07	0.07
Oct.	10	110.690	110.45	110.17	110.73	0.12	110.77	−0.08	−0.07
Nov.	11	110.923	110.59	110.29	110.89	0.13	110.85	0.07	0.07
Dec.	12	110.873	110.68	110.41	110.94	0.11	111.01	−0.14	−0.13
Jan. '83	13	110.677	110.68	110.49	110.86	0.08	111.06	−0.38	−0.34
Feb.	14	110.688	110.68	110.55	110.81	0.06	110.94	−0.26	−0.23
Mar.	15	110.735	110.70	110.59	110.80	0.05	110.87	−0.14	−0.12
Apr.	16	110.975	110.78	110.65	110.91	0.06	110.85	0.13	0.12
May	17	110.950	110.83	110.70	110.96	0.05	110.97	−0.02	−0.02
June	18	111.905	111.15	110.84	111.47	0.14	111.01	0.89	0.80
July	19	111.825					111.60	0.22	0.20
Aug.	20	112.117					111.74	0.38	0.34
Sept.	21	112.229					111.87	0.35	0.32
Oct.	22	111.866					112.01	−0.14	−0.13
Nov.	23	112.035					112.14	−0.11	−0.10
Dec.	24	112.136					112.28	−0.14	−0.13

Source: Bureau of Labor Statistics, U.S. Department of Labor

Table 4-14 presents a double exponential smoothing forecast for the civilian labor force. Column 1 presents actual data for January 1982 through December 1983. The object of this exercise is to compute forecast values for July–December 1983, given the data for the prior eighteen months.

The single exponential smoothing statistic (S_t^1) was computed using a value for alpha of 0.3 and the results are shown in column 2. Note that for January 1982 (t = 1), the average of the January and February labor force levels is used to initialize the process ($S_1^1 = 109.289 = (109.075 + 109.503)/2$). Thereafter, the statistic is computed as in equation 4-1. For instance, for February 1982 the value is found as below.

$$S_2^1 = \propto * X_2 + (1 - \propto) * S_1^1 \qquad (4\text{-}1)$$

$$= 0.3 * (109.503) + 0.7 * (109.289)$$

$$= 109.353$$

It is clear from comparing the actual values to these estimates that the S_t^1 estimates tend to lag the actual trend, although as can be seen for the January–March 1983 values, the single exponential smoothing statistic adapts more quickly than would a moving average because of the high weight given S_{t-1}^1.

Column 3 presents the computed values for the double exponential smoothing statistic (S_t^2). Again, the value for January 1982 is equal to the average of the January and February actuals. The February 1982 double exponential smoothing statistic is computed as in equation 4-2.

$$S_2^2 = \alpha * S_2^1 + (1 - \alpha) * S_1^2 \qquad (4\text{-}2)$$

$$= 0.3 * (109.353) + 0.7 * (109.289)$$

$$= 109.308$$

The constant term and coefficient of time for the linear exponential smoothing equation (4-3) are computed separately and presented in columns 4 and 5, respectively. These values are estimated for February 1982 using equations 4-4 and 4-5 as shown below,

$$a_2 = 2 * S_2^1 - S_2^2 \qquad (4\text{-}4)$$

$$= (2 * 109.353) - 109.308$$

$$= 109.398$$

$$b_2 = \frac{\alpha}{1 - \alpha} * (S_2^1 - S_2^2) \qquad (4\text{-}5)$$

$$= 0.3/0.7) * (109.353 - 109.308)$$

$$= 0.019$$

resulting in an estimating equation (4-3) for the next month. The results are shown in column 6. The value for March 1982 is computed below.

$$FX_3 = a_2 + b_2 * T \qquad (T = 1) \qquad (4\text{-}3)$$

$$= 109.398 + 0.019 * (1)$$

$$= 109.417$$

Columns 7 and 8 present the error (actual minus estimate) in millions and as a percent of the actual, respectively. Analysis of the forecast errors for the March 1982–June 1983 period show the errors are small and, more important, that they tend to stabilize. For July through December 1983, the equation estimated for June 1983 is used as the basis for estimation. Thus the value of T increases from 1 in July to 6 in December. The errors are small and acceptable.

One of the attractions of this method is that once a worksheet is set up—either manually, with the computations done on a calculator, or, as is increasingly common, on a computer using a "spreadsheet' program (as was used for Table 4-14)—different values of alpha can be tried until the one-period ahead estimates converge on a set which provides the lowest error. These can then be used for the out-of-sample forecast. Moreover, the technique is sparing in its data needs. Finally, as actual data become known, the error patterns can be analyzed again and the forecast modified. The opportunities to use the double exponential smoothing approach are many in economic forecasting. In particular, the method is helpful in situations where econometric or other causal methods leave a sizable unexplained residual.[12]

The *autoregressive integrated moving average,* or ARIMA, method is very complex and its successful use in forecasting is an art acquired with experience. Indeed, C.W.J. Granger has noted that "it has been said to be so difficult that it should never be tried for the first time."[13] A thorough discussion of the ARIMA technique is beyond the scope of this text. In light of its acceptance and growing use in forecasting, however, a brief overview of some of the main features of this technique is provided. Readers interested in a more detailed discussion of ARIMA should consult one of the books which examine the subject in depth.[14]

Like other time series methods, the ARIMA technique uses past values of a data series to forecast future values. Four conditions are required of a time series used to construct an ARIMA model. First, the series must be determined by a *stochastic* process. This means the values in the series are randomly drawn from a probability distribution with particular statistical properties (mean and variance). The randomness is captured in the stochastic error term (ε_t). Second, the most recent value of the series is assumed to

---

[12] Other, more sophisticated, exponential smoothing methods exist. For a discussion of some of these see Steven C. Wheelwright and Spyros Makridakos, *Forecasting Methods for Management* (New York: John Wiley, 1980), pp. 54–81. For examples, see Wheelwright and Makridakis, *Interactive Forecasting,* pp. 87–110; and Bails and Peppers, *Business Fluctuations,* pp. 349–77.

[13] C.W.J. Granger, *Forecasting in Business and Economics* (New York: Academic Press, 1980), p. 64.

[14] A good introduction to the nature and main aspects of the ARIMA method are provided in Granger, *Forecasting in Business and Economics,* Ch. 3. A well-paced, accessible discussion is in Pindyck and Rubinfeld, *Econometric Models,* Chs. 13–17. The original source on this technique is G.E.P. Box and G.M. Jenkins, *Time Series Analysis* (San Francisco: Holden-Day, 1970). A less difficult source is C. Nelson, *Applied Time Series Analysis* (San Francisco: Holden-Day, 1973).

be *linearly* related to past values and error terms. Third, it is required that the process which generates the series is *stationary,* or can be transformed through differencing into a stationary process. This means that the properties of the stochastic process—its mean, variance, and probability distribution—must not change as the time period lengthens. Fourth, it is necessary that the models can be stated in *equation* form with fixed coefficients.

There are three basic parts to an ARIMA model, although all three need not be present in a particular model.

(1)   The series can be described by an *autoregressive (AR)* component, such that the most recent value (X_t) can be estimated by a weighted average of past values in the series going back p periods as in 4-6.

$$X_t = \emptyset * X_{t-1} + \cdots + \emptyset_p * X_{t-p} + \delta + \varepsilon_t \qquad (4\text{-}6)$$

where $\emptyset_p$ = the weights of the lagged values,
δ = a constant term related to the series mean, and
ε_t = the stochastic error.

(2)   The series can have a *moving average (MA)* component based on a q period moving average of the stochastic errors as in 4-7.

$$X_t = \overline{X} + \varepsilon_t - \Theta_1 * \varepsilon_{t-1} - \cdots - \Theta_q * \varepsilon_{t-q} \qquad (4\text{-}7)$$

where $\overline{X}$ = the mean of the series,
Θ_q = the weights of the lagged error terms, and
ε_t = the stochastic errors.

(3)   Most economic series are not stationary, but instead display trend or cyclical movements over time. Most series, however, can be   made stationary by differencing. For instance, first differencing is the period-to-period change in the series,

$$\Delta X_t = X_t - X_{t-1}$$

second differencing is the period-to-period change in first differences,

$$\Delta^2 X = \Delta X_t - \Delta X_{t-1}$$

and so forth. The order of the differencing is denoted as d. Once forecast values are found for a d order differenced series, they can be converted back to the original form by *integrating (I)* or summing the series d times.

An ARIMA model is described as an ARIMA(p,d,q) where p, d, and q are, respectively: (p) the number of lagged autoregressive terms, (d) the order of the differencing needed to make the series stationary, and (q) the number of lagged stochastic errors in the moving average component. Of course, all of these properties may not be present; in which case one or more of the characteristics (p, d, or q) may equal zero. Thus, there are six possible types of ARIMA models.

ARIMA(p,0,0), or an *AR(p)*, is a pure autoregressive model with p autoregressive terms of a stationary time series.

ARIMA(p,d,0), or an *ARI(p,d)*, is a pure autoregressive model with p autoregressive terms of a d order differenced time series.

ARIMA(0,0,q), or a *MA(q)*, is a pure moving average model of q lagged stationary stochastic error terms.

ARIMA(0,d,q), or an *IMA(d,q)*, is a pure moving average model of q lagged d order differenced stochastic error terms.

ARIMA(p,0,q), or an *ARMA(p,q)*, is a mixed p term autoregressive, q term moving average, undifferenced model.

ARIMA(p,d,q) is a mixed p term autoregressive, q term moving average, d order differenced model.

There are three phases to an ARIMA analysis: (1) identification, (2) estimation, and (3) diagnostic checking. *Identification* is the phase in which the analyst determines the type of ARIMA process which is most appropriate to capture the behavior of the time series. This is done by examining the plot of the autoregressive function, or *correlogram,* of the data. The correlogram is a plot of the correlations of lag k in the sample data, computed as in 4-8.

$$r_k = \frac{\sum\limits_{t=k+1}^{n} (X_t - \overline{X})(X_{t-k} - \overline{X})}{\sum\limits_{t=1}^{n} (X_t - \overline{X})^2} \tag{4-8}$$

FIGURE 4-8a   Correlogram for AR(p) model
FIGURE 4-8b   Correlogram for MA(q) model

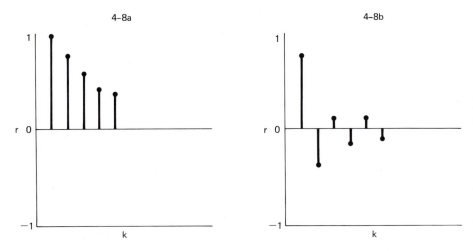

When these sample correlations are plotted, the distinctive patterns typical of an AR(p) or MA(q) process can be looked for. Figure 4-8a shows a typical correlogram for an AR(p). Note that the values decline gradually, but quickly, and then fluctuate around zero. Figure 4-8b shows a typical correlogram for an MA(q). Again the values decline, but even more quickly than for the AR(p), and then fluctuate around zero. If the sample correlations for a series do not decline quickly (say, within five periods), or at all, this is a sign that the series is not stationary and that it should be differenced one or more times until it does decline quickly.

In practice, identification requires the most art (judgment) in an ARIMA analysis. The more experience the analyst has, the easier the identification of the process. Two guidelines may be helpful: simple (p, q, or p + q less than 5) processes are more likely to yield better results (because they are easier to estimate) than complex ones, and a number of alternative processes should be considered.

The *estimation* phase requires specification of the weights (Øps and Θqs) of the estimated ARIMA process. The values of the weights are related to the values of the sample correlations as in 4-9 and 4-10 so that the weights can be estimated in an iterative manner.

$$r_k = Ø^k \qquad (4\text{-}9)$$

where k = p

$$r_k = \frac{\Theta}{1 - \Theta^2} \qquad (4\text{-}10)$$

for k = 1

$$r_k = 0$$

for k > 1

The actual nonlinear estimation process is quite difficult. Fortunately, there are a number of computer programs which perform this estimation.

Diagnostic checking refers to the analysis of how well the chosen model fits data outside the sample period. In order to be able to check known data, it is important to estimate the model for a subsample of the data, saving some of the final data points for checking purposes. Forecast results for these data, estimated from all the models under consideration, can be compared with the out-of-sample actuals, and the "best" model chosen for a "live" or *ex ante* forecast of unknown values.

The ARIMA approach is best used for short-period forecasts. It is more complex than other time series methods and requires extensive experience before it can be used with confidence. Finally, as with all time series methods, an ARIMA forecast is based on the past behavior of the series itself. It says nothing about the causal relationships underlying the economic process being forecast. This fact presents an obvious shortcoming to the forecaster wishing to consider "what if" scenarios and, more important, no insight is provided as to how the outcome will change if "other conditions" change. To deal with this last problem the forecaster is likely to prefer a behavioral or causal model estimated using regression analysis.

II. REGRESSION ANALYSIS

One of the most common approaches in economic forecasting is the estimation of regression equations to convert a hypothesized relationship between two or more sets of data into a precise mathematical relationship. In regression analysis an equation with specific coefficients and known properties is fitted to the data so that the squared differences between the actual value of the variable being estimated (the dependent variable) and its estimated value are less than would be the case using any other approach. Because of this property, regression analysis is often referred to as a *least squares* analysis.

Regression analysis forms the basis for econometrics, for which there is a vast literature.[15] The present section has a narrower scope with three aims: (1) to outline the basic concepts of regression analysis; (2) to indicate some of the areas of potential problems in using the technique, with suggestions of how such problems can be avoided and/or corrected; and (3) to provide an example of the use of regression analysis in forecasting economic activity.

In practice, forecasters perform regression analyses with the aid of a computer. This greatly reduces the number of tedious and often complex computations which have to be performed. A danger is that the process becomes so easy that results which violate one or more of the assumptions on which regression analysis is based may be accepted when they should be rejected. To avoid this danger the forecaster should keep in mind the main steps in calculating the basic statistical properties of a regression analysis. This provides the forecaster with better insights for analyzing the results a computer spews forth and deciding whether to accept or reject these results as a basis for forecasting. In order to highlight these characteristics a step-by-step simple two-variable regression analysis will be described, including a discussion of the principal statistics which must be calculated, and then a sample regression will be computed.

---

[15] The texts cited in footnote 1 may be consulted.

A two-variable regression model is an attempt to specify an exact, usually linear, relation for two sets of data between which a prior assumption (hypothesis) has proposed an economic relationship.[16] Thus, one variable, the dependent, is assumed to be a function of the other, the independent. The aim is to derive an equation which can be used to forecast future values of the dependent variable, given forecast values for the independent variable. An example is the consumption function, cited in Chapter Two, where real personal consumption expenditures are assumed to be a function of real disposable (after-tax) income.

$$c = f(y - T) \tag{4-11}$$

Normally, regression analysis requires that the function be specified in linear form. For the consumption function this is quite easy.

$$c = c_0 + b * yd \tag{4-11a}$$

where
$$b = MPC$$

In estimating this equation using a sample of data for personal consumption expenditures (C72) and disposable personal income (YD72), both expressed in billions of constant 1972 dollars, the equation contains an additional term (u) which is the stochastic error term.

$$C72 = a + b * YD72 + u \tag{4-12}$$

The error term can arise from three sources: (1) The value of the dependent variable (real consumer spending) in a period may be explained by factors other than the value of the independent variable (real disposable income); (2) there may be an element of randomness in the dependent variable which can not be captured statistically; and (3) there may be errors of measurement in either or both variables.

In addition to the assumption that the relationship is linear, there are three other basic assumptions which underlie regression analysis, all related to the error term, u. First, the error term is assumed to have a zero mean and constant variance (σ^2). That is, for a large number of observations the average error—$\bar{u} = \Sigma u/n$, where n is the number of observations—will equal zero, and the variance $\sigma^2 = \Sigma(u - \bar{u})^2/(n - 1)$—is a constant. Second,

---

[16] It is essential that a hypothesis about the relationship exists prior to attempts to estimate it. The estimated regression equation merely provides statistical evidence on the amount of variation in the dependent variable that is accounted for, "explained" by, the variation in the independent variable. The analysis does not prove causality; that depends on the rigor of the hypothesis specification. Regression analysis does permit different forms of the data to be used to arrive at the "best" version of the equation.

the errors associated with each observation are assumed to be statistically uncorrelated. That is, the errors are random and there is no relationship between an error at one time and an error at another time. When this is not true, *serial correlation* exists. Third, the errors are assumed to be distributed normally around the average value of zero. If it is true that the errors have a zero mean and are unrelated, this is a reasonable assumption. Moreover, it permits the further assumption that the estimated value of the dependent variable is also normally distributed.

When these assumptions hold, the error term can be dropped from the equation (since on average it is zero) and an estimated equation as in 4-13 can be used for forecasting future values of the dependent value.

$$C72e = \hat{a} + \hat{b} * YD72 \qquad (4\text{-}13)$$

Where the parameters to be estimated, $\hat{a}$ and $\hat{b}$, are called *best linear unbiased estimators* (BLUE) of the true parameters, a (the constant term) and b (the slope, in this case the Marginal Propensity to Consume) are denoted as such by carets.

The parameters, and thus the equation, are estimated using pairs of observed data for real consumer spending and real disposable income. The estimated equation has two important properties: (1) the estimated values for real consumer spending (C72) for given values of real disposable income (YD72) may differ from the observed values (C72), but the sum of these differences, or residuals—$\Sigma(C72)\text{-}C72_e)$—will equal zero; and (2) the sum of the squares of these differences—$\Sigma(C72-C72_e)^2$—will be less than would result from any other method of estimation. (This is why the estimators are called "best" estimators; they have minimum variance.) The values for the two parameters—$\hat{a}$ and $\hat{b}$—are found by using the *normal equations*.[17] When the sum of the squared residuals is minimized (by taking partial derivatives with respect to each of the estimated parameters and setting them equal to zero) the normal equations for a two variable regression equation are derived. The resulting normal equations are shown in equations 4-14a and 4-14b.

$$\Sigma C72 = n * \hat{a} + \hat{b} * \Sigma YD72 \qquad (4\text{-}14a)$$

and $\qquad \Sigma(YD72 * C72) = \hat{a} * \Sigma YD72 + \hat{b} * (\Sigma YD72)^2 \qquad (4\text{-}14b)$

The equations for estimating $\hat{a}$ and $\hat{b}$ are derived by solving the normal equations simultaneously as in 4-15a and 4-15b.

[17] The interested reader can check any statistics or econometrics text (e.g., Salvatore, *Theory and Problems of Statistics and Econometrics*, pp. 117, 124–25) for the derivation of these equations.

$$\hat{b} = \frac{\Sigma(YD72 * C72) - n * (\overline{YD72} * \overline{C72})}{\Sigma(YD72)^2 - n * (\overline{YD72})^2} \tag{4-15a}$$

and
$$\hat{a} = \overline{C72} - b * (\overline{YD72}) \tag{4-15b}$$

That is, $\hat{b}$ is equal to the difference between the summed products of the two variables ($\Sigma(YD72 * C72)$) and the product of the number of observations (n), the mean of the independent variable ($\overline{YD72}$), and the mean of the dependent variable ($\overline{C72}$), all divided by the difference between the sum of the squared independent variables ($\Sigma(YD72)^2$) and the product of the number of observations (n) and the mean of the independent variable squared (($\overline{YD72})^2$). In turn $\hat{a}$ is equal to the difference between the mean of the dependent variable ($\overline{C72}$) and the product of the estimator $\hat{b}$ and the mean of the independent variable ($\overline{YD72}$).

The estimated parameters, $\hat{a}$ and $\hat{b}$, can then be substituted in equation (4-13) and the estimated values of the dependent variable (C72e) calculated from actual values of the independent variable (YD72). It is usual that when the estimated values of the dependent variable are compared to the actual values, small differences, or residuals (e), will result. In this case

$$e = (C72 - C72e) \tag{4-16}$$

These residuals are one measure of the "goodness of fit" of the estimated equation, and should always be examined. (They will of course sum to zero.) Examination of the residuals may offer useful information about how well the equation "fits" the data and may suggest another variable which may account for an especially large residual. As a measure of the "goodness of fit" of the equation, however, the residuals are less than ideal. In particular, since the residuals will reflect the units in which the dependent variable is measured, the residuals can not be viewed on a standardized basis from equation to equation.

There are at least four additional statistics which should always be computed in order to arrive at a fuller evaluation of the statistical properties of an estimated equation and its parameters before it is used for forecasting. These are: (1) the standard error of the regression (SER, also called the standard error of estimate); (2) the standard errors and t statistics of the estimated parameters; (3) the coefficient of determination (R^2) for the equation; and (4) the Durbin-Watson statistic.

The *standard error of the regression* (s) is based on the residual variance (s^2), an estimate of the true variance (σ^2) of the relationship, based on the sample of data used. (See equation 4-17.) It is a measure of the error of the estimating equation, and is equal to the square root of the sum of the squared residuals (Σe^2) divided by the degrees of freedom (the number of observations minus the number of estimated parameters, in this case n-2).

$$\text{SER} = s = \sqrt{\frac{\Sigma e^2}{n-2}} = \sqrt{\frac{\Sigma(C72 - C72e)^2}{n-2}} \qquad (4\text{-}17)$$

The meaning of the standard error of the regression is that for any value of the independent variable; the true value of the dependent variable will lie within $\pm s$ of the estimated value some 68% of the time and within $\pm 2s$ about 95% of the time. Because the square of the standard error of the regression (s^2) is an estimate of the residual variation of the dependent variable (σ^2), it is also useful in computing other statistics.

The *standard errors* and *t statistics* of the estimated coefficients â and b̂ are used to determine the significance of these parameters. That is they are used to determine whether â and, more importantly, b̂ are statistically different from zero. The assumption that the errors (residuals) are normally distributed makes the use of the t distribution possible.

The standard error of b is equal to the square root of the variance of b̂, $s_{\hat{b}}^2$, which is equal to the square of the standard error of the regression (s^2) divided by the squared sum of the deviations of the independent variable ($\Sigma(YD72 - \overline{YD72})^2$).

$$s_{\hat{b}} = \sqrt{s_{\hat{b}}^2} = \sqrt{\frac{s^2}{\Sigma(YD72 - \overline{YD72})^2}} \qquad (4\text{-}18)$$

The t statistic is equal to the coefficient (b̂) divided by the standard error ($s_{\hat{b}}$).

$$t_{\hat{b}} = \frac{\hat{b}}{s_{\hat{b}}} \qquad (4\text{-}19)$$

A rule of thumb is, if t is 2 or more, then the coefficient is said to be significant; that is, there is a 95% probability that it is nonzero.

The standard error of â ($s_{\hat{a}}$), the constant term, is equal to the square root of its variance ($s_{\hat{a}}^2$), which is equal to the square of the standard error of estimate (s^2) times the quotient of the sum of the squares of the independent variable ($\Sigma(YD72)^2$) divided by the product of the number of observations (n) times the sum of the squared deviations of the independent variable ($\Sigma(YD72 - \overline{YD72})^2$).

$$s_{\hat{a}} = \sqrt{s_{\hat{a}}^2} = \sqrt{\left(\frac{\Sigma(YD72)^2}{n * \Sigma(YD72 - \overline{YD72})^2}\right) * s^2} \qquad (4\text{-}20)$$

The t statistic for â is calculated as for $\hat{b}$. The t test is often not met for the constant coefficient, but this is a less serious result than failure of the t test for $\hat{b}$.

$$t_{\hat{a}} = \frac{\hat{a}}{s_{\hat{a}}} \tag{4-21}$$

The *coefficient of determination* (R^2) is the most often used measure of the goodness of fit of an estimated regression equation. It measures the proportion of total variation in the dependent variable which is "explained," or accounted for, by the variation in the independent variables. Thus, the value of the R^2 must fall between 0 and 1.[18] The coefficient of determination is equal to one minus the ratio of the residuals to the sum of the squared deviations of the dependent variable.

$$R^2 = 1 - \frac{\Sigma e^2}{\Sigma (C72 - \overline{C72})^2} \tag{4-22}$$

As stated above, the coefficient of determination is one of the most often used descriptive statistics. It must be used very carefully, however. A high R^2 value does not necessarily prove the goodness of fit. Indeed, regressions on time series data often yield a high R^2 simply because the series both follow a linear trend. Because of this fact, serial correlation is often a problem.

The *Durbin-Watson statistic* (D-W) is used to test for the presence of first-order serial correlation. The D-W is equal to the ratio of the sum of the squared differences in residuals to the sum of the squared residuals.

$$D\text{-}W = \frac{\sum_{t=2}^{n} (e_t - e_{t-1})^2}{\sum_{t=1}^{n} e_t^2} \tag{4-23}$$

Note that the numerator cannot include a difference for the first observation in the sample, since no earlier observation is available. The Durbin-Watson statistic is then compared to critical values depending on the number of observations and the number of independent variables. A table of Durbin-Watson critical values lists upper (d_u) and lower (d_l) values for combinations of n (the number of observations) and k (the number of independent variables). There are six possible results for the Durbin-Watson statistic, summarized in Table 4-15.

---

[18] The adjusted coefficient of determination ($\overline{R}^2$), associated with multiple regression analysis (see below), must be corrected for the diminished degrees of freedom due to the use of additional independent variables. In this case, $\overline{R}^2$ may be less than 0. See equation 4–35b.

TABLE 4-15   Results for the Durbin-Watson Statistic[19]

VALUE OF D-W	RESULT
$(4 - d_1) < $ D-W $ < 4$	Negative serial correlation is present
$(4 - d_u) < $ D-W $ < (4 - d_1)$	Result is indeterminate ("grey area")
$2 < $ D-W $ < (4 - d_u)$	No serial correlation present
$d_u < $ D-W $ < 2$	No serial correlation present
$d_1 < $ D-W $ < d_u$	Result is indeterminate ("grey area")
$0 < $ D-W $ < d_1$	Positive serial correlation is present

As a general rule, the D-W should be close to 2 for there to be no serial correlation. If serial correlation is present it biases the standard errors. Thus the t test may suggest a coefficient is significant when it is not.

Serial correlation is a particular problem in estimating equations with time series data. There are several methods for correcting it. One of the most frequently used, the Cochrane-Orcutt Procedure,[20] can be simply described. When first order serial correlation is present the error terms are functionally related to the error term in the prior period.

$$\hat{e}_t = \rho * e_{t-1} + v_t \qquad (4\text{-}24)$$

Where rho (ρ) is unknown and v is an error term which meets the assumptions of econometrics (zero mean, constant variance, and normally distributed). Rho can be calculated by performing the regression in first difference terms, where

$$C72e_t - \rho * C72e_{t-1} = \hat{a} * (1 - \rho) + \hat{b} * (YD72_t - \rho * YD72_{t-1}) \qquad (4\text{-}25)$$

This of course, involves re-estimating all the other regression coefficients and statistics, using a generalized least squares method, a chore that is easily done on a computer.

At times, an equation in which serial correlation is present may have to be accepted. The criteria for doing so (indeed, for accepting any regression equation) is its ability to forecast. One way to judge this ability is to estimate the equation over a sub-period of that for which the data are available. This permits the forecaster to test the forecast properties of the equation by estimating values for more recent periods and comparing the forecast results to the actual values. (This is known as *ex post* forecasting.) If the residuals

[19] J. Durbin and G.S. Watson, "Testing for Serial Correlation in Least Squares Regressions," *Biometrika* 38 (1951), 159–77.

[20] D. Cochrane and G.H. Orcutt, "Application of Least Squares Regressions to Relationships Containing Autocorrelated Error Terms," *Journal of the American Statistical Association*, 44 (1947), 32–61.

are small the forecaster may choose to use the equation despite the presence of serial correlation.

Table 4-16 shows a worksheet for computing the regression parameters and summary statistics for the simple consumption function hypothesized in equation 4-13. The first two columns present quarterly data, expressed at annual rates, for real consumption and real disposable income, respectively, for the sixteen quarters from first quarter 1970 through fourth quarter 1973.[21] The sums and means for these data are shown at the bottom of each column. Thus, the summed real consumption values ($\Sigma C72 = \Sigma Y$) equal \$11,495.5 billion and the mean ($\overline{C72} = \overline{Y}$) equals \$718.47 billion, while the summed real disposable income values ($\Sigma YD72 = \Sigma X$) equal \$12,823 billion and the mean ($\overline{YD72} = \overline{X}$) equals \$801.44 billion. Columns 3 and 4 present the cross products for the two variables and the squared values for the independent variable (YD72). Substituting the summed values of these two columns along with the means of the two variables into equation 4-15a permits estimation of the regression coefficient on real disposable income. This computation, shown in Table 4-17, yields a value for $\hat{b}$ of 0.8513. As an initial impression, this appears a reasonable value for the marginal propensity to consume. When this value is substituted into equation 4-15b along with the means, the constant term, $\hat{a}$, is calculated (shown in Table 4-17) as 36.19.

In order to test the significance of these regression parameters, estimated values for real consumer spending (C72e) must be found and the errors (residuals) calculated by comparing these estimates to the actual values for consumer spending. Column 9 of Table 4-16 presents values for C72e found by solving equation 4-26 for the given values of YD72.

$$C72e_t = 36.19 + 0.8513 * YD72_t \qquad (4\text{-}26)$$

The errors and squared errors are presented in columns 10 and 11, respectively.

The standard error of the regression is estimated in equation 4-17 in Table 4-17 from the sum of the squared errors as 8.42. One way to normalize this value, or express it free of the units of measurement, is to express it as a percent of the mean of the dependent variable. This results in a normalized standard error of 1.2%. This implies that roughly two-thirds of the time the estimated value of real consumption using equation 4-26 will be within $\pm 1.2\%$ of the actual value and that 95% of the time it will be within $\pm 2.4\%$ of the actual value. Substituting the square of the standard error of the regression

---

[21] In general, more than sixteen observations are desired. (It is recommended to use at least thirty.) This is because, with two estimated parameters and only sixteen observations, only fourteen degrees of freedom remain. These may be too few to perform tests of statistical significance. Fewer observations are used in this case to reduce the complexity of the computations. The Table also follows the standard practice of labeling the dependent variable as Y (Y = C72) and the independent variable as X (X = YD72).

TABLE 4-16   Worksheet for Simple Regression Estimation

Period	REAL CONSUMPTION Y (1)	REAL DISPOSABLE INCOME X (2)	X * Y (3)	X^2 (4)	$x = X - \overline{X}$ (5)
1970: I	667.40	737.40	492140.76	543758.76	−64.04
II	670.50	752.50	504551.25	566256.25	−48.94
III	676.50	760.10	514207.65	577752.01	−41.34
IV	673.90	756.20	509603.18	571838.44	−45.24
1971: I	687.00	771.10	529745.70	594595.21	−30.34
II	693.30	779.90	540704.67	608244.01	−21.54
III	698.20	780.70	545084.74	609492.49	−20.74
IV	708.60	785.20	556392.72	616539.04	−16.24
1972: I	718.60	792.00	569131.20	627264.00	−9.44
II	731.10	798.70	583929.57	637921.69	−2.74
III	741.30	812.40	602232.12	659993.76	10.96
IV	757.10	838.10	634525.51	702411.61	36.66
1973: I	768.80	855.20	657477.76	731367.04	53.76
II	766.80	862.30	661211.64	743561.29	60.86
III	769.70	867.90	668022.63	753250.41	66.46
IV	766.70	873.30	669559.11	762652.89	71.86
Sums:	11495.50	12823.00	9238520.21	10306898.89	0.00
Means:	718.47	801.44			

$b = .8513$ $s_b = .0486$ $t_b = 17.53$ $R^2 = .9564$
$a = 36.19$ $s_a = 38.97$ $t_a = 0.93$ D-W $= .3986$
$s = 8.42$

Source: *National Income and Product Accounts,* Bureau of Economic Analysis, U.S. Department of Commerce.

(the variance) and the sum of the deviations of the independent variable about its mean (from column 6, Table 4-16) in equation 4-18, the standard error of the coefficient on real disposable income (s_b) can be estimated as shown in Table 4-17. Similarly, the standard error of the constant term (s_a) can be calculated as in equation 4-20 in Table 4-17. Dividing these values into the estimated coefficients yields the t statistics for each coefficient. As can be seen from Table 4-17, the t statistic for $\hat{b}$ equals 17.53 suggesting the coefficient is highly significant, while the t statistic for the constant, $\hat{a}$, is found to be not significant with a value of 0.93.

The overall explanatory power of the regression can be assessed by examining the value of the coefficient of determination (R^2). This statistic is computed by substituting the sum of the squared errors (column 11, Table 4-16) in equation 4-22. The R^2 is found in Table 4-17 to equal 0.9564, implying 95.64% of the variation in real consumer spending is explained by the variation in real disposable income.

TABLE 4-16

			ESTIMATED REAL CONSUMPTION	RESIDUAL		SERIAL CORRELATION
x^2 (6)	$y = Y - \overline{Y}$ (7)	y^2 (8)	Ye (9)	e (10)	e^2 (11)	$(e_t - e_{t-1})^2$ (12)
4100.80	−51.07	2608.02	663.95	3.45	11.88	
2394.88	−47.97	2301.00	676.81	−6.31	39.79	95.16
1708.79	−41.97	1761.38	683.28	−6.78	45.94	0.22
2046.43	−44.57	1986.37	679.96	−6.06	36.69	0.52
920.36	−31.47	990.28	692.64	−5.64	31.83	0.17
463.86	−25.17	633.47	700.13	−6.83	46.70	1.42
430.04	−20.27	410.82	700.81	−2.61	6.84	17.80
263.66	−9.87	97.39	704.65	3.95	15.64	43.15
89.07	0.13	0.02	710.43	8.17	66.68	17.73
7.49	12.63	159.55	716.14	14.96	223.85	46.19
120.18	22.83	521.27	727.80	13.50	182.22	2.14
1344.14	38.63	1492.37	749.68	7.42	55.06	36.95
2890.41	50.33	2533.23	764.24	4.56	20.82	8.17
3704.24	48.33	2335.91	770.28	−3.48	12.12	64.71
4417.26	51.23	2624.64	775.05	−5.35	28.61	3.49
5164.22	48.23	2326.25	779.65	−12.95	167.60	57.72
30065.84	0.00	22781.97	11495.50	0.00	992.26	395.53

The Durbin-Watson statistic—showing the presence or absence of first-order serial correlation—is calculated by substituting the sum of the squared errors (column 11, Table 4-16) and the sum of the squared differences in the error terms (column 12, Table 4-16) into equation 4-23 in Table 4-17. It should be noted that there is one less term (15) in the sum of the squared differences in the errors (numerator) than in the sum of the squared errors (denominator). The greater the number of observations the less important is this fact. The resulting value of 0.40 is low and indicates the presence of first-order serial correlation.[22]

[22] The critical values for the Durbin-Watson statistic with one independent variable and sixteen observations are: $d_l = 0.84$, $d_u = 1.09$, for the 1% level of significance; and $d_l = 1.10$, $d_u = 1.37$ for the 5% level of significance. Since in this case the estimated Durbin-Watson Statistic is less than the lower value in all cases, the hypothesis of no serial correlation must be rejected.

TABLE 4-17   Calculation of Regression Statistics

$C72 = \hat{a} + \hat{b} * YD72$

(4-15a) $\hat{b} = \dfrac{\Sigma(X * Y) - (n * \bar{X} * \bar{Y})}{\Sigma X^2 - (n * \bar{X}^2)} = \dfrac{9{,}238{,}520.21 - (16 * 801.44 * 718.47)}{10{,}306{,}898.89 - (16 * (801.44)^2)} = 0.8513$

(4-15b) $\hat{a} = \bar{Y} - \hat{b} * \bar{X} = 718.47 - (0.8513 * 801.44) = 36.19$

(4-13) $Ye_t = \hat{a} + \hat{b} * X_t = 36.19 + 0.8513 * X_t$

(4-16) $e_t = Y_t - Ye_t$

(4-17) $SER = s = \sqrt{\dfrac{\Sigma e^2}{n-2}} = \sqrt{\dfrac{992.26}{14}} = 8.42$

(4-18) $s_{\hat{b}} = \sqrt{\dfrac{s^2}{\Sigma(X - \bar{X})^2}} = \sqrt{\dfrac{70.90}{30{,}065.84}} = 0.0486$

(4-20) $s_{\hat{a}} = \sqrt{s^2 * \left(\dfrac{\Sigma X^2}{n * (X - \bar{X})^2}\right)} = \sqrt{70.90 * \left(\dfrac{10{,}306{,}898.89}{16 * 30{,}065.84}\right)} = 38.97$

(4-19) $t_{\hat{b}} = \dfrac{\hat{b}}{s_{\hat{b}}} = \dfrac{0.8513}{0.0486} = 17.53$ (4-21) $t_{\hat{a}} = \dfrac{\hat{a}}{s_{\hat{a}}} = \dfrac{36.19}{38.97} = 0.93$

(4-22) $R^2 = 1 - \left(\dfrac{\Sigma e^2}{\Sigma(Y - \bar{Y})^2}\right) = 1 - \left(\dfrac{992.26}{22{,}781.97}\right) = 0.9564$

(4-23) $D\text{-}W = \dfrac{\displaystyle\sum_{t=2}^{16}(e_t - e_{t-1})^2}{\displaystyle\sum_{t=1}^{16} e_t^2} = \dfrac{395.53}{992.26} = 0.40$

The results of the regression analysis are summarized below.

$$C72e_t = \hat{a} + \hat{b} * YD72_t$$

coefficients	t statistics
$\hat{a} = 36.19$	(0.93)
$\hat{b} = 0.8513$	(17.53)

$$R^2 = 0.9564 \quad D\text{-}W = 0.40 \quad SER = 8.42\ (1.17\%)$$

The lack of significance of the constant term is not a serious matter. The fact that the value of $\hat{b}$ is plausible, given prior expectations, and significant is more important. Moreover, the value of R^2 is high and the standard error of the regression is fairly low. The poor results of the Durbin-Watson test, however, place all the other results in question, especially the significance of $\hat{b}$.

The existence of first-order serial correlation is a common, but serious, problem with estimating regression equations from time series data. It should be removed by an autocorrelation correction procedure. In this case, a Cochrane-Orcutt correction was performed as shown in the computer output in Figure 4-9. The results are shown below.

$$C72e_t = \hat{a} + \hat{b} * YD72_t$$

coefficients	t statistics
$\hat{a} = 114.70$	(1.80)
$\hat{b} = 0.7136$	(7.11)
rho = 0.86	(6.57)

$$R^2 = 0.9838 \quad D\text{-}W = 1.00 \quad SER = 4.96 \ (0.69\%)$$

The value of the constant term has increased and is now significant at the 95% level. The coefficient on real disposable income, $\hat{b}$, is lower at 0.7136, but still highly significant and a reasonable estimate of MPC. The value of rho is high at 0.86, and the Durbin-Watson statistic has only moved into the "grey" area at the 1% level. The value of R^2 has increased slightly, and the standard error of the regression has declined.

When the equation was used to forecast the values of real consumer spending in 1974 the results shown in Table 4-18 were found. The results show that the equation generally underestimated actual consumption in these four quarters, but by small amounts (less than 1% in all but one quarter). Among the possible explanations is that some other variable in addition to real disposable income exerts an important effect on the level of real consumer spending.

Multiple Regression Analysis

Real world economic relationships are quite complex. For instance, the total level of real consumer spending is almost certainly a result of more influences than just the level of real disposable income. In other words, economic models only approximate reality by focusing on the main forces

TABLE 4-18   Forecast of Real Consumer Spending (C72)

$$C72e_t = 114.70 + 0.7136 * YD72_t$$

	ACTUAL	FORECAST	ERROR	ERROR AS PERCENT OF ACTUAL
	(IN BILLIONS OF 1972 DOLLARS)			
74 : 1	761.2	757.5	3.7	0.49%
74 : 2	764.1	757.3	6.8	0.89
74 : 3	769.4	757.2	12.2	1.59
74 : 4	756.5	751.2	5.3	0.70

QUARTERLY(1970:1 TO 1973:4)   16 OBSERVATIONS
DEPENDENT VARIABLE: C72

COEFFICIENT	STD. ERROR	T-STAT	INDEPENDENT VARIABLE
144.698	80.32	1.802	CONSTANT
0.713632	0.1003	7.114	YD72
0.858851	0.1308	6.567	RHO

1)

R-BAR SQUARED: 0.9838
DURBIN-WATSON STATISTIC: 1.0000
STANDARD ERROR OF THE REGRESSION: 4.962   NORMAL-
IZED: 0.006906

RESIDUALS(ERR)

1970:1	−1.809
1970:2	−8.174
1970:3	−1.005
1970:4	−1.317
1971:1	0.992
1971:2	−1.106
1971:3	3.206
1971:4	6.676
1972:1	5.649
1972:2	8.947
1972:3	2.741
1972:4	−0.162
1973:1	1.516
1973:2	−5.618
1973:3	0.284
1973:4	−6.058

DATE	ACTUAL	FITTED	* MARKS ACTUAL VALUES
1970:1	667,400	669,209	*
1970:2	670,500	678,674	*††
1970:3	676,500	677,505	*
1970:4	673,900	675,217	*
1971:1	687,000	686,008	*
1971:2	693,300	694,406	*
1971:3	698,200	694,994	−*
1971:4	708,600	701,924	──*
1972:1	718,600	712,951	−*
1972:2	731,100	722,153	──*
1972:3	741,300	738,559	−*
1972:4	757,100	757,262	*
1973:1	768,800	767,284	*
1973:2	766,300	771,918	*†
1973:3	769,700	769,416	*
1973:4	766,700	772,758	*††

	1974:1	1974:2	1974:3	1974:4	1975:1	1975:2	1975:3
C72	757,523	757,313	757,225	751,196	747,222	780,343	770,992

	1975:4
C72	775,975

FIGURE 4-9 Least squares with first-order autocorrelation correction

which affect the dependent variable. This fact poses two problems for the economic forecaster. First, there may be theoretically sound relationships which are no help because of the difficulty in forecasting values for one or more of the independent variables. (For instance, a stock market index's past performance may account for a high degree of the variation in household spending. The poor track record of stock market forecasts, however, underscores the profound difficulty of using such a measure as an "explanatory"[23] variable in a forecast model.) The second problem posed by a more complex model is the need to estimate an increased number of forecast parameters. Fortunately, the method of *multiple regression analysis* provides a means to address this second problem.

Multiple regression analysis is an extension of the simple (two-variable) regression analysis discussed above. In this case, however, the variation in the dependent variable is explained by variation in two or more independent variables. Often, both the explanatory and econometric properties of a relationship can be enhanced by the addition of one or more further variables. It should be remembered, however, that the forecaster is attempting to model an economic relationship, not merely to optimize statistical measures. Thus, the forecaster should carefully specify the relationship, in particular, determining expectations about the sign and magnitude of the coefficients to be estimated.

Returning to the consumption function analyzed above, it seems possible that a more complex consumption model might yield better results. In particular, although the estimated coefficients on real disposable income in both the uncorrected and corrected forms were of the expected magnitude (0.85 and 0.71, respectively) for the marginal propensity to consumer (MPC), and despite the high degree of variation explained (the R^2 equaled 0.95 and 0.98, respectively), there were two problems. First, there was evidence of serial correlation, which could not be completely ruled out even after a Cochrane-Orcutt correction was performed. Second, were the errors which emerged when the estimated equation was used to forecast 1974. In its corrected form the equation underestimated consumption in each of the four quarters. One possible explanation of both problems is that some other important explanatory variable may have been left out of the model.

A possible candidate may be the unemployment rate (RU), on the assumption that consumers feel inhibited from spending when the unemployment rate is high, and are encouraged when it is falling. Thus, an inverse relationship is posited. When it is recalled that a severe recession was underway throughout 1974, such a relationship appears more likely. A revised consumption equation can, therefore, be hypothesized as in 4-27.

$$C72_t = a + b_1 * YD72 + b_2 * RU_t \qquad (4\text{-}27)$$

---

[23] The term *explanatory* variable is used here and elsewhere in this text to refer to the role an independent variable plays in "explaining" the variation in a dependent variable.

where a = a constant term

   b_1 = the marginal propensity to consume, with an expected value between 0 and 1 (in fact, the value should be in the range of the simple regression estimates of 0.70 to 0.85)

   b_2 = the coefficient on the unemployment rate, expected to be negative.[24]

Estimating this relationship requires multiple regression analysis since there are now two explanatory variables. The parameters and measures of significance for a multiple regression equation are estimated in a manner similar to the sequence followed in simple regression analysis, but, as might be expected, the computations are more complex. Indeed, the usual approach—and the only practical approach when more than two explanatory variables are involved—is to use matrix algebra. A discussion of the matrix algebra required to estimate large multiple regression equations is beyond the scope of this chapter.[25] Moreover, as a practical matter such computations are likely to be performed using a computer. However, in order to highlight some of the particular aspects of multiple versus simple regression, the three variable (one dependent, two explanatory variables) case will be described, first in general terms, and then for the relationship specified by equation 4-27 from first quarter 1970 through fourth quarter 1973.

A general specification of the multiple regression equation with two explanatory variables is shown in 4-28.

$$Y_t = a + b_1 * X_{1t} + b_2 X_{2t} + u_t \qquad (4\text{-}28)$$

where Y_t = the dependent variable

   X_{1t} = the first independent variable

   X_{2t} = the second independent variable

   u_t = the stochastic error term

all of which are time series containing t observations

a = the constant term

b_1, b_2 = the coefficients of the independent variables

---

[24] Note that *a priori*, or expected, values for the coefficients are specified before estimation. Regression analysis should not consist of simply throwing variables into a computer program. There should be some economic basis for the hypothesized relationship, reflected in the specification.

[25] The reader wishing to consult a more rigorous general (matrix-based) discussion of multiple regression can consult: Pindyck and Rubinfeld, *Econometric Models and Economic Forecasts;* Intriligator, *Econometric Models, Techniques, and Applications;* or Johnston, *Econometric Methods.*

The four basic assumptions of simple regression—(1) there is a linear relationship, (2) the error terms have zero means and constant variance, (3) there is no serial correlation in the error terms, and (4) the errors are normally distributed—are all assumed for the multiple regression case. The assumption of a linear relationship needs some elaboration. It is assumed that the dependent variable is linearly related to each of the explanatory variables, assuming the other is held constant. In addition it is assumed that in the multiple regression case there is no linear relationship between the explanatory variables—they are independent of each other. When this assumption is violated, *multicollinearity* exists. In general, some multicollinearity exists in most complex economic relationships, but the problems become most serious when the correlation between explanatory variables is high.

If the assumptions of regression analysis are met, multiple regression analysis provides a least squares estimate of the dependent variable. This means that the squared sum of the residuals (where the residual, e_t, equals the difference between the actual value of the dependent variable, Y_t, and its estimated value, Ye_t) is minimized. The squared sum of the residuals for the three variable (one dependent, two independent) regression equation are shown in equation form in 4-29.

$$\Sigma e_t^2 = \Sigma(Y_t - Ye_t)^2 = \Sigma(Y_t - \hat{a} - \hat{b}_1 * X_{1t} - \hat{b}_2 * X_{2t})^2 \qquad (4\text{-}29)$$

When this relationship is minimized by taking partial derivatives with respect to each of the estimated parameters ($\hat{a}$, $\hat{b}_1$, and $\hat{b}_2$) and setting them equal to zero, the normal equations can be derived.[26]

$$\Sigma Y_t = n * \hat{a} + \hat{b}_1 * \Sigma X_{1t} + \hat{b}_2 * \Sigma X_{2t} \qquad (4\text{-}30a)$$

$$\Sigma X_{1t}Y_t = \hat{a} * \Sigma X_{1t} + \hat{b}_1 * \Sigma X_{1t}^2 + \hat{b}_2 * \Sigma X_{1t}X_{2t} \qquad (4\text{-}30b)$$

$$\Sigma X_{2t}Y_t = \hat{a} * \Sigma X_{2t} + \hat{b}_1 * \Sigma X_{1t}X_{2t} + \hat{b}_2 * \Sigma X_{2t}^2 \qquad (4\text{-}30c)$$

The three normal equations can be solved for the three parameters. The algebra can be more easily expressed if the solution equations are in deviations. For instance, y is the deviation of the dependent variable ($y = Y_t - \overline{Y}$) about its mean. In deviation form, the regression coefficients are solved for as in 4-31a through 4-31c.

$$\hat{b}_1 = \frac{(\Sigma x_1 y)(\Sigma x_2^2) - (\Sigma x_2 y)(\Sigma x_1 x_2)}{(\Sigma x_1^2)(\Sigma x_2^2) - (\Sigma x_1 x_2)^2} \qquad (4\text{-}31a)$$

[26] See Pindyck and Rubinfeld, *Econometric Models*, pp. 54–56.

$$\hat{b}_2 = \frac{(\Sigma x_2 y)(\Sigma x_1^2) - (\Sigma x_1 y)(\Sigma x_1 x_2)}{(\Sigma x_1^2)(\Sigma x_2^2) - (\Sigma x_1 x_2)^2} \qquad (4\text{-}31b)$$

$$\hat{a} = \overline{Y} - b_1 * \overline{X}_1 - b_2 * \overline{X}_2 \qquad (4\text{-}31c)$$

These estimates provide the estimation parameters of equation 4-32, from which estimated values of the dependent value (Ye_t) can be derived, and the residuals (e_t) and squared residuals (e_t^2) calculated.

$$Ye_t = \hat{a} + \hat{b}_1 * X_{1t} + \hat{b}_2 * X_{2t} \qquad (4\text{-}32)$$

The values of the parameters themselves (or even the squared residuals) do not supply sufficient information about the significance and explanatory power of either the individual independent variables or the relationship as a whole to allow use of the estimated equation for forecasting. Thus, there are a number of further statistics that should be computed to judge the equation's usefulness in forecasting. These are described below and their equations given in Table 4-19.

The *standard error of the regression* (also called standard error of estimate) provides one measure of the closeness of fit of the regression. Moreover, it is used to estimate some of the other measures of significance. As can be seen from equation 4-33 in Table 4-19, it is estimated by taking the square root of the sum of the squared residuals divided by the adjusted degrees of freedom (the number of observations, n, less the number of estimated parameters including the constant, k). *Adjusted* degrees of freedom are used in multiple regression analysis to offset the improvement in significance that results merely from adding explanatory variables. The interpretation of the standard error of the regression is that the true value of Y will lie within ±s of Ye 68% of the time and within ±2s 95% of the time.

The *standard errors of the coefficients* of the independent variables are used to test the significance of the estimated coefficients of the explanatory variable. Estimation of the standard error of the constant term is cumbersome, but usually not of importance, so it is not shown here.[27] As can be seen from equations 4-34a and 4-34b, in Table 4-19, these statistics are related to the standard error of the regression. The standard errors of the coefficients can be used to derive the t statistic for each of the coefficients, thus providing a measure of the significance of each coefficient similar to the method for a simple regression equation.

The *coefficient of multiple determination* (R^2) provides a measure of goodness of fit. However, in multiple regression analysis the R^2 should be

---

[27] The equation for estimating the standard error of the constant term in a three-variable regression equation is shown in Salvatore, *Theory and Problems of Statistics and Econometrics*, p. 151. Multiple regression computer programs usually provide estimates of $s_{\hat{a}}$.

TABLE 4-19   Multiple Regession Statistics

1. *Standard Error of the Regression*

$$s = \sqrt{\frac{\Sigma e_t^2}{n - k}} \qquad (4\text{-}33)$$

where n = the number of observations
k = the number of estimated parameters (including the constant term)

2. *Standard Error of Independent Variable Coefficients*

$$s_{\hat{b}_1} = \sqrt{s^2 * \left(\frac{\Sigma x_2^2}{(\Sigma x_1^2 \Sigma x_2^2) - (\Sigma x_1 x_2)^2}\right)} \qquad (4\text{-}34a)$$

$$s_{\hat{b}_2} = \sqrt{s^2 * \left(\frac{\Sigma x_1^2}{(\Sigma x_1^2 \Sigma x_2^2) - (\Sigma x_1 x_2)^2}\right)} \qquad (4\text{-}34b)$$

$$t_{\hat{b}_1} = \frac{\hat{b}_1}{s_{\hat{b}_1}} \qquad t_{\hat{b}_2} = \frac{\hat{b}_2}{s_{\hat{b}_2}}$$

3. *Coefficient of Multiple Determination*

$$R^2 = 1 - \frac{\Sigma e^2}{\Sigma y^2} \qquad (4\text{-}35a)$$

Adjusted

$$\bar{R}^2 = 1 - (1 - R^2) * \frac{n - 1}{n - k} \qquad (4\text{-}35b)$$

4. *F Test*

$$F = \frac{\dfrac{\Sigma y^2}{(k - 1)}}{\dfrac{\Sigma e^2}{(n - k)}} = \frac{(R^2)}{(1 - R^2)} * \frac{(n - k)}{(k - 1)} \qquad (4\text{-}36)$$

adjusted for the lessened degrees of freedom associated with the use of additional explanatory variables. This adjustment is shown in equation 4-35b in Table 4-19.

The *Durbin-Watson statistic* is estimated as in equation 4-23 and, as in the simple regression case, it provides a measure of the presence or absence of serial correlation.

Finally, the *F Test statistic,* which measures the ratio of explained to unexplained variation, provides a measure of the overall significance of the regression. This statistic is computed as in equation 4-36 in Table 4-19. Its value is then compared to the critical value for the appropriate number of observations and degrees of freedom from an F Table. If above the critical value, the null hypothesis that there is no relationship can be rejected.

TABLE 4-20   Worksheet for Multiple Regression Estimation

	REAL CONSUMP-TION	REAL DISPOS-ABLE INCOME	UNEMPLOY-MENT RATE	y	x_1	x_2	x_1y
	Y	X_1	X_2	(4)	(5)	(6)	(7)
	(1)	(2)	(3)				
Period							
1970: I	667.40	737.40	4.17	−51.07	−64.04	−1.19	3270.32
II	670.50	752.50	4.76	−47.97	−48.94	−0.60	2347.47
III	676.50	760.10	5.18	−41.97	−41.34	−0.18	1734.88
IV	673.90	756.20	5.82	−44.57	−45.24	0.47	2016.18
1971: I	687.00	771.10	5.93	−31.47	−30.34	0.58	954.68
II	693.30	779.90	5.92	−25.17	−21.54	0.57	542.07
III	698.20	780.70	6.00	−20.27	−20.74	0.65	420.32
IV	708.60	785.20	5.97	−9.87	−16.24	0.62	160.24
1972: I	718.60	792.00	5.79	0.13	−9.44	0.44	−1.24
II	731.10	798.70	5.68	12.63	−2.74	0.33	−34.58
III	741.30	812.40	5.61	22.83	10.96	0.26	250.29
IV	757.10	838.10	5.33	38.63	36.66	−0.03	1416.32
1973: I	768.80	855.20	4.98	50.33	53.76	−0.38	2705.93
II	766.80	862.30	4.92	48.33	60.86	−0.44	2941.56
III	769.70	867.90	4.82	51.23	66.46	−0.54	3404.96
IV	766.70	873.30	4.80	48.23	71.86	−0.56	3466.02
Sums:	11495.50	12823.00	85.68	0.00	0.00	0.00	25595.43
Means:	718.47	801.44	5.36				

$\hat{b}_1 = .8598$ $\hat{s} = 8.56$ $R^2 = .9582$ D-W = .4523

$\hat{b}_2 = 2.9449$ $\hat{s}_{\hat{b}_1} = .0508$

$\hat{a}_0 = 13.60$ $\hat{s}_{\hat{b}_2} = 4.0450$ $\bar{R}^2 = .9517$ $F = 148.82$

Sources: Real Consumption and Real Disposable Income—*National Income and Product Accounts,* Bureau of Economic Analysis, U.S. Department of Commerce. Unemployment rate—Bureau of Labor Statistics, U.S. Department of Labor.

The consumption function hypothesized in equation 4-27 can be used to illustrate the estimation of a multiple regression of real consumer spending ($C72 = Y$) on real disposable income ($YD72 = X_1$) and on the unemployment rate ($RU = X_2$). Values for these three variables from first quarter 1970 through fourth quarter 1973 are presented in columns 1 to 3 of Table 4-20.[28] The other values needed to calculate the regression parameters and statistics are presented in the remaining columns.

[28] As was true for the simple regression analysis, sixteen observations are generally regarded as too few on which to perform a multiple regression analysis (twice as many would be preferred). However, for ease of presentation this example is limited to only sixteen quarters of data.

x_2y (8)	x_1x_2 (9)	x_1^2 (10)	x_2^2 (11)	y^2 (12)	ESTIMATED REAL CONSUMPTION Y_e (13)	RESIDUAL e (14)	e^2 (15)
60.52	75.88	4100.80	1.40	2608.02	659.92	7.48	55.99
28.54	29.12	2394.88	0.35	2301.00	674.64	−4.14	17.13
7.34	7.23	1708.79	0.03	1761.38	682.41	−5.91	34.93
−20.72	−21.04	2046.43	0.22	1986.37	680.94	−7.04	49.58
−18.09	−17.44	920.36	0.33	990.28	694.08	−7.08	50.08
−14.22	−12.17	463.86	0.32	633.47	701.61	−8.31	69.12
−13.07	−13.38	430.04	0.42	410.82	702.54	−4.34	18.81
−6.07	−9.99	263.66	0.38	97.39	706.32	2.28	5.21
0.06	−4.11	89.07	0.19	0.02	711.64	6.96	48.51
4.11	−0.89	7.49	0.11	159.55	717.07	14.03	196.78
5.82	2.80	120.18	0.07	521.27	728.65	12.65	160.13
−0.97	−0.92	1344.14	0.00	1492.37	749.92	7.18	51.57
−18.87	−20.16	2890.41	0.14	2533.23	763.59	5.21	27.13
−21.02	−26.48	3704.24	0.19	2335.91	769.52	−2.72	7.39
−27.41	−35.56	4417.26	0.29	2624.64	774.04	−4.34	18.83
−26.77	−39.88	5164.22	0.31	2326.25	778.62	−11.92	142.18
−60.84	−86.97	30065.84	4.73	22781.97	11495.50	0.00	953.39

The deviations around their means for real consumer spending, real disposable income, and the unemployment rate are presented in columns 4 to 6, respectively.

The cross products of the deviations are presented in columns 7 to 9; the squared deviations in columns 10 to 12.

Substituting the appropriate summed deviation products from columns 7 through 12 into equations 4-31a through 4-31c, the estimated coefficients are shown at the bottom left of Table 4-20. Thus, equation 4-37 can be derived.

$$C72e_t = 13.60 + 0.86 * YD72_t + 2.94 * RU_t \qquad (4\text{-}37)$$

While it can readily be seen that the estimated value of the MPC is close to the expected range, the coefficient on the unemployment rate does not have the expected sign. This, by itself indicates a serious problem. Nevertheless, the analysis can be continued and the remaining statistics computed to determine the source of the problem.

The first step is to calculate the estimated values for real consumption (Ye_t) over the sample period. These values are shown in column 13 of Table 4-20. The associated errors and squared error terms are presented in columns 14 and 15. The sum of the squared errors is important for computing measures of "goodness of fit."

The first gauge of how well the relationship explains the variation in real consumer spending is provided by the standard error of the regression. The value of 8.56 suggests that estimates derived using this equation will be within $8.56 billion of the actual real consumption amount 68% of the time and within $17.1 billion 95% of the time. The standard error can be normalized (i.e., made free of the units it is measured in) by dividing it by the mean of the dependent variable in the sample period. In this case the normalized standard error of the regression is 1.2%, similar to the result for the simple regression equation analyzed above. The standard errors of the coefficients on real disposable income and the unemployment rate are 0.05 and 4.04, respectively. The t statistics can be derived by dividing the estimated coefficients by their standard errors. The t statistic for b_1 is 16.94, well in excess of the critical value of 2.16 required to state with 95% confidence that there is a significant relationship between real consumer spending and disposable income. On the other hand, the t statistic for b_2 is only 0.73, suggesting that there is not a significant relationship between real consumption and the unemployment rate. This result is consistent with the failure to find the expected negative coefficient.

Despite the poor results for the hypothesized consumption-unemployment rate relationships, the adjusted coefficient of determination (R^2) is quite high, indicating that 95.2% of the variation in real consumption is explained by the variation in the independent variables. Moreover, the F statistic at 148.82 is well in excess of the critical value of 6.7 (for three parameters and thirteen degrees of freedom) needed to reject the null hypothesis that there is no relationship with 99% certainty. However, the Durbin-Watson statistic is low (0.45), indicating positive serial correlation. As in the simple regression case, the presence of serial correlation means that the standard errors of the coefficients are biased downward and, thus, the t statistics may indicate that a coefficient is statistically significant (different from zero) when it is not.

The evidence of serial correlation suggested that a Cochrane-Orcutt transformation should be performed. The results of this computation are shown below in the format in which future regression analyses will be presented in this text.

$$C72e_t = \hat{a} + \hat{b}_1 * YD72_t + \hat{b}_2 * RU_t$$

	coefficients	t statistics	
$\hat{a} =$	164.3	(1.91)	
$\hat{b}_1 =$	0.70	(6.10)	(4-38)
$\hat{b}_2 =$	−2.41	(−0.42)	
rho =	0.88	(5.50)	

$$\overline{R}^2 = 0.9829 \quad D\text{-}W = 0.92 \quad SER = 5.09 \ (0.71\%) \quad F = 432.1$$

These results show improvement in the summary statistics due to the removal of the bias caused by the serial correlation: the adjusted coefficient of determination, the standard error of the regression, and the F statistic all show a greater degree of explained variation; more important, the Durbin-Watson statistic has now moved into the "grey" area at the 1% level of significance. The coefficient on real disposable income has declined to 0.70, roughly the same as the simple regression result after correcting for serial correlation, and remains highly significant. The coefficient on the unemployment rate now shows the expected negative sign, but the t statistic still indicates the relationship is not significant. The value of rho is somewhat high, suggesting that a similar result might have been derived by performing the analysis in first difference form.

Forecast results for 1974, based on the corrected version of equation 4-27, similar to those presented in Table 4-18 for the corrected version of equation 4-13, are presented below. The results are not as good as for the simple regression. This is clear from the larger error shown in Table 4-21

TABLE 4-21   Forecast of Real Consumer Spending (C72)

$$C72e_t = 164.30 + 0.70 * YD72_t - 2.41 * RU_t$$

	ACTUAL	FORECAST	ERROR	ERROR AS PERCENT OF ACTUAL
	BILLIONS OF 1972 DOLLARS			
74:1	761.2	756.8	4.4	0.58%
74:2	764.1	756.3	7.8	1.02
74:3	769.4	755.2	14.2	1.85
74:4	756.5	746.9	9.7	1.28

compared to those shown in Table 4-18. It is likely that these larger errors are due to the inclusion of the unemployment rate which was found to be insignificant.

III. ERROR ANALYSIS AND FORECAST EVALUATION

One point that emerges from the foregoing discussion is that all the examples of forecast methods produced estimates which to some extent differed from the actual values. In other words, the estimates only equaled the actual values when an error term was included as in 4-39, where A_t is the actual

$$A_t = E_t + e_t \tag{4-39}$$

value at time t, E_t is the estimate at time t, and e_t is the error ($e_t = A_t - E_t$) at time t. It is an uncomfortable fact of economic forecasting life that forecasts are subject to, and usually contain, errors. Nevertheless, every effort should be made to minimize and anticipate forecast errors.

A further problem is posed by the fact that, while errors in estimating a forecast method can be determined, the errors in the forecast period itself cannot be known until the actual value of the variable being forecast is itself known. Thus, by the time the error is known, the forecast is wrong. In order to limit the damage such errors pose it is even more vital to derive some expectation of future errors and, if necessary, to include estimates of the errors in the forecast.

There are several error analysis procedures that a forecaster should follow before adopting a particular forecast method. A simple, but valuable, procedure is to examine the errors in the estimation period to see if there is any pattern. Figure 4-10 shows plots of errors over the estimation period for the two consumption functions described above in both the uncorrected form and corrected for first order serial correlation. The serial correlation in the errors for the uncorrected equations is apparent from the wave-like pattern of the errors. On the other hand, the error patterns for the corrected equations, particularly for the simple relationship on real disposable income alone, display more randomness, with many of the errors closer to zero. The dotted lines on the graphs indicate the range of one standard error for each of the regressions. Once again, the corrected forms display a desirable narrowing in this range. Such a basic look at the error patterns in the estimation period yields some information about the likely errors. Nevertheless, little direct guidance is offered about the future error pattern.

A useful procedure to gain insight to the errors that can be expected in an actual forecast situation—called *in vitro* forecasting—is to perform an *ex*

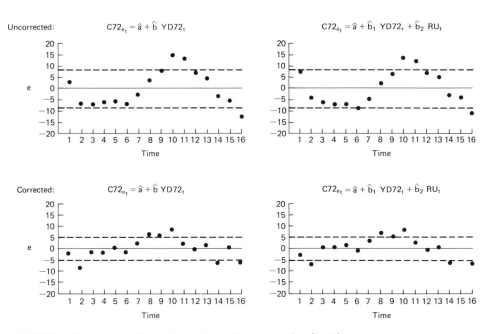

FIGURE 4-10   Error patterns for estimated consumption functions

post forecast. An *ex post* forecast is one using the estimated equation to forecast values for a period later than that used for estimation for which actual values are known. The errors which then result give more information about how the forecast method will work *ex ante*—that is, in the period for which actuals are unknown. Two criteria must be weighed in choosing the *ex post* period: (1) it should be long enough to let the forecast "settle in," but (2) the estimation period should not be so distant in time from that to be forecast—the *ex ante* forecast period—that shifts in the relationship may become important. Thus, for a four-quarter *ex ante* forecast, an estimation period which ends four quarters (one year) earlier would be useful since it allows a four-quarter (one year) *ex post* forecast period.

   Ex post forecasts were performed for the four quarters of 1974 for the two versions of the consumption function examined above: the results for the simple consumption function (Version I, using real disposable income alone as an explanatory variable) were presented in Table 4-18; the results for the more complex function (Version II, including the unemployment rate as an additional explanatory variable) were shown in Table 4-21. There are a number of quantitative measures of the forecast errors which can be made, which provide some insight to the nature of the error pattern of the forecast process.

The first such measure is the *mean error* (ME) which is simply the average error, computed as in 4-40.

$$ME = \frac{\Sigma e}{n} \qquad (4\text{-}40)$$

The mean error provides an indication of whether the forecast over- or under-predicts the actual value—in other words, the bias. Table 4-22 presents the errors and percent errors for the two corrected versions of the consumption function. As can be seen, the mean errors are both positive, suggesting the equations under-predict the actuals. (This can be confirmed by inspecting the quarterly errors, all of which are positive, indicating under-prediction: the actuals exceed the forecast values.) While, in general, bias is undesirable, there may be conditions where the cost of over-prediction is greater than under-prediction (or vice versa). In such cases, a forecast approach that is biased in the preferred direction may be chosen.

In cases where a high degree of forecast accuracy is sought and under- and over-prediction are equally undesirable, the mean error may not be the best evaluative measure because offsetting errors (over- and under-predictions of equal or near-equal size) lower the mean error. In such a case, the *mean absolute error* (MAE), which measures the average of the absolute value of the errors—without regard to sign—as in equation 4-41 may be a

$$MAE = \frac{\Sigma |e|}{n} \qquad (4\text{-}41)$$

more useful statistic. (In Table 4-22, since all the errors are positive, the mean error and the mean absolute errors are equal.) The *mean absolute*

TABLE 4-22   Ex Post Forecast Error Analysis

Version I: $C72e_t = 114.70 + 0.71 * YD72_t$

Version II: $C72e_t = 164.30 + 0.70 * YD72_t - 2.41 * RU_t$

	VERSION I ERRORS	% ERRORS	VERSION II ERRORS	% ERRORS
74 : 1	3.7	0.49%	4.4	0.58%
74 : 2	6.8	0.89	7.8	1.02
74 : 3	12.2	1.59	14.2	1.85
74 : 4	5.3	0.70	9.7	1.28
ME	7.0		9.025	
MAE	7.0		9.025	
RMSE	7.695		9.694	
MAPE		0.918		1.182

percent error (MAPE) is analogous, but measures the mean of the absolute errors as a percentage of the actual value as in equation 4-42. This has the advantage of normalizing the errors.

$$\text{MAPE} = \frac{\Sigma |\%e|}{n} \tag{4-42}$$

Finally, if large errors impose a greater cost than small errors, the *root mean square error* (RMSE) is a better criteria. For this measure, the average of the squared errors is taken—thus, penalizing large errors—and then the square root is taken so as to scale the error with the value being forecast.[29] Equation 4-43 depicts the root mean square error.

$$\text{RMSE} = \sqrt{\frac{\Sigma e^2}{n}} \tag{4-43}$$

In Table 4-22, the root mean square errors for each version are close to the mean errors and the mean absolute errors. In each case, Version I—the simple consumption function—yields lower errors and would be selected. The mean absolute percentage error of just less than 1% suggests that the forecast values for 1975 based on equation 4-26 might be increased by 1% based on the *ex post* forecast for 1974.

Ex post forecasting is an important preparatory step for an *ex ante* forecast. In Part II of this text, the forecast examples will be for periods for which the actual data are known. The prevalence of errors in these forecast examples underscores the difficulty of economic forecasting: even when the values of the independent or past dependent variables are known, forecast errors occur. A more stringent test of a forecast model—usually applied for a more complex, multi-equation model—is the technique known as *ex post dynamic simulation*. This method uses forecast rather than actual values of the independent variables to estimate the dependent variable(s) over some period which is beyond the estimation period, but for which actual values for all values are known. Thus, an *ex post dynamic* simulation more nearly

---

[29] The mean square error (MSE), equal to the squared sum of the errors divided by the number of observations (shown below), has a special function. The mean square

$$\text{MSE} = \frac{\Sigma e^2}{n}$$

error can be decomposed into three components: the bias, the variance, and a residual unexplained error term. Discussions of this procedure can be found in: Jacob Mincer and Victor Zarnowitz, "The Evaluation of Economic Forecasts" in Jacob Mincer, ed., *Economic Forecasts and Expectations* (New York: National Bureau of Economic Research, 1969); and Robert B. Platt, "Statistical Measures of Forecast Accuracy," in Butler, Kavesh, and Platt, eds., *Methods and Techniques of Business Forecasting* (Englewood Cliffs, NJ: Prentice-Hall, 1974). Used purely as a measure of forecast accuracy, the RMSE is superior to the MSE since it is expressed in the same scale as the variable being forecast.

replicates the conditions under which an *ex ante* forecast is performed. The sources for error are greater, however, coming from errors in the estimated relationship and in the independent variable estimation. If a simple *ex post* forecast is performed first, the errors attributable to the relationship alone (when explanatory variables are known exactly) can be determined. An *ex post dynamic* simulation performed subsequently will indicate the additional error due to errors in variables. Thus, the forecaster may find that, while a particular relationship has a low error associated with it, the errors associated with forecasting the explanatory variables are likely to be large and, as a result, make the relationship less useful for forecasting.

SUMMARY

This chapter has aimed at refreshing the reader's knowledge of statistical forecasting methods. More detailed discussions should be sought in the works referenced. The chapter also follows a sequence that the forecaster might find useful in preparing to forecast. This involves graphing the data and "looking" at it through a variety of transformations. It may also lead to the conclusion that the best approach to forecasting a particular activity measure is a method based on the data series' behavior in the past—a time series method. Alternatively, the forecaster may wish to model the economic activity being forecast on a hypothesized relationship estimated by regression analysis. In any event, errors are likely because the exact economic process is more complex than the forecaster's model. These errors should also be carefully analyzed. They provide vital information about the likely success of the forecast.

QUESTIONS FOR REVIEW AND RESEARCH

4-1   Using monthly data for 1982 and 1983, compute first differences, monthly percent changes, annualized monthly percent changes, and year-over-year percent changes for employment as measured by the BLS payroll survey. Contrast these statistics with those shown in Tables 4-2 through 4-5 for the Household survey data.

4-2   Using monthly data from issues of the *Survey of Current Business,* analyze the seasonally adjusted and not seasonally adjusted data for housing starts for the years 1976 through 1979. What conclusions can you draw about the seasonal pattern of housing starts?

4-3   The business cycle that ran from the January 1980 peak to the July 1981 peak was unusually short. For this reason, an average cycle which excluded the cycle might be useful for forecasting. Using the data in Table 4-10, recompute the average cycle shown in Table 4-11 for only the first five cycles shown. Then compare the average of six cycles and the average of five cycles to the cycle which peaked in July 1981. Do the MAE, MAPE, and RMSE of these two comparisons suggest that the five- or the six-cycle average is a better basis for forecasting?

4-4 Using the data on population in Table 4-13, compute three- and six-month moving averages for the percent changes. From these, forecast the levels for 1983 and compute the errors compared to the actuals. On the basis of the error statistics (MAE, MAPE, and RMSE) for the three-, six-, and twelve-month moving averages of the percent changes, which appears to be the best (lowest error) forecasting method and why?

4-5 Compute double exponential smoothing forecasts of the civilian labor force using values for alpha of 0.25 and 0.35. Compare the resulting forecasts for July-December 1983 with the results in Table 4-14. Again, using error analysis statistics, determine which alpha results in the best *ex post* forecast. Extend the forecasts to January-June 1984 and re-examine the error analysis statistics. Has the best value for alpha from the July-December 1983 *ex post* forecast remained the best forecast in 1984?

4-6 Perform a regression using quarterly data with personal income as the dependent variable and payroll employment as the independent variable. Indicate the *a priori* assumptions that suggest these data might be related. Analyze the regression results in light of these *a priori* assumptions. Might a relationship between payroll employment and consumer spending be hypothesized?

5

INDICATOR FORECASTING
Employment, income, and retail sales

An economic forecast is not prepared in a vacuum. Forecasting is a continuous process, reflecting and responding to changing economic and business conditions. In this sense a forecast is never really complete. It only reflects the forecaster's expectations, given the conditions that exist and are expected to exist at the time the forecast is prepared. As these conditions change—and they will almost always differ to some extent from expectations—the forecast must be adjusted. Thus, the forecaster is also an economic analyst, monitoring developments and assessing their implications for recent and future developments.

There are many measures of economy-wide, industry, and firm activity which provide ongoing readings of the state of the economy and which can be used to assess the degree to which a forecast is "on track." Constantly tracking the actual movements of economic measures is an important part of the continuous process of forecasting.

In many cases, these measures of specific economic activities may serve as inputs to a regularly prepared forecast. For instance, personal income may be used as an input in forecasting consumption. Thus, a sudden change in the monthly pattern of personal income growth may signal the need to alter the forecast for personal consumption expenditures and, in turn, for the sales of a company's products. In other instances, a particular measure—say, retail sales of autos—may be the key measure which the firm—a tire manufacturer—gears its business to. Thus, the monthly reports on retail sales of autos provide a standard against which the firm's sales forecast can be evaluated. Yet another example is the case where the response of economic and monetary policymakers to a measure—for instance, the unemployment rate—is likely to affect the business environment for a firm or industry.

USES OF SHORT-TERM INDICATOR FORECASTING

The discussion above points out the usefulness of monitoring measures of economic activity which are less aggregate than the quarterly National Income and Product Account reports. In addition to monitoring the flow of information about recent economic conditions, it is often useful to prepare forecasts of the near-term trends for such indicators. There are three broad reasons for preparing such forecasts.

First, as indicated above, a particular measure or set of measures may serve as input to a more comprehensive forecast. As will be described in Chapter 8, most forecasts contain both *exo*genous and *endo*genous variables. The former are generated outside the forecast model, and thus are independent of it, while the latter are solved within the model. While exogenous variables are determined outside a model, they still have to be estimated. Except in rare cases where the variable is exactly known—such as a time variable, or may be assumed from some other source—such as defense expenditures as projected in the Federal Budget—these inputs must themselves be forecast. The forecasts of these measures will often be based on sub-models using higher frequency data than the overall forecast. (For instance, a quarterly GNP model may use the consumer price index as an input, and the CPI may be forecast using monthly data.)

A second case is where a particular measure of less-aggregate economic activity is itself the basic indicator that a firm gears its operations to. For instance, in the case of the tire manufacturer, the pattern of future car sales is of much greater importance than the growth of total GNP. (Of course, as the forecast horizon is extended, GNP growth will have an important bearing on the number of new cars sold.) Thus, the tire company's forecasters may put far greater effort into forecasting near-term auto sales so as to aid management in setting production and inventory policies.

Finally, stock, financial, and commodity markets react directly to the announcement of current economic statistics. Hence, forecasters employed by firms active in these markets estimate the likely level (or change) for such measures in advance, so that the firm's traders can develop conditional strategies. For instance, the announcement of an increase of five-tenths of one percent in the unemployment rate may cause varying reactions in different markets. The financial markets may view this as a sign that inflationary pressures have lessened, so the Federal Reserve can safely relax monetary policy, and thus short-term interest rates may decline. The stock market may view rising unemployment as a sign of worsening business conditions, thus driving down stock prices (assuming the beneficial effect of falling interest rates does not provide an offset—markets are interdependent). Commodity markets may respond in an even more complex fashion: the decline in interest rates eases the burden of carrying speculative positions— an upward influence on prices; on the other hand, the prospect of a weakening economy casts doubts on the future demand for some basic commodities—a downward influence on prices. In each case, however, a well-considered forecast will provide the traders with useful information that may serve as a basis for taking a position.

A STRUCTURAL APPROACH

As indicated above, there are many reasons for forecasting disaggregated indicators of economic activity. It is important, however, not to view these measures as separate from overall trends in economic activity. This and the two following chapters describe an approach to estimating a variety of indicators which: track general macroeconomic developments, are measures of specific economic activities, and relate to one another.

Even in the case where one indicator is the primary focus of a forecaster's efforts, to forecast it in a structural way—where that indicator is related to the behavior of others—is a desirable, methodological approach. This is all the more true when a number of measures are being tracked; for instance, to be used as exogenous inputs in a larger model.

This approach examines the main monthly measures in seven groups, similar to those described in section II of Chapter 3. First are *labor market* measures: population, labor force, employment, and unemployment. Using estimates for these and related variables, estimates of *personal income* can then be made. This reflects the fact that, in the main, personal income reflects payment for labor services. Consumer spending is related to income, and a major part of consumer spending is for durable and nondurable goods—which are captured by monthly *retail sales* data. The flow from employment, to income, to retail sales is a vital linkage in this structural approach. It permits the forecaster to anticipate and modify forecasts in one measure that arise out of changes in another. Moreover, retail sales have a special role for forecasters in consumer goods producing industries. Quite often in such a case, one component of retail sales—automobile tires, to repeat an example—may be the major market the firm sells in, and thus, the overall aim of the forecast.

The task of forecasting economic activity is complicated by the existence of inflation. For instance, a forecast of personal income or retail sales must take account not only of the changes in real activity but also the impact of price changes. Thus, it is necessary to examine and forecast *price changes* at both the producer and consumer levels. This topic is addressed in Chapter 6.

Changes in the level of *inventories* are the fifth group of indicators. The change in inventories results from three factors: production, sales, and the level of stocks on hand desired by the firm (the intended inventory/sales ratio). While all three factors are important, sales are the most volatile and the least subject to control by the firm. A separate and important area of activity occurs in the *housing* sector. Housing starts are a focal point for many industries—such as lumber producers and carpet manufacturers—which are directly, or indirectly involved in residential construction. Finally, *industrial production* measures the final goods, intermediate goods, materials, and utility output of the economy. As such, production responds to sales—both actual and expected—and changes in inventories. Detailed examples of forecasts for these last three measures are offered in Chapter 7.

There are two advantages to utilizing the linkages between these variables. Explicitly linking forecasts of, say employment, personal income, retail sales, and industrial production, permits the forecaster to modify expectations for other measures in response to the release of new data for one measure. For instance, if an explicit forecast linkage does exist among these four measures, and new data become available on the level of employment, it is possible for the forecaster to use this information to modify not only the subsequent forecasts of employment, but also those for the other variables as well. The second advantage of a linked structural approach is that it is less costly than a more formal econometric approach. Construction and maintenance of a simultaneous equation model is expensive in terms of both intellectual and financial resources. Such a model requires many equations, rigorous econometric techniques, and a great deal of data. This type of exercise is usually beyond the resources of a forecasting department and is best left to one of the commercial vendors of such models. The approach described here is perhaps less elegant, but within the resources of a small forecasting group, and it may well yield results which are equally valid.

An important source of information and guidance to a forecaster is the recent behavior of economic activity. As stated at the beginning of this chapter, forecasts are not made in a vacuum; rather, forecasting should be viewed as a continuous process. This does not mean that a forecast is just an extrapolation, but rather that the near future is more likely to be vaguely similar to the recent past than vastly different from it. Often, economists have only limited, and sometimes faulty, information on the recent state of economic activity. Nevertheless, whatever information is available is useful in fixing the environmental parameters for the forecast period. For instance, if a forecast of the next twelve months is made in a recessionary environment this will have different implications than if the economy is expanding. Similarly, whether inflation has recently been subsiding or accelerating has different forecast implications.

Moreover, since forecasts are usually updates (rather than performed for the first time), the actual performance of indicators can be compared to the previous forecast values—the forecast's track record—and these comparisons may suggest ways of improving the forecast. A large error in one month may be identified as the result of some special factor and incorporated in future forecasts.

A third point concerns the role the forecaster's *judgment* plays in forecasting. This role cannot be underestimated. The forecaster is an economist, not merely a technician. It should be apparent in the following sections, and indeed throughout the rest of the text, that judgment plays a crucial role. Even the selection of a particular method may require judgment between competing approaches.

LABOR MARKET MEASURES

Labor market conditions are the correct starting point for short-term forecasting. In the short term, labor is the most variable of the inputs to the production process—capital inputs vary only slowly over time, while materials are used in relatively fixed proportions to output. Moreover, the utilization of labor inputs—in terms of both the number of workers and the intensity (number of hours worked per worker)—is a key determinant, along with wage rates, of income. In turn, the availability of income is a basic factor underlying the final demand for goods and services.

There are several basic forces which affect labor market conditions. Principal among these are: (1) the population pool available for employment; (2) the participation rates of various age and sex groups in the labor force; (3) the state of economic activity, both recent and prospective (the phase of the business cycle); and (4) the age and work experience of job seekers, particularly the relative number of workers seeking: to change jobs, to regain lost employment (laid-off workers), to re-enter the job market after an absence, and to seek first-time employment.

The starting point for forecasting labor market conditions is *population*. An appropriate population measure is the civilian noninstitutional population sixteen years and over (POP16&)—a useful starting point for two reasons. First, this group encompasses the actual and potential segment of the population which is economically active. Second, it is a fairly easy measure to forecast in the short term; all the potential members of this group have been born, and its growth can be seen to be quite stable over time.[1] Figure 5-1 depicts the trend for this series over the post-war period.

There are several possible approaches to forecasting this series. If a long-term forecast has been done or is available to the forecaster (see Chapter 10) it is likely that a forecast—most likely at an annual frequency—may already exist. If so this can be interpolated to derive estimates of the monthly levels. This is especially appropriate for an aggregate measure of population such as this one where the monthly changes are quite regular. Alternatively, separate estimates can be made of the number of persons entering (immigrants and those turning sixteen) or leaving (as a result of joining the armed forces, emigration, institutionalization, or death) this group. Making such separate estimates is an arduous task where the benefit in extra precision may not equal the cost in time.

A quicker, cheaper, and possibly equally accurate approach is to use a simple time series method. As was seen in Chapter 4 first differences provide a good method of tracking the changes in this measure. Table 5-1 presents: (1) the levels and first differences for the civilian noninstitutional population 16 years and older for the months of 1981 and 1982, (2) actual levels for 1983, (3) forecast levels for 1983, and (4) the errors expressed as a percentage of the actual level.[2] The forecast method applies the average monthly change (first difference) for 1981–82 to each month of 1983. Examination of the forecast, actuals, and errors points out two things: (1) the errors are small; but (2) the errors cumulate—that is, an error early in the forecast period

---

[1] There are minor discontinuities in the series around census dates which the Bureau of the Census has attempted to smooth.

[2] In this and other examples, 1983 is treated as a forecast period. This *ex post* forecast approach permits comparison of the forecast values to actual values. In all cases the estimation method uses data only for periods prior to 1983.

FIGURE 5-1   Civilian population 16 and over

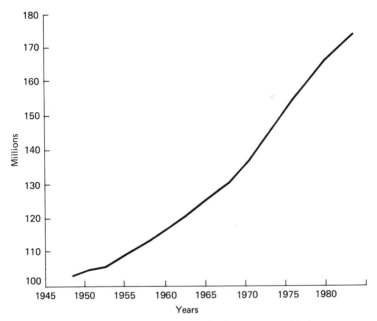

Source: Bureau of Labor Statistics, U.S. Department of Labor.

remains and affects all subsequent estimates. This is a common result with time series methods; once the forecast gets off track it tends to stay off track. However, if the forecast is updated regularly, these errors can be reduced by inclusion of new information in the forecast process. (For instance, if a twenty-four month moving average of the first differences is used, the errors will diminish.) It can further be shown that, in this case, using first differences results in a slightly smaller error by December 1983 (0.14% versus 0.21%) than if, say, the average monthly percent change in population during 1981–82 (0.11%) had been applied.

A more important measure of labor market conditions is the size of the *labor force*. This can be viewed as a factor of two variables: (1) the size of the population available for work; and (2) the portion of that population which is active in the labor market—the participation rate. The foregoing discussion demonstrated that the population over 16 can be forecast simply and fairly accurately. Thus, the key to a labor force forecast is the participation rate.

Table 5-2 presents monthly data for the civilian labor force (labor force), along with the population data examined above, and derived participation rates. The participation rates are derived by dividing the value for the labor force in a particular month, by the population, and then multiplying the

TABLE 5-1   Civilian Noninstitutional Population 16 Years and Over

	ACTUAL LEVELS	FIRST DIFFERENCES	FORECAST LEVELS	PERCENT ERROR (%)
		(IN MILLIONS)		
Date				
JAN 1981	169.104	.221		
FEB	169.280	.176		
MAR	169.453	.173		
APR	169.641	.188		
MAY	169.829	.188		
JUN	170.042	.213		
JUL	170.246	.204		
AUG	170.399	.153		
SEP	170.593	.194		
OCT	170.809	.216		
NOV	170.996	.187		
DEC	171.166	.170		
JAN 1982	171.335	.169		
FEB	171.489	.154		
MAR	171.667	.178		
APR	171.844	.177		
MAY	172.026	.182		
JUN	172.190	.164		
JUL	172.364	.174		
AUG	172.511	.147		
SEP	172.690	.179		
OCT	172.881	.191		
NOV	173.058	.177		
DEC	173.199	.141		
JAN 1983	173.354		173.379	−0.01%
FEB	173.505		173.559	−0.03
MAR	173.656		173.739	−0.05
APR	173.794		173.919	−0.07
MAY	173.953		174.099	−0.08
JUN	174.125		174.279	−0.09
JUL	174.306		174.459	−0.09
AUG	174.440		174.639	−0.11
SEP	174.602		174.819	−0.12
OCT	174.779		174.999	−0.13
NOV	174.951		175.179	−0.13
DEC	175.121		175.359	−0.14
MEAN		.180		
STANDARD ERROR		.020		
MAPE				0.088

Source: Bureau of Labor Statistics, U.S. Department of Labor, and the author's calculations.

TABLE 5-2 Population, Labor Force, and Participation Rates

Date	POPULATION (IN MILLIONS) (1)	ACTUALS LABOR FORCE (IN MILLIONS) (2)	PARTICIPATION RATE (%) (3)	POPULATION (IN MILLIONS) (4)	FORECAST LABOR FORCE (5)	PARTICIPATION RATE (%) (6)	ERROR (IN MILLIONS) (7)	PERCENT ERROR (8)
JAN 1981	169.104	108.025	63.88					
FEB	169.280	108.267	63.96					
MAR	169.453	108.597	64.09					
APR	169.641	108.965	64.23					
MAY	169.829	109.207	64.30					
JUN	170.042	108.434	63.77					
JUL	170.246	108.589	63.78					
AUG	170.399	108.681	63.78					
SEP	170.593	108.257	63.46					
OCT	170.809	108.977	63.80					
NOV	170.996	109.169	63.84					
DEC	171.166	108.882	63.61					
JAN 1982	171.335	109.075	63.66					
FEB	171.489	109.503	63.85					
MAR	171.667	109.664	63.88					
APR	171.844	109.901	63.95					

MAY	172.026	110.542	64.26					
JUN	172.190	110.133	63.96					
JUL	172.364	110.399	64.05					
AUG	172.511	110.473	64.04					
SEP	172.690	110.679	64.09					
OCT	172.881	110.690	64.03					
NOV	173.058	110.923	64.10					
DEC	173.199	110.873	64.01					
JAN 1983	173.354	110.677	63.84	173.379	110.847	63.93	-.170	-0.15
FEB	173.505	110.688	63.80	173.559	110.962	63.93	-.274	-0.25
MAR	173.656	110.735	63.77	173.739	111.077	63.93	-.342	-0.31
APR	173.794	110.975	63.85	173.919	111.192	63.93	-.217	-0.20
MAY	173.953	110.950	63.78	174.099	111.307	63.93	-.357	-0.32
JUN	174.125	111.905	64.27	174.279	111.422	63.93	.483	0.43
JUL	174.306	111.825	64.15	174.459	111.537	63.93	.288	0.26
AUG	174.440	112.117	64.27	174.639	111.652	63.93	.465	0.41
SEP	174.602	112.229	64.28	174.819	111.767	63.93	.462	0.41
OCT	174.779	111.866	64.00	174.999	111.882	63.93	-.016	-0.01
NOV	174.951	112.035	64.04	175.179	111.998	63.93	.037	0.03
DEC	175.121	112.136	64.03	175.359	112.113	63.93	.023	0.02
Mean 1981–82			63.93					
Mean 1983			64.01					
RMSE							.309	
MAPE								.234

Source: Bureau of Labor Statistics, U.S. Department of Labor, and author's calculations.

result by 100 so as to express it as a percentage. Thus, the value for January 1981 indicates that 63.88% of the economically active population was in the labor force, either employed or looking for work.

The problem is to forecast values for the labor force in 1983. A simple approach is to assume that the average participation rate over some recent period will apply to the forecast period. In this case, the average participation rate for the twenty-four months of 1981–82 was assumed to hold for 1983. By multiplying the forecast values for population found in Table 5-1 (shown in column 4) by this average participation rate (column 6), values for the labor force can be estimated for each month in 1983 (column 5). As can be seen from column 7, the errors (actual less forecast) are quite small overall, varying between an under-estimate of .483 million (0.4%) in June and an over-estimate of .357 million (0.3%) in May. The errors arise from two sources reflecting the fact that forecast labor force (LF_e) is itself based on two forecast variables: population ($POP16\&_e$) and the participation rate (RP_e), such that:

$$LF_e = POP16\&_e \times RP_e \qquad (5\text{-}1)$$

Thus, to the extent that (1) the population values forecast in Table 5-1 tended to over-estimate the true values, and (2) the participation rate was held constant rather than allowed to vary as it actually does, the forecast labor force values reflect these effects.

There are two further points that should be kept in mind in forecasting the labor force; these points become even more important for other variables. First, although the forecast shown is made for a full twelve months, new data will become available monthly. This allows the forecaster to take advantage of this new information in modifying the forecast. For instance, the actual participation rate for January 1983 is 63.84% compared to the average of 63.93% over the prior twenty-four months. If the forecaster uses, say a twenty-four month moving average to estimate the participation rate over the forecast period, the inclusion of the January 1983 value for the participation rate and the exclusion of the January 1981 value will take account of more recent data and remove the effect of distant data. (In December 1983 the forecast value for the participation rate would be 63.99% using this method.) This is a wholly appropriate method for forecasting the participation rate as it increases the sensitivity of the forecast to recent information. (Indeed, a similar approach can be applied to the forecast of population; a moving average of the first differences can be used.) A question the forecaster should consider is whether the small changes which result warrant updating the forecast each month, or whether less frequent updates—say, every three months—will suffice. Such an approach would lessen the cumulative errors from mis-forecasts of the population and the

TABLE 5-3   Seasonal Factors for Labor Force

	1978	1979	1980	1981	1982	AVERAGE
Month						
Jan.	.988	.988	.989	.989	.990	.989
Feb.	.988	.987	.988	.988	.989	.988
Mar.	.991	.991	.991	.991	.992	.991
Apr.	.991	.991	.991	.990	.990	.991
May	.992	.993	.994	.994	.994	.993
June	1.016	1.015	1.014	1.014	1.013	1.014
July	1.021	1.020	1.020	1.020	1.019	1.020
Aug.	1.014	1.013	1.012	1.013	1.013	1.013
Sept.	1.000	1.000	.999	1.000	.999	1.000
Oct.	1.004	1.004	1.003	1.002	1.001	1.003
Nov.	1.000	1.001	1.000	1.000	.999	1.000
Dec.	.998	.998	.997	.997	.996	.997
SUM	12.003	12.001	11.998	11.998	11.995	11.999

Source: Bureau of Labor Statistics, U.S. Department of Labor.

participation rate. These values are then shown to be the result of a moving average forecast method.

$$POP16\&_{e,t+1} = POP16\&_t + MA(\Delta POP16\&) \tag{5-2}$$

and

$$RP_{e,t+1} = MA(RP) \tag{5-3}$$

where

$$MA(X) = \frac{1}{n} * \sum_{t=1}^{n} X_t \tag{5-4}$$

This utilizes the most recent data so as to keep the forecast responsive (in this case n = 24).

The second point concerns the seasonal and cyclical characteristics of a data series. The forecaster should be aware of seasonal and cyclical influences on a data series because quite often they may have major short-term effects. Table 5-3 lists the monthly seasonal factors for the labor force for each of the five years between 1978 and 1982, and the average seasonal factor for each month in the five-year period.[3] While the seasonal pattern is generally rather smooth, the summer months (June through August) stand out as a period of above-average seasonal changes in the labor force. These

[3] The seasonally adjusted value for the labor force is equal to the raw (not seasonally adjusted) value divided by the seasonal factor. In turn, the seasonal factor can be derived by dividing the raw value by its seasonally adjusted value. The Bureau of Labor Statistics computes and updates seasonal factors once a year by a method similar to that described in Chapter 4.

movements reflect the seasonal flows into and out of the labor force of students and graduates seeking summer or first-time employment. It should be recognized that the seasonal adjustment process attempts to smooth these flows, but in any year there may be over- or under-adjustment due to changing population or economic conditions. Thus, there is the possibility of "residual seasonality"—a purely seasonal movement which is not adequately adjusted for by the seasonal factors. Often a forecaster can anticipate such residual seasonality, and adjust the forecast accordingly.

The problem of cyclical influence is harder to deal with. While the labor force is not the most cyclical of economic indicators, it does have cyclical characteristics. One of the most pronounced of these is the "discouraged worker" syndrome: "persons not in (the) labor force who want a job now but are not looking because they think they cannot get a job."[4] These workers are not counted in the labor force at all. This is a factor which is likely to hold down the participation rate—and thus the labor force—in a period of economic weakness, and, in turn, raise both measures when the economy is expanding. This can be seen in Figure 5-2 which shows the trend in the labor force during the 1946–1983 period, with recessions shown by the bars. While it is not easy to anticipate cyclical turns, they do sometimes signal themselves in advance. Moreover, many times a short-term forecast is prepared during a period when the near-term cyclical behavior of the economy is discernable, at least as to whether the economy is weakening or strengthening.

The incorporation of both seasonal and cyclical effects in forecasting requires the use of judgment by the forecaster. In much of the rest of this chapter, judgment plays an even larger role. This is certainly the case with the decomposition of the labor force into its two components: employment and unemployment.

The growth of the labor force is somewhat cyclical, but its division between *employment* and *unemployment* mainly reflects the strength (or weakness) of overall economic growth. Briefly, when the economy is growing at or above its trend rate most of the increase in the labor force occurs as increased employment; whereas when the economy is growing below trend, a larger portion of the labor force growth is reflected in rising unemployment and a slower rate of increase in employment; when the economy is in recession, unemployment is likely to rise rapidly, while employment is likely to decline. Moreover, these cyclical effects may be exacerbated by seasonal labor force flows.

The role of judgment in constructing forecasts of employment and unemployment is, thus, much greater than for the labor force. Once again, it

[4] Geoffrey H. Moore, *Business Cycles, Inflation, and Forecasting,* National Bureau of Economic Research Studies in Business Cycles, No. 24 (Cambridge, MA: Ballinger Publishing Co., 1980), p. 132.

FIGURE 5-2   Civilian labor force

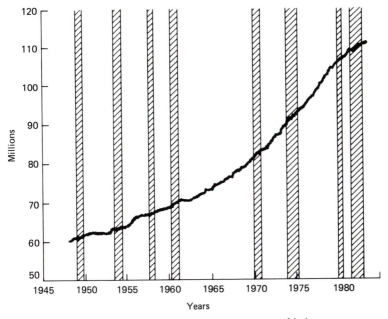

Source: Bureau of Labor Statistics, U.S. Department of Labor.

must be emphasized that a forecaster is not typically forecasting in a vacuum, or *de novo*. Rather, forecasts are typically updates (revisions) to past forecasts, given a background of recent information about the performance of the economy. Errors can be adjusted for as they become evident, though this is not to say that the process is easy or that errors are quickly corrected—sometimes the forecaster merely makes new ones.

Once again, the case of constructing a twelve-month forecast for 1983, given complete information about 1982 and earlier years, will be examined.[5] Monthly data for 1981 and 1982 will be used as the basis for the forecast. A longer time series could be used, and this could well yield better results when using simple time series methods, but it is not followed here because of expositional constraints. Moreover a longer time series may tell the forecaster more about the trend rate of growth (that is the average growth rate over a long period) or the cyclical behavior of the series.

In general, employment shows a more regular growth pattern than unemployment. For this reason, it is recommended that employment be forecast directly, and unemployment (and hence, the unemployment rate) be determined as the residual, or difference between the labor force and em-

---

[5] Typically, such a forecast would be performed in January, when freshly benchmarked seasonal factors are available.

ployment. Table 5-4 presents the levels for employment (household survey), the first differences, the monthly percent changes, and year-over-year percent changes in 1981 and 1982.

The first differences and monthly percent changes display considerable variation, reflecting the impact of the 1981–82 recession—which began in July 1981 and ended in November 1982—on employment. In five of the last seven months of 1981 and in eight months during 1982, employment declined. A forecast approach based on average changes—either first differences or percent changes—such as was used in forecasting population and the labor force would be inappropriate. Such an approach, which assumes regularity in the time series trend, would ignore an important irregularity:

TABLE 5-4   Employment (household survey) Trends: 1981–82

Date	LEVELS	FIRST DIFFERENCES	MONTHLY PERCENT CHANGES	YEAR-YEAR
	(IN MILLIONS)			
JAN 1981	99.951	.319	0.36	0.09
FEB	100.217	.266	0.27	0.18
MAR	100.609	.392	0.39	0.83
APR	101.074	.465	0.46	1.82
MAY	101.096	.022	0.02	2.07
JUN	100.379	−.717	−0.71	1.64
JUL	100.705	.326	0.32	1.96
AUG	100.638	−.067	−0.07	1.90
SEP	100.013	−.625	−0.62	1.01
OCT	100.324	.311	0.31	1.03
NOV	100.155	−.169	−0.17	0.66
DEC	99.585	−.570	−0.57	0.03
JAN 1982	99.682	.097	0.10	−0.27
FEB	99.810	.128	0.13	−0.41
MAR	99.754	−.056	−0.06	−0.85
APR	99.598	−.156	−0.16	−1.46
MAY	100.179	.581	0.58	−0.91
JUN	99.653	−.526	−0.53	−0.72
JUL	99.503	−.150	−0.15	−1.19
AUG	99.563	.060	0.06	−1.07
SEP	99.412	−.151	−0.15	−0.60
OCT	99.146	−.266	−0.27	−1.17
NOV	99.036	−.110	−0.11	−1.12
DEC	98.979	−0.57	−0.06	−0.61
Annual Averages:				
1981	100.396	−.004	0.00	1.10
1982	99.526	−.050	−0.05	−0.86

Source: Bureau of Labor Statistics, U.S. Department of Labor, and the author's calculations.

namely, the cyclical downturn in 1981–82. Moreover, 1983 proved to be a year of recovery, a development that was recognized early in the year.

The importance of these cyclical forces suggests that a cyclical approach should be used in forecasting employment. Table 5-5 presents employment data for the thirteen months following the five business cycle troughs prior to the 1981–82 recession, and indexes based on the trough month. For instance, the value of 62.631 million in April 1958—the trough month for the recession which began in August 1957—is divided into the employment levels for each of the subsequent thirteen months, and the quotients are then multiplied by 100 to produce the index. A period of thirteen months is chosen to conform to the forecast period, January through December 1983, which ends thirteen months after the November 1982 trough. The average index for the five cycles (column 6, Table 5-5) can then be used to forecast values for 1983.

Table 5-6 presents 1983 forecast values for employment, unemployment, and the unemployment rate. The forecast values presented in the upper panel of Table 5-6, are based on the previously forecast values for the labor force from Table 5-2. Employment is forecast by multiplying the average cyclical index values from Table 5-5 times the level of employment in November 1982 (the trough month).[6] The level of unemployment is then found by subtracting the forecast value for employment from the forecast value for the labor force in each month, while the forecast values for the unemployment rate are equal to unemployment divided by the labor force, expressed as a percentage. The lower panel presents the actual data for each of these measures in 1983.

Comparison of the forecast and actual values shows that while the forecast values were generally close to the actuals through May 1983, the forecast employment growth underestimated actual employment gains during the rest of 1983. Indeed, by December, the actual level of employment was 1.33 million higher than forecast. Moreover, since the labor force estimates were quite close to the actual levels, virtually all of the above-forecast employment gain was accompanied by a greater-than-forecast fall off in unemployment, and a sharp reduction in the unemployment rate.

The results in Table 5-6 point out the relevance of the dictum "if you must forecast, forecast often." Conditions can change quickly, as they did in 1983. A forecast prepared at the start of the year is likely to have missed the speed with which economic activity recovered as the year progressed. There are no absolute safeguards against wrong forecasts, but their damage can be limited by frequent monitoring and updates. Presumably, a forecaster monitoring the business situation carefully would have noticed signs that economic activity was reviving strongly. This points out, once again, the impor-

---

[6] The cyclical index is used in the form: level in trough month = 1.000.

TABLE 5-5   Employment (13 months from cycle trough)

	APR 1958 (1)	FEB 1961 (2)	NOV 1970 (3)	MAR 1975 (4)	JULY 1980 (5)	AVERAGE (6)	NOV 1982 (7)
			(IN MILLIONS)				
Month from Trough							
T	62.631	65.588	78.650	85.187	98.891		99.036
T+1	62.874	65.850	78.594	85.189	98.920		98.979
T+2	62.730	65.374	78.864	85.451	99.208		
T+3	62.745	65.449	78.700	85.355	99.328		
T+4	63.012	65.993	78.588	85.894	99.534		
T+5	63.181	65.608	78.987	86.279	99.632		
T+6	63.475	65.852	79.139	86.234	99.951		
T+7	63.470	65.541	78.547	86.370	100.217		
T+8	63.549	65.919	79.305	86.456	100.609		
T+9	63.868	66.081	79.539	86.665	101.074		
T+10	63.684	65.900	79.689	87.400	101.096		
T+11	64.267	66.108	79.918	87.672	100.379		
T+12	64.768	66.538	80.297	87.985	100.705		
T+13	64.699	66.793	80.471	88.416	100.638		

	APR 1958 (1)	FEB 1961 (2)	NOV 1970 (3)	MAR 1975 (4)	JULY 1980 (5)	AVERAGE (6)	NOV 1982 (7)
			(INDEXES: TROUGH = 100)				
Month from Trough							
T	100.00	100.00	100.00	100.00	100.00	100.00	100.00
T+1	100.39	100.40	99.93	100.00	100.03	100.15	99.94
T+2	100.16	99.67	100.27	100.31	100.32	100.15	
T+3	100.18	99.79	100.06	100.20	100.44	100.13	
T+4	100.61	100.62	99.92	100.83	100.65	100.53	
T+5	100.88	100.03	100.43	101.28	100.75	100.67	
T+6	101.35	100.40	100.62	101.23	101.07	100.93	
T+7	101.34	99.93	99.87	101.39	101.34	100.77	
T+8	101.47	100.50	100.83	101.49	101.74	101.21	
T+9	101.98	100.75	101.13	101.74	102.21	101.56	
T+10	101.68	100.48	101.32	102.60	102.23	101.66	
T+11	102.61	100.79	101.61	102.92	101.50	101.89	
T+12	103.41	101.45	102.09	103.28	101.83	102.41	
T+13	103.30	101.84	102.32	103.79	101.77	102.60	

Source: Employment Levels—Bureau of Labor Statistics, U.S. Department of Labor; indexes calculated by author.

TABLE 5-6   Forecasts of Labor Market Conditions for 1983

	LABOR FORCE	EMPLOYMENT INDEX	EMPLOYMENT LEVEL	UNEMPLOYMENT	UNEMPLOYMENT RATE
	(1)	(2)	(3)	(4)	(5)
Jan.	110.847	1.0015	99.185	11.662	10.5
Feb.	110.962	1.0013	99.165	11.797	10.6
Mar.	111.077	1.0053	99.561	11.516	10.4
Apr.	111.192	1.0067	99.700	11.492	10.3
May	111.307	1.0093	99.957	11.350	10.2
June	111.422	1.0077	99.799	11.623	10.4
July	111.537	1.0121	100.234	11.303	10.1
Aug.	111.652	1.0156	100.581	11.071	9.9
Sept.	111.767	1.0166	100.680	11.087	9.9
Oct.	111.882	1.0189	100.908	10.974	9.8
Nov.	111.998	1.0241	101.423	10.575	9.4
Dec.	112.113	1.0260	101.611	10.502	9.4
				ACTUALS	
Jan.	110.677	1.0012	99.154	11.523	10.4
Feb.	110.688	1.0014	99.172	11.516	10.4
Mar.	110.735	1.0028	99.316	11.419	10.3
Apr.	110.975	1.0058	99.606	11.369	10.2
May	110.950	1.0073	99.762	11.188	10.1
June	111.905	1.0172	100.743	11.162	10.0
July	111.825	1.0221	101.225	10.600	9.5
Aug.	112.117	1.0247	101.484	10.633	9.5
Sept.	112.229	1.0287	101.876	10.353	9.2
Oct.	111.866	1.0296	101.970	9.896	8.8
Nov.	112.035	1.0360	102.606	9.429	8.4
Dec.	112.136	1.0394	102.941	9.195	8.2

Notes: (1) Forecast from Table 5-2 (millions)
      (2) Forecast is for "Average Index" from Table 5-5 (trough value = 1.0000)
      (3) Forecast equals index value in column 2 times level in November 1982 (millions)
      (4) Labor Force less Employment (millions)
      (5) Unemployment divided by Labor Force (percent)

tance of an economist's analysis as compared to the mere technical use of time series methods in forecasting.

The employment measure discussed above is based on the BLS House-hold Survey and measures total employment relative to the civilian labor force. The employment series based on the BLS Survey of Establishments (or Payrolls) is somewhat narrower in coverage (see Chapter 3), but yet an important measure of economic activity. Payroll employment, as this mea-sure is referred to, is an input to the official estimates of industrial production and personal income and thus may be useful for deriving forecasts for these measures.

There are two approaches suggested for forecasting payroll employment, both of which can be described briefly. The first approach recognizes relationships between this aggregate measure and others—especially household employment—and may be labeled a "top-down" approach. The other approach acknowledges the components—employment by industry—within the total measure and attempts to use this structure to develop a "bottom-up" approach. It is recommended that both approaches be followed in order to establish greater confidence in the forecasts which emerge. However, since the "top-down" approach is simpler, it may be more efficient for frequent forecast updates, saving the "bottom-up" approach for major revisions to a forecast. These two approaches will be used again in forecasting other measures of economic activity.

In this case the "top-down" approach relates total payroll employment to total household employment, using the forecast values for total household employment (see Table 5-6) to derive values for payroll employment. This recognizes that the two series measure the same activity even if in slightly different ways. Figure 5-3 charts the employment levels from the household and payroll surveys, and the ratio of the payroll to the household survey levels, from 1946 through 1983. While it can be seen that the ratio of the two employment surveys has followed an upward trend since 1950, most of the growth occurred in the early 1950s and 1960s. (In 1950 the ratio averaged 76.67%; in 1960, 82.35%; and in 1970, 90.10%, compared to 89.38% in 1983.) The much stabler recent trend of the ratio suggests that a moving average of it would be a useful approach to a forecast of payroll employment in 1983.

Table 5-7 shows: the actual levels for employment measured by both surveys for 1981–83; the difference in millions between the two employment measures; their ratio (payroll series relative to household series); and the 1983 forecast values for household employment (from Table 5-6) and for payroll employment. The payroll employment forecast is based on a twelve month moving average of the ratio of payroll employment to household employment multiplied by the level of household employment. That is:

$$EP_t = MA(EP/EH) * EH_t \tag{5-5}$$

$$= \left(\frac{1}{12} * \sum_{i=1}^{12} (EP/EH)_{t-i} \right) * EH_t$$

where EP is equal to the level of payroll employment and EH, is equal to the levels of household employment forecast in Table 5-6.

A moving average is a valid approach because, although there is a trend to the ratio of payroll to household employment, this trend has shown little growth in recent years. Therefore, a moving average provides as good

FIGURE 5-3   Employment measures

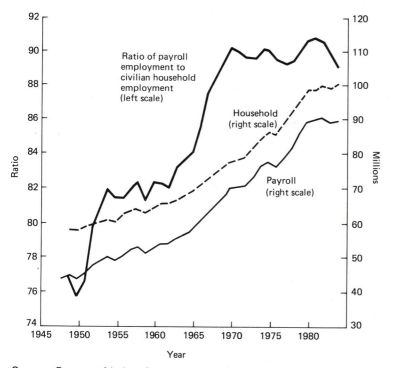

Source: Bureau of Labor Statistics, U.S. Department of Labor and the author's calculations.

an approximation of the trend as any other method.[7] Indeed, for the first eight months of 1983, this method produces quite accurate forecast results (RMSE = .303). The results for the final four months of 1983 err by roughly twice as much. This mainly reflects the earlier error in the forecasts of household employment. The main point is that the forecast for payroll employment is consistent with—indeed, is based on—the forecast of household employment.

The alternative—"bottom-up"—method for forecasting payroll employment is to focus on the major components. This is a more complex approach. Payroll employment data is reported not only in total, but also by major industry segments: manufacturing versus services and other non-manufacturing, private versus government employees. The approach here is to disaggregate the total into components about which the forecaster may make some reasonable assumptions.

---

[7] In particular, a time trend for this ratio estimated for 1970–82 yields a slope of 0.00016. Methods such as exponential smoothing do not provide better forecast results.

TABLE 5-7 Payroll Employment: "Top-Down" Approach

	HOUSEHOLD (a) (1)	PAYROLL (a) (2)	DIFFERENCE (3)	RATIO (4)	HOUSEHOLD (f) (5)	PAYROLL (f) (6)	ERROR (a-f) (7)	% ERROR (8)
	(IN MILLIONS)			%	(IN MILLIONS)			
Date								
JAN 1981	99.951	90.920	9.031	90.96				
FEB	100.217	90.990	9.227	90.79				
MAR	100.609	91.030	9.579	90.48				
APR	101.074	91.128	9.946	90.16				
MAY	101.096	91.131	9.965	90.14				
JUN	100.379	91.322	9.057	90.98				
JUL	100.705	91.484	9.221	90.84				
AUG	100.638	91.424	9.214	90.84				
SEP	100.013	91.411	8.602	91.40				
OCT	100.324	91.295	9.029	91.00				
NOV	100.155	91.041	9.114	90.90				
DEC	99.585	90.730	8.855	91.11				
JAN 1982	99.682	90.396	9.286	90.68				
FEB	99.810	90.417	9.393	90.59				
MAR	99.754	90.207	9.547	90.43				
APR	99.598	90.024	9.574	90.39				
MAY	100.179	90.016	10.163	89.86				
JUN	99.653	89.775	9.878	90.09				
JUL	99.503	89.450	10.053	89.90				

164

AUG	99.563	10.299	89.264	89.66			
SEP	99.412	10.177	89.235	89.76			
OCT	99.146	10.208	88.938	89.70			
NOV	99.036	10.251	88.785	89.65			
DEC	98.979	10.314	88.665	89.58			
JAN 1983	99.154	10.269	88.885	89.64	99.185	89.290	-.405	-0.46
FEB	99.172	10.426	88.746	89.49	99.165	89.186	-.440	-0.50
MAR	99.316	10.502	88.814	89.43	99.561	89.450	-.636	-0.72
APR	99.606	10.516	89.090	89.44	99.700	89.492	-.402	-0.45
MAY	99.762	10.341	89.421	89.63	99.957	89.644	-.223	-0.25
JUN	100.743	10.899	89.844	89.18	99.799	89.484	.360	0.40
JUL	101.225	11.073	90.152	89.06	100.234	89.798	.354	0.39
AUG	101.484	11.736	89.748	88.44	100.581	90.039	-.291	-0.32
SEP	101.876	11.025	90.851	89.18	100.680	90.025	.826	0.91
OCT	101.970	10.886	91.084	89.32	100.908	90.180	.904	0.99
NOV	102.606	11.251	91.355	89.03	101.423	90.608	.747	0.82
DEC	102.941	11.342	91.599	88.98	101.611	90.724	.875	0.96
MEAN ERROR							0.15
RMSE						.587	
MAPE							0.60

Difference = Household Survey − Payroll Survey Totals

Ratio = (Payroll/Household) * 100

a = actual

f = forecast

Source: Bureau of Labor Statistics, U.S. Department of Labor

There are at least five such components that can be so considered. These are: manufacturing, with a further breakdown into durable and nondurable manufacturing; nonmanufacturing goods producers—mining and construction; and services, of which private service industries—including transportation, utilities, trade, and finance—can be distinguished from governmental service employment. Table 5-8 shows data for these series for 1981–83. The series can be viewed as determined mainly by either cyclical forces (manufacturing, especially of durables, and construction) or secular trends. Decomposing total payroll employment into these subgroups eases the forecasting problem and highlights a basic fact of economic activity. Most activities grow in a fairly trend-like manner, compared to those few activities—for instance durable manufacturing and construction—which impart most of the cyclical pattern of overall economic activity. Thus, to the extent the cyclical components can be isolated from the trend-like, the forecasting process is made easier.

The "bottom-up" method for forecasting payroll employment can be viewed in four steps: (1) time trends (or other time series methods) are used to forecast the trend-like components; (2) structural forecasts are made for the cyclical components[8]; (3) the forecast levels for the subgroups are totaled to arrive at a forecast of total payroll employment; and (4) the results from this forecast can be compared to results from a "top-down" forecast. A detailed example will not be described here, though the process outlined above and the data in Table 5-8 allow the interested reader to perform such a forecast.

Two further series contained in the Payroll Survey are useful inputs in a structured indicator forecast. These are: (1) average weekly hours per worker on nonagricultural payrolls (*average workweek*) and (2) average hourly earnings of production and nonsupervisory workers (*average hourly earnings*). These data are reported in total and by the same subgroups as payroll employment with one exception. The average workweek and average hourly earnings for government workers are not reported (and neither hours nor earnings cover supervisory or nonproduction workers).

These series can be forecast using methods similar to those for payroll employment. However the "top-down" approach would not be based on the household employment forecast. Rather, time series methods could be used to forecast the workweek and hourly earnings on the basis of past data. Table 5-9 shows data from the payroll survey for total employment, average workweek, and average hourly earnings for 1981–83 in columns 1–3. Aggregate employee-hours, shown in column 4, is the product of employment and

---

[8] Either cyclical indexes can be used, or regression equations can be estimated. For instance, in a structured model, durable manufacturing employment can be related to industrial production, and construction employment can be related to housing starts. In the absence of forecast values for industrial production and housing starts, the unemployment rate may be used as a cyclical proxy.

TABLE 5-8   Payroll Employment: "Bottom-Up" Approach (millions)

		MANUFACTURING		MINING &	SERVICES	
			NON-	CONSTRUC-		
	TOTAL	DURABLE	DURABLE	TION	PRIVATE	GOVERNMENT

Date						
JAN 1981	90.920	12.140	8.051	5.409	49.124	16.196
FEB	90.990	12.100	8.051	5.365	49.282	16.192
MAR	91.030	12.128	8.052	5.399	49.308	16.143
APR	91.128	12.186	8.074	5.270	49.477	16.121
MAY	91.131	12.206	8.091	5.206	49.549	16.079
JUN	91.322	12.221	8.097	5.336	49.647	16.021
JUL	91.484	12.231	8.127	5.362	49.757	16.007
AUG	91.424	12.204	8.093	5.356	49.854	15.917
SEP	91.411	12.153	8.086	5.347	49.905	15.920
OCT	91.295	12.070	8.040	5.335	49.920	15.930
NOV	91.041	11.922	8.010	5.310	49.879	15.920
DEC	90.730	11.751	7.968	5.273	49.824	15.914
JAN 1982	90.396	11.625	7.903	5.183	49.807	15.878
FEB	90.417	11.561	7.889	5.220	49.889	15.858
MAR	90.207	11.469	7.839	5.175	49.853	15.871
APR	90.024	11.350	7.810	5.147	49.856	15.861
MAY	90.016	11.289	7.789	5.148	49.922	15.868
JUN	89.775	11.169	7.749	5.083	49.938	15.836
JUL	89.450	11.095	7.707	5.041	49.938	15.669
AUG	89.264	10.961	7.705	5.006	49.907	15.685
SEP	89.235	10.862	7.693	4.975	49.921	15.784
OCT	88.938	10.605	7.673	4.929	49.871	15.780
NOV	88.785	10.577	7.645	4.909	49.882	15.772
DEC	88.665	10.559	7.634	4.868	49.846	15.758
JAN 1983	88.885	10.594	7.650	4.942	49.946	15.753
FEB	88.746	10.608	7.637	4.804	49.955	15.742
MAR	88.814	10.617	7.650	4.763	50.060	15.724
APR	89.090	10.689	7.687	4.783	50.218	15.713
MAY	89.421	10.708	7.705	4.854	50.330	15.744
JUN	89.844	10.844	7.738	4.936	50.605	15.721
JUL	90.152	10.961	7.772	4.991	50.748	15.680
AUG	89.748	11.022	7.771	5.037	50.244	15.674
SEP	90.851	11.081	7.790	5.064	51.055	15.861
OCT	91.084	11.235	7.829	5.104	51.144	15.775
NOV	91.355	11.326	7.856	5.140	51.306	15.785
DEC	91.599	11.394	7.877	5.163	51.415	15.795

Source: Bureau of Labor Statistics, U.S. Department of Labor

the average workweek indexed on a 1977=100 base. Column 5 presents similar index levels for aggregate weekly earnings, which is equal to the product of aggregate employee hours (column 4) and average hourly earnings (column 3). These data will be useful in forecasting other indicators, particularly personal income and industrial production.

TABLE 5-9 Employment, Average Workweek, and Hourly Earnings
(payroll survey data)

Date	EMPLOYMENT (MILLIONS)	AVERAGE WORKWEEK (HOURS)	AVERAGE HOURLY EARNINGS (DOLLARS)	AGGREGATE EMPLOYEE-HOURS 1977=100	AGGREGATE WEEKLY EARNINGS 1977=100
JAN 1981	90.920	35.5	7.00	108.7	144.9
FEB	90.990	35.3	7.05	107.6	144.5
MAR	91.030	35.3	7.10	108.1	146.2
APR	91.128	35.4	7.14	108.4	147.4
MAY	91.131	35.3	7.19	108.5	148.6
JUN	91.322	35.2	7.23	108.2	149.0
JUL	91.484	35.3	7.27	108.8	150.7
AUG	91.424	35.2	7.34	108.5	151.7
SEP	91.411	35.0	7.37	107.8	151.3
OCT	91.295	35.1	7.40	107.7	151.8
NOV	91.041	35.1	7.45	107.3	152.3
DEC	90.730	35.0	7.46	106.3	151.0
JAN 1982	90.396	34.3	7.52	104.2	149.3
FEB	90.417	35.1	7.53	106.1	152.2
MAR	90.207	34.9	7.54	105.5	151.5
APR	90.024	34.9	7.59	105.2	152.1
MAY	90.016	35.0	7.65	105.6	153.9
JUN	89.775	34.9	7.67	105.0	153.4
JUL	89.450	34.9	7.71	104.8	153.9
AUG	89.264	34.8	7.74	104.2	153.6
SEP	89.235	34.8	7.72	103.9	152.8
OCT	88.938	34.7	7.77	102.9	152.3
NOV	88.785	34.7	7.79	102.5	152.1
DEC	88.665	34.8	7.82	102.4	152.5
JAN 1983	88.885	35.1	7.88	104.1	156.2
FEB	88.746	34.5	7.91	102.2	154.0
MAR	88.814	34.8	7.91	103.1	155.3
APR	89.090	34.9	7.95	104.0	157.5
MAY	89.421	35.1	7.97	105.0	159.4
JUN	89.844	35.1	8.00	105.7	161.1
JUL	90.152	35.0	8.03	106.1	162.3
AUG	89.748	35.0	7.98	105.3	160.1
SEP	90.851	35.2	8.08	107.5	165.4
OCT	91.084	35.3	8.13	108.1	167.4
NOV	91.355	35.2	8.13	108.3	167.7
DEC	91.599	35.3	8.16	108.7	169.0

Source: Bureau of Labor Statistics, U.S. Department of Labor

PERSONAL INCOME

The labor market measures discussed in the previous section are useful not only as forecast results, but also as inputs for forecasting personal income. This is because payments for labor services—in the form of wages and salaries—comprise the largest part of personal income. Personal income, in turn, fuels consumer spending, the largest component of GNP. Thus, personal income connects employment and consumer spending in an employment-income-spending stream, which is a basic element of this structural approach to indicator forecasting.

A "bottom-up" approach, in which major components are forecast separately and then combined to form a total, will be followed in forecasting personal income. This allows the forecaster to take advantage of other information specific to particular components in constructing the forecast.

Wage and salary payments are by far the largest single portion of personal income, accounting for over 60% of the total in recent years. Moreover, these payments are directly related to employment, hours worked, and hourly earnings. Wage and salary payments are thus a logical place to begin a personal income forecast for two reasons. First, this series is such a major component of personal income. Second, since wage and salary payments result from measures already forecast—employment, average workweek, and hourly earnings—successful estimation of this aggregate appears likely. Table 5-10 sheds further light on this relationship. The first column, titled Earnings, is equal to the product of payroll employment (in million workers), hours worked per worker per week (in hours), and hourly earnings (in dollars per worker-hour). Thus, Earnings are expressed in billion dollars per week.

$$\text{EARNINGS} = \text{EMPLOYMENT} \times \text{AVERAGE WORKWEEK} \\ \times \text{HOURLY EARNINGS}$$

$$\text{billion dollars/week} = \text{million workers} \times \text{hours/week} \\ \times \text{dollars/worker-hour}$$

Column 2 shows the monthly percent change for the EARNINGS data in column 1. Wage and Salary payments (WSP), in billions of dollars at annual rates, are presented in column 3, while the monthly percent changes are shown in column 4. Column 5 provides monthly data on personal income (PI) in billions of dollars at annual rates, while the last column shows wage and salary payments as a percent of total personal income.

The values of the EARNINGS' levels are lower than the values of the wage and salary payments. (Compare columns 1 and 3.) This mainly reflects the fact that EARNINGS are expressed at weekly rates, while wage and salary payments are expressed at annual rates. Multiplying the EARNINGS

TABLE 5-10   Wage and Salary Payments

	EARNINGS $ BILLIONS (1)	% CHANGE (2)	WAGE & SALARY PAYMENTS $ BILLIONS (3)	% CHANGE (4)	PERSONAL INCOME $ BILLIONS (5)	WSP/PI % (6)
Date						
JAN 81	22.594	1.93	1444.5	1.34	2316.9	62.3
FEB	22.644	0.22	1450.3	0.40	2336.5	62.1
MAR	22.815	0.76	1460.3	0.69	2361.4	61.8
APR	23.033	0.96	1468.0	0.53	2375.1	61.0
MAY	23.130	0.42	1477.5	0.65	2390.6	61.8
JUN	23.241	0.48	1489.0	0.78	2416.9	61.6
JUL	23.478	1.02	1500.6	0.78	2463.7	60.9
AUG	23.621	0.61	1513.6	0.87	2494.6	60.7
SEP	23.579	−0.18	1522.8	0.61	2514.3	60.6
OCT	23.713	0.57	1529.1	0.41	2513.4	60.8
NOV	23.807	0.40	1532.4	0.22	2518.7	60.8
DEC	23.690	−0.49	1530.2	−0.14	2517.6	60.8
JAN 82	23.316	−1.58	1536.5	0.41	2518.1	61.0
FEB	23.897	2.49	1545.8	0.61	2530.2	61.1
MAR	23.738	−0.67	1546.1	0.02	2535.0	61.0
APR	23.847	0.46	1551.8	0.37	2549.0	60.9
MAY	24.102	1.07	1568.0	1.04	2568.0	61.1
JUN	24.031	−0.29	1571.7	0.24	2572.5	61.1
JUL	24.069	0.16	1578.9	0.46	2589.8	61.0
AUG	24.043	−0.11	1579.2	0.02	2586.7	61.1
SEP	23.974	−0.29	1581.2	0.13	2597.4	60.9
OCT	23.979	0.02	1583.1	0.12	2617.8	60.5
NOV	24.000	0.09	1583.1	0.00	2633.1	60.1
DEC	24.129	0.54	1591.8	0.55	2645.0	60.2

(1) Earnings = Payroll Employment × Average Workweek × Average Hourly Earnings (billions of dollars, weekly rates)
(2) Monthly percent changes in Earnings
(3) Wage and Salary Payments (billions of dollars, annual rates)
(4) Monthly percent changes in Wage and Salary Payments
(5) Personal Income (billions of dollars, annual rates)
(6) Wage and Salary Payments as a percent of Personal Income
Sources: Data for Earnings: Bureau of Labor Statistics, U.S. Department of Labor and author's calculations
All other data: Bureau of Economic Analysis, U.S. Department of Commerce.

data by 52 would annualize the data and make the two series more comparable. A greater source of concern is the fact that the monthly percent changes
for the two series appear to show little similarity. Were there a more consistent pattern between the two monthly percent change series, the monthly
percent changes for Earnings could be used directly to forecast the level of
Wage and Salary payments. Such a relationship is shown in equation (5-6).

$$WSP_t = (1 + \%\Delta \ EARNINGS_t) \times WSP_{t-1} \qquad (5\text{-}6)$$

An alternative forecast approach would be to apply the year-over-year percent changes for EARNINGS to the level of wage and salary payments twelve months prior to the month being forecast. This approach smooths the differences in monthly growth rates for the two series. Inspection of the monthly percent changes suggests that this is a likely result: large differences in monthly percent changes between the series in one month appear to be at least partly reversed in later months. (Compare the cumulative percent changes between October 1981 and February 1982.) This can be represented in a form slightly different than equation 5-6, such as equation 5-7 below.

$$WSP_t = (1 + Y/Y \ \%\Delta \ EARNINGS_t) \times WSP_{t-12} \qquad (5\text{-}7)$$

Examination of the year-over-year percent changes for the two series (not shown, but calculable) shows that the changes in EARNINGS are more variable than for Wage and Salary payments. This may reflect the fact that EARNINGS include the workweek and hourly earnings for production workers but not for nonproduction and supervisory workers. This is because the workweek does not vary much (if at all) for the latter groups and these groups are usually paid on weekly, monthly, or annual salary bases rather than at the hourly rates production workers are paid. Thus, while EARNINGS of production workers are subject to three types of cyclical pressures—on employment, length of the workweek, and hourly earnings—other workers are usually only subjected to cyclical pressure on employment. EARNINGS, as a result, show more cyclical movement than Wage and Salary payments, and this produces more volatile monthly and year-to-year percent changes in the former than in the latter measure.

Nevertheless, EARNINGS should be a useful proxy for wage and salary payments. One further way to test this hypothesis and develop forecasts of wage and salary payments based on EARNINGS, is to fit a regression to the data. This equation is in the form shown by (5-8).

$$WSP_t = a + b * EARNINGS_t \qquad (5\text{-}8)$$

coefficients	*t statistics*
a = 562.244	(3.77)
b = 39.07	(8.91)
rho = 0.998	(38.67)

$$\overline{R}^2 = .9976 \quad D\text{-}W = 1.65 \quad SER = 6.98$$

The equation was estimated from January 1979 through December 1982. The adjusted coefficient of determination ($\overline{R}^2$) is high, suggesting that 99.8% of the variation in wage and salary payments is accounted for by EARNINGS. Both the constant term and the coefficient on EARNINGS are significant at the 95% level and the Durbin-Watson statistic suggests an absence of serial correlation after a Cochrane-Orcutt correction is performed. However, the value of rho is nearly equal to one, suggesting that it might be better to re-estimate the relationship in first difference form. This is done in equation 5-8a.

$$\Delta WSP_t = a + b * \Delta EARNINGS_t \qquad \text{(5-8a)}$$

coefficients	t statistics
a = 6.03	(7.63)
b = 24.98	(5.91)

$$\overline{R}^2 = .4470 \quad D\text{-}W = 2.11 \quad SER = 4.24$$

The Durbin-Watson statistic for this version indicates an absence of serial correlation without the need for a Cochrane-Orcutt correction; the constant term and the coefficient on the change in EARNINGS are significant, but the $\overline{R}^2$ is much lower. Low values of $\overline{R}^2$ often result for regressions in first difference form reflecting the greater variation inherent in a series of changes than in levels. The basically strong relationship between these variables was confirmed by the high value for $\overline{R}^2$ in equation 5-8. Thus, equation 5-8a can be used despite the low value of $\overline{R}^2$, and the results can be used to forecast the level of wage and salary payments in a two step process as shown below.

$$\Delta WSP_t = 6.03 + 24.98 * \Delta EARNINGS_t \qquad \text{(5-8a)}$$

where $\qquad \Delta WSP_t = WSP_t - WSP_{t-1}$

and $\qquad \Delta EARNINGS_t = EARNINGS_t - EARNINGS_{t-1}$

so $\qquad WSP_t = WSP_{t-1} + \Delta WSP_t \qquad \text{(5-8b)}$

Table 5-11 presents forecast comparisons for wage and salary payments in 1983. The actual data are presented in column 1 of the upper panel. Columns 2–4 of the upper panel present forecasts of wage and salary payments based on the three methods discussed above. Column 2 is based on monthly percent changes for EARNINGS applied to the prior month's level of wage and salary payments (equation 5-6). It should be noted that while the January 1982 forecast is based on the actual level of wage and salary payments in December 1982, all subsequent forecast values are, in turn, based on previous forecast levels. Forecast II, in column 3, is based on the year-over-year percent changes in EARNINGS times the level of wage and salary

TABLE 5-11   Forecasts of Wage and Salary Payments: 1983 (billion dollars, annual rates)

		FORECASTS		
	ACTUAL (1)	I (2)	II (3)	III (4)
Date				
JAN 83	1608.9	1621.9	1620.1	1609.2
FEB	1606.3	1584.9	1566.6	1605.8
MAR	1616.8	1621.6	1592.3	1618.1
APR	1632.1	1634.7	1608.5	1629.6
MAY	1652.2	1651.7	1627.4	1645.6
JUN	1660.9	1666.3	1650.0	1663.6
JUL	1673.5	1668.1	1662.1	1669.7
AUG	1680.5	1655.7	1646.5	1672.8
SEP	1691.8	1732.3	1704.2	1705.8
OCT	1710.6	1711.5	1725.8	1705.4
NOV	1715.3	1710.9	1724.5	1716.7
DEC	1726.0	1731.1	1740.6	1727.4

**Forecast Errors
(as percent of actual)**

	I	II	III
JAN 83	−0.81	−0.70	−0.02
FEB	1.33	2.47	0.03
MAR	0.30	1.52	−0.08
APR	−0.16	1.45	0.15
MAY	0.03	1.50	0.40
JUN	−0.33	0.66	−0.16
JUL	0.32	0.68	0.23
AUG	1.48	2.02	0.46
SEP	−2.39	−0.73	−0.83
OCT	−0.05	−0.89	0.30
NOV	0.26	−0.54	−0.08
DEC	−0.30	−0.85	−0.08
MEAN ERROR	−0.03	0.55	0.03
MAPE	0.65	1.17	0.24
RMSE	15.9	21.5	5.5

FORECAST I: $WSP_t = (1 + \%\Delta EARNINGS_t) \times WSP_{t-1}$

FORECAST II: $WSP_t = (1 + Y/Y\%\Delta EARNINGS_t) \times WSP_{t-12}$

FORECAST III: $WSP_t = WSP_{t-1} + (6.03 + 24.98 \times (\Delta EARNINGS_t))$

* FORECAST ERRORS = $(WSP_a - WSP_e)/WSP_a \times 100$

MAPE = Mean Absolute Percent Error

RMSE = Root Mean Square Error

payments twelve months earlier (equation 5-7). Thus, unlike Forecast I, the twelve-month forecast is based on actual, known levels for wage and salary payments.[9] Forecast III, presented in column 4, is based on the estimated regression (equation 5-8a) of the first differences in wage and salary payments on the first differences in EARNINGS with equation 5-8b used to derive the final estimates. The bottom panel shows the percent errors in each month for each method (actual less forecast divided by the actual value of wage and salary payments), the mean of these percent errors, the mean absolute percent error (MAPE), and the root mean square error (RMSE) expressed in billion dollars for each method.

As can be seen, the third method—using equations 5-8a and 5-8b—provides the best forecast by virtue of having the lowest MAPE and RMSE.[10] Indeed, the results are surprisingly good; by December 1983 the error is less than 0.1%. This is reassuring because wage and salary payments represent such a large part of total personal income.

While wage and salary payments comprise the largest portion of personal income, reference to Table 3-1 shows that the other components are important in terms of the activities measured. Moreover, the variations in these activities account for a good deal of the variation in total personal income.

It is tempting, at this point, to forecast total personal income (PI) by dividing the forecast values of wage and salary payments (WSP) from Table 5-11 by an estimate of the ratio of the two concepts (WSP/PI from Column 6, Table 5-10). This would be a mistake for two reasons. First, the ratio (WSP/PI) has been far from stable. Indeed, the ratio has displayed a downward trend. Thus, it would be necessary to forecast the trend for the ratio, adding a further source of uncertainty to the overall forecast. A second, more important, reason for not forecasting personal income in this way is that such an approach ignores important information the forecaster should be aware of.

The alternative is to forecast at least some of the remaining components of personal income directly. Rather than attempt to forecast each of the remaining portions of personal income separately—an arduous task—it is desirable to isolate those components: (1) which are major sources of variation, and (2) about which the forecaster has some knowledge. Table

---

[9] For this example the actual values for EARNINGS were used. In an *ex ante* forecast, this would only be possible for a one month (month-ahead) forecast. For forecasts beyond the next month, forecast values of EARNINGS and the percent changes would be used. This introduces a further potential source of error, namely the errors in the forecast of the level of EARNINGS. This example avoids this potential error in order to focus solely on the difference due to the three methods.

[10] Any additional errors which would arise from using forecast values of EARNINGS rather than the actual values (as used in the *ex post* analysis) would likely have similar effects on all three methods. The forecast levels of EARNINGS would be used directly in III, and as a basis to derive the percent changes in I and II.

5-12 presents data on the levels and first differences (in billion dollars) of non-wage and salary income, and three of its components. These components are: (1) personal interest income; (2) net transfer payments (transfer payments less personal contributions for social insurance); and (3) other income (including other labor income, proprietors' income, rental income, and dividends). Each of the first two of these components changes in response to known economic forces and, thus, can be forecast with some degree of success. The remaining "other" category is less than half of non-wage and salary income and shows, on the whole, small monthly movements which can be forecast using a time series approach.

Interest income reflects the interest received by individuals. An important source of the variation in this component over short periods,[11] therefore, would seem to be changes in interest rates. If this is true, then a regression of personal interest income on interest rates should provide a basis for forecasting. Among the variety of interest rate series, the six-month Treasury bill rate is chosen for three reasons. First, this series displays sufficient variation to account for the variation in the dollar change in personal interest income. Second, this is a popular issue with individual investors and thus, an important source of personal interest income. Third, increasingly in recent years, six-month Treasury bill rates have been used by banks in setting CD and other interest rates paid on deposits. Indeed, with the advent of new depository instruments—such as Money Market Mutual Funds and Money Market Deposit Accounts—this rate has become even more important as an indicative rate.

The forecast approach has two stages: (1) personal interest income in period t (PII_t) is equal to its value in period $t - 1$ (PII_{t-1}) plus the first difference in period t (ΔPII_t); (2) where the first difference is estimated as a function of the six-month Treasury bill rate (TBILL6).

$$PII_t = \Delta PII_t + PII_{t-1} \qquad (5\text{-}9)$$

$$\Delta PII_t = a + b * TBILL6_t \qquad (5\text{-}9a)$$

coefficients	t statistics
a = −1.711	(−0.394)
b = 0.449	(1.221)
rho = 0.672	(5.47)

$\overline{R}^2 = 0.546$ D-W = 1.61   SER = 2.79

---

[11] Over periods longer than a year, a further source of variation in interest income may be changes in the savings habits of the public. Over brief periods, however, these can be assumed to remain fairly constant.

TABLE 5-12 Personal Income Less Wage and Salary Payments (Billion dollars, seasonally adjusted annual rates)

Date	NON-WAGE & SALARY INCOME		INTEREST INCOME		NET TRANSFERS		OTHER INCOME	
	LEVEL	$ CHANGE	LEVEL	$ CHANGE	LEVEL	$ CHANGE	LEVEL	$ CHANGE
JAN 81	872.4	6.3	300.1	9.0	220.7	-6.9	351.6	4.2
FEB	886.2	13.8	309.0	8.9	221.5	0.8	355.7	4.1
MAR	901.1	14.9	317.1	8.1	224.3	2.8	359.7	4.0
APR	907.1	6.0	323.8	6.7	223.7	-0.6	359.6	-0.1
MAY	913.1	6.0	328.1	4.3	223.6	-0.1	361.4	1.8
JUN	927.9	14.8	337.4	9.3	225.2	1.6	365.3	3.9
JUL	963.1	35.2	350.4	13.0	240.0	14.8	372.7	7.4
AUG	981.0	17.9	363.7	13.3	239.5	-0.5	377.8	5.1
SEP	991.5	10.5	371.7	8.0	241.2	1.7	378.6	0.8
OCT	984.3	-7.2	366.1	-5.6	241.1	-0.1	377.1	-1.5
NOV	986.3	2.0	364.3	-1.8	244.3	3.2	377.7	0.6
DEC	987.4	1.1	363.8	-0.5	246.4	2.1	377.2	-0.5
JAN 82	981.6	-5.8	363.6	-0.2	241.3	-5.1	376.7	-0.5
FEB	984.4	2.8	364.6	1.0	243.0	1.7	376.8	0.1
MAR	988.9	4.5	366.5	1.9	247.1	4.1	376.1	-0.7
APR	997.2	8.3	371.5	5.0	251.3	4.2	374.4	-1.7
MAY	1000.0	2.8	373.0	1.5	252.8	1.5	374.2	-0.2
JUN	1000.8	0.8	371.1	-1.9	253.5	0.7	376.2	2.0
JUL	1010.9	10.1	368.2	-2.9	266.2	12.7	376.5	0.3
AUG	1007.5	-3.4	363.9	-4.3	266.4	0.2	377.2	0.7
SEP	1016.2	8.7	362.2	-1.7	270.3	3.9	383.7	6.5
OCT	1034.7	18.5	361.7	-0.5	280.1	9.8	392.9	9.2
NOV	1050.0	15.3	363.3	1.6	288.3	8.2	398.4	5.5
DEC	1053.2	3.2	364.3	1.0	289.9	1.6	399.0	0.6

Source: Bureau of Economic Analysis, U.S. Department of Commerce

Equation 5-9a was estimated from January 1979 through December 1982. The regression results, at first glance, are disappointing. The coefficient on the Treasury bill rate suggests that personal interest income increases $0.4 billion for each one percentage point of yield. Thus, a 6% Treasury bill rate suggests an increase in personal interest income of just under $1 billion per month (after taking account of the constant term and assuming a zero forecast error in the prior month); a 12% Treasury bill rate would result in a $3.7 billion increase in personal interest income. The coefficient is only significantly different from zero at the 90% level, however. This is one reason for the low $\overline{R}^2$ value, although a low $\overline{R}^2$ is anticipated since the dependent variable is a dollar change. The Durbin-Watson statistic indicates an absence of serial correlation after a Cochrane-Orcutt correction.

Despite its flaws, this equation form showed better qualities than alternatives tried. Moreover, the forecast results using equations 5-9 and 5-9a (see column 3, Table 5-13) provided acceptable forecasts for 1983 based on the values for the MAPE and RMSE. Thus, it was decided to use equation 5-9a recognizing its flaws.[12]

Net transfer payments are equal to all transfer payments to persons less personal contributions for social insurance. Transfers mainly include retirement payments—including social security benefits—unemployment benefits, and welfare payments. There are two aspects of the first two of these components which can be used to forecast movements in transfer payments. First, social security benefits were adjusted for changes in the price level each July between 1975 and 1982. (In 1983, the adjustment was shifted to the following January.) In other words, social security benefits are subject to a cost of living adjustment. This adjustment is equal to the percent change in the CPI or in average hourly earnings in the year ending three months earlier, whichever is greater. Consequently, the alert forecaster can estimate this increase, thus reducing the irregular movements in net transfers. (Note the large first differences in July 1981 and 1982 in Table 5-12.)

A second effect on transfer payments which can be isolated is that from unemployment insurance benefits. These are assumed to show a direct relationship with the unemployment rate.

In addition to the above effects on transfer payments, scheduled increases in personal contributions for social insurance can be anticipated and adjusted for. (These increases typically take effect in January.)

Combining all these facts, a forecast of net transfers should include: (1) a relationship with the unemployment rate, (2) an adjustment to reflect the annual cost-of-living increase made to social security benefits, and (3) a downward adjustment for increases in personal contributions to social secu-

---

[12] Once again, actual values for the six-month Treasury bill rate were used to produce the estimates of personal interest income shown in Table 5-13. In an *ex ante* forecast, forecast values would be used.

TABLE 5-13 Personal Income and Its Components: 1983 (billion dollars, seasonally adjusted annual rates)

	PERSONAL INCOME (1)	WAGES & SALARIES (2)	INTEREST INCOME (3)	NET TRANSFERS (4)	OTHER INCOME (5)
			FORECAST VALUES		
JAN 83	2660.8	1609.2	364.1	288.4	399.1
FEB	2651.5	1605.8	360.1	281.1	404.5
MAR	2666.8	1618.1	356.2	284.2	408.3
APR	2686.5	1629.6	356.1	287.5	413.3
MAY	2706.8	1645.6	355.5	287.4	418.3
JUN	2735.1	1663.6	357.6	290.2	423.7
JUL	2747.5	1669.7	360.4	289.3	428.1
AUG	2755.3	1672.8	365.7	285.8	431.0
SEP	2792.3	1705.8	371.3	284.1	431.1
OCT	2799.9	1705.4	375.9	282.9	435.7
NOV	2820.8	1716.7	379.1	281.9	443.1
DEC	2849.3	1727.4	381.9	289.6	450.4
			ACTUAL VALUES		
JAN 83	2652.6	1608.9	360.0	278.8	404.9
FEB	2650.5	1606.3	356.0	281.9	406.3
MAR	2670.1	1616.8	355.7	285.2	412.4
APR	2689.0	1632.1	355.0	285.1	416.8
MAY	2719.3	1652.2	356.9	287.9	422.3
JUN	2732.6	1660.9	359.4	287.2	425.1
JUL	2747.6	1673.5	364.4	283.4	426.3
AUG	2756.4	1680.5	370.2	281.9	423.8
SEP	2781.6	1691.8	375.2	280.8	433.8
OCT	2812.5	1710.6	378.3	279.8	443.8
NOV	2833.5	1715.3	380.9	287.4	449.9
DEC	2859.6	1726.0	384.0	289.5	460.1
			ERRORS		
JAN 83	−8.2	−0.3	−4.1	−9.6	5.8
FEB	−1.0	0.5	−4.1	0.8	1.8
MAR	3.3	−1.3	−0.5	1.0	4.1
APR	2.5	2.5	−1.1	−2.4	3.5
MAY	12.5	6.6	1.4	0.5	4.0
JUN	−2.5	−2.7	1.8	−3.0	1.4
JUL	0.1	3.8	4.0	−5.9	−1.8
AUG	1.1	7.7	4.5	−3.9	−7.2
SEP	−10.7	−14.0	3.9	−3.3	2.7
OCT	12.6	5.2	2.4	−3.1	8.1
NOV	12.7	−1.4	1.8	5.5	6.8
DEC	10.3	−1.4	2.1	−0.1	9.7
MEAN ERROR	2.7	0.4	1.0	−2.0	3.2
MAPE	0.23	0.24	0.72	1.15	1.10
RMSE	8.1	5.5	3.0	4.2	5.4

(1) Forecast values of Personal Income equal the sum of its components

(2) Forecast values based on Forecast III, Table 5-11

(3) Forecast values based on Equations 5-9 and 5-9a

(4) Forecast values based on Equations 5-10 and 5-10a

(5) Forecast values derived from double exponential smoothing of data for 1981–82, alpha = 0.25

rity. It was found that, as with the relationship for wage and salary payments (equation 5-8), when the relationship was performed in level form the value of $\overline{R}^2$ was high (0.998) but a Cochrane-Orcutt correction was needed which used a rho equal to 0.97. Thus it was decided to estimate the relationship in first difference form as in equations 5-10 and 5-10a.

$$NTP_t = NTP_{t-1} + \Delta NTP_t \tag{5-10}$$

where $\Delta NTP_t = a + b * \Delta RU_t + SSCOLA - FICA \tag{5-10a}$

$$\begin{array}{ll} coefficients & t\ statistics \\ a = 2.35 & (2.41) \\ b = 5.19 & (1.23) \end{array}$$

$$\overline{R}^2 = 0.012 \quad D\text{-}W = 2.29 \quad SER = 5.43$$

The low $\overline{R}^2$ can be ignored because of the high value found when the relationship was estimated in level form. SSCOLA and FICA are Dummy variables for Social Security Cost-of-Living Adjustments and changes in Social Security taxes, respectively.[13] The estimated values for 1983 are shown in column 4 of Table 5-13.

Examining the values for "other income" in Table 5-12, it can be seen that the variations depicted by the first differences are less erratic than for the other components. In fact, this component was estimated by double exponential smoothing in which the value of alpha was set equal to 0.25. As can be seen from Table 5-13, the estimates were reasonably close to the actual values for 1983. In fact, when each month's values for the components in columns 2 through 5 are summed, the estimated values of personal income (column 1 in the upper panel of Table 5-13) that result are quite close to the actual values (shown in the second panel of Table 5-13). Note that the MAPE for total personal income is less than for any of the four component series. This result partly reflects the effects of offsetting errors among the components.

Personal income, thus, can be forecast with acceptable results using only a modest amount of additional information. The wage and salary component is estimated using the constructed series EARNINGS, which is equal to the product of payroll employment, the average workweek, and average hourly earnings. Personal interest income is estimated from the six-month

[13] The value for SSCOLA is zero: in all months except July for 1975–82; all months in 1983; and would be zero for all months except January in 1984 and later. In the months when it is not equal to zero, SSCOLA equals the year-to-year percentage change in the CPI for urban wage earners three months earlier. Similarly, the value for FICA is zero in all months other than January and equal to the dollar increase in social insurance payments due to legislated increases in the base and withholding rate changes that occur in January.

Treasury bill rate. Net transfers are estimated from the unemployment rate, with specific adjustments made for the cost-of-living adjustment to social security benefits and increases in personal social security contributions. All other income payments—equal to about 16% of total personal income—are estimated using double exponential smoothing. All the independent variables, except for the six-month Treasury bill rate, were estimated above in the section on labor market measures. Thus, the estimates of labor market measures and of personal income are related and the forecasts are consistent.

There are doubtless ways to lessen the errors in the estimates of personal income. Nevertheless, the results achieved meet two important criteria: (1) they are mainly based on estimates of labor market measures previously estimated and, thus, are consistent with those results; and (2) they yield acceptable results for an *ex post* forecast for 1983—a difficult year to have forecast because of the strong cyclical recovery which occurred. The approach used in forecasting personal income also presented an example of a way in which regression and time series methods can be combined in constructing a forecast. These methods will be followed in the sections below.

RETAIL SALES

Consumer spending logically extends the pattern of economic activities that includes employment and income. Employment generates income which, in turn, is largely spent on consumer goods and services. Moreover, consumption fuels the economy: not only because it directly comprises nearly two-thirds of total GNP, but also because it is the source of the derived demand for investment goods and even for a large part of government services.

Retail sales, in turn, comprise a major portion of personal consumption expenditures. Most purchases of durable and nondurable goods are made at retail outlets.[14] In Chapter 2, consumption was hypothesized to be a function of income. Thus, since retail sales are a large portion of consumption, it follows that retail sales are also likely to be a function of personal income. This hypothesis is tested below only partly to confirm the earlier theory of consumer demand. More important, in the context of this chapter is the fact that if a relationship between personal income and retail sales can be found it would fit the structured approach followed so far. That is, the estimates for personal income—largely based on estimated employment measures—could be used to derive estimates for retail sales, thus maintaining the consistency, or structure, of the forecasts.

---

[14] As noted in Chapter 3, BEA uses retail sales data to construct the estimates of personal consumption expenditures for durable and nondurable goods.

Figure 5-4 presents a scatter plot of retail sales (on the vertical axis) and personal income (on the horizontal axis) for the sixty months from January 1978 through December 1982. It can be seen that a close, though not perfect, relationship does appear to exist.

A logical first step to a retail sales forecast is to estimate a relationship between retail sales measured in billions of dollars, (seasonally adjusted *monthly* rates) and personal income (measured in billions of dollars, seasonally adjusted *annual* rates). Equation 5-11 presents the results of a regression analysis of the data shown in Figure 5-4.

$$RST_t = a + b * PI_t \qquad (5\text{-}11)$$

coefficients	*t statistics*
a = 18.69	(4.88)
b = 0.0279	(16.08)
rho = 0.8433	(11.64)

$$\overline{R}^2 = .9904 \quad D\text{-}W = 2.19 \quad SER = 0.828$$

FIGURE 5-4   Retail sales and personal income (1978–1982)

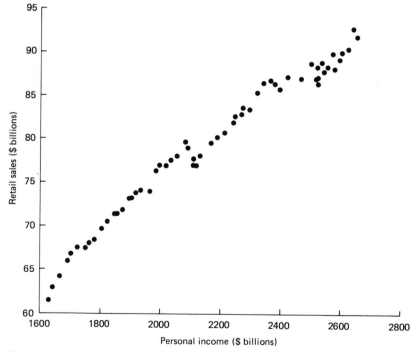

Source: U.S. Department of Commerce.

(In the equation, RST equals total retail sales and PI equals personal income).

The regression results appear quite good: the adjusted $\overline{R}^2$ indicates that much of the variation in retail sales is accounted for by variation in personal income; the Durbin-Watson statistic indicates an absence of autocorrelation in the residuals after a Cochrane-Orcutt correction is performed; the standard error of the regression is low; and the t statistics are all significant. Moreover, the coefficient for personal income—b—when multiplied by twelve[15] suggests that 33.5% of each additional dollar of income is reflected in retail sales for durable and nondurable goods. This is close to the just-under 40% of personal income accounted for by consumption expenditures on durable and nondurable goods in 1978–82.

The most basic test of equation 5-11, however, is how well it forecasts retail sales. Such an evaluation can be made by performing an *ex post,* out-of-sample forecast for 1983. Table 5-14 presents a comparison between actual monthly levels and percent changes for retail sales in 1983 (columns 1 and 2), and forecast levels and percent changes derived by substituting actual personal income values in equation 5-11 (columns 3 and 4). The monthly forecast errors (actual minus forecast values) in billions of dollars are presented in column 5, while the errors as percentages of actual values are presented in column 6. Three summary measures of the errors are presented at the bottom of the Table: the mean error, which takes account of the net impact of over- and under-estimates; the mean absolute percentage error (MAPE), which is not diminished by offsetting errors; and the root mean square error (RMSE), which penalizes large errors.

It can be seen that the forecast under-estimated the strong pick-up in retail sales in the first half of 1983, although it generally captured the growth pattern in the second half of the year. The mean error shows that the equation under-estimated average sales growth by $0.7 billion in 1983, while the RMSE value of nearly $0.9 billion shows that some of the errors—particularly for April through June—were quite large. The MAPE suggests that, on average, even when the actual values of personal income in the current month and retail sales in the prior month[16] were known, the equation resulted in a forecast error of nearly 0.8% per month.

Thus, while equation 5-11 provided fairly sensitive forecasts of the pattern of retail sales in 1983, it would be desirable to reduce the size of the errors in certain months. In particular, it is desirable to capture more of the strong cyclical rise that occurred in the first half of the year. There are

---

[15] The coefficient is multiplied by twelve so as to make retail sales, measured at monthly rates, consistent with personal income, measured at annual rates.

[16] Retail sales in the prior month are used to estimate the error term (the difference between actual retail sales and the values derived from substituting the independent variable into the estimated regression equation). This error term is in turn multiplied by the value of rho to adjust for the effects of serial correlated residuals.

TABLE 5-14   Total Retail Sales: Actual and Forecast, 1983

	ACTUAL (1)	PERCENT CHANGE (2)	FORECAST* (3)	PERCENT CHANGE (4)	ERROR (a-e) (5)	PERCENT ERROR (6)
JAN	92.526	0.72	92.172	0.34	.354	0.38
FEB	92.211	−0.34	92.315	0.15	−.104	−0.11
MAR	93.804	1.73	92.980	0.72	.824	0.88
APR	95.125	1.41	93.961	1.05	1.164	1.22
MAY	97.239	2.22	95.985	2.15	1.254	1.29
JUN	98.638	1.44	97.193	1.26	1.445	1.47
JUL	98.832	0.20	98.478	1.32	.354	0.36
AUG	98.277	−0.56	98.534	0.06	−.257	−0.26
SEP	99.537	1.28	98.562	0.03	.975	0.98
OCT	100.923	1.39	98.894	1.35	1.029	1.02
NOV	101.896	0.96	100.922	1.03	.974	0.96
DEC	102.438	0.53	101.976	1.05	.462	0.45
MEAN ERROR					.706	
MAPE						0.72
RMSE					.875	

* Forecast based on equation 5-11.
Source: Actual data: Bureau of the Census, U.S. Department of Commerce

two steps which appear likely to enhance the forecast accuracy of retail sales.

First, as with personal income, it may be preferrable to follow a "bottom-up," or more disaggregated, approach to forecasting retail sales. Consideration of how disaggregated the forecast approach should be depends on a careful evaluation of the costs and benefits. A forecast prepared for a retail establishment or a manufacturer of particular consumer products might require separate equations for each of the eleven major retail groups reported on by the Census Bureau,[17] and even detailed projections by product lines. Such a detailed forecast is necessarily expensive in terms of time and computational cost. While this cost may be justified for a business closely allied to retailing, it is unlikely to be worth the increased cost to a forecaster seeking retail sales estimates as a part of a general forecast of economic activity. A less costly alternative would be to split retail sales into durable and nondurable components. A major reason for trying this approach is the belief that, since durable goods are usually more costly than nondurables, they are likely to show a stronger cyclical pattern. Durable purchases can be postponed in times of weak economic activity and increased strongly as the economy picks up. Since nondurable goods tend to comprise a greater pro-

[17] See Chapter 3, Section II.

portion of necessities—food and clothing, in particular—these purchases can be hypothesized to be less responsive to the pace of economic activity.

The second step is to include an explanatory variable that is explicitly cyclical in nature in the estimation of the more cyclical retail sales component(s). Thus, in the simplified model outlined here, the estimation of retail sales of durable goods (RSD) would include a cyclical variable, while estimation of retail sales of nondurable goods (RSN) would not. A choice for a cyclical variable among those considered so far is the unemployment rate (RU), which is hypothesized to have an inverse relationship to RSD: an increase in the unemployment rate is expected to exert a negative effect on RSD; a decrease in RU is expected to exert a positive effect on RSD. Retail sales of both durables and nondurables are expected to be directly related to increases in personal income.

Thus, a simple disaggregated approach to forecasting retail sales can be performed as in equation 5-12, 5-12a, and 5-12b.

$$RST = RSD + RSN \qquad\qquad (5\text{-}12)$$

where
$$RSD = a + b_1 * PI + b_2 * RU \qquad (5\text{-}12a)$$

$$RSN = a + b_1 * PI \qquad\qquad (5\text{-}12b)$$

Table 5-15 presents summary statistics for equations 5-11, 5-12a, and 5-12b. Note that the equation for durable retail sales was estimated over a longer period (January 1970–December 1982) in addition to the five-year period (January 1978–December 1982) over which all three equations were estimated. This longer estimation was performed because the estimated coefficient on the unemployment rate in the 1978–82 version of equation 5-12a, while showing the expected negative sign, could not be regarded as significantly different from zero according to the t statistic. It was thought that a longer estimation period might improve the results. Unfortunately, the coefficient on unemployment for the 1970–82 can only be regarded as significantly different from zero 70% of the time due to the slight improvement of the t statistic. Still, the t statistic is low enough in both periods to suggest the unemployment rate should be dropped from the equation. Out-of-sample forecasts for 1983, using the 1970–82 version equation 5-12a, performed better (had lower values for the MAPE and the RMSE) than either a version without the unemployment rate for either period or the 1978–82 version of equation 5-12a. For this reason it was decided to use the version of equation 5-12a with the unemployment rate.

One bit of additional information offered by the 1978–82 versions of all three equations is that when the coefficients on personal income for RSD (0.0062) and for RSN (0.0211) are summed (0.0273) they approximate the coefficient on personal income for total retail sales (0.0279) in equation 5-11.

TABLE 5-15 Regression Results For Estimating Retail Sales

| | COEFFICIENTS | | | | | | | |
	CONSTANT	PERSONAL INCOME	UNEMPLOYMENT RATE	rho	R̄²	D-W	SER	ESTIMATION PERIOD
I. *RST*	18.69	0.0279		0.8433	0.9904	2.19	0.828	78:1–82:12
	(4.88)	(16.08)		(11.64)				
II. *RSD$_a$*	2.411	0.0109	−0.1338	0.9503	0.9927	2.01	0.522	70:1–82:12
	(1.21)	(9.45)	(−0.63)*	(36.06)				
RSD$_b$	12.81	0.0062	−0.1586	0.7888	0.8277	1.84	0.710	78:1–82:12
	(4.74)	(3.42)	(−0.41)*	(8.33)				
III. *RSN*	8.004	0.0211		0.9504	0.9874	2.56	0.361	78:1–82:12
	(2.29)	(12.81)		(22.58)				

I. Equation 5-11
II. Equation 5-12a
III. Equation 5-12b
Numbers in parentheses are t statistics
* Not significant at the 95% level

The other regression results for all the equations are quite good. The values of R² are high in all cases. The Durbin-Watson statistics all indicate an absence of serial correlation after Cochrane-Orcutt corrections are performed. Finally, but importantly, the coefficients on personal income are significant and, as noted, consistent with the coefficient estimated for the total retail sales equation.

Once again, the most important test of these equations is how well they forecast actual retail sales in 1983. Table 5-16 presents forecast results for equations 5-12, 5-12a, and 5-12b. The top panel presents actual levels and monthly percent changes for total, durable, and nondurable retail sales. The middle panel presents the forecast levels and percent changes, while the bottom panel shows the errors in billions of dollars and as a percentage of the actuals.

On balance, the mean error, MAPE, and RMSE for total retail sales using this disaggregated approach are lower than the results using equation 5-11. (See Table 5.14.) Moreover, the disaggregated version showed smaller under-estimates in the April–June period when sales rose rapidly and, consequently, the RMSE is lower overall ($0.6 billion versus $0.9 billion). Comparing the components it can also be seen that equation 5-12a picks up the more rapid growth in retail sales of durables. The errors for nondurable retail sales are quite small, although the mean error indicates a slight bias towards overestimation, mainly from September onwards.

An important point should be noted about the forecast results in Table 5-14 and Table 5-16. Since actual values of personal income were used and actual values of retail sales in the prior month were used to calculate the error adjustment (rho times the difference between the actual and unadjusted estimate), these forecasts should be viewed as *ex post,* out-of-sample, month-ahead forecasts. In other words, in practice (*ex ante*), the errors can only be kept this low if the forecast is made monthly for the next month's value. Such forecast occasions often occur, but they are not the most frequent case. Moreover often a forecaster is asked to forecast six, twelve, or more months in advance, in which case both the values for the independent variables and the forecast errors will themselves be estimates.

In order to see this distinction more clearly, *ex post,* out-of-sample, partly dynamic forecasts for 1983 were performed. These forecasts used the forecast personal income values from Table 5-13 and the forecast values of the error terms for retail sales to estimate values for retail sales in the twelve months of 1983.[18] Table 5-17 presents the results of such a forecast for equation 5-11. The errors become appreciably larger by May and remain

---

[18] This and the analysis in Table 5-18 are only ''partly'' dynamic simulations because (1) while forecast personal income values are used, the personal income estimates themselves are based on actual data, and (2) actual values for the unemployment rate in 5-12a were used. In a fully dynamic simulation all input variables would be forecast values.

TABLE 5-16 Actual Versus Forecast Retail Sales Total, Durable, and Nondurable: 1983 (billions of dollars, seasonally adjusted monthly rates)

	TOTAL*	PERCENT CHANGE	DURABLE*	PERCENT CHANGE	NON-DURABLE*	PERCENT CHANGE
				ACTUAL		
Jan.	92.526	0.72	28.955	1.10	63.571	0.56
Feb.	92.211	−0.34	28.840	−0.40	63.371	−0.31
Mar.	93.804	1.73	29.986	3.97	63.818	0.71
Apr.	95.125	1.41	30.671	2.28	64.454	1.00
May	97.239	2.22	31.705	3.37	65.534	1.68
June	98.638	1.44	32.790	3.42	65.848	0.48
July	98.832	0.20	32.597	−0.59	66.235	0.59
Aug.	98.277	−0.56	31.951	−1.98	66.326	0.14
Sept.	99.537	1.28	32.905	2.99	66.632	0.46
Oct.	100.923	1.39	33.882	2.97	67.041	0.61
Nov.	101.896	0.96	34.641	2.24	67.255	0.32
Dec.	102.438	0.53	35.532	2.57	66.906	−0.52
				FORECAST		
Jan.	92.232	0.40	28.821	0.63	63.411	0.30
Feb.	92.320	0.10	28.909	0.31	63.411	0.00
Mar.	93.127	0.87	29.183	0.95	63.944	0.84
Apr.	94.138	1.09	30.102	3.15	64.036	0.14
May	96.408	2.41	31.101	3.32	65.308	1.99
June	97.623	1.26	31.815	2.30	65.809	0.77
July	99.077	1.49	32.920	3.47	66.157	0.53
Aug.	99.024	−0.05	32.614	−0.93	66.410	0.38
Sept.	99.071	0.05	32.219	−1.21	66.850	0.66
Oct.	100.507	1.45	33.218	3.10	67.289	0.66
Nov.	101.567	1.05	34.066	2.55	67.501	0.32
Dec.	102.663	1.08	34.829	2.24	67.834	0.49

	LEVELS	PERCENT	LEVELS	PERCENT	LEVELS	PERCENT
				ERRORS		
Jan.	.294	0.32	.134	0.46	.160	0.25
Feb.	−.109	−0.12	−.069	−0.24	−.040	−0.06
Mar.	.677	0.72	.803	2.68	−.126	−0.20
Apr.	.987	1.04	.569	1.85	.418	0.65
May	.831	0.85	.604	1.91	.226	0.35
June	1.015	1.03	.975	2.97	.039	0.06
July	−.245	−0.25	−.323	−0.99	0.78	0.12
Aug.	−.747	−0.76	−.663	−2.08	−.084	−0.13
Sept.	.466	0.47	.686	2.08	−.219	−0.33
Oct.	.416	0.41	.664	1.96	−.248	−0.37
Nov.	.329	0.32	.575	1.66	−.246	−0.37
Dec.	−.225	−0.22	.703	1.98	−.927	−1.39
MEAN ERROR	.307		.388		−.081	
MAPE		0.54		1.74		0.36
RMSE	.607		.618		.331	

* RSD forecast based on 1970–82 version of equation 5-12a
  RSN forecast based on 1978–82 version of equation 5-12b
  RST forecast using sum of results for RSD and RSN

Source: Actual data: Bureau of the Census, U.S. Department of Commerce

TABLE 5-17   Total Retail Sales: Actual and Forecast, 1983

	ACTUAL (1)	PERCENT CHANGE (2)	FORECAST* (3)	PERCENT CHANGE (4)	ERROR (a-e) (5)	PERCENT ERROR (6)
JAN	92.526	0.72	92.401	0.59	.125	0.13
FEB	92.211	−0.34	92.226	−0.19	−.015	−0.02
MAR	93.804	1.73	92.724	0.54	1.080	1.15
APR	95.125	1.41	93.334	0.66	1.791	1.88
MAY	97.239	2.22	93.951	0.66	3.288	3.38
JUN	98.638	1.44	94.784	0.89	3.854	3.91
JUL	98.832	0.20	95.166	0.40	3.666	3.71
AUG	98.277	−0.56	95.414	0.26	2.863	2.91
SEP	99.537	1.28	96.472	1.11	3.065	3.08
OCT	100.923	1.39	96.706	0.24	4.217	4.18
NOV	101.896	0.96	97.307	0.62	4.589	4.50
DEC	102.438	0.53	98.118	0.83	4.320	4.22
MEAN ERROR					2.737	
MAPE						2.75
RMSE					3.143	

* Forecast based on equation 5-11, using forecast values for Personal Income (from Table 5-13) and estimated retail sales values in prior month for error adjustment

larger throughout the rest of 1983. (Compare column 5 for Table 5-14 and 5-17.) The summary error statistics are also a good deal larger for this partly dynamic forecast. Table 5-18 presents results from a similar forecast using equations 5-12, 5-12a, and 5-12b. Again the errors in Table 5-18 are larger than those for Table 5-17, mainly reflecting the under-estimates for RSD in the second half of the year. Nevertheless, comparison of the monthly errors and the summary error statistics for total retail sales in Table 5-17 and Table 5-18 indicates a more pronounced superiority for the disaggregated version.

The higher errors for the partly dynamic forecast are not surprising. One message to the forecaster is that, to the extent possible, the forecast results should be monitored closely against the actual values so that serious differences can be spotted and, if possible, judgmentally adjusted.

SUMMARY

The economic measures examined in this chapter represent an important series of economic activities. The sequence leading from employment changes, to income changes, to changes in consumer spending for durable and nondurable goods provides a core source of macroeconomic momentum. The forecast approaches outlined provide a means to trace the related

TABLE 5-18 Actual Versus Forecast Retail Sales Total, Durable, and Nondurable: 1983 (billions of dollars, seasonally adjusted monthly rates)

			ACTUAL			
	TOTAL*	PERCENT CHANGE	DURABLE*	PERCENT CHANGE	NON-DURABLE*	PERCENT CHANGE
Jan.	92.526	0.72	28.955	1.10	63.571	0.56
Feb.	92.211	−0.34	28.840	−0.40	63.371	−0.31
Mar.	93.804	1.73	29.986	3.97	63.818	0.71
Apr.	95.125	1.41	30.671	2.28	64.454	1.00
May	97.239	2.22	31.705	3.37	65.534	1.68
June	98.638	1.44	32.790	3.42	65.848	0.48
July	98.832	0.20	32.597	−0.59	66.235	0.59
Aug.	98.277	−0.56	31.951	−1.98	66.326	0.14
Sept.	99.537	1.28	32.905	2.99	66.632	0.46
Oct.	100.923	1.39	33.882	2.97	67.041	0.61
Nov.	101.896	0.96	34.641	2.24	67.255	0.32
Dec.	102.438	0.53	35.532	2.57	66.906	−0.52

			FORECAST			
Jan.	92.495	0.69	28.910	0.94	63.584	0.58
Feb.	92.281	−0.23	28.863	−0.16	63.418	−0.26
Mar.	92.860	0.63	29.092	0.79	63.768	0.55
Apr.	93.578	0.77	29.367	0.95	64.211	0.69
May	94.313	0.79	29.649	0.96	64.664	0.71
June	95.303	1.05	30.017	1.24	65.285	0.96
July	95.829	0.55	30.259	0.80	65.570	0.44
Aug.	96.137	0.32	30.381	0.40	65.756	0.28
Sept.	97.413	1.33	30.855	1.56	66.558	1.22
Oct.	97.760	0.36	31.022	0.54	66.738	0.27
Nov.	98.538	0.80	31.341	1.03	67.197	0.69
Dec.	99.528	1.00	31.712	1.18	67.817	0.92

			ERRORS			
	LEVELS	PERCENT	LEVELS	PERCENT	LEVELS	PERCENT
Jan.	.031	0.03	.045	0.15	−.013	−0.02
Feb.	−.070	−0.08	−.023	−0.08	−.047	−0.07
Mar.	.944	1.01	.894	2.98	.049	0.08
Apr.	1.547	1.63	1.304	4.25	.243	0.38
May	2.926	3.01	2.056	6.48	.870	1.33
June	3.335	3.38	2.773	8.46	.562	0.85
July	3.003	3.04	2.338	7.17	.665	1.00
Aug.	2.140	2.18	1.570	4.91	.570	0.86
Sept.	2.124	2.13	2.050	6.23	.074	0.11
Oct.	3.163	3.13	2.860	8.44	.303	0.45
Nov.	3.358	3.30	3.300	9.53	.058	0.09
Dec.	2.910	2.84	3.820	10.75	−.911	−1.36
MEAN ERROR	2.118		1.916		.202	
MAPE		2.15		5.79		0.55
RMSE	2.429		2.240		.486	

* RSD forecast based on 1970–82 version of equation 5-12a
  RSN forecast based on 1978–82 version of equation 5-12b
  RST forecast using sum of results for RSD and RSN

Source: Actual data: Bureau of the Census, U.S. Department of Commerce.

impacts of these changes and a structure around which forecasts of other economic variables can be constructed.

These examples should not be viewed as comprising a static model. The forecast equations are simple and can be improved. Rather, the methodology presented in this chapter can be viewed as typical of that to be followed in constructing an iterative, but relative set of disaggregated indicator forecasts.

Chapter 6 provides a similar approach for generating inflation forecasts, while Chapter 7 presents approaches for forecasting investment and production measures.

QUESTIONS FOR REVIEW AND RESEARCH

5-1   The participation rate (RP) is a derived concept, equal to the labor force (LF) divided by the population 16 years and over (POP16&). For forecasting purposes, however, it was shown in equation 5-1 that the labor force can be forecast as the product of the participation rate and the population 16 years and over, each of which are themselves forecast using moving average techniques (RP by a moving average of its past levels; POP16& by a moving average of past first differences).

    (a)   Using the data in Table 5-2, prepare alternative forecasts for the labor force in 1983 based on twelve-month and twenty-four month moving averages of the first differences for POP16& and of the levels of the RP.

    (b)   Compare and evaluate these alternatives with the actual labor force levels in 1983.

    (c)   Explain why a moving average of less than twelve months would be inappropriate.

5-2   Actual employment growth (as measured by the Household Survey) in the thirteen months following the November 1982 business cycle trough exceeded the average growth in the five preceeding cyclical upturns (see Table 5-5).

    (a)   Compute an index for the thirteen months after the November 1982 trough.

    (b)   Compare the effects on the average cycle index of (i) replacing the monthly index levels after the April 1958 trough with those following the November 1982 trough, and (ii) computing the average cycle index over all six upturns.

    (c)   The recessions which ended in April 1958 and March 1975 were as severe as was the 1981–82 recession. Evaluate how well analysis of employment trends in the downturns and upturns surrounding just these troughs would have served as a guide to the employment rebound in 1983.

    (d)   Discuss what your findings in parts (b) and (c) of this question suggest about the relationship between the severity of a decline and the speed of recovery in employment in business cycles.

5-3   It was suggested that (payroll) employment in durable manufacturing and mining and construction is more cyclical than in nondurable manufacturing and services. Analyze this suggestion by constructing and comparing cycle indexes (peak: July 1981 = 100, and trough: November 1982 = 100) for: (i) the total of durable manufacturing and mining and construction employment, and (ii) nondurable manufacturing and service employment based on data in Table 5-8.

5-4   As businesses experience declining sales in a recession they attempt to reduce production and labor expense. Labor costs are trimmed by: (i) laying off workers, (ii) reducing the length of the workweek, or (iii) some combination of (i) and (ii). Using the data in Table 5-9, discuss the relative effects of these alternative approaches during the 1981–82 recession and indicate how employers responded—between rehiring workers and lengthening the workweek—during the 1983 upturn.

5-5   High and rising interest rates are generally regarded as adverse for continued economic growth—they increase the costs of financing for interest-sensitive spending sectors such as: consumer durables, housing, business fixed investment, and inventories. In particular, high and rising interest rates were widely cited as a contributing factor to the 1981–82 recession. High and rising interest rates also bolster personal interest income, as reflected in equation 5-9a. Graph the behavior of the six-month Treasury bill rate and personal interest income for the months of 1981–83 and evaluate the extent to which the positive effects of high, rising interest rates on income (and presumably spending) may mitigate their negative effects on interest-sensitive spending.

5-6   The Table below presents monthly data for 1983 on retail sales—total, durables, and by automotive dealers—in billions of dollars, and unit sales of domestic and foreign autos at seasonably adjusted annual rates in millions.

Retail Sales

	TOTAL	DURABLE GOODS	AUTOMOTIVE DEALERS	UNIT AUTO SALES
Jan.	92.526	28.955	16.323	8.5 mil.
Feb.	92.211	28.840	16.348	8.2
Mar.	93.804	29.986	17.169	8.4
Apr.	95.125	30.671	17.689	8.5
May	97.239	31.705	18.350	9.1
June	98.638	32.790	19.236	10.1
July	98.832	32.597	18.901	10.0
Aug.	98.277	31.951	18.053	8.8
Sept.	99.537	32.905	18.857	9.1
Oct.	100.923	33.882	19.620	9.7
Nov.	101.896	34.641	20.286	9.5
Dec.	102.438	35.532	21.164	10.5

Since retail sales by automotive dealers account for such a large share of retail sales of durables, any means to estimate these sales more accurately should reduce the forecast error for retail sales of durables and, thus, for total retail sales. Unit auto sales data become available roughly one week before the monthly retail sales report is released.

Using the data in the Table for 1983, evaluate the usefulness of unit auto sales data in preparing one-month forecasts for retail sales. Contrast the results from such an approach with the forecast results presented in Table 5-16.

5-7   Wage and salary payments may be regarded as a core component of personal income. Consumer purchases of nondurable goods fall more into the category of necessities than luxuries and, thus, may be assumed to grow more in line with "core" income. Test this hypothesis by estimating a regression of retail sales of nondurable goods on wage and salary payments and contrast the forecast results for 1983 with the results, using equation 5-12b.

6

INDICATOR FORECASTING
Inflation

Most labor market measures are reported in terms of the number of workers employed or unemployed, or the number of hours worked. These are measures of real activities without distorting effects from changing prices. Personal income and retail sales, on the other hand, are, like most economic indicators, reported in dollars. Since the purchasing power of a dollar changes—or, in other words, prices change—these reports do not always provide a clear picture of real activity over time. Instead, they reflect the combined effects of changes in economic activity and in prices.

Because so many economic indicators are reported in "current" (market) price terms, it is necessary to separate the price effects from the "real" effects—the change in activity excluding price changes—in order to discern the true pattern of economic activity. For instance personal income grew by 8.1% between December 1982 and December 1983. Over the same time span, the consumer price index for all urban workers rose 3.8%. Thus, much of the increase in personal income during 1983 was eroded by rising prices and only a bit more than half the total increase reflected enhanced purchasing power. Put another way, while personal income grew at an average monthly rate of 0.65% in 1983, consumer prices rose 0.31% per month, so that real purchasing power (ignoring tax changes) increased on average by 0.34 per month due to the growth of personal income alone.[1]

The need to separate price from real effects in many measures of economic activity is the chief reason why a forecast of price changes is an essential item in nearly all economic forecasts. Moreover, the experience of volatile, but on the whole rapid and unanticipated, inflation during the late 1960s and throughout the 1970s has focused the attention of many economists on the nature and causes of inflation so as to improve the ability to forecast it. This last topic has received a great deal of attention in recent years and has spawned a vast literature.[2] A complete discussion of the many issues raised and theories offered for explaining inflationary processes— which are more often at odds than in agreement—is beyond the scope of this text. A brief discussion of some of the main approaches is in order, however, for two reasons. First, given the complexity of the forecast problem and the

---

[1] This is simply the increase in personal income exclusive of the change in price level, or real personal income (pi).

$$pi = PI/CPI$$

Real personal income differs from real disposable personal income in that tax and nontax payments are subtracted from personal income and then deflated by the price level to derive the latter. A fully comprehensive measure of purchasing power would also take into account changes in real wealth and the availability of credit.

[2] A brief, representative list includes D.E.W. Laidler and J.M. Parkin, "Inflation: A Survey," *The Economic Journal,* No. 340 (Dec. 1975), 741–809; Helmut Frisch, "Inflation Theory 1963–75: A Second Generation Survey," *Journal of Economic Literature,* 15, No. 4 (Dec. 1977), 1289–1317; Peter I. Berman, *Inflation and the Money Supply in the United States: 1956–1977* (Lexington, MA: D.C. Heath, 1978); Otto Eckstein, *Core Inflation* (Englewood Cliffs, NJ: Prentice-Hall, 1982); Arthur M. Okun and George L. Perry, eds., *Curing Chronic Inflation* (Washington, D.C: The Brookings Institution, 1978); John S. Flemming, *Inflation* (London: Oxford University Press, 1976).

lack of agreement on the nature of the process itself, a forecaster may well prefer to use more than one method to derive an inflation forecast. Similar results reached by disparate methods may bolster confidence in the forecast on the part of both the forecaster and the managers for whom the forecast is prepared. Divergent results reached by differing methods on the other hand, may offer clues as to which assumed conditions account for the differences and, thus, where the major risks lie. Second, inflation forecasts may be required in varying detail by different businesses—a forecast of the overall inflation rate might be sufficient for a financial firm, while a detailed forecast by commodity groups might be required by a manufacturer. Differing methods provide a range of forecast detail.

Four approaches are discussed in this chapter, referred to as: (I) the monetary approach, (II) the expectations/momentum approach, (III) the factor input costs approach, and (IV) the stage of processing approach. The examination of each of these approaches includes a discussion of the theoretical background, practical steps in adapting these theories to forecast needs, and an *ex post* forecast for 1983.

I MONETARY APPROACH

The monetary approach stems from the monetarist view of inflation, most boldly stated by Milton Freidman: "Inflation is always and everywhere a monetary phenomenon."[3] In essence, according to this approach, the relation between money and prices is rooted in the quantity theory of money, expressed by the equation of exchange. This equation, in its strict form, states that the quantity of money (M) times its velocity (V), or turnover, (assumed to be constant by strict quantity theorists) equals nominal output (Y), composed of a price (P) component and real output (Q) (see Chapter 2).

$$M \times V = Y = P \times Q \qquad (6\text{-}1)$$

Stated in terms of growth rates and assuming that (a) there is constant (or nearly constant) growth of velocity, and (b) that real output growth occurs at a stable trend rate, the equation can be restated to show a proportionality between growth in the money stock and inflation.

$$\%\Delta P = a + f(\%\Delta M) \qquad (6\text{-}1a)$$

In this form, a, the constant term, captures the effects of non-trend growth in real output and velocity.

[3] Milton Friedman, *The Counter Revolution in Monetary Theory* (London: Institute of Economic Affairs, for the Wincott Foundation, 1970), Occasional Paper No. 33, p. 24.

A recent study by Berman[4] provides a basis for using this relationship for forecasting inflation rates. Berman found that between 1963 and 1971 roughly 78% of the variability in inflation—measured as the annualized quarterly percentage change in the implicit GNP deflator—was accounted for by a ten-quarter distributed lag[5] on the annualized quarterly percentage changes in the narrowly defined money stock (M1). Moreover, his results confirmed the general stability of the constant term, a. Berman's estimated relationship was of the form

$$\%\Delta P_t = a + \sum_{i=0}^{10} w_i * \%\Delta M_{t-i} \qquad (6\text{-}2)$$

where the w_is are the distributed lag weights.[6] Table 6-1 presents Berman's results for equation 6-2 estimated for the period from second quarter 1963 through second quarter 1971. (Mid 1963 was chosen as the starting point because by then a structural change due to the inclusion of vault cash in bank reserves was completed; mid 1971 was chosen as the end so as to exclude the effects of the wage-price freeze that began in August 1971).

The constant had the expected negative sign. The sum of the distributed lag weights was greater than one and suggested that a permanent one percentage point increase in money supply growth would produce an increase of 1.4 percentage points in the rate of inflation. Berman confirmed by testing alternative specifications that a lag of ten quarters plus the current quarter provided the best money supply growth-inflation relationship.

Berman used this equation to simulate an out-of-sample forecast through 1975, the results for which are presented in Table 6-2. Two aspects of these results are notable. First, the forecast inflation rates show much less volatility than the actuals, reflecting the moderating effects of the long lag on money supply growth. (This is so even for the period prior to 1973:IV.) Second, the errors become much larger between 1973:IV and 1975:I when nonmonetary forces (mainly the sharp OPEC-induced rise in energy prices) were largely responsible for faster inflation. Berman showed that when the simulation is continued beyond 1975 the errors decrease again. He concluded that this suggests that the nonmonetary forces had a one-time effect. Whether one accepts this explanation, this development does pose a warning: money supply growth alone does not always explain all inflation.

[4] Peter I. Berman, *Inflation and the Money Supply in the United States: 1956–1977* (Lexington, MA: D.C. Heath, 1978).

[5] The polynomial distributed lag technique used by Berman and below was first described by Shirley Almon, "The Distributed Lag Between Capital Appropriations and Expenditures," *Econometrica,* 33 (1965), 178–96; this article has been reprinted in Arnold Zellner, ed., *Readings in Economic Statistics and Econometrics* (Boston: Little, Brown, 1968), pp. 516–36.

[6] Berman, *Inflation and the Money Supply,* pp. 17–65.

TABLE 6-1   **Annualized Quarterly Percent**
Changes in the GNP Deflator
Based on Lagged M1,
1963 : II–1971 : II (Berman Study)
Regression Statistics

LAG PERIOD	CONSTANT −2.67 WEIGHTS	t STATISTIC (−4.29) t STATISTICS
0	0.16	(3.31)
1	0.15	(5.92)
2	0.14	(5.45)
3	0.12	(4.80)
4	0.11	(4.94)
5	0.10	(5.01)
6	0.09	(4.21)
7	0.10	(3.88)
8	0.12	(4.86)
9	0.15	(6.61)
10	0.20	(4.31)
Summed Weights	1.42	(10.43)
$\bar{R}^2$	0.78	
D-W	2.58	
SER	0.81	

Reprinted by permission of the publisher, from
Peter I. Berman, *Inflation And the Money Supply in
the United States,* 1956–1977 (Lexington, MA:
Lexington Books, D.C. Heath and Co., 1978), p. 71.

Berman's results do provide a basis for forecasting inflation based on
money supply growth. It must be recognized in advance, however, that such
a simple model is unlikely to explain a complicated process like inflation
fully. What it does provide is a "baseline" forecast of some of the main
"demand side" influences on inflation that can be modified when other
influences are also considered.

Because the structured approach followed in Chapter 5 looked at
monthly changes in economic measures, two modifications to Berman's
approach are made. First, instead of forecasting the annualized quarterly
percentage changes in the GNP deflator, this approach aims at forecasting
the annualized monthly percentage changes in the consumer price index for
all urban workers (CPIU) and then deriving simple monthly percentage
changes. The CPIU is the most widely watched measure of inflation, partly
because of its timeliness. Moreover, monthly percentage changes are more
consistent with the monthly data on personal income and retail sales examined already.

TABLE 6-2   Actual and Forecast Inflation
(Berman Study), 1971 : III–1975 : IV
(annualized quarter-to-quarter %
changes)

	ACTUAL	FORECAST	ERROR
1971 : III	3.3%	4.8%	−1.5%
IV	3.5	4.3	−0.8
1972 : I	5.6	4.7	0.9
II	2.8	5.4	−2.6
III	3.4	6.2	−2.8
IV	4.6	6.9	−2.3
1973 : I	5.7	7.2	−1.5
II	6.8	7.3	−0.5
III	7.3	7.4	−0.1
IV	9.2	7.2	2.0
1974 : I	9.1	6.7	2.4
II	10.9	6.5	4.4
III	11.0	6.7	4.3
IV	11.9	6.3	5.6
1975 : I	10.3	5.4	4.9
II	5.6	5.2	0.4
III	7.1	4.9	2.2
IV	6.1	4.3	1.8
MAE			2.28
RMSE			2.76

Error = Actual − Forecast
Source: Berman, *Inflation and the Money Supply*, p. 97

Second, instead of using annualized quarterly percentage changes in M1 as the dependent variable, year-over-year percentage changes in monthly levels are used. This makes estimation of the independent variable somewhat easier and reduces the errors due to mis-forecasts of M1 growth. For a twelve-month forecast, most of the year-over-year growth in M1 is known for the earliest months of the forecast period. As the forecast period lengthens, the year-over-year growth can be approximated using the Federal Reserve's announced growth targets for M1 in combination with past growth rates that remain applicable. It requires some judgment on the part of the forecaster to decide which growth rate within the target range to choose, but the problem is limited. More important, the year-over-year growth rates are easier to compute than annualized quarterly changes, with less risk of error.[7]

[7] The Chairman of the Federal Reserve Board provides Congress with monetary growth targets twice a year—usually in February and July. In addition, modifications to these targets are announced in the Federal Open Market Committee's (FOMC) minutes. For a twelve-month forecast made in December, the January estimate of year-over-year M1 growth is fairly simple,

TABLE 6-3   Percent Change in CPIU Based on Lagged M1: 1963–82 Regression Statistics

CONSTANT (t STATISTIC)			−6.34 (−4.47)		
LAG PERIOD	WEIGHTS	(t STATISTICS)	LAG PERIOD	WEIGHTS	(t STATISTICS)
0	0.0505	(1.23)*			
1	0.0536	(1.51)*	17	0.0761	(4.35)
2	0.0565	(1.87)	18	0.0758	(4.42)
3	0.0592	(2.32)	19	0.0754	(4.62)
4	0.0617	(2.87)	20	0.0747	(4.86)
5	0.0640	(3.52)	21	0.0738	(5.17)
6	0.0661	(4.21)	22	0.0728	(5.52)
7	0.0680	(4.80)	23	0.0715	(5.84)
8	0.0697	(5.15)	24	0.0700	(5.93)
9	0.0712	(5.22)	25	0.0684	(5.61)
10	0.0725	(5.09)	26	0.0665	(4.88)
11	0.0736	(4.88)	27	0.0644	(4.00)
12	0.0745	(4.67)	28	0.0622	(3.19)
13	0.0752	(4.50)	29	0.0597	(2.53)
14	0.0758	(4.38)	30	0.0571	(2.01)
15	0.0761	(4.31)	31	0.0542	(1.61)*
16	0.0762	(4.30)	32	0.0512	(1.30)*
Summed Weights	2.2182	(9.22)			
rho	0.3837	(5.97)			
$\bar{R}^2$	0.5557				
D-W	2.12				
SER	2.91				

* t statistics not significant at 95% level

Equation 6-2a shows this modified form.

$$\%\Delta CPIU_t = a + \sum_{i=0}^{32} w_i * (\%\Delta Y/Y(M_{t-i})) \qquad (6\text{-}2a)$$

Note that in order to conform to Berman's ten quarter lag specification, a thirty-two-month lag (plus the current month) is required. Table 6-3 presents the regression results for equation 6-2a, estimated from 1963 through 1982. Some care is necessary in comparing these results to Berman's because

since eleven-twelfths is known. For the July estimate, only half the growth is known; the rest must be estimated. Only the estimate for the following December would rely totally on a forecast of the year-over-year growth in M1. However, this estimate is one of only thirty-three lagged M1 growth rates used to estimate the monthly change in the inflation rate. Thus, while the potential of a mis-forecast of M1 growth leading to a forecast error of inflation increases as the forecast period lengthens, this risk is partly reduced by the long lag which includes mainly known data. As always, frequent updates and monitoring will help limit such errors.

TABLE 6-4   Actual and Forecast Percent Changes in CPIU: 1983* (annualized and simple monthly % changes)

	ANNUAL RATES			MONTHLY RATES		
	ACTUAL	FORECAST	ERROR	ACTUAL	FORECAST	ERROR
Jan.	3.80	3.94	−0.14	0.31	0.32	−0.01
Feb.	−0.80	6.99	−7.79	−0.07	0.56	−0.63
Mar.	0.80	5.45	−4.65	0.07	0.44	−0.37
Apr.	8.50	6.27	2.23	0.68	0.51	0.17
May	5.40	9.44	−4.04	0.44	0.75	−0.31
June	2.50	8.47	−5.97	0.21	0.68	−0.47
July	4.50	7.57	−3.07	0.37	0.61	−0.24
Aug.	4.50	8.53	−4.03	0.37	0.68	−0.31
Sept.	4.50	8.76	−4.26	0.37	0.70	−0.33
Oct.	4.90	8.94	−4.04	0.40	0.72	−0.32
Nov.	4.50	9.24	−4.74	0.37	0.74	−0.37
Dec.	2.80	9.17	−6.37	0.23	0.73	−0.50
Dec.–Dec. % Change				4.08	7.70	
MEAN ERROR			−3.91			−0.31
MAE			4.28			0.34
RMSE			4.68			0.37

* Using equation 6-2a as estimated in Table 6-3

equation 6-2a is specified at a monthly frequency. The constant term has the expected negative sign and is significant. However, its value, at 6.34, is more than twice as high. This suggests that the effects of nontrend velocity and real output growth were greater over the longer estimation period. The sum of the lagged weights is also higher (2.22). Moreover, the amount of explained variation (shown by the value of $\bar{R}^2$) is less at 56%. These results suggest that, while money supply growth was still an important determination of inflation over this longer estimation period, other factors had increased in importance. For one thing, the effects of the two oil price shocks of 1973–75 and 1979–80 are included in the estimation period for equation 6-2a, while they were not in Berman's equation.[8] The lagged weights are distributed in an inverse saucer shape, whereas Berman's weights followed a more saucer shaped pattern, This may point to some modest change in the relationship between money supply growth and velocity—increases in money supply affect inflation more slowly—though the differences are small and may reflect the altered specification.

Table 6-4 presents forecast percent changes in CPIU for 1983 and compares these results to the actual percent changes in annualized and simple monthly rates. The forecast rates were estimated using equation 6-2a

    [8] See Berman, *Inflation and the Money Supply,* pp 43–76. In particular see Table 3-1 page 43 and Table 3-3 page 52, lengthened sample estimates.

in annualized monthly percent change terms. These rates were then reduced to simple monthly percent changes by taking the twelfth root. As with Berman's results, the forecast inflation rates are less volatile than the actuals (ranging from a low of 3.9% in January to a high of 9.4% in May for the forecasts, compared to a low of -0.8% in February and a high of 8.5% in April for the actuals). The forecast rates over-estimated inflation, on average (as measured by the Mean Error) by 3.9% in 1983, or by just over 0.3% per month. Indeed, ignoring the effects of offsetting errors, the Mean Absolute Error was 4.3% (0.3%, monthly) and the Root Mean Square Error was 4.7% (0.4%, monthly), roughly two percentage points higher than Berman found for mid 1971 through 1975. These results suggest nonmonetary factors were probably quite important in keeping inflation low. Among possible factors were: ample food and oil supplies, and a strong recovery-induced growth in productivity. The forecast inflation rates derived by this monetary approach nevertheless provide a starting point upon which a more detailed inflation forecast can be built. Past monetary growth does appear to provide a theoretical basis for a forecast of the "central path" inflation that is likely to follow. Careful analysis of other influences can be used to reduce the errors.

II EXPECTATIONS/MOMENTUM APPROACH

One result of the rapid inflation of the late 1960s and the 1970s was to increase popular awareness about the rate of price change. In turn, this greater awareness of past inflation became the basis for expectations based on past inflation. This view of past inflation is not neutral: suppliers in the factor and goods market will attempt to attain price (wage) increases which at least match their expectations for general inflation. One result is that these inflation expectations get built into the price system—they are partly self-fulfilling. This reasoning forms the basis, then, for another approach to inflation forecasting which assumes: (1) expectations about future inflation are based on past inflation experience, (2) these expectations are incorporated in costs and prices, (3) thus, imparting a *momentum* to inflation.[9]

Practically, this approach suggests that current inflation is a function of inflation expectations, which in turn are based on past inflation rates. This can be stated in functional form as in equations 6-3 and 6-3a below.

$$\%\Delta P_t = f(\%\Delta P_t^e) \tag{6-3}$$

[9] A strong statement of this approach, the rational expectations theory, stems from the writing of Muth and Sargent. For two articles see: J.F. Muth, "Rational Expectations and the Theory of Price Movements," *Econometrica,* 39, (1961) 315–50; and T.J. Sargent, "Anticipated Inflation and the Nominal Rate of Interest," *Quarterly Journal of Economics,* 86 (1972), 212–51.

where
$$\%\Delta P_t^e = \sum_{i=1}^{n} w_i * \%\Delta P_{t-i} \qquad (6\text{-}3a)$$

The variable $\%\Delta P_t^e$ represents inflation expectations in period t. Equation 6-3 states that the current period's percentage change in prices is a function of the current period's inflation expectations. Specifying an expectations variable is a difficult task, made even harder by the range of expectations theories. The *rational expectations* theory, in its strong form, states that if economic agents are rational they will form their expectations on the basis of the "correct" economic theory. The weaker form states that if a theory proves wrong, economic agents will recognize this fact and revise their expectations accordingly. Moreover, the theory on which rational expectations are based may be simply a rule of thumb which has worked well in the past. This form of the rational expectations theory is close to *adaptive expectations* theories which view current expectations as the result of a learning process: the errors between past expectations and actual outcomes are used to form current expectations. John Flemming shows how rational and adaptive expectations can be combined to reflect the way in which the public forms inflation expectations.[10] Equation 6-3a reflects this approach by stating that current inflation expectations are equal to some weighted average of past inflation rates. This captures the "rule of thumb" aspect of the weaker rational expectations approach and is consistent with the learning process which underlies the adaptive expectations approach. The use of only past inflation rates as explanatory variables, however, recognizes the difficulty—perhaps the impossibility—of determining exactly how inflation expectations are formed. For forecasting purposes, the two equations can be combined in a form such as equation 6-4.

$$\%\Delta CPIU_t = \sum_{i=1}^{12} w_i * (\%\Delta Y/Y(CPIU_{t-i})) \qquad (6\text{-}4)$$

Two points about the specification of equation 6-4 should be noted. First, the past inflation rates are expressed as year-over-year percentage changes in CPIU. This assumes that: (1) the public thinks of inflation in annual rate terms; but (2) their expectations are adapted gradually to recent experience over an extended period. Using year-over-year rates allows known data to be used. The second point to be noted is the assumption that the lag is twelve months. This assumption was tested by using shorter and longer lags. The shorter lags did not explain as much variation as the twelve-month lag, and longer lags provided little or no increase in the amount of explained variation. Moreover, there is a certain plausibility to the suggestion that the

---

[10] See Flemming, *Inflation*, pp. 62–68.

TABLE 6-5   Monthly Percent Changes in CPIU
Based on Lagged Inflation: 1970–82
Regression Statistics

LAG PERIOD	WEIGHTS	(t STATISTICS)
1 month	0.0371	(1.71)
2 months	0.0291	(2.75)
3 months	0.0218	(6.69)
4 months	0.0152	(2.27)
5 months	0.0093	(0.85)*
6 months	0.0042	(0.32)*
7 months	−0.0002	(−0.02)*
8 months	−0.0039	(−0.36)*
9 months	−0.0069	(−1.00)*
10 months	−0.0091	(−2.83)
11 months	−0.0106	(−1.04)*
12 months	−0.0114	(−0.54)*
Summed Weights	0.0745	
rho	0.3910	
$\overline{R}^2$	0.44	
D-W	2.12	
SER	0.26	

* Denotes t statistic not significant at 95% level.

inflation experiences during the past year have the greatest relevance to current expectations. It should be recognized that equation 6-4 is a simplification which assumes that the inflation expectations of many owners of different factors of production can be aggregated. A more complete specification would show individual input costs as functions of the inflation expectations of the factor owners and other relevant determinants.

The regression statistics for equation 6-4 are presented in Table 6-5. The lag weights are positive and decline steadily in value for the first six months. This suggests, quite reasonably, that while inflation expectations are formed on the basis of inflation experiences over an extended period, the most recent experiences have the greatest weight. More interesting is the shift from positive to negative weights after a six-month lag. This is a quite common result with estimates of inflation expectations based on a distributed lag of past inflation. Modigliani and Sutch[11] have called attention to the possibility of two types of adaptive inflation expectations: extrapolative and regressive expectations. Inflation expectations are extrapolative when individuals believe that inflation in the future will rise from current levels, while regressive expectations are based on the belief that over time inflation will

[11] Franco Modigliani and Richard Sutch, "Innovations in Interest Rate Policy," American Economic Review, LVI, No. 2 (May 1966), 185–87.

regress towards "more normal" (lower) levels. It is possible to reconcile the coexistence of both types of expectations if it is assumed that near-term expectations are likely to be extrapolative, but as these expectations become more futuristic (i.e., as the lag lengthens), they take on a greater degree of regressiveness. Only one of the statistics for the weights beyond the fourth month is significant at the 95% level. This is not important as these weights are near zero in any event. The summed weights when multiplied by twelve (so as to annualize the dependent variable, the monthly inflation rate) equal 0.89. This suggests that a permanent one percentage point increase in the inflation rate over the past twelve months will result in just under a one percent annualized rate of inflation in the current month.

The other summary statistics—the adjusted coefficient of determination, the Durbin-Watson statistic, and the standard error of the regression—are nearly equal in value to those for equation 6-2a. Equation 6-4 was estimated without a constant term, as a constant had no economic meaning. However, there were only minor changes in the other statistics when 6-4 was estimated to include a constant term (which had a value of 0.09).

Forecasts of the monthly percentage change in the CPIU for 1983, estimated using equation 6-4 and actual data for the year-over-year percentage change in CPIU, are presented in Table 6-6. In general, the results are quite good: somewhat more of the month-to-month volatility is captured

TABLE 6-6   Actual and Forecast Percent Changes in CPIU: 1983* (annualized and simple monthly % changes)

	ANNUAL RATE			MONTHLY RATES		
	ACTUAL	FORECAST	ERROR	ACTUAL	FORECAST	ERROR
Jan.	3.80	0.00	3.80	0.31	0.00	0.31
Feb.	−0.80	2.80	−3.60	−0.07	0.23	−0.30
Mar.	0.80	0.84	−0.04	0.07	0.07	0.00
Apr.	8.50	1.45	7.05	0.68	0.12	0.56
May	5.40	4.53	0.87	0.44	0.37	0.07
June	2.50	3.29	−0.79	0.21	0.27	−0.06
July	4.50	2.06	2.44	0.37	0.17	0.20
Aug.	4.50	2.67	1.83	0.37	0.22	0.15
Sept.	4.50	2.67	1.83	0.37	0.22	0.15
Oct.	4.90	2.80	2.10	0.40	0.23	0.17
Nov.	4.50	3.17	1.33	0.37	0.26	0.11
Dec.	2.80	3.17	−0.37	0.23	0.26	−0.03
Dec.–Dec. % Change				4.08	2.44	
MEAN ERROR						0.11
MAE						0.18
RMSE						0.23

* Using equation 6-4 as estimated in Table 6-5.

than with equation 6-2a (see Table 6-3), the December–December inflation estimate is slightly closer to the actual at 2.4% versus 4.1%, but now underestimates the actual, and the MAE and RMSE are slightly smaller. In short, equation 6-4 appears to provide a reasonably good estimate of inflation in 1983 and does so on the basis of easily obtainable data—the rate of past inflation. This last point highlights a benefit of this approach, namely that only past inflation rates are needed for a forecast. Thus, by producing the forecast sequentially—one month at a time—a consistent forecast can be easily produced.

The main drawback with the expectations approach seems to be the lack of any insight into the fundamental influences on price determination; it is only assumed that these inflation expectations shape the negotiation of input costs.

III   FACTOR INPUT COSTS APPROACH

In microeconomic theory, output prices are equal to the sum of all the factor input costs—the sum of the price of each factor used times the share of each factor in total inputs used to produce one unit of output. This is also true in fact, at the macroeconomic level. Thus, the change in output prices, inflation, can be explained by examining the changes in input costs pressures. Analysis of inflation as a result of changes in factor input costs have had a prominent place in the literature on inflation, and on its causes in recent years.[12] This approach is a desirable one for forecasting inflation because it isolates the sources of inflationary pressures in a more complete way than the expectations approach.

In general, factor inputs can be classed in two groups: labor and nonlabor. Labor costs per unit of output are equal to compensation per hour less any offset from productivity changes. Nonlabor payments per unit of output include profits, depreciation, net interest payments, and indirect taxes. Output prices, as measured by the GNP deflator, can be shown to be equal to a weighted sum of unit labor costs and unit nonlabor payments. Or, in percentage change terms, inflation equals a weighted sum of the percentage change

---

[12] A sampling includes many lengthy studies appearing in the *Brookings Papers on Economic Activity* (*BPEA*) in recent years: Robert J. Gordon, *BPEA*, No. 1 (1970), 8–41; George L. Perry, "Changing Labor Markets and Inflation," *BPEA*, No. 3 (1970), 441–48; William D. Nordhaus, "The Worldwide Wage Explosion," *BPEA*, No. 2 (1972), 431–64; George L. Perry, "Determinants of Wage Inflation Around the World," *BPEA*, No. 2 (1975), 403–35; George L. Perry, "Inflation, in Theory and Practice," *BPEA*, No. 1 (1980), 207–41: and Charles L. Schultze, "Some Macro Foundations for Micro Theory," *BPEA*, No. 2 (1981), 521–76. This last article draws on and develops the views presented in Arthur M. Okun, *Prices and Quantities: A Macroeconomic Analysis,* (Washington, D.C.: The Brookings Institution, 1981). In addition, Otto Eckstein, *Core Inflation,* offers an important contribution to the topic.

in unit labor costs and the percentage change in unit nonlabor payments.

$$\%\Delta PGNP = w_1 * \%\Delta ULC + w_2 * \%\Delta UNLP \qquad (6\text{-}5)$$

There are three caveats concerning equation 6-5. First, the weighted sums of the percentage changes in unit labor costs and unit nonlabor payments will not always completely account for all inflation. Eckstein has separated inflation into three components: (1) core inflation, (2) demand inflation, and (3) shock inflation.[13] Equation 6-5 captures the first and most of the second of these components, but little if any of the third. The second caveat is related; equation 6-5 refers to inflation as measured by the GNP deflator, not the CPIU. In general, the shock component is somewhat greater in the CPIU (because of its fixed-weight structure) than in the GNP deflator. Thus, the estimates derived from equation 6-5 are better used as measures of the underlying—or, to use Eckstein's term, core—inflation rate than the inflation rate observed by movements in the CPIU. Finally, the GNP deflator, unit labor costs, unit nonlabor payments, and productivity are measured quarterly rather than monthly. Thus, this approach does not yield monthly inflation forecasts directly. However, insights to underlying inflation pressures—and where those pressures are most intense between labor and nonlabor costs—can be gained. This information can then be used to supplement estimates derived from other approaches to derive monthly forecasts.

Unit labor costs account for roughly two-thirds of total output costs and are more homogenous in composition than unit nonlabor payments. Thus, input cost analysis focuses mainly on unit labor costs and estimates inflation based on the year over year percentage change in unit labor costs. In estimating the percentage change in unit labor costs it it necessary to break the concept down to its most basic component and then work the estimate up from there.

The percentage change in unit labor costs is equal to the percentage change in hourly labor compensation less the percentage change in productivity. The major source of changes in compensation are changes in hourly earnings. Thus, estimation of the percentage change in average hourly earnings is the starting point for estimating compensation. Productivity equals private business output—basically, GNP less government and other nonbusiness output—divided by hours worked. This can be approximated if the forecaster has available a forecast of real GNP and its major components. Thus, unit labor costs are derived in a four-step sequence: (1) percentage changes in hourly earnings are estimated; (2) these estimates are then used

---

[13] Eckstein, *Core Inflation,* pp. 7–34.

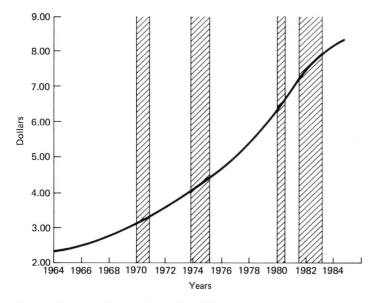

Source: Bureau of Labor Statistics, U.S. Department of Labor

FIGURE 6-1 Average hourly earnings

to derive forecast percentage changes in compensation per hour; (3) levels and percentage changes in productivity are subtracted[14] from the percentage changes in compensation per hour; (4) to derive estimates of the percentage change in unit labor costs.

The crucial step is the estimate of the percentage change in hourly earnings. An examination of hourly earnings data from the mid 1960s through 1983, as in Figure 6-1, shows that hourly earnings have increased fairly steadily over time. However, it is reasonable to suspect that the growth in earnings is affected by labor market conditions: earnings are likely to rise faster in periods of tight labor supply conditions, and more slowly when excess labor supply obtains. On these bases, a relationship such as equation 6-6 can be hypothesized, in which the percentage change in earnings per hour (ERN/H) is assumed to be a function of a time trend (TIME) and the inverse of the unemployment rate (1/RU). Regression statistics for equation 6-6 in which the dependent variable measures the year-over-year percentage change in average hourly earnings for private nonfarm production workers—are shown below.

---

[14] To be more precise, the quotient of the current quarter's value for compensation per hour divided by its value in the prior quarter is, in turn, divided by the current quarter's value for productivity divided by its value in the prior quarter.

$$\%\Delta Y/Y(ERN/H) = a_0 + a_1 * TIME + a_2 * (1/RU) \qquad (6\text{-}6)$$

coefficients	t statistics
$a_0 = -1.53$	(-0.76)
$a_1 = 0.023$	(5.24)
$a_2 = 5.28$	(1.41)
rho $= 0.81$	(17.60)

$$\bar{R}^2 = 0.87 \quad D\text{-}W = 2.20 \quad SER = 0.42$$

The equation was estimated with monthly data for the years 1967 through 1980. The value for the coefficient on time (a_1) states that hourly earnings have a trend rate of increase of 0.23% per month, all other conditions equal. However, the coefficient, a_2, points out the inverse relationship between earnings growth and the unemployment rate. For instance, an unemployment rate of 5% is associated with annual earnings growth of 1.056% per month, while at a 10% unemployment rate annual earnings growth would be 0.528% slower.

Table 6-7 presents actual and forecast levels and year-over-year percentage changes for average hourly earnings, monthly and quarterly averages, for 1983. (The forecast levels were calculated by multiplying the actual year-earlier level by the forecast year-over-year percentage change; for instance the value of $7.86 in January 1983 is equal to $7.52, the value for January 1982, multiplied by 1.0448). The errors are, for the most part, small and the forecasts provide good estimates of the actual levels and percentage changes in average hourly earnings.[15]

Compensation per hour includes hourly earnings, but with major differences: (1) compensation is adjusted for changes in employment mix between high-paid and low-paid workers, while hourly earnings are not; (2) compensation covers all workers, while hourly earnings cover only production workers; and (3) compensation per hour also includes employer contributions for social insurance and other private benefits. In order to go from the hourly earnings estimate to an estimate of hourly compensation, a simple "bridge" equation as in equation 6-7 is estimated.

$$\%\Delta Y/Y(COMP/H) = a_0 + a_1 * \%\Delta Y/Y(ERN/H) \qquad (6\text{-}7)$$

coefficients	t statistics
$a_0 = 3.23$	(3.05)
$a_1 = 0.68$	(5.14)
rho $= 0.88$	(14.27)

$$\bar{R}^2 = 0.88 \quad D\text{-}W = 1.46 \quad SER = 0.52$$

---

[15] This equation can also be used to estimate the hourly earnings component of the variable, earnings, which was used to forecast wage and salary payments in Chapter 5.

TABLE 6-7   Average Hourly Earnings, Private Nonfarm Production Workers: 1983

	ACTUAL LEVELS	YEAR-OVER-YEAR PERCENT CHANGE	FORECAST LEVELS	YEAR-OVER-YEAR PERCENT CHANGE	PERCENT ERROR
Jan.	$7.88	4.79	$7.86	4.48	0.31
Feb.	7.91	5.05	7.86	4.45	0.60
Mar.	7.91	4.91	7.89	4.66	0.24
Apr.	7.95	4.74	7.94	4.56	0.19
May	7.97	4.18	7.99	4.43	−0.25
June	8.00	4.30	7.98	3.98	0.32
July	8.03	4.15	8.03	4.11	0.04
Aug.	7.98	3.10	8.05	3.96	−0.86
Sept.	8.08	4.66	7.96	3.13	1.53
Oct.	8.13	4.63	8.11	4.42	0.22
Nov.	8.13	4.36	8.13	4.41	−0.04
Dec.	8.16	4.35	8.15	4.19	0.16
MEAN ERROR					0.20
MAE					0.10
RMSE					0.37
		QUARTERLY AVERAGES			
I	7.90	4.91	7.87	4.53	0.38
II	7.97	4.41	7.97	4.32	0.09
III	8.03	3.97	8.01	3.73	0.24
IV	8.14	4.45	8.13	4.34	0.11

Equation 6-7 was estimated in year-over-year percentage changes using quarterly data from 1967 through 1980. Panel I in Table 6-8 presents actual and forecast index levels and year-over-year percentage changes for compensation per hour in 1983. The percent errors represent the difference between the actual and the forecast year-over-year percent change in hourly compensation. In this case, forecasts for 1981 and 1982 were also performed. Thus, the forecast index levels were found by applying the forecast percent changes in 1983 to forecast index levels in 1982. In general the forecast was quite accurate, although there was an average over-estimate of nearly 0.6% in the year-to-year growth in hourly compensation.

Productivity in the private business sector equals private business output divided by total hours worked (the number of employees times the average number of hours worked) expressed as an index with 1977 equal to 100. Productivity can be approximated if the forecaster has available a quarterly forecast of real GNP and its components. Private business output can be roughly approximated as equal to real GNP less real government spending.

TABLE 6-8 Compensation per Hour, Productivity, and Unit Labor Costs: 1983

Panel I

	INDEX OF COMPENSATION/HOUR 1977 = 100		YEAR-OVER-YEAR PERCENT CHANGE		PERCENT ERROR
	ACTUAL	FORECAST	ACTUAL	FORECAST	
I	160.8	162.2	6.28	7.18	−0.90
II	162.6	162.7	5.93	5.97	−0.04
III	164.1	165.0	5.12	5.67	−0.54
IV	165.9	167.1	4.80	5.55	−0.75
MEAN ERROR					0.56
MAE					0.56
RMSE					0.64

Panel II

	ACTUAL			ESTIMATED		
	PRODUCTIVITY 1977 = 100	YEAR-OVER-YEAR PERCENT CHANGE	OUTPUT = GNP72−G72 1977 = 100	HOURS WORKED 1977 = 100	OUTPUT/HOUR 1977 = 100	YEAR-OVER-YEAR PERCENT CHANGE
I	101.6	1.60	108.0	104.1	104.5	4.50
II	103.4	3.50	112.0	105.6	106.1	6.24
III	104.0	3.48	114.3	106.6	107.2	6.75
IV	104.7	3.97	116.3	108.5	107.2	6.51

Panel III

	UNIT LABOR COST 1977 = 100		YEAR-OVER-YEAR PERCENT CHANGES		PERCENT ERROR
	ACTUAL	FORECAST	ACTUAL	FORECAST	
I	158.3	155.2	4.63	5.39	−0.76
II	157.2	153.2	2.34	2.39	−0.05
III	157.8	153.8	1.54	2.02	−0.48
IV	158.4	155.8	0.83	1.77	−0.94
MEAN ERROR					−0.56
MAE					0.56
RMSE					0.65

Source: Actual data: Bureau of Labor Statistics, U.S. Department of Labor

Hours worked can be approximated by multiplying payroll employment by the average workweek.[16] When these two constructed series are indexed on a 1977 = 100 basis and the index of estimated output is divided by the index of estimated hours worked (as in Panel II of Table 6-8) the resulting index of output per hour-worked is derived. As can be seen from Table 6-8, the estimated levels and year-over-year percent changes for productivity (output/hour) were somewhat greater than the actuals.

The forecast index of compensation per hour can be divided by the estimated index of output per hour to derive a forecast of the index of unit labor costs in the private business sector. As shown in Panel III of Table 6-8, the resulting forecast index values were somewhat less than the actuals for 1983, but the year-over-year percent changes followed the pattern of the actuals quite well—decelerating as the year progressed—although the growth in Unit Labor Costs was overestimated, on average, by the same amount as hourly compensation.

Estimation of unit nonlabor payments is less straightforward than for unit labor costs. For one thing, there are four distinct components—per unit payments for: depreciation, indirect business taxes, net interest expense, and profits—each of which poses an estimation problem. Moreover, the relative contribution of each of these components to total nonlabor payments shifts from quarter to quarter. A regression of unit nonlabor payments on these components would, therefore, be inappropriate: the shifting relative contributions are in conflict with the assumption of stable regression coefficients. On the other hand, the detailed data that would need to be known to construct accurate quarterly estimates of unit nonlabor payments present a formidable obstacle to such an approach.

Because it is still desirable to derive some insight into the source of inflationary pressures—between labor and nonlabor inputs—an alternative approach can be followed.

The approach is a three-stage, iterative one: (1) a "first stage" estimate of inflation is derived on the basis of unit labor cost *alone* (all concepts are expressed in year-over-year percentage change terms); (2) after estimating the coefficients (weights) for equation 6-5—which relates inflation to the weighted changes in unit labor costs and unit nonlabor payments—the "first stage" estimated values for inflation and the values for the change in unit labor costs, already forecast in Table 6-8, can be substituted, and the values for the change in unit nonlabor payments can then be solved; (3) the resulting forecast changes in unit nonlabor payments and unit labor costs can then be substituted into an estimated version of equation 6-5 to derive a "second stage" estimate of inflation.

---

[16] The estimates in Panel II of Table 6-8 were derived using payroll employment and the average workweek as on Table 5-9.

The relationship between inflation and unit labor costs shown in equation 6-8 was estimated from 1967 through 1980, with the results shown.

$$\%\Delta Y/Y(PGNP) = a + b * \%\Delta Y/Y(ULC) \qquad (6\text{-}8)$$

coefficients	t statistics
a = 4.92	(3.28)
b = 0.22	(4.18)
rho = 0.96	(25.04)

$$\bar{R}^2 = 0.93 \quad \text{D-W} = 1.09 \quad \text{SER} = 0.58$$

The results require careful interpretation. The $\bar{R}^2$ is high, suggesting that a large amount of the variation in inflation is explained by the variation in the change in unit labor costs. However, the value of the constant term is large and significant—suggesting that, if unit labor costs were unchanged, inflation would be just below 5%—and the value of the coefficient on unit labor costs (b), while significant, is low—suggesting that a 10% increase in unit labor costs would add only 2.2% to the inflation rate. Moreover, despite the high value of rho, the Durbin-Watson statistic still suggests serious autocorrelation. All these results point to the absence of an important explanatory variable. This is not an unexpected result: it was assumed in equation 6-5 that unit nonlabor payments is an important explanatory variable for inflation. For this reason, the forecast inflation rates for 1983 which result from equation 6-8 (shown as "Inflation I" in Table 6-9) should only be used in an interim forecast.

The coefficients (weights) of equation 6-5, relating inflation to the changes in *both* unit labor costs and unit nonlabor payments, were estimated from 1967 through 1980.

$$\%\Delta Y/Y(PGNP) = w_1 * \%\Delta Y/Y(ULC) + w_2 * \%\Delta Y/Y(UNLP) \quad (6\text{-}5a)$$

coefficients	t statistics
w_1 = 0.54	(26.51)
w_2 = 0.26	(23.25)
rho = 0.98	(74.77)

$$\bar{R}^2 = 0.99 \quad \text{D-W} = 2.05 \quad \text{SER} = 0.17$$

As expected, most (99%) of the variation in inflation is explained by this relationship. The Durbin-Watson statistic now signals the absence of serious autocorrelation after a Cochrane-Orcutt correction, though the value of rho remains high. In addition, the standard error of the regression is only

TABLE 6-9   Inflation and Input Costs: 1983 (year-over-year percent changes)

		ACTUAL	
	INFLATION[1]	UNIT LABOR COST	UNIT NONLABOR PAYMENTS
I	4.60	4.63	3.15
II	4.07	2.34	5.88
III	4.04	1.54	8.64
IV	4.06	0.83	10.28

		FORECASTS		
	INFLATION 1[2]	ULC[3]	UNLP[4]	INFLATION II[5]
I	4.81	5.39	−6.59	4.43
II	4.00	2.39	6.36	6.28
III	4.04	2.02	6.86	3.98
IV	4.04	1.77	9.17	4.48

		PERCENT ERRORS (ACTUAL-FORECAST)		
I	−0.21	−0.76	9.74	0.17
II	0.07	−0.05	−0.47	−2.21
III	0.00	−0.48	1.79	0.06
IV	0.02	−0.94	1.11	−0.42
MEAN ERROR	−0.03	−0.56	3.04	−0.60
MAE	0.08	0.56	3.28	0.72
RMSE	0.11	0.65	4.99	1.13

(1) Year-over-year percent change in GNP deflator
(2) Estimates derived from equation 6-8
(3) Estimates derived in Table 6-8
(4) Estimates derived from equation 6-5b
(5) Estimates derived from equation 6-5a
Source: Actual data: Bureau of Labor Statistics, U.S. Department of Labor

one-quarter of that for equation 6-8. Finally, the values of the coefficients approximate the relative contribution of labor (.54/.80 = 67%) and nonlabor inputs (.26/.80 = 33%) in production.

Rearranging equation 6-5 to solve for the change in unit nonlabor payments provides

$$\%\Delta Y/Y(UNLP) = 1/w_2 * \%\Delta Y/Y(PGNP) - w_1/w_2 * \%\Delta Y/Y(ULC)$$

When this relationship is estimated directly, using regression analysis as in equation 6-5b (where $b_1 = 1/w_2$ and $b_2 = w_1/w_2$), the results are, as shown below, quite good.

$$\%\Delta Y/Y(UNLP) = b_1 * \%\Delta Y/Y(PGNP) + b_2 * \%\Delta Y/Y(ULC)$$

		coefficients	t statistics	(6-5b)
$1/w_2 =$	3.82	$b_1 =$ 3.46	(23.22)	
$-w_1/w_2 =$	-2.05	$b_2 =$ -1.97	(-30.29)	
		rho = 0.97	(46.06)	

$$\bar{R}^2 = 0.98 \quad D\text{-}W = 2.06 \quad SER = 0.62$$

Finally, the estimated values for unit labor costs and unit nonlabor payments can be substituted in equation 6-5b to re-estimate the year-over-year percentage change in inflation. Indeed, the whole sequence can be performed over again until the analyst is satisfied that the inflation forecast is stable.

Forecast results for 1983 compared to the actual year-over-year percentage changes are presented as Inflation II in Table 6-9. The results show that (1) except for the second quarter, inflationary trends, as measured by the GNP deflator, were closely approximated by equation 6-5b for 1983, and (2) the relative contributions of unit labor costs and unit nonlabor costs are captured. In particular, this iterative approach did capture the tendency for nonlabor payments to increase strongly during 1983. On balance, Inflation I, the method based solely on Unit Labor Costs, provided a more accurate inflation forecast in 1983. This is not always so (in 1981, Inflation II was more accurate; in 1982 both methods provided good results).

The factor input costs approach is in many ways the most satisfactory approach to inflation forecasting. It permits the analyst to focus on the ongoing pressures from input costs on output prices and to draw operational conclusions about their likely future intensity or subsidence.

IV   STAGE OF PROCESSING APPROACH

The stage of processing approach can be described briefly. In the absence of a detailed sectoral price model this approach is more an analytical than a forecasting tool. As discussed in Chapter 3, the Bureau of Labor Statistics publishes detailed data on producer and consumer prices. While it is possible to analyze these data in considerable detail, analysis is only practical if much information on each price category can be brought to bear. This is generally impossible in the absence of detailed, and costly, sectoral models.

It is, however, possible to separate the components that are basically trend-like or cyclical in behavior from those which respond chiefly to forces of specific supply and demand, and which, therefore, supply much of the shock or irregular movement to prices.

The two principal sources of shocks to overall prices in recent years have been the food and energy components. It is often possible to determine in advance if food or energy prices are likely to exert greater-than- or less-than-average pressures based on evidence about recent or prospective grain harvests and actions affecting prices by OPEC or government policies. Thus, a breakdown of producer and consumer prices by product groups, and within product groups by stage of processing, as in Table 6-10 is a useful tool in isolating expected prices pressures.

Specific price assumptions can then be made for food and energy prices, while all other prices can be assumed to move in accordance with the results of one of the other three approaches discussed above. Clearly, application of this approach cannot be described in any but the most general terms. The forecaster's own experience in application is the only useful

TABLE 6-10   Inflation by Stage of Processing

	DECEMBER–DECEMBER PERCENT CHANGES							
	1976	1977	1978	1979	1980	1981	1982	1983
Food Prices								
Crude (PPI)	−4.1%	1.3%	18.3%	10.3%	10.3%	−13.8%	1.7%	8.3%
Intermediate (PPI)	3.9	−1.3	14.3	7.9	16.5	−12.7	0.1	9.4
Finished (PPI)	−2.4	6.7	11.6	7.2	7.8	1.5	2.1	2.4
Consumer (CPI)	1.3	7.7	11.7	10.0	10.0	4.3	3.2	2.6
Energy Prices								
Producer (PPI)	−7.1	30.9	8.9	58.4	27.2	13.8	−0.3	−9.3
Consumer (CPI)	7.9	7.2	8.0	37.4	21.3	11.9	1.3	−1.9
Other Commodity Prices								
Crude (PPI)	10.1	6.2	15.5	26.1	18.6	10.1	−0.8	1.3
Intermediate (PPI)	5.9	6.7	8.3	16.7	12.3	7.2	0.2	1.5
Finished (PPI)	6.9	5.2	8.3	9.4	10.8	7.7	4.8	1.9
Consumer (CPI)	5.6	4.6	7.6	8.8	9.8	5.9	5.7	5.1
Other Services								
Consumer (CPI)	6.7	7.8	9.4	13.7	14.0	13.0	3.3	4.9
Total Consumer Prices	4.8	6.6	9.1	13.4	12.1	8.9	3.9	3.8

Source: Bureau of Labor Statistics, U.S. Department of Labor

method of reducing the forecasting errors resulting from one of the other three approaches described above.

QUESTIONS FOR REVIEW AND RESEARCH

6-1   Many monetarist economists argue that a rise in the overall price level—inflation—need not have followed the increase in oil prices by OPEC in 1973–74. If money supply growth had been kept at a constant low rate (assuming that the trend growth in velocity would have allowed real GNP to grow at its long-run potential rate of around 3%, a noninflationary money growth rate would have been 1% to 2%) the immediate effect would have been a loss of purchasing power according to this view. Subsequently, either: (1) the resulting fall off in demand for oil and oil products would have made the oil price rise difficult to sustain, or (2) if oil demand were price inelastic in the short run, demand for other (less necessary) products would have fallen off due to reduced purchasing power, leading to downward pressures on the prices of the affected products. Instead, the monetarists maintain, money supply growth was allowed to accelerate, thus accommodating the oil price increase and, so, resulting in a generalized price increase.

   (1)   In order to evaluate this argument, contrast: (a) the actual rate of inflation (measured by the CPIU) between 1973 and 1983, with (b) inflation rates estimated, using the regression parameters presented in Table 6-3 and actual money supply (M1) growth, and (c) inflation rates using the regression parameters presented in Table 6-3 and a constant 1 1/2% annual rate of money supply growth.

   (2)   Evaluate the merits of the monetarist case based on your results. In particular, address the question of whether price shocks for particular commodities can lead to generalized inflation under a constant money growth policy.

   (3)   Discuss some of the effects on other economic activity measures that might have resulted from such a policy.

6-2   Expectations of future inflation may influence and affect a wide range of economic activities. Briefly discuss the likely influences and effects of inflation expectations on the economic actions of:

   (a)   Consumers
   (b)   Producers/Retailers
   (c)   Employees
   (d)   Employers
   (e)   Investors
   (f)   Borrowers
   (g)   Lenders

   Evaluate equation 6-4, which attempts to capture the net effect of all these inflation expectations, in light of the differing roles inflation expectations play for the economic agents listed above.

6-3   In the short run, labor costs were stated to have the primary input cost effect on output prices. Analyze this assertion in light of microeconomic theory and empirical data for the nonfarm business sector on hourly earnings, unit labor costs, productivity, and unit nonlabor payments for the years since 1970 (annual data are presented in the statistical tables of the *Economic Report of the President*).

(a) Plot the percentage changes in hourly earnings, unit labor costs, and output prices. Does the volatility in labor costs tend to explain the volatility in output prices?

(b) Can you suggest other variables which might explain more of the movement in prices? Do these variables present forecast problems?

6-4 Using the results found in the text for inflation in 1983 based on (a) the monetary approach, (b) the expectations/momentum approach, and (c) the factor input cost approach, suggest which were the main sources of inflation in 1983. Extend this analysis for the most recent twelve-month period for which data are available. (Check the most recent issue of the *Survey of Current Business*.)

6-5 Based on an analysis of consumer and producer price index data by stage of processing, determine the main sources of inflationary pressure during the past year. Evaluate the extent to which these pressures are: microeconomic in nature—reflecting particular supply/demand pressures—or macroeconomic—reflecting the state of overall economic activity.

7

INDICATOR
FORECASTING
*Inventories, housing,
and production*

Chapter 5 was concerned with that portion of economic activity focused on consumer spending by households. The analysis commenced with employment, proceeded with the translation of employment into spending power in the form of personal income, and concluded with the exercise of this spending power represented by retail sales to consumers. Thus, to a great extent, Chapter 5 dealt with major monthly indicators of *demand*.

This chapter, in contrast, focuses on monthly measures of *supply*—the adjustment of the stock of business inventories and industrial production. In addition, housing start activity—which combines elements of supply and demand—are examined. Inventory adjustment, because it aids the distribution and production of final goods, and housing starts, because of the long-term nature of the asset, may also be viewed as investment-type activities in contrast to the consumption-oriented activities in Chapter 5. Moreover, production not only responds to these other consumer- and investment-type demands, but is also a source of the demand for labor services which evoke changes in employment.

This last point is a key one to the theme that has run through Part II: the individual indicators of economic activity are related. Indeed, when all these measures are viewed as interrelated economic activities it can be readily recognized that when the chain ends in a forecast of industrial production, it also begins again as an impetus to employment, income, and spending. In other words, the forecasts are linked, should be consistent, and must be *iterated* to insure consistency.

BUSINESS INVENTORIES

Business investment in stock (inventories) is one of the most volatile of economic activities. There are two main reasons for this. First, inventories are held to meet future sales, usually in excess of expected sales—in order to have some stock to display and/or to provide a buffer against sudden surges in demand. Thus, if sales change there is likely to be an even larger response in the form of a change in inventory investment. Second, in all but the smallest businesses there is likely to be some lag between a change in sales and the desired response in inventory investment. Indeed, during this lag period an unintended change in inventories may occur which requires an even greater corrective action when the sales change is recognized.

For instance, suppose a business has monthly sales totaling $100,000 and desires an inventory/sales ratio of 1.5. In other words, a stock of goods on hand worth $150,000 is desired to meet expected sales each month. If sales should suddenly fall to $95,000 (down 5%) in one month, the new desired level of inventories would be $142,500 (1.5 × $95,000). It is likely, however, that, as the falloff in sales was unexpected, inventory investment at the former rate would have occurred and the unsold goods (worth $5,000) would also have piled up. Thus, actual inventories worth $155,000 would be on hand, resulting in an inventory/sales ratio of 1.63 ($155,000/$95,000). If

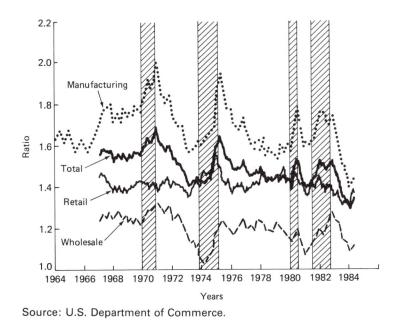

Source: U.S. Department of Commerce.

FIGURE 7-1   Inventory/sales ratios (total, manufacturing, wholesale, and retail trade)

no further decline in sales takes place, inventories must be reduced by $12,500 (to reduce stocks from the actual level of $155,000 to the new desired level of $142,500). Clearly, if a further falloff in sales occurs, inventory investment must be cut even more. A reverse process applies if sales increase unexpectedly: inventories will prove too low, the inventory/sales ratio will fall below the desired level, and inventory investment will have to increase.[1]

The volatility in inventory investment makes forecasting the level of business inventories especially difficult. This task is made harder by the fact that inventory/sales ratios have shown a secular decline—interrupted by cyclical increases—since the mid 1960s (see Figure 7-1) reflecting technological and managerial improvements in the process of inventory control. Recognizing these difficulties, expectations about the accuracy of inventory forecasting are limited: the basic trend movements in inventories will, it is hoped, be captured, but large forecast errors are to be expected, and the errors are likely to be even larger near cyclical turning points. Nevertheless, a forecast of inventory levels should add to the forecasters' understanding of potential economic activity as a whole, and of the forces likely to shape it.

---

[1] One result of the magnified effects of a change of sales on the inventory/sales ratio is the need for large adjustments to production. For instance, in the case cited, the need to reduce the value of inventories by $12,500 would likely be achieved through a cut in production equal to this amount. This relationship is discussed below in the section on industrial production.

Efforts to determine theoretical relationships in order to explain inventory investment have been made by Lovell, Mack, and Blinder[2] among others. These studies have examined a wide range of influences including: the costs of financing inventories, optimal costs (the cost of excess stocks contrasted with the cost of lost sales due to inadequate inventories), and the state of capacity utilization and its implications for future supply flows. These analyses tend to be very complex and require a great deal of data. One basic component of all inventory theories, however, is the relationship to sales.

The approach followed here is to forecast business inventories based primarily on sales. While this is necessarily a simple approach, it maintains the interrelated scheme followed in Chapters, 5 and 6. Business inventories include stocks held by manufacturers, wholesalers, and retailers. These different businesses hold different types of inventories (for instance, manufacturers hold stocks of raw materials, goods in process, and finished goods, while retailers hold only finished goods), in varying relation to sales, and are subject to different-length lags between sales and changes in inventory investment. As a result, it is necessary to forecast inventories for each of these sectors and then to sum up the total level of business inventories.[3]

The approach discussed here involves three-steps. First, sales of manufacturers and wholesalers will be forecast using the already-forecast levels of retail sales. Second, inventory/sales ratios for each sector will be derived based on past trends. Finally, the forecast sales level will be multiplied by the forecast inventory/sales ratio. The product represents a basic forecast of inventory levels. Judgment as to the likely cyclical impacts on inventories, above and beyond those captured, must then be used to arrive at a final forecast.

Retail sales represent a basic part of the final demand for goods. To a considerable extent, manufacturers' and wholesalers' sales reflect an earlier response to this demand. That is, goods sold at retail in one month can be assumed to have been sold by a manufacturer either directly to the retailer or first to a wholesaler and then to the retailer in the current or some earlier month. When viewed as an ongoing process, retail sales can thus be viewed as a determining factor of the level of manufacturers', and of wholesalers' sales (or shipments).

Manufacturers' shipments (SM) are forecast as a function of total retail sales (RST) in the prior month and the unemployment rate (RU) in the

---

[2] Michael A. Lovell, "Manufacturers' Inventories, Sales Expectations, and the Acceleration Principle," *Econometrica* (July 1961), pp. 293–314; Ruth P. Mack, *Information, Expectations, and Inventory Fluctuation: A Study of Materials Stock on Hand and on Order* (New York: Columbia Univ. Press for the National Bureau of Economic Research, 1967); Alan S. Blinder, "Retail Inventory Behavior and Business Fluctuations," *Brookings Papers on Economic Activity, 1981,* No. 2, 443–505.

[3] Total nonfarm business inventories in the National Product and Income Accounts also include stocks held by non-merchant wholesalers, not covered in the measures considered here. These stocks are small (less than 4% of total nonfarm inventories in 1983).

current month, used as a proxy for cyclical effects. This function was estimated using regression analysis from January 1970 through December 1980.
The results for equation 7-1 are shown below.

$$SM_t = a + b_1 \times RST_{t-1} + b_2 \times RU_t \tag{7-1}$$

$$
\begin{array}{ll}
coefficients & t\ statistics \\
a = -11.027 & (-4.99) \\
b_1 = 2.159 & (78.14) \\
b_2 = -0.763 & (-2.14) \\
rho = 0.616 & (8.76)
\end{array}
$$

$$\bar{R}^2 = 0.997 \quad D\text{-}W = 2.42 \quad SER = 1.829$$

The results conform to expectations: manufacturers' shipments are positively related to lagged retail sales and the coefficient (b_1) suggests that there
are roughly $2.16 of shipments by manufacturers for every $1 worth of retail
sales in the prior month; the negative coefficient for the unemployment rate
(b_2) suggests, as expected, that shipments are likely to decline when economic activity weakens (as reflected in an increase in the unemployment
rate). It should also be noted that equation 7-1 maintains the basic concept of
the structural approach: the independent variables are previously-forecast
measures. Thus, the forecast of manufacturers' shipments is consistent with
forecasts made in Chapter 5.

Wholesalers' shipments prove more difficult to forecast. Attempts at
estimating an equation for wholesalers' shipments, based on measures already forecast, failed. In the end, a two-step approach was followed. Since
forecasts of manufacturers' shipments and retail sales are available, total
sales by manufacturers, wholesalers, and retailers (SM&W&R) were forecast using equation 7-2, in which personal income (PI) and the unemployment rate (RU) in the same month and retail sales in the prior month
(RST_{t-1}) are independent variables. Wholesalers' shipments can then be
estimated as in equation 7-2a where the estimated values for manufacturers'
shipments and retail sales are subtracted from the estimated levels for total
sales. Regression results for January 1970 through December 1980 are shown
below.

$$SM\&W\&R_t = a + b_1 * PI_t + b_2 * RU_t + b_3 * RST_{t-1} \tag{7-2}$$

$$
\begin{array}{ll}
coefficients & t\ statistics \\
a = -9.846 & (-1.56) \\
b_1 = 0.154 & (10.20) \\
b_2 = -2.010 & (-2.40) \\
b_3 = 0.225 & (0.55) \\
rho = 0.878 & (20.04)
\end{array}
$$

$$\bar{R}^2 = 0.999 \quad D\text{-}W = 2.386 \quad SER = 2.213$$

$$SW_e = SM\&W\&R_e - SM_e - RST_e \qquad (7\text{-}2a)$$

The results are as expected except for the low, insignificant coefficient for lagged retail sales.

Table 7-1 presents data on the actual levels, forecast levels, and errors for total, manufacturers', wholesalers', and retail sales for 1983. It can be seen that the errors for manufacturers' and wholesalers' shipments are much larger than those for retail sales, but that the errors diminish in the last five months of 1983. This may be due to the volatility of sales expectations in early 1983: while it was generally recognized that consumer demand was rising, the robustness of the pick-up—in consumer demand and in the economy at large—was not expected, and recognized quite late. A possible source of improvement—following Mack's analysis—might be to relate

TABLE 7-1   Sales: Total, Manufacturers, Wholesalers, and Retailers: 1983 (billions of dollars)

	TOTAL SALES AND SHIPMENTS (1)	MANUFACTURERS' SHIPMENTS (2)	WHOLESALERS' SHIPMENTS (3)	RETAIL SALES (4)
	ACTUAL LEVELS			
Jan.	345.890	159.020	94.344	92.526
Feb.	342.742	158.184	92.347	92.211
Mar.	348.227	161.809	92.614	93.804
Apr.	351.012	162.997	92.890	95.125
May	360.488	166.603	96.646	97.239
June	368.971	171.756	98.577	98.638
July	370.181	171.408	99.941	98.832
Aug.	373.283	174.112	100.894	98.277
Sept.	379.229	177.521	102.171	99.537
Oct.	382.457	177.324	104.210	100.923
Nov.	386.564	180.875	103.793	101.896
Dec.	395.682	186.352	106.892	102.438
	FORECAST LEVELS			
Jan.	346.843	163.173	91.438	92.232
Feb.	351.141	168.273	90.548	92.320
Mar.	353.521	166.258	94.136	93.127
Apr.	356.656	172.383	90.135	94.138
May	364.123	173.893	93.822	96.408
June	369.320	178.964	92.732	97.623
July	377.932	182.660	96.195	99.077
Aug.	377.204	180.766	97.414	99.024
Sept.	382.995	181.178	102.746	99.071
Oct.	390.245	186.897	102.841	100.507
Nov.	392.410	188.246	102.596	101.567
Dec.	396.824	190.657	103.504	102.663

TABLE 7-1   Continued

	TOTAL SALES AND SHIPMENTS (1)	MANUFACTURERS' SHIPMENTS (2)	WHOLESALERS' SHIPMENTS (3)	RETAIL SALES (4)
		ERRORS (5)		
Jan.	−0.953	−4.153	2.906	0.294
Feb.	−8.399	−10.089	1.799	−0.109
Mar.	−5.294	−4.449	−1.522	0.677
Apr.	−5.644	−9.386	2.755	0.987
May	−3.635	−7.290	2.824	0.831
June	−0.349	−7.208	5.845	1.015
July	−7.751	−11.252	3.746	−0.245
Aug.	−3.921	−6.654	3.480	−0.747
Sept.	−3.766	−3.657	−0.575	0.466
Oct.	−7.795	−9.573	1.369	0.416
Nov.	−5.846	−7.371	1.196	0.329
Dec.	−1.142	−4.305	3.388	−0.255
MEAN ERROR	−4.541	−7.116	2.268	0.307
MAPE	1.24%	4.19%	2.66%	0.54%
RMSE	5.248	7.532	2.958	0.222

(1) Forecast levels derived from equation 7-2
(2) Forecast levels derived from equation 7-1
(3) Forecast levels derived from equation 7-2a
(4) Forecast levels derived from equation 5-16
(5) Errors equal actual levels minus forecast levels
Source: Actual data from Bureau of the Census, U.S. Department of Commerce.

shipments to a distributed lag (three to six months) of retail sales representing expected sales.

Inventory/Sales (I/S) ratios can be forecast using a combination of time series and regression methods. The first step is to construct twelve-month moving averages of actual I/S ratios as in equation 7-3.

$$ISAVG = MA(I/S) = \frac{1}{12} \times \sum_{t=1}^{12} (I/S)_t \qquad (7\text{-}3)$$

The resulting moving average captures the gradual change in the I/S ratios over time and permits the estimation of first approximations for the forecast period. It was found that these moving average approximations could then be improved upon by fitting a regression of the actual I/S ratio to its moving average as in equation 7-4.

$$I/S = a + b \times ISAVG \qquad (7\text{-}4)$$

TABLE 7-2   Regression Statistics: Inventory/Sales Ratios

	COEFFICIENTS					
	CONSTANT	ISAVG	rho	$\bar{R}^2$	D-W	SER
Manufacturing	0.0742	0.9542	0.9030	0.937	1.920	0.029
	(0.2)	(4.5)	(21.1)			
Wholesale	0.0077	0.9880	0.9000	0.935	2.117	0.019
	(0.03)	(4.7)	(20.7)			
Retail	−0.0335	1.0226	0.8133	0.760	1.686	0.017
	(−0.1)	(3.8)	(15.0)			

Numbers in parenthesis are t statistics

The results for these regressions are shown in Table 7-2. Note that the constants are all small and insignificant.

Table 7-3 presents the resulting forecasts of the I/S ratios for manufacturers, wholesalers, and retailers in 1983. The forecast I/S ratios all slightly overstate the actual I/S ratios (see the mean errors). The forecasts of the I/S ratios resulted in smaller errors (compare the mean absolute percent errors for the forecasts in Table 7-3 with those in Table 7-1) than for sales and shipments. Once again, the results for the retail I/S ratio have the smallest errors.

Table 7-4 (shown on page 228) presents actual and forecast levels, and errors for total, manufacturing, wholesale, and retail inventories. The errors are large, particularly for manufacturers. This reflects a compounding of the errors in the shipments forecast and those in the forecast of the I/S ratio. As noted above, the shipments forecast might be improved by using a distributed lag on retail sales. Since the greater part of the error for forecast inventory levels stems from the errors in the forecast of manufacturers' and wholesalers' shipments, a considerable reduction in the errors in the inventories levels might be expected from this change.

In the end, inventory forecasts are among the most judgmental of indicator forecasts. A forecast approach such as described above, however, provides a baseline from which adjustments can be made.

HOUSING STARTS

Residential construction, like business investment in inventories, is a highly cyclical activity. Housing starts, the most widely-watched monthly indicator of this activity,[4] provide a good signal of near-term trends for the sector, and

---

[4] Of three monthly measures, starts are intermediate between permit authorizations and sales.

TABLE 7-3 Inventory/Sales Ratios: Manufacturers, Wholesalers, and Retailers: 1983

	MANUFACTURERS	WHOLESALERS	RETAIL
	ACTUAL LEVELS		
Jan.	1.647	1.219	1.354
Feb.	1.650	1.239	1.384
Mar.	1.593	1.237	1.354
Apr.	1.581	1.237	1.342
May	1.550	1.175	1.329
June	1.500	1.148	1.316
July	1.503	1.142	1.311
Aug.	1.488	1.132	1.333
Sept.	1.460	1.132	1.328
Oct.	1.464	1.121	1.316
Nov.	1.437	1.127	1.321
Dec.	1.397	1.105	1.326
	FORECAST LEVELS (1)		
Jan.	1.708	1.258	1.365
Feb.	1.641	1.227	1.355
Mar.	1.646	1.243	1.385
Apr.	1.588	1.243	1.355
May	1.575	1.238	1.329
June	1.546	1.181	1.335
July	1.494	1.149	1.311
Aug.	1.497	1.142	1.314
Sept.	1.479	1.131	1.330
Oct.	1.451	1.129	1.326
Nov.	1.450	1.115	1.314
Dec.	1.423	1.122	1.322
MEAN ERROR	−0.019	−0.014	−0.002
MAPE	1.56%	1.52%	0.84%
RMSE	0.030	0.025	0.016

(1) Forecast from equation 7-4

Source: Actual data: Bureau of the Census, U.S. Department of Commerce

are used in constructing the quarterly GNP estimate. The highly cyclical nature of housing starts (see Figure 7-2), however, makes them, like inventory levels, difficult to forecast. However, insights into the likely direction and intensity of housing start activity can be gained from an approach that forecasts single-family and multi-family starts separately based on the main forces affecting each category.

Among the many differences between single-family and multi-family home building, perhaps the most significant is the source of demand for the structure. Single-family units are usually intended for sale to owner occu-

TABLE 7-4 Inventories: Total, Manufacturers, Wholesalers, and Retailers: 1983 (billions of dollars)

	TOTAL	MANUFACTURERS	WHOLESALERS	RETAILERS
		ACTUAL LEVELS		
Jan.	502.209	261.901	115.030	125.278
Feb.	503.043	261.042	114.425	127.576
Mar.	499.370	257.803	114.569	126.998
Apr.	500.263	257.748	114.902	127.613
May	501.035	258.281	113.557	129.197
June	500.615	257.661	113.172	129.782
July	501.379	257.699	114.124	129.556
Aug.	504.284	259.074	114.227	130.983
Sept.	506.984	259.168	115.674	132.142
Oct.	509.171	259.569	116.825	132.777
Nov.	511.453	259.873	116.958	134.622
Dec.	514.336	260.426	118.067	135.843
		FORECAST LEVELS		
Jan.	519.696	278.770	115.029	125.897
Feb.	512.409	276.213	111.102	125.094
Mar.	519.695	273.703	117.011	128.981
Apr.	513.324	273.729	112.038	127.557
May	518.097	273.819	116.152	128.126
June	516.498	276.655	109.516	130.327
July	513.392	272.974	110.528	129.890
Aug.	511.921	270.556	111.247	130.118
Sept.	515.915	267.945	116.206	131.764
Oct.	520.618	271.239	116.107	133.272
Nov.	520.863	273.009	114.395	133.459
Dec.	523.071	271.220	116.131	135.720
		ERRORS		
Jan.	−17.487	−16.869	0.001	−0.619
Feb.	−9.366	−15.171	3.323	2.482
Mar.	−20.325	−15.900	−2.442	−1.983
Apr.	−13.061	−15.981	2.864	0.056
May	−17.062	−15.538	−2.595	1.071
June	−15.883	−18.994	3.656	−0.545
July	−12.013	−15.275	3.596	−0.334
Aug.	−7.637	−11.482	2.980	0.866
Sept.	−8.931	−8.777	−0.532	0.378
Oct.	−11.447	−11.670	0.718	−0.495
Nov.	−9.410	−13.136	2.563	1.163
Dec.	−8.735	−10.794	1.936	0.123
MEAN ERROR	−12.613	−14.132	1.339	0.180
MAPE	2.51%	5.45%	1.98%	0.65%
RMSE	13.225	14.412	2.553	1.101

Errors equal actual levels minus forecast levels

Source: Actual data from Bureau of the Census, U.S. Department of Commerce

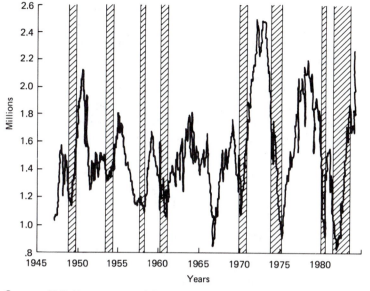

Source: U.S. Department of Commerce.

FIGURE 7-2   Housing starts (seasonally adjusted annual rates)

pants. Thus, the demand for single-family housing is like that for other consumer durables, with two special features: (1) the purchase price is far greater, and (2) because of high cost it is usually financed by borrowing (mortgaging) over a much longer term than for other durable goods. Multi-family dwellings, on the other hand, are usually intended for rental occupation. As such, the demand for multi-family housing is more similar to that for other investment goods: based on the likely stream of income (rents) the units will produce.

Because of the different motives that prompt single-family and multi-family housing starts, it can be concluded that either different forces or similar forces but with varying importance underlie each activity. Two basic forces affecting the demand for single-family starts are: (1) credit availability, and (2) affordability. The availability of credit for home purchase is a key variable affecting single-family starts and, because there are cyclical influences on credit availability, this accounts for much of the cyclical nature of housing start activity. As mentioned above, the high cost of a new home purchase makes the availability of credit essential. In "normal" times, contractors and home buyers compete with other consumer borrowers, businesses, and government borrowers for credit. In the mature stage of an expansion, business borrowers (who can, or believe they can, offset high financing costs by their expected returns), government units, and, to a lesser extent, consumers of other durable goods (whose loans are usually for a smaller amount over a shorter term) tend to "squeeze" mortgage borrowers out of the credit markets. Thus, reduced mortgage availability typically leads to a falloff in housing starts and eventually a decline in overall economic activity: recession. After a recession has been underway for some months, credit conditions ease—there is a falloff in business borrowing for investment in inventories and fixed capital, and durable consumption usually declines. The lessened demand for credit from these two sources eases the squeeze on mortgage lending and, thus, a pick-up in housing starts can begin. Thus, housing start activity often leads the rest of the economy at both cyclical downturns and upturns. The level of mortgage interest rates is one variable which can be used to capture the impact of credit availability on housing start activity.[5] An inverse relationship would be expected: when mortgage rates rise, housing starts decline, and vice versa.

Affordability is likely to be nearly as great a concern to single-family home buyers as credit availability. Thus, some measure of income should also be included as a factor affecting demand. The expectation here is that as income rises affordability also increases, and housing starts will rise.

The demand for multi-family starts is also likely to be affected in a similar manner by credit availability; that is, rising mortgage rates are likely to depress starts. The response, however, is unlikely to be as strong as in the case of single-family starts. For one thing, developers of multi-family housing units often have a greater variety of funding sources available to them.[6] Affordability, as measured by income, is less likely to be a major influence on multi-family starts. Since these units are mainly intended as investments, some measure of economic conditions can be used to reflect the likely climate for achieving the income stream which the units are intended to earn. The unemployment rate is a likely prospect for such a variable. When the unemployment rate is high, it may be inferred that economic conditions are likely to be weak and thus multi-family starts will decline. Conversely, a lower unemployment rate suggests a stronger economy and increased multi-family starts.

Total housing starts can be forecast using a three step model. First, single-family starts (HUSTS1) are forecast, as in equation 7-5, on the basis of the effective mortgage interest rates for new homes (RMORT) and the level of personal income (PI). Second, multi-family starts (HUSTS2&) are

[5] A more complete approach might be to use the spread (difference in hundredths of a percentage point) between effective mortgage lending rates and some short-term money market instruments—such as CD or Treasury bill rates which banks and thrift institutions, the main sources of mortgage lending, use to fund new home loans. Such an approach requires a more detailed analysis of credit conditions and the sources of funds to mortgage lending institutions. The benefits from such a detailed analysis are unlikely to warrant the cost for a general purpose economic forecast. However, if the forecast of housing starts is vital—for instance, one prepared for a savings bank or a homebuilder—this more detailed approach should be followed.

[6] Notably insurance companies, but also, in the case of large developers, direct access to the bond market.

forecast, as in equation 7-6, on the basis of the effective mortgage interest rates (RMORT) and the unemployment rate (RU). Finally, equation 7-7, which is merely an identity, adds the forecast levels for single-family and multi-family starts to arrive at an estimate of the level of total housing starts (HUSTS).

$$HUSTS1 = a_1 + b_1 \times RMORT + c_1 \times PI \qquad (7-5)$$

$$HUSTS2\& = a_2 + b_2 \times RMORT + d_2 \times RU \qquad (7-6)$$

$$HUSTS = HUSTS1 + HUSTS2\& \qquad (7-7)$$

The regression results for equation 7-5 (estimated from January 1972 through December 1981) are shown below.

$$
\begin{aligned}
a_1 &= 1.99 & (10.12) \\
b_1 &= -0.17 & (-4.26) \\
c_1 &= 0.00052 & (2.52) \\
rho &= 0.82 & (14.18)
\end{aligned}
$$

$$\overline{R}^2 = 0.88 \quad D\text{-}W = 2.32 \quad SER = 0.093$$

The regression results for equation 7-6 (estimated over the same period) are also shown below.

$$
\begin{aligned}
a_2 &= 1.63 & (5.20) \\
b_2 &= -0.076 & (-2.83) \\
d_2 &= -0.039 & (-1.20) \\
rho &= 0.94 & (28.76)
\end{aligned}
$$

$$\overline{R}^2 = 0.91 \quad D\text{-}W = 2.76 \quad SER = 0.074$$

For single-family starts (expressed in million units at an annual rate), the results are quite good. The coefficient on the mortgage rate is negative, as expected, and significant; the coefficient suggests that for every one percentage point rise in the mortgage rate, single-family starts decline by 170,000 units at an annual rate. The coefficient on personal income is positive, as expected, and also significant: for each $1 billion increase in personal income, single-family housing starts rise at an annual rate of 520. (When the unemployment rate was included in the equation for single family starts, it was found to have a near-zero, insignificant coefficient.)

The results for multi-family starts are not quite so good. The coefficient on the mortgage rate is negative and smaller than for single-family starts as expected, suggesting a one percentage point increase in the mortgage rate will result in an annual decline in multi-family starts of 76,000. The coefficient on the unemployment rate also has the expected negative sign, suggesting that starts decline at an annual rate of 39,000 for every one percentage point increase in the unemployment rate. However, the t statistic indicates the coefficient is not significant at the 95% confidence level, but rather (by interpolation) at the 88% level. Equation 7-6 was, however, the best of many versions tried and can be used—with caution—for forecast purposes.

Table 7-5 presents actual and forecast levels of total, single-family, and

TABLE 7-5   Housing Starts: Total, Single-, and Multi-Family in 1983 (millions of units, seasonally adjusted annual rates)

	TOTAL	SINGLE-FAMILY	MULTI-FAMILY
		ACTUAL LEVELS	
Jan	1.64	1.09	0.55
Feb	1.71	1.07	0.64
Mar	1.59	1.02	0.58
Apr	1.55	1.03	0.52
May	1.78	1.15	0.63
June	1.74	1.12	0.62
July	1.79	1.05	0.75
Aug	1.87	1.12	0.75
Sept	1.68	1.04	0.64
Oct	1.67	1.02	0.66
Nov	1.73	1.07	0.66
Dec	1.69	1.02	0.67
Annual Average	1.70	1.07	0.64
		FORECAST LEVELS	
Jan	1.38	0.92	0.45
Feb	1.69	1.14	0.55
Mar	1.64	1.04	0.60
Apr	1.84	1.21	0.63
May	1.54	1.04	0.49
June	1.86	1.22	0.64
July	1.75	1.14	0.61
Aug	1.84	1.11	0.73
Sept	1.86	1.14	0.72
Oct	1.81	1.15	0.66
Nov	1.72	1.07	0.65
Dec	1.76	1.12	0.64
Annual Average	1.72	1.11	0.61
MEAN ERROR	−0.02	−0.04	0.02
MAPE	7.25%	8.15%	10.33%
RMSE	0.16	0.08	0.08

Source: Actual data from Bureau of the Census, U.S. Department of Commerce

multi-family housing starts in 1983. The estimates for single-family starts are, on the whole, somewhat closer than for multi-family starts (as indicated by the values for the mean absolute percent errors, which normalize the errors and thus make them comparable). On an annual average basis the level of single-family starts is slightly over-estimated, while multi-family starts are slightly under-estimated. Moreover, since some of the errors for single-family and multi-family starts are offsetting, the forecast levels of housing starts provide close estimates of the actual levels (with a lower MAPE than for either of the components).

The forecast results confirm that the simple equations discussed above provide useful insights into housing start activity for a twelve-month span, and that the three variables are indeed important forces on housing start demand. As with all measures examined, frequent monitoring and the use of judgment can improve the usefulness of this simple forecast approach.

INDUSTRIAL PRODUCTION

The industrial production index is a measure of the output of the nation's factories, utilities, and mines. While industrial production comprises only a portion of total economic activity,[7] it can be said to represent the hard core of the U.S. economy. Industrial production represents the supply of newly made goods in the economy. Much nonindustrial activity is associated with the industrial sector. For instance, banking, law, and advertising provide support to industrial firms, while the trade sector sells the output of the industrial sector. Consequently, the industrial production index is one of the most representative coincident indicators of overall economic activity.

Production is a supply concept; it responds to demand. In the theoretical condition known as steady-state equilibrium, production will equal demand, reflected by sales. In fact, however, the economy is almost never in steady-state equilibrium. In disequilibrium, changes in inventories account for the difference between sales and production. If sales increase more than businesses expect, inventories will be drawn down to meet the unexpected rise in demand. Thus, the inventory/sales ratio will decline and production will have to be increased to restore the ratio to its desired level. Conversely, if sales increase less than businesses expect or decline unexpectedly, the excess supply will go into inventories, raising the inventory/sales ratio. In this case, production will have to be cut.

Thus, industrial production is expected to be: (1) directly related to sales—as sales rise production will be increased, as sales decline production

---

[7] Importantly, industrial production does not include the output of the service sector. In 1983, services accounted for 47.2% of real GNP and 73.4% of nonagricultural payroll employment.

will be cut; and (2) inversely related to the inventory/sales ratio—when the inventory/sales ratio increases production will be cut, when the inventory/sales ratio declines production will increase. In addition, to capture the cyclical response more fully, an inverse relationship with the unemployment rate can be posited.

Industrial production can be disaggregated into a number of components, but three suggest themselves strongly and will be used in this approach. These three components are: (1) manufacturing production, (2) output of gas and electric utilities, and (3) mining output. These three components, when multiplied by their weights,[8] add to the industrial production index as in equation 7-8.

$$IPI = w_1 \times IPIM + w_2 \times IPIU + w_3 \times IPIMI \qquad (7\text{-}8)$$
$$w_1 = .8795$$
$$w_2 = .0569$$
$$w_3 = .0636$$

The total industrial production index (IPI) equals the weighted sum of the index for manufacturing (IPIM), the index for utilities (IPIU), and the index for mining (IPIMI). All indexes are expressed as 1967 = 100.0

The production index for manufacturing can be approximated most closely using the assumptions outlined above. Equation 7-9 presents this specification with regression coefficients estimated for 1972–82.

$$IPIM = a_1 + b_1 \times SM + c_1 \times ISM + d_1 \times RU \qquad (7\text{-}9)$$

$$
\begin{aligned}
a_1 &= 139.7 & (9.76) \\
b_1 &= 0.29 & (4.48) \\
c_1 &= -10.89 & (-1.88) \\
d_1 &= -2.94 & (-5.82) \\
rho &= 0.970 & (37.01)
\end{aligned}
$$

$$\overline{R}^2 = .99 \quad D\text{-}W = 1.90 \quad SER = 1.094$$

The high $\overline{R}^2$ suggests that the equation accounts for most of the variation in the industrial production index for manufacturing and all the coefficients have the expected sign and are significant. The coefficient on sales suggests a 0.3 percentage point increase in industrial production for each $1 billion increase in manufacturers' shipments. The coefficient on the inventory/sales ratio suggests that the production index would decline 10.9 percentage points if the I/S ratio is increased a full point. (Such a large change is un-

[8] For a discussion of the weighting of the Index, see "Revision of Industrial Production Index," *Federal Reserve Bulletin* (Aug. 1979).

likely; from 1967 through 1983, the manufacturing I/S ratio ranged from a low of 1.397 to a high of 2.013.) Finally, the coefficient on the unemployment rate suggests that the production index declines 2.9 percentage points for each one percentage point rise in the unemployment rate.

The production index for utilities poses a special problem because utility output cannot be stored as inventory. Thus, it can be inferred that utility production is merely a response to current demand. In this case, demand will be proxied by the noninstitutional population aged 16 and over. In addition, to capture cyclical effects on demand for utility output, the unemployment rate will be used as a cyclical proxy. Equation 7-10 presents this specification. Estimated regression coefficients for 1972–82 are also shown below.

$$IPIU = a_2 + b_2 \times POP + c_2 \times RU \qquad (7\text{-}10)$$

$$
\begin{aligned}
a_2 &= -109.6 \quad (-8.52) \\
b_2 &= 1.86 \quad (20.20) \\
c_2 &= -1.89 \quad (-3.50) \\
rho &= 0.68 \quad (10.31)
\end{aligned}
$$

$$\overline{R}^2 = .97 \quad \text{D-W} = 2.09 \quad \text{SER} = 2.63$$

Once again, a great deal of the variation in production is explained by the equation as reflected in the high $\overline{R}^2$ value. The coefficients have the expected signs and are significant. The coefficient on population suggests an increase of nearly 1.9 percentage points in production for every 1 million increase in population. The coefficient on the unemployment rate suggests that production will decline by 1.9 percentage points for every percentage point rise in the unemployment rate. The fact that this coefficient is less than that found for manufacturing production reflects the less cyclical nature of utility production compared to manufacturing production. In downturns, business demand for gas and electricity is likely to be reduced, but only a very severe downturn would lead to a noticeable cut in household demand for these services.

The production index for mining poses different forecasting problems. Mining is an earlier stage in the production process than those examined so far. Mining output is seldom sold as finished product, but rather as raw material input to other industries. For this reason the demand for mining can be viewed as derived from manufacturing demand. If this hypothesis is correct, then manufacturing production in some earlier period can be used as a proxy for the demand side of an equation in which the production index for mining is the supply side. Another important factor in accounting for the trend in mining production in recent years has been the role played by strikes. This effect is captured by use of a dummy variable for strikes.[9]

The production index for mining (IPIMI) can, thus, be estimated using equation 7-11, in which a one-month lag of the production index for manufacturing ($IPIM_{t-1}$) and a dummy variable for strikes (STRIKEDMY) are the independent variables. The estimated regression coefficients are shown below.

$$IPIMI_t = a_3 + b_3 \times IPIM_{t-1} + f_3 \times STRIKEDMY_t \qquad (7\text{-}11)$$

$$
\begin{aligned}
a_3 &= 91.48 & (6.30) \\
b_3 &= 0.22 & (2.05) \\
f_3 &= -2.48 & (-3.30) \\
rho &= 0.96 & (45.17)
\end{aligned}
$$

$$\overline{R}^2 = .96 \quad \text{D-W} = 1.39 \quad \text{SER} = 2.08$$

The amount of explained variation, measured by the $\overline{R}^2$, is nearly as high as for the equations for manufacturing and utility production. The coefficient on the lagged manufacturing production index has the expected positive sign and is significant. The coefficient suggests that a 1 percentage point increase in the prior month's manufacturing index would produce a 0.2 percentage point rise in the index for mining. The coefficient on the strike dummy also has the expected negative sign, is significant, and suggests that the production index for mining would show an average decline of 2.5 percentage points in a strike month. In fact, for the seven identified strike months from 1972 through 1980, mining production declined by 2.71 percentage points.

Table 7-6 presents actual and forecast index levels for 1983 for the total, manufacturing, utility, and mining industrial production indexes. The forecast levels for the total industrial production index were found by substituting the forecast levels for the three component indexes into equation 7-8.

The forecast of manufacturing production yields quite good results. The mean absolute percentage error is less than 1%, the other summary error statistics are reassuringly low, and, most important, the strong December 1982 to December 1983 growth is captured quite well. Although the forecast overstates growth, this is minor, given the sharpness of the cyclical rebound in manufacturing production during 1983. The forecast of production by utilities performed less well against the actual performance: the mean absolute percentage error is more than twice as large as that for manufactur-

---

[9] Between January 1972 and December 1980, there were a number of major strikes in the mining industry and a larger number of, generally, brief wildcat strikes. A value of 1 was assigned to the months in which major strikes occurred: August and November 1974; July 1975; July 1976; and December 1977 through February 1978. All other months were assigned a value of 0.

TABLE 7-6   Industrial Production Indexes: Total, Manufacturing, Utilities, and Mining: 1983 (1967 = 100.0)

	TOTAL	MANUFACTURING	UTILITIES	MINING
		ACTUAL LEVELS		
Jan	137.4	136.7	184.4	121.9
Feb	138.1	138.2	183.0	115.6
Mar	140.0	140.4	188.2	112.6
Apr	142.6	143.1	192.7	111.6
May	144.4	145.1	192.9	112.8
June	146.4	147.4	192.0	112.6
July	149.7	150.6	200.9	115.0
Aug	151.8	152.8	205.4	116.1
Sept	153.8	155.1	204.5	117.1
Oct	155.0	156.2	200.7	118.3
Nov	155.3	156.4	200.2	121.1
Dec	156.2	156.8	208.0	123.7
		FORECAST LEVELS		
Jan	139.0	137.3	188.5	118.6
Feb	138.4	136.4	187.4	122.3
Mar	141.2	140.1	186.7	116.1
Apr	142.2	141.1	190.4	113.4
May	145.4	144.7	193.6	112.6
June	147.8	147.3	193.9	113.6
July	149.0	148.6	194.1	113.5
Aug	151.9	151.4	199.7	116.0
Sept	155.1	154.7	203.4	116.9
Oct	156.2	156.0	203.2	117.9
Nov	155.7	155.5	199.2	118.8
Dec	158.7	158.8	200.0	121.3
MEAN ERROR	−0.82	0.58	1.07	−0.21
MAPE	0.69%	0.68%	1.69%	1.68%
RMSE	1.21	1.24	4.07	2.69
		% CHANGE DECEMBER TO DECEMBER		
ACTUAL	15.5	16.6	12.1	4.5
FORECAST	16.5	18.3	5.4	3.9

Source: Actual data from Board of Governors, Federal Reserve Board

ers, but the forecast December-December growth was more than twice as rapid as actual. The forecast for mining production shows a large mean absolute percentage error, but the December-December forecast is close to actual. Overall, the forecast production index performs well compared to the actual as measured by the summary error statistics and the December-December growth rates. This largely reflects the high weight of manufacturing in the total and the relatively good results of the forecast for this component. It is especially encouraging that the forecasts captured so much of the strong cyclical rebound in 1983.

Good estimates of industrial production can be very useful to a forecaster. Industrial production is one of four coincident indicators used by BEA to construct its index of coincident indicators. Since World War II the industrial production index has turned within one month of all cyclical turning points. Thus, an indicative forecast such as the one described above, can be used to anticipate future turning points. Moreover, although industrial production was examined last in this sequential approach to indicator forecasting, in reality, where forecasts are constantly monitored and updated, a forecast of industrial production may be used to improve other forecasts. For instance, payroll employment forecasts can be analyzed to insure consistency with the industrial production forecast. In this way, the separate forecasts of monthly measures of economic activity can be made consistent with each other through successive iterations and comparisons.

STRUCTURAL AND SPOT FORECASTING: THE USE OF JUDGMENT

This and the prior two chapters have been concerned with developing methods of forecasting key monthly indicators of economic activity. Underlying this approach is the basic concept that these forecasts are *interrelated*. As such, the forecast relationships, when viewed together, constitute a *model* of macroeconomic activity. It is easy to lose sight of this basic point when considering the details of forecasting each indicator. Yet building an indicative model was the purpose of the exercise.

The Structural Approach

The structural approach outlined in Part II has a number of strengths and at least two weaknesses. Among the strengths are:

(1) using fairly few assumed or exogenous variables and simple techniques, twelve-month forecasts for a wide variety of economic activities can be forecast at relatively low cost in terms of computation and time;

(2) because these forecasts are related—they build upon one another—their consistency is assured;

(3) viewed together, these measures encompass enough varied activities to provide a good indication of the likely strength and direction of overall economic activity; and

(4) individually, the forecasts provide insights to the sources of overall economic strength or weakness.

The two chief weaknesses of the approach are:

(1) as the *ex post* forecasts show, large errors do occur, especially in the more distant months;
(2) forecast errors in one measure can lead to errors in others (for instance, since the unemployment rate is used as an input in estimating many of the other indicators, a large forecast error in the unemployment rate will distort many of the other forecast values).

In order to lessen the impact of such built-in forecast errors, it is necessary to modify the forecast by using all available information and applying the forecaster's own judgment to the model's results. The starting point in this process is viewing the structural model developed in its proper context. It is a tool designed to generate a "baseline" forecast of economic outcomes based on a series of past relationships.[10] While the "baseline" forecast reflects outcomes based on average past relationships, in any period, specific forces or events may overwhelm these relationships. An alert forecaster can use these factors to modify a "baseline" forecast judgmentally.

There are a series of steps which should be followed in using judgment to modify a "baseline" forecast. In practice, forecasts are subject to nearly constant testing by the release of new monthly data. Thus, it is not necessary to wait six months to find out if a forecast is on track. Forecast errors can be analyzed as fresh data are released and the forecast updated. The actual value for any measure is likely to differ from its forecast value. The first step in modifying a forecast is to determine whether the difference is within the normal range of variation around a forecast trend—for instance, consistent with the standard error of the estimated relationship—or whether it represents a large enough error to suggest a departure from trend.

If the error is small, it may be ignored and assumed that subsequent values will remain close to or on the forecast path. If the error is large, it must be decided whether some temporary disturbance—such as more severe than normal weather conditions, a strike, or some policy action—can account for a "blip" in the trend, which will quickly reverse with no lasting effect. Of greater concern is a large error which the forecaster can not attribute to an identifiable temporary force. In this case, the forecast will have to be altered in a significant way.

The occurrence of a large, unexpected, and seemingly non-temporary, error is an important signal that basic economic conditions may be changing. In such a case, there are two basic ways to modify the forecast: (1) a *level adjustment* can be made, in which all subsequent forecast values are adjusted up or down by the error (either in absolute or percentage terms) until more information can be brought to bear; or (2) a *trend adjustment,* reflect-

---

[10] Some of these relationships are behavioral relationships—a measure is forecast on the basis of a theoretical linkage to one or more other measures—and some are time series relationships—a measure is forecast based solely on past values of itself.

ing a fundamental change in the trend of the measure, may be required. The first of these options is a temporary expedient; if the error is not repeated, it may be sufficient; if errors in the same direction recur, a trend adjustment is required.

A further step which is helpful in modifying structural forecasts is to prepare spot, one-month forecasts as well. Normally there is more information available to make a one-month forecast than for a twelve-month indicative forecast. A few examples will make this point clear.

Spot Forecasting

Employment/Unemployment. Newspaper accounts of layoffs or scarcity in finding skilled labor provide a background against which judgments about current labor market conditions can be formed. BLS also publishes weekly data on the number of initial claims for unemployment insurance and the total number of unemployed workers covered by unemployment insurance. In addition, there are specific seasonal effects on labor market conditions—the number of students expected to look for work in the summer months, or the impact of harsher than normal winter weather on employment—that may help refine a forecast for a given month and suggest something about subsequent months.

Income. Since employment data is released roughly two weeks before personal income, actual data on employment, hours worked, and hourly earnings can be used to prepare an estimate of wage and salary payments. Similarly, knowledge of the number of unemployed helps to refine the estimate of transfer payments (part of which are unemployment insurance benefits). Sudden changes in other components—personal interest payments, dividends, farm income, and changes in social security benefits or payments—are also likely to be better known and, thus, permit improved forecasts.

Retail sales. 10-day reports on unit auto sales are released by domestic manufacturers three to five days after the end of each period. These reports can be used to forecast retail sales of autos—roughly 20% of total retail sales. In addition, major chain stores usually report their sales on a year-over-year basis just after the month ends and before the retail sales report is released. These sales account for another 15-20% of total retail sales. The translation of unit car sales and chain store sales to retail sales of autos and of department stores is tricky—sometimes unit car sales rise while dollar sales decline. Nevertheless, they do provide an insight into the strength of consumer buying.

Inflation. Agricultural and other commodities prices are reported on a daily basis in many newpapers. Also, specific factors which affect certain prices—the supply-demand situation for petroleum, changes in excise and property taxes, scheduled changes in new car prices, and utility rate changes—may be known in advance. The stage of processing approach is especially useful for estimating near-term price index changes.

Inventories.   Recent sales and production trends provide a basis for refining near-term forecasts of the change in inventory levels. In addition, reports by the National Association of Purchasing Managers on the current state of sales, inventories, and orders supply useful information about business intentions to invest in inventories.

Housing starts.   Knowledge of mortgage rate movements may point to a change in home building. Government-subsidized programs for multi-family starts often undergo programmed changes which may induce a spurt or sudden falloff in starts in a particular month. Also, since home building is so subject to weather conditions, harsher than normal weather—especially during the winter months—may result in a greater than seasonal falloff. Conversely, milder than normal winter weather may permit a larger than seasonal increase in starts.

Industrial production.   Data on employment and hours worked provide a basis for forecasting production. In addition, weekly production statistics are reported for many major industries in *Business Week, U.S. News and World Report,* and other industrial publications.

If the one-month "spot" forecast for a given indicator differs from the indicative twelve-month forecast, the former should be used to modify the latter. A useful way to do this is: (1) substitute the one-month forecast into the indicative trend; (2) assume that the following two or three months will more closely resemble the spot forecast than the indicative forecast; and (3) so, return to the former forecast path gradually. If a gradual return to the old forecast path requires unlikely changes in the near-term months, then the return to trend can be stretched out or the trend changed. The advantage of this method is that the forecaster is likely to know more about the forces affecting the indicator in question over the next one, two, or three months than over the next twelve. Indeed, many of the twelve-month forecast approaches developed in the chapter relied on only a small number of the determining economic forces; others could be identified, but not forecast easily. When the forecast period is shortened to one to three months, many more of these influences can be intelligently guessed at.

By analyzing monthly forecast errors and performing one-month ahead spot forecasts, the errors in a twelve-month indicative forecast can be reduced. This recognizes that indicator forecasting is an ongoing process. Whether the time and expense involved justify performing these modifications every month depends on the uses to which the forecast will be put. An alternative is to modify the forecast every three months. If accurate forecasts are constantly important, then updates should be performed monthly; one benefit will be that constant updates should result in smaller revisions. On the other hand, if the economic forecast is chiefly used for annual budget planning, less frequent updates are acceptable.

QUESTIONS FOR REVIEW AND RESEARCH

7-1   A linkage between retail sales and manufacturers' shipments was suggested. Discuss and evaluate the posited relationship on the basis of theory and empirical trends. Test alternative forms of equation 7-1 using: (a) three- and six-month moving averages of retail sales, and (b) three- and six-month distributed lags of retail sales as indicators of expected demand. Do any of these forms provide better estimates of manufacturers shipments for 1983? If so, indicate the theoretical—as distinct from the purely econometric—reasons for your conclusion.

7-2   Discuss and evaluate the behavior of the inventory/sales ratios for manufacturers, wholesalers, and retailers in 1969–71, 1973–76, and 1979–83. Construct cyclical indexes based on the peak month for each cycle (as was done for household employment in Chapter 5). Does this approach present a better basis for forecasting the I/S ratios than the method based on equations 7-3 and 7-4?

7-3   Contrast the trends for durable and nondurable inventories and sales for the three periods cited in question 7-2. Do the differences in behavior suggest that such a disaggregated forecast approach yields better results than the approach followed in the chapter?

7-4   Housing start activity is susceptible to seasonal effects from milder than normal or severer than normal winter weather: milder than normal weather permits a greater amount of building to occur than under normal winter conditions; severer than normal storms and low temperatures prevent building from taking place. Using both seasonally adjusted and not seasonally adjusted data (from the *Survey of Current Business* and its supplement, *Business Statistics*), analyze the seasonal effects on housing starts for the past ten years. (See Robert B. Stoddard, "The Impact of Weather on Housing Starts in The First Quarter of 1984," *Federal Reserve Bank of New York Quarterly Review,* 9, No.1, 34–35 for an example of how such an analysis might be conducted.)

7-5   Examine the relationship between total hours worked in the nonfarm economy (payroll employment times average weekly hours) and industrial production. Does this constitute a useful alternative forecast approach for industrial production?

7-6   Use the forecast levels of industrial production in Table 7-6 to estimate payroll employment. Contrast your results with the results in Chapter 5. Discuss how such an iterative analysis can be used to test the consistency of forecast results for employment, personal income, and industrial production.

7-7   Prepare one-month and three-month forecasts for the economic measures listed below.
      (a)   Civilian labor force
      (b)   Civilian employment—household basis
                            —payroll basis

(c)   Civilian unemployment rate
(d)   Personal income
(e)   Retail sales
(f)   All urban consumer price index
(g)   Total business inventories
(h)   Housing starts
(i)   Industrial production

Distinguish between the extra information that can be used to forecast one month ahead and the more standard factors which affect the three-month forecast. To what extent do the one-month judgment factors have an effect on three-month forecast?

8

MEDIUM-TERM
MACROECONOMIC
FORECASTING

INTRODUCTION

One of the most common business uses of economic forecasts is in planning. This includes both medium-term (the next one or two years) *operational* planning and longer term *strategic* planning. Typically in the latter case, annual updates are made to the underlying forecast assumptions, which are stated in broad, general terms.[1] Because the medium-term economic forecast is likely to be the basis for a firm's planned operations over the next one or two years, however, a greater standard of detail and accuracy is required.

This chapter discusses the desired qualities and some of the chief problems likely to be encountered in construction of medium-term macroeconomic forecasts. This is done through outlining an *ex post* forecast for 1983. Medium-term macroeconomic forecasts create a needed link between the indicator forecasts discussed in Part II and the industry forecasts covered in Chapter 11.

A structural approach to forecasting economic indicators, as outlined in Part II, provides useful insights to the likely performance of a large number of economic indicators. Moreover, since the forecasts are related, they provide a consistent set of forecasts for a range of economic activities. It is difficult, however, to derive an overall view of economic activity using any one of these indicators—rather, some constructed measure, based on a weighted average of the indicators, is needed. Gross National Product is such a measure.

This chapter is mainly concerned with forecasting GNP, its components, and related measures; thus, it extends and broadens the activities discussed in Part II. GNP is widely regarded by economists as the broadest measure of macroeconomic activity. Indeed, the determination of national output, income, and their components are at the core of the study of macroeconomics. Forecasting these measures is, thus, an exercise in applied macroeconomic theory. Preparation of GNP forecasts is, perhaps, the most nearly universal function performed by business economists.

It should be remembered that the GNP forecast is generally of more interest to the forecaster than to the manager for whom it is prepared. At best, the insightful business manager may view a GNP forecast as a necessary basis for more directly useful forecasts of costs, input supplies, sales demand, product prices, and revenues. In many cases, management may only be concerned with these "bottom line" concepts, and may regard a forecast of GNP as a fairly abstract exercise. Forecasting these industry-specific concepts comprises the subject matter of Chapter 11. It is a central theme of this text, however, that business economists can best forecast industry- or firm-specific concepts based on an underlying macroeconomic forecast.

---

[1] Long-term forecasts are the subject of Chapter 10.

AIMS AND LIMITATIONS

Medium-term GNP forecasts are usually prepared for quarterly frequencies, but expressed at seasonally adjusted annual rates. That is, GNP and its components are estimated for a three-month span and then multiplied by four. Thus, the annualized GNP for a particular quarter measures the total amount of goods and services produced (or incomes received) in the quarter as if it were for a full year. (To derive an annual total, an average of the quarterly levels is taken.) Forecasting GNP provides an overall measure of the economy's performance; forecasting the components provides a sense of which sectors are relatively strong or weak; while forecasting at a quarterly frequency exposes the contours of economic performance during a year or some longer period.

This last point is important to the business forecaster and the operational planner. It is not enough for planning purposes to be told that economic activity will increase (or decrease) by 3% over the next year. More important is whether economic activity is likely to: (a) rise strongly early in the year, but then lose momentum; (b) increase in tempo throughout the year; or (c) grow at a steady rate. For the same reason, it is often more useful to express growth at fourth quarter to fourth quarter rates rather than at average year over average year growth rates. The former measures growth *during* a single year; the latter captures part of the growth in one year and part of the growth in the prior year—it is more ambiguous.

It is useful to forecast overall economic activity on both the product (or expenditure) and income accounts. The product account approach provides insight to the sectors which will record above- or below-average growth. This is particularly useful to a firm whose business is sensitive to a sector or sub-sector: for instance, the carpet manufacturing business which is sensitive to consumer demand for durable goods and, on a more forward looking basis, to residential construction expenditures. Of course, all sectors have some impact; if demand for automobiles is expected to be strong, then demand for carpets—when viewed as a competing good—may suffer. A separate forecast of the income account shows how the proceeds from production are shared among the factors of production. This also serves as a useful check on the product account forecast—both approaches measure the same concept.

Standard practice for forecasting product-side GNP is to perform separate forecasts for real (or *constant* dollar) GNP and inflation.[2] This permits a distinction between the forces of real growth and inflation. While it requires forecasting a larger number of unknown values, forecasting each of the two

---

[2] Clearly if forecasts of real GNP and inflation are available, a nominal (or *current* dollar) GNP forecast can be derived by multiplying the constant dollar levels by the price indexes for each component.

components of nominal GNP separately—the real and the price components—offers the advantage of distinguishing between the two sets of forces which affect each of these processes.

An important conclusion that can be drawn from the forecast examples in Part II is that forecasting economic measures accurately is very difficult. Many of the *ex post* forecasts in Part II showed that, even when a method—whether based on simple time series or regression estimates—provides close approximations to the actual data for the estimation period, and even when actual data are used for determining variables in an out-of-sample forecast, the forecast errors may be large. In forecasting those relatively narrow measures of economic activity, it was clear that a great deal of judgment—based on the forecaster's knowledge of economic theory and prevailing conditions, supplemented by common sense—was needed to modify initial estimates so they could be used as final forecasts.[3] Even so, frequent updates and revisions are needed.

This is at least equally true for forecasts of the broader economic measures of GNP. Accurate forecasting is never easy—whether for narrow, single-activity measures, or broad aggregates. Thus, forecast accuracy is nearly always relative within some expected and (prior-determined) acceptable range of error. This inevitable fact of forecasting life should be recognized by the forecaster and made clear to those who make decisions based on the forecasts. An approximately correct forecast is still useful: it indicates a probable outcome and eliminates many improbable ones.

FORECAST APPROACH: ECONOMETRIC OR CONSENSUS

Medium-term GNP forecasts can be derived in a number of ways. At one extreme, the forecaster can use one of the large, simultaneous equation, econometric models developed by commercial vendors.[4] These are all powerful models which provide detailed forecasts for many sectors and subsectors of the U.S. economy. Moreover, they emphasize the interrelationships

---

[3] The forecast examples in this text all share an advantage that forecasters do not actually have. Since the examples are for past periods, the actual values are known and can be contrasted with the forecast results. In a real forecast situation, actual values are not known; yet the knowledge that the raw forecast value is likely to contain some error requires that adjustments be made. A useful approach is to confine the estimation to a period shorter than that for which data exist. The most recent data can then be contrasted with out-of-sample, *ex post* forecast values and the errors analyzed. The resulting *ex post* error pattern offers some insight to the error pattern likely to prevail in the *ex ante* forecast period.

[4] A large number of such models is available to subscribers, including those from: Chase Econometric Associates; Data Resources, Inc. (DRI); Merrill-Lynch Economics; Townsend-Greenspan, Inc.; and Wharton Econometric Forecasting Associates. These all provide subscriber services that allow the user to accept the vendor's forecast solutions, or the ability to modify the model's assumptions—and thus the solution.

and sensitivities between sectors, allowing the forecaster to trace the impacts on one sector of a change in some other variable. They have three drawbacks, however. First, they are costly. Second, the model's conceptual framework and input assumptions are those of its developers. While it is possible for the user to change assumptions—and occasionally even to modify equations—the model fundamentally reflects someone else's approach. Third, even these complex models are subject to large errors.[5]

An approach at the other extreme is to derive a consensus forecast drawn from the published forecasts of others. A large variety of macroeconomic forecasts prepared by governmental and private entities are available at little or no cost. The Federal government's forecast, prepared by the Council of Economic Advisors, is presented along with the *Budget of the United States Government* in January and revised in July. The Federal Reserve Board states its economic forecast assumptions twice a year (in February and July) as part of the testimony of the Chairman of the Board of Governors before the Joint Economic Committee. The Congressional Budget Office prepares its own macroeconomic forecast at the time of the President's Budget message and updates the forecast as needed. A sampling of private forecasts is published each February by the Federal Reserve Bank of Richmond in its publication, *Business Forecasts*.

Deriving a consensus forecast has the great advantage of being inexpensive, and assures that the resulting forecast will be no more inaccurate than the forecasts on which it is based—of course it will perform no better if the consensus is wrong. This approach still requires a great deal of judgment; first, in selecting the forecasts to be used, and second, in deciding how to weight these inputs. A major disadvantage compared to econometric forecasting is that, since the coefficients between economic activity variables and the aggregates they affect are not known, it is difficult to modify the forecast in response to changed conditions.

An approach which combines elements of each of the two approaches outlined above will be described in the rest of this chapter. The aim is to develop: (1) a set of simple equations for those sectors which are most sensitive to changing economic conditions; while (2) basing the forecasts of other sectors on external forecasts and judgment. Such an approach retains the desirable quality of econometric models (capturing inter-sectoral sensitivities), but at less cost than if a full simultaneous model were constructed. Moreover, a key aim will be to keep the model simple and manageable—judgmental forecasts will be used for certain sectors difficult to model (such

---

[5] Stephen K. McNees, an economist at the Federal Reserve Bank of Boston, has prepared evaluations of the forecast records of major forecasting models. Articles presenting those findings appear in the September/October issue of the *New England Economic Review*, published by the Federal Reserve Bank of Boston.

as government spending and exports). This allows the resulting forecast to reflect the forecaster's own theoretical approach and judgment. This type of eclectic approach has been recommended by McNees and Perna.[6]

AN ECLECTIC APPROACH TO GNP FORECASTING

The approach to forecasting GNP described in the remainder of this chapter combines econometric and judgmental methods. This is intended as an exemplary, not a definitive approach. Indeed, compared to the state of the art, the approach is quite simple. Its merit is in presenting an eclectic approach which captures some of the sensitivities of an econometric model at far less cost. Moreover, the need to reach judgments about many of the sectors and inputs forces the forecaster to think of the "story" that must underlie the forecast. In particular, the key judgments which much be made—on the future value of input variables, the forecast for some sectors, and on the error patterns—highlight the risks to the forecast and suggest where adjustments should be made if the near-term values go off track.

The product account will be considered first, and in greater detail, for two reasons. First, the product or expenditure components of GNP can be considered in "real" terms—corrected for inflation. This allows the analysis to focus more directly on the major cyclical forces shaping the near-term economic environment. Second, and related, this approach assumes that in the medium term the macroeconomy responds mainly to changes in effective demand,[7] which can more easily be seen by examining the product account rather than the income account.

Deflators for the main product sectors will be determined next. This permits construction of current dollar GNP. The income account will then be constructed. The forecast of personal income, which accounts for two-thirds of GNP, derived in Part II, provides a useful input. (Indeed, forecasts based on the approaches discussed in Part II will be used as inputs—or exogenous variables—for forecasting sectors on the product side as well.) The other components of the income account will be forecast largely using judgmental methods to derive forecasts consistent with the product account results.

---

[6] Stephen K. McNees and Nicholas S. Perna, "Forecasting Macroeconomic Variables: An Eclectic Approach," *New England Economic Review,* The Federal Reserve Bank of Boston (May/June, 1981), pp. 15–30.

[7] This is one of the main points made by Keynes in Chapter 3 of *The General Theory.* See John Maynard Keynes, *The General Theory of Employment, Interest, and Money* (London: Macmillan, 1936), pp. 23–34.

Real GNP Forecast: Product (Expenditure) Account

The product account structures the GNP in terms of the traditional sectoral model—consumption, investment, net exports, and government spending—as shown in 8-1.

$$GNP = C + I + (X\text{-}M) + G \qquad (8\text{-}1)$$

Standard practice is to separate investment (I) into three components: residential investment (RES), business fixed investment (BFI), and the change in business inventories (ΔINV). Because the change in business inventories may be unintended, it is desirable to view GNP as composed of final sales (FS)—GNP minus the change in business inventories—and the change in inventories. Thus, the identity shown above can be rearranged.

$$GNP = FS + \Delta INV = C + RES + BFI + (X\text{-}M) + G + \Delta INV \qquad (8\text{-}1a)$$

When viewed in constant dollar—"real" or deflated—terms these accounting categories become economic activity measures; in particular, measures of sectoral demand. Estimation of these sectoral demands form the core of the macroeconomic forecast. Figure 8-1 shows a flow chart of the model used to derive product side GNP. The model is arranged in a seven-step sequence combining equation-based and judgmental estimates. There are seven exogenous input variables: population aged sixteen and over, the unemployment rate, inflation (the year-over-year percentage change in the CPIU), domestic car sales, the prime rate, housing starts, and the capital stock. Values for four of these input variables—population, unemployment rate, inflation, and housing starts—can be derived using the methods described in Part II. The prime rate can be forecast as described in Chapter 9. The capital stock is estimated recursively using past levels and the change in the capital stock, or net investment, as described below. Domestic car sales are forecast judgmentally on the basis of recent activity analysis.

The model is solved a quarter at a time. This permits the use of lagged variables, as in the equation for imports which are based on lagged real GNP. This is clearly a simple framework. This simplicity is a virtue in that it limits the amount of input data that has to be estimated. Moreover, it does provide a fairly complete view of the behavior of the major GNP sectors. The role the forecaster's judgment plays can not be over-stressed. Even for those sectors which are forecast on the basis of equations, judgment must be exercised in determining the error patterns—for the resulting equation estimates will nearly always contain errors. Exports, government spending and the inventory/sales ratio are forecast entirely on the basis of judgment.

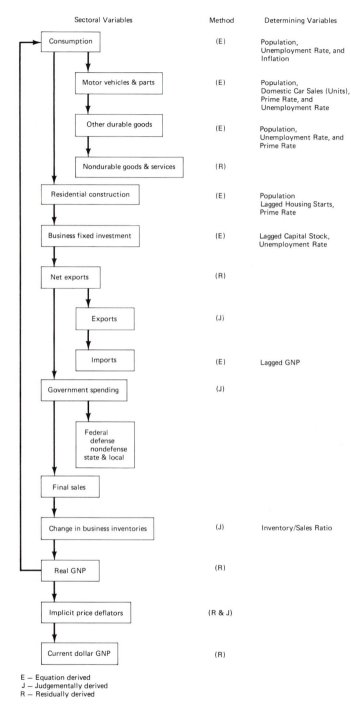

Sectoral Variables — Method — Determining Variables

Consumption — (E) — Population, Unemployment Rate, and Inflation

Motor vehicles & parts — (E) — Population, Domestic Car Sales (Units), Prime Rate, and Unemployment Rate

Other durable goods — (E) — Population, Unemployment Rate, and Prime Rate

Nondurable goods & services — (R)

Residential construction — (E) — Population Lagged Housing Starts, Prime Rate

Business fixed investment — (E) — Lagged Capital Stock, Unemployment Rate

Net exports — (R)

Exports — (J)

Imports — (E) — Lagged GNP

Government spending — (J)

Federal defense nondefense state & local

Final sales

Change in business inventories — (J) — Inventory/Sales Ratio

Real GNP — (R)

Implicit price deflators — (R & J)

Current dollar GNP — (R)

E — Equation derived
J — Judgementally derived
R — Residually derived

FIGURE 8-1   Real GNP forecast (product/expenditure side) flow chart

As McNees and Perna point out[8] there are a number of external sources for these values including the forecasts contained in the *Economic Outlook* of the Organization of Economic Cooperation and Development (OECD) for exports, and the *Budget of the U.S. Government* for Federal spending.

The major sector forecasts, with examples for the four quarters of 1983, will be described briefly in sequence.

Consumption.   Real consumer spending levels are estimated first, and fulfill a central role in the forecast of real GNP. This largely reflects the fact that since consumption is by far the largest component of GNP, changes in the level of consumption are bound to account for much of the movement in total GNP. Moreover, recognizing, as Adam Smith and Keynes did, that consumption is the end of all economic activity, the consumption forecast can aid the forecaster in making judgments about other GNP components. For instance, investment is more likely to increase when consumption is growing: increases in consumer demand induce expansion in the plant and equipment needed to produce the added consumer goods, while rising consumer sales lead to increased investment in inventories. Conversely, falling consumer demand dampens fixed investment and requires inventory cuts.

The approach followed at this stage forecasts consumer demand on the basis of non-income variables which account for: (1) an underlying momentum (or trend growth) in consumption, and (2) "environmental" forces which lead to periodic variations around this trend.[9] The population over sixteen years of age is used to capture the underlying momentum, or trend growth in consumption. This assumes that under neutral conditions—in which economic activity is experiencing neither a cyclical downturn nor a recovery—consumption demand will grow in line with population. Among the economic conditions which lead to departures from the trend growth in consumption are unemployment and inflation. When the unemployment rate is high and rising, the fear of unemployment is likely to inhibit consumer demand. When the unemployment rate is declining, consumers may feel more secure about their own economic futures and, thus, increase consumption. A similar relationship is likely between inflation and consumer demand: in periods of rising inflation, consumers may postpone spending; and when inflation is subsiding, consumption is likely to pick up.[10] Such a relationship is depicted in equation 8-2.

---

[8] McNees and Perna, "Forecasting Macroeconomic Variables," pp. 18–19.

[9] The central relationship between consumption and disposable personal income will be examined in a second equation when the income account is analyzed. The results of both equations can then be compared and used in reaching a final judgmental forecast of consumption. This *iterative* method is an important part of the eclectic approach. It allows the forecaster to consider a number of forces; in particular, it avoids relying on forecast values of income alone.

[10] An alternative view gained currency in the late 1970s, suggesting that consumers were responding to rapid inflation by going into debt to "buy in advance": the prospect that prices

$$C72 = a + b_1 * POP16\& + b_2 * RU + b_3 * INFLAT \qquad (8\text{-}2)$$

coefficients	t statistics
a = −776.02	(−29.63)
b_1 = 10.79	(40.56)
b_2 = −10.45	(−7.32)
b_3 = −3.72	(−5.21)
rho = 0.66	(6.27)

$$\overline{R}^2 = 0.998 \quad \text{D-W} = 1.845 \quad \text{SER} = 4.938$$

C72 represents personal consumption expenditures in billions of constant (1972) dollars. (In this and other equations, constant dollar values will be indicated by the suffix "72".) The equation was estimated at a quarterly frequency from first quarter 1967 through fourth quarter 1980. The coefficients all have the expected signs and are significant. The coefficient for population (POP16&) states that real consumption spending will rise by $10.8 billion for every one million increase in population. The coefficients for the environmental variables, on the other hand, show that real consumer spending declines by just under $10.5 billion for a one percentage point increase in the unemployment rate (RU) and by $3.7 billion for every one percent increase in the inflation rate (INFLAT). Thus, with stable rates of unemployment and inflation, consumption will rise in proportion to the increase in population; when the unemployment rate and/or inflation are increasing, these worsening economic conditions will offset part or all of the positive influence of the rise in population; and if the unemployment rate and/or inflation are subsiding, the improved economic condition(s) will enhance the population-induced growth in consumption.

The adjusted coefficient of multiple determination ($\overline{R}^2$) is high, indicating that 99.8% of the variation in real consumption in the sample period is accounted for by the relationship specified by equation 8-2. The Durbin-Watson statistic indicates no serial correlation (d_u at the 5% level for 56 periods and three independent variables is 1.60). A Cochrane-Orcutt correction was necessary, however, to raise the Durbin-Watson statistic to an acceptable value. The use of the Cochrane-Orcutt procedure raises a question of how to interpret the value of rho in preparing an out-of-sample forecast. In an *ex post,* out-of-sample forecast, the value of rho multiplied by the error (the actual value minus the estimated value) in the prior period can be added to the result otherwise yielded by the estimated equation. The error

---

would go even higher induced consumers to bring forward their purchases by use of credit, which would be paid back in depreciated currency. This is an extreme, short-term view. See Gina Rogers and William Springer, "Risks from the Consumption Sector," in Allen R. Sanderson, ed., *DRI Readings in Macroeconomics* (New York: McGraw-Hill, 1981), pp. 90–102.

pattern which results for the *ex post* forecast can then be used as a basis for generating an error pattern for the *ex ante* forecast period. Indeed, the need for such a basis highlights one of the values of performing an *ex post,* out-of-sample forecast.

The standard error of the regression (SER) is \$4.9 billion, suggesting that a forecast for 1983 would be within ±0.5% of the actual value two-thirds of the time and within ±1.0% of the actual value 95% of the time.

Table 8-1 compares quarterly and annual levels for actual and estimated values for real consumption in 1983. Errors for this *ex post* forecast are shown both in billions of constant dollars and as a percentage of the actual level. In addition the root mean square error (RMSE) and mean absolute percentage error (MAPE) for the four quarters are shown. The quarterly errors are small, ranging from an under-estimate of 1.1% in the second quarter to an over-estimate of 0.9% in the third quarter. The average real consumption value for all of 1983 is over-estimated by less than 0.1% and the fourth quarter-fourth quarter growth rate was accurate. The root mean square error of \$15.3 billion and the mean absolute percent error of 0.7% further attest to the accuracy of the estimates. Given the importance of consumption to the overall real GNP, this is a reassuring finding.

In fact, 1983 was a year of recovery for the U.S. economy marked by strong consumption growth. This growth largely reflected a sharp decline in the unemployment rate (from 10.7% at the end of 1982 to 8.5% at the end of 1983) and reduced inflation (subsiding from a 4.5% rate to 3.3%). These improved cyclical conditions bolstered the "trend" growth in real consumption resulting from population growth alone. In general, consumption of

TABLE 8-1   Actual Versus Forecast Values for Real GNP Components: 1983 (personal consumption expenditures)

	I	II	III	IV	ANNUAL AVERAGE	IV Q–IV Q GROWTH
			QUARTERS			
	(BILLIONS OF CONSTANT 1972 DOLLARS)					
Actual	986.7	1010.6	1016.0	1032.2	1011.4	5.4%
Forecast	993.8	999.0	1024.7	1030.7	1012.0	5.4
Error (Act-Fcst)	−7.1	11.6	−8.7	1.5	−0.6	0.0
-as % of Actual	−0.7%	1.1%	−0.9	0.1	−0.1	
	RMSE = \$15.3 Billion			MAPE = 0.7%		

durable goods is much more subject to these cyclical forces, while consumer spending on nondurable goods and services usually follows a more trend-like pattern.

For this reason, it is useful to forecast durable consumption directly, based on the forces likely to account for its variability, while treating consumption of nondurable goods and services as residuals. It should be noted that this approach only allocates the already forecast level of total consumer spending from equation 8-2 among its components. Because nondurable and service consumption, in total, is treated as a residual, this approach is not equivalent to a "bottom-up" estimate of consumption. The implied level of combined nondurable and service consumption may, however, provide insights to the likelihood of the implied *ex ante* error pattern for total consumption. If the implied growth for consumption of nondurables and services differs greatly from its long-term trend growth, this may be a sign that the forecast of durable or total consumption needs to be adjusted. This type of refinement is most easily performed by adjusting the error pattern. Attention to these types of details—departures from trend in the trend-like components, and scrutiny of the implied error patterns—highlights the iterative nature of this overall approach.

Durable consumption can be divided between spending for motor vehicles and parts and spending for all other consumer durables. This recognizes the importance of the automobile industry to U.S. economic performance and cyclical behavior.

Real consumer spending for motor vehicles and parts (CDMV&P72) is hypothesized to be a function of four variables: population over age sixteen, unit sales of new domestically-produced automobiles (CARSDOM), the unemployment rate, and the prime rate (RPRIME). The population variable again serves as a measure of underlying trend demand; as population increases, it is assumed that consumer spending on motor vehicles and parts will also increase. Unit sales of domestically-produced cars comprise an important part of CDMV&P72, and are also assumed to have a direct relationship. This variable is exogenously determined on the bases of analysis of recent sales rates and judgment.[11] The unemployment rate serves as a cyclical proxy, though consumer attitude surveys do show that consumers are reluctant to commit themselves to such a large expenditure as a new car when the unemployment rate is high and rising. An inverse relationship between real consumer spending on motor vehicles and parts and the interest rate is expected.

---

[11] Unit car sales can be forecast by an equation-based approach which uses such variables as: the driving-age population, the stock of existing cars, new car prices, interest rates, and an index of operating costs (including price indices for gasoline, parts, and repairs). The need to forecast some of these variables judgmentally remains.

Equation 8-3 presents the estimated parameters for this relationship.

$$CDMV\&P72 = a + b_1 * POP16\& + b_2 * CARSDOM$$
$$+ b_3 * RU + b_4 * RPRIME \quad (8\text{-}3)$$

coefficients	t statistics
a = −113.58	(−32.81)
b_1 = 0.92	(20.30)
b_2 = 4.32	(17.14)
b_3 = −0.87	(−3.30)
b_4 = −0.58	(−4.33)

$$\overline{R}^2 = 0.986 \quad D\text{-}W = 1.483 \quad SER = 1.207$$

The equation was estimated at a quarterly frequency from first quarter 1967 through fourth quarter 1980. All the coefficients are significant and have the expected signs. The coefficient on population suggests an increase of $0.9 billion for every one million increase in population. For each one million unit rise in unit car sales, the equation suggests a $4.3 billion increase in CDMV&P72. Real consumption of motor vehicles and parts will decline, however, for each one percentage point increase in the unemployment rate (by $0.9 billion) and in the prime rate (by $0.6 billion). Note that more than 8% of the inverse effect of the unemployment rate on total consumption is accounted for by the effect on consumption of motor vehicles and parts (b_3 = −0.87 from equation 8-3 divided by b_2 = −10.45 from equation 8-2), though CDMV&P72 accounts for less than 6% of C72. This reflects the much greater cyclical responsiveness of consumer demand for motor vehicles than of consumption generally.

The $\overline{R}^2$ is again high, indicating 98.6% of the variation in real consumer spending on motor vehicles and parts is accounted for by the variation in the combined independent variables in equation 8-3. The Durbin-Watson statistic at 1.48, however, is in the "grey area" at both the 5% (d_1 = 1.41, d_u = 1.72) and the 1% (d_1 = −1.25, d_u = 1.55) levels of significance, providing neither conclusive evidence of the presence or absence of serial correlation. The standard error of the regression at $1.2 billion is proportionately larger than for equation 8-2, suggesting that the estimate is likely to be within ±4% of the actual value in 1983 95% of the time.

In fact, the estimated values of CDMV&P72 under-estimated the actual values in all four quarters of 1983 as can be seen in Table 8-2—from 4.1% in the first quarter to 9.2% in the fourth quarter. Real consumption of motor vehicles and parts surged by nearly 21% in 1983 (compared to estimated growth of nearly 16%), but the quarterly growth was quite uneven. The full year growth reflected the strong cyclical response of this spending

TABLE 8-2   Actual Versus Forecast Values for Real GNP Components: 1983 (consumer durables: motor vehicles and parts)

	I	II	III	IV	ANNUAL AVERAGE	IV Q–IV Q GROWTH
	QUARTERS					
	(BILLIONS OF CONSTANT 1972 DOLLARS)					
Actual	60.9	69.1	69.1	73.0	68.0	20.7%
Forecast	58.4	63.1	64.0	66.3	63.0	15.8
Error (Act-Fcst)	2.5	6.0	5.1	6.7	5.0	4.9
-as % of Actual	4.1%	8.7%	7.4%	9.2%	7.4%	
	RMSE = $8.2 Billion			MAPE = 7.4%		

sector to the wider economic recovery, while the quarterly volatility reflected the shifting demand-supply balance for autos in 1983.[12]

Real consumption of all other consumer durables (CDO72) is forecast using the same variables, with the exception of unit car sales. Population is again assumed to have a direct relationship, while the unemployment rate and the prime rate are assumed to be inversely related to real consumption of other durables for similar reasons. Equation 8-4 presents parameters for these relationships.

---

[12] After three years of declining sales and bulging inventories, U.S. auto manufacturers had finally trimmed production and stocks to sustainable levels relative to sales by late 1982. As the recovery gathered strength in early 1983, auto demand strengthened, so that by mid year, inventories were depleted to such an extent that demand for some popular models could not be supplied. The manufacturers—mindful of past over–responses to what proved only temporary sales spurts—raised production only gradually. By early 1984, auto production and supplies had returned to a state of balance with still-strong demand.

The quarterly growth pattern for CDMV&P72 during 1983 reflects this unevenness. Indeed, when the forecast growth pattern is compared, as in the table below, the degree to which the equation captured this unusually sporadic pattern is surprising.

Consumption of Motor Vehicles and Parts: 1983 (real growth at seasonally adjusted annual rates)

	I	II	III	IV
Actual	2.7%	65.8%	0.0%	24.6%
Forecast	8.3	36.3	5.8	15.2

$$\text{CDO72} = a + b_1 * \text{POP16\&} + b_2 * \text{RU} + b_3 * \text{RPRIME} \qquad (8\text{-}4)$$

	coefficients	t statistics
	a = −122.86	(−27.52)
	b_1 = 1.32	(33.36)
	b_2 = −2.02	(−8.26)
	b_3 = −0.18	(−1.80)
	rho = 0.45	(3.60)

$$\overline{R}^2 = 0.994 \quad \text{D-W} = 1.748 \quad \text{SER} = 0.996$$

The equation was estimated at a quarterly frequency from first quarter 1967 through fourth quarter 1980. The results conform to those found above for total consumption and consumption of motor vehicles and parts. CDO72 increases by $1.3 billion for each one million rise in population. Consumption of non-auto durables declines, however, for each one percentage point rise in the unemployment rate (by $2.0 billion) and in the prime rate (by $0.2 billion). The response to a rise in the unemployment rate is even larger than in the case of CDMV&P72 and disproportionately large relative to the response for total consumption—nearly 20% of the response for total consumption (b_2 = −2.02 from equation 8-4 divided by b_2 = −10.45 from equation 8-2), although other durable consumption accounts for only about 9% of total real consumption.

Once again the $\overline{R}^2$ is high, indicating that 99.4% of the variation in CDO72 is accounted for by the relationship specified in equation 8-4. The Durbin-Watson statistic is in excess of the upper limit (d_u = 1.60 for 56 quarters and three independent variables), but again only after performing a Cochrane-Orcutt correction. The value of rho is quite low, however. The standard error of the regression is also low, suggesting the estimated value will be within ±2% of the 1983 actual 95% of the time.

TABLE 8-3   Actual Versus Forecast Values For Real GNP Components: 1983 (consumption of other durable goods)

	Quarters				Annual Average	IV Q − IV Q Growth
	I	II	III	IV		
	(Billions of Constant 1972 Dollars)					
Actual	85.0	87.3	88.8	92.2	88.3	11.5%
Forecast	85.4	87.1	89.6	91.8	88.5	9.9
Error (Act − Fcst)	−0.4	0.2	−0.8	0.4	−0.2	1.6
−as % of Actual	−0.5%	0.2%	−0.9%	0.4%	−0.2%	
	RMSE = $0.5 Billion			MAPE = 0.5%		

The results for 1983, presented in Table 8-3 show small errors, ranging from an over-estimate of $0.8 billion in the third quarter to an under-estimate of $0.4 billion in the fourth quarter. The root mean square error is only $0.5 billion.

As noted above, real consumption of nondurable goods and services (CN&S72) are forecast as a residual. That is, the forecast levels for real consumer spending on motor vehicles and parts and for other durable goods are subtracted from the forecast level for total real consumer spending.

$$CN\&S72 = \widehat{C72} - \widehat{CDMV\&P72} - \widehat{CDO72} \qquad (8\text{-}5)$$

Bearing in mind the usual trend-like pattern for nondurable and service consumption, the forecaster can once again adjust the error patterns of the other, equation-estimated, results if the growth pattern for CN&S72 appears unlikely. Finally, the forecast levels for CN&S72 can be split to derive separate estimates of real consumer spending of nondurable and of services.

Residential construction expenditures.   Real spending on residential construction is also a volatile, cyclically related sector of the product account. Most (roughly two-thirds) of the total is for new housing units. Consequently, there is a close relationship between real spending for residential construction (RES72) and housing starts (HUSTS). The relationship is not exact, however; construction of new housing units takes time, and much of the spending—and actual construction activity—occurs in the one or two quarters following that in which the unit is started. The model for RES72, therefore, posits a positive relationship to housing starts, but with a three-quarter—the current and two preceding quarters—distributed lag.

Population pressures can also be expected to exert a positive effect on real residential construction spending. In addition, as already noted in Chapter 7, housing construction and purchases are sensitive to interest rate movements. Thus, an inverse relationship is expected between RES72 and the prime rate.[13]

---

[13] The prime rate is used instead of the effective mortgage rate on new homes in order to minimize the inputs to this overall GNP model (since the prime rate is already included in the estimation of real consumption of durable goods). The interest rate effect, regardless of the rate used, is somewhat understated in equation 8-6 since the estimates of housing starts already contain an interest rate effect (see equations 7-26 and 7-27).

These relationships are presented in equation (8-6)

$$RES72 = a + \sum_{n=0}^{2} b_{1n}*HUSTS_{t-n} + b_2*POP16\& + b_3*RPRIME \quad (8-6)$$

	coefficients	t statistics
a =	−34.803	(−13.01)
b₁ n = 0 =	4.759	(3.34)
n = 1 =	11.764	(6.65)
n = 2 =	3.375	(2.85)
b₂ =	0.380	(16.37)
b₃ =	−0.507	(−4.60)

$$\overline{R}^2 = 0.980 \quad D\text{-}W = 1.623 \quad SER = 1.315$$

The equation was estimated quarterly from first quarter 1967 through fourth quarter 1980. The coefficients on housing starts all show the expected positive signs. They also confirm that most of the construction activity occurs in the quarter following the housing start: RES72 rises by $4.8 billion for each one million increase in housing starts during the current quarter, $11.8 billion for each one million increase in the prior quarter, and $3.4 billion for each one million rise in starts two quarters earlier. These lagged effects are important because they suggest that RES72 will show only a muted response to a sudden change in housing start activity.[14]

The impact of a change in population is less than for consumption: RES72 increases by less than $0.4 billion for a one million increase in population. While population growth does exert upward pressure on spending for residential construction, other factors — possibly the high cost of new homes relative to household income and credit conditions — prevent this pressure from being instantly relieved.

Real residential construction spending is inversely affected by rising interest rates, declining by $0.5 billion for each one percentage point rise in the prime rate. This almost certainly understates the interest rate effect, largely because much of the adverse interest rate effect is already included in the estimation of housing starts.

A high value of $\overline{R}^2$ indicates that most of the variation in real residential construction (98%) is accounted for by the relationship specified in equation 8-6. The Durbin-Watson statistic of 1.62 is just inside the "grey area" at the 5% level of significance ($d_1 = 1.45$, $d_u = 1.68$), but suggests no serial correlation at the 1% level ($d_1 = 1.28$, $d_u = 1.51$). The standard error of the regres-

---

[14] One interpretation of the lag weights is that some 23% (4.759/(4.759 + 11.764 + 3.375)) of the total real spending on housing construction occurs in the quarter in which the unit is started, nearly 60% occurs in the following quarter, and a further 17% two quarters following the start of construction.

sion, however, is fairly high, suggesting that the estimated value will only be within ±5% of the actual value 95% of the time.

The estimated values for 1983, as shown in Table 8-4, exceeded the actuals in all four quarters, but the errors diminished during the course of the year.

TABLE 8-4　Actual Versus Forecast Values For Real GNP Components: 1983 (residential construction)

	Quarters				Annual Average	IV Q – IV Q Growth
	I	II	III	IV		
	(Billions of Constant 1972 Dollars)					
Actual	45.5	52.6	56.8	55.8	52.7	37.4%
Forecast	53.0	59.0	60.9	61.7	58.6	28.2
Error (Act − Fcst)	−7.5	−6.4	−4.1	−5.9	−5.9	9.2
−as % of Actual	−16.5%	−12.2%	−7.2%	−10.6%	−11.2%	
	RMSE = $6.1 Billion		MAPE = 11.6%			

This pattern largely reflected the very sharp recovery in housing starts early in 1983. (Housing starts rose from an annual rate of 1.29 million units in fourth quarter 1982 to 1.69 million in first quarter 1983 and then held near or slightly above this level through the rest of the year.)

Business fixed investment.　Real spending by business on plant and equipment is both affected by cyclical forces and is itself an important source of cyclical volatility. Both of these aspects are important for forecasting business fixed investment: the response to past cyclical movements will influence the current level of real capital spending; in turn, the induced change in investment will itself be a source of current cyclical movement in the overall economy and will induce future investment responses.

The reaction of business fixed investment to cyclical developments can be described by the *accelerator* principle. The accelerator results from three relationships.

First, it is assumed that businesses desire to maintain a fairly constant relationship (k) between the real nonresidential capital stock (KBFI72) and real output (GNP72). The desired capital/output ratio is determined by the supplies of productive factors, and by the way in which these factors are combined in production—in other words the state of technology. Factor supplies and technology can be assumed to be relatively fixed in the short term, so that the desired capital/output ratio (k) is also stable in the short run, or at least changes very slowly.

$$k = KBFI72/GNP72 \qquad (8\text{-}7)$$

or $$KBFI72 = k * GNP72$$

Second, it should be noted that net new investment measures the change in the capital stock. Business fixed investment, however, is measured in gross terms in the National Product Account; that is, measured business fixed investment (BFI72) includes net investment in new capital (BFI72n) and a larger portion that represents replacement of worn-out or obsolete capital (BFI72r). Both portions of business fixed investment are related to the capital stock. But, whereas net investment results in a change in the capital stock, replacement investment results in no net change in the capital stock. Indeed, the amount of replacement investment in a quarter is a function of the past level of the capital stock.

$$BFI72 = BFI72n + BFI72r \qquad (8\text{-}8)$$

where $\qquad BFI72n = \Delta KBI72 = KBFI72_t - KBFI72_{t-1}$

The third relationship, the accelerator itself, follows from 8-7 and 8-8 and states that net business fixed investment (the change in the capital stock) is proportional (by a factor equal to the capital/output ratio) to the change in real output.

$$BFI72n = k * \Delta GNP72 \qquad (8\text{-}9)$$

Equation 8-9, however, does not fully capture the cyclical impacts on business fixed investment. In recession, the change in real output is negative, and, therefore net business fixed investment will not merely decline; rather it will be negative. Negative net investment is achieved by allowing the level of replacement investment to decline. In other words, when real GNP declines: gross investment declines (the change in gross investment is negative), no net new investment takes place,[15] and replacement investment declines (the change in replacement investment is negative). In expansions, real GNP increases and gross investment increases because net new investment is positive and replacement investment increases.[16]

when $\qquad \Delta GNP72 > 0: \Delta BFI72 > 0 \qquad \begin{cases} BFI72n > 0 \\ \\ \Delta BFI72r > 0 \end{cases}$

---

[15] Algebraically, net new investment should be negative. But viewed as an activity, the only way in which the capital stock can decrease is if worn out capital is not replaced. Thus, viewing the two parts of gross investment as activities, for there to be a decline in gross investment there must be no new net investment activity and replacement activity must be reduced.

[16] In the unlikely situation where there is no change in real output (stagnation) and no technological innovation, net investment would be zero but replacement investment would still occur at a constant rate. Thus, gross investment would also be constant.

when $\quad\quad \Delta GNP72 < 0: \Delta BFI72 < 0 \quad \begin{cases} BFI72n = 0 \\ \\ \Delta BFI72r < 0 \end{cases}$

Business fixed investment is also a transmitter of cyclical disturbances to the rest of the economy. This happens in two ways. First, business fixed investment itself is a significant portion of real GNP, accounting for about 9% to 12% of the total. Thus, sharp changes in the level of investment produce direct changes in the level of real GNP. The second effect of cyclical changes in business fixed investment on GNP is through the spending *multiplier*. Changes in investment activity lead to changes in the employment of factors in the production of investment goods and, thus, to changes in the income received by these factor owners. These income changes, in turn, lead to changes in spending for other goods, and these spending changes will themselves set off accelerator-induced changes in investment. The combined effects of the multiplier and accelerator, therefore, produce ripples of spending changes throughout the economy. This interaction has been noted as an important source of cyclical movement.[17]

A forecast of real business fixed investment should take into account both the normal relationship to the capital stock—which results in replacement investment—and some account of cyclical forces. The Bureau of Economic Analysis estimates the end-of-year gross and net capital stock for the business, household, and government sectors on current and constant (1972) dollar bases. These estimates are prepared by a perpetual inventory method.[18] In essence, this method adds to the existing capital stock the business fixed investment that occurs each year less discards of old capital and less sales (plus purchases) to (from) other sectors. Data on discards and ex sector sales[19] are also available from BEA on current and constant dollar bases at annual frequencies. (See footnote 18.) These data can be converted to quarterly frequencies and used in combination with estimates of business

[17] The interaction between the multiplier and accelerator was first described in an article by Samuelson. See Paul A. Samuelson, "Interactions between the Multiplier Analysis and the Principle of Acceleration," *The Review of Economic Statistics, XXI*, No. 2 (May 1939), 75–78. This article has been reprinted in American Economic Association, *Readings in Business Cycle Theory* (Philadelphia: Blakiston Co.), 1950, pp. 261–69.

[18] A discussion of these estimates is in Allan H. Young and John C. Musgrave, "Estimation of Capital Stock in the United States," Dan Usher, ed., *The Measurement of Capital* (Chicago: Univ. of Chicago Press, 1980), pp. 23–81. A more detailed discussion of methdology and data for the estimation is contained in Bureau of Economic Analysis, *Fixed Reproducible Tangible Wealth in the United States, 1925–79* (Washington, DC: U.S. Government Printing Office, 1982).

[19] Sales of used business capital to other sectors typically consist of sales of used automobiles to the household sector. The only significant instances of net purchases by the business sector were purchases of capital from the federal government of war surplus following the two World Wars and the Korean War.

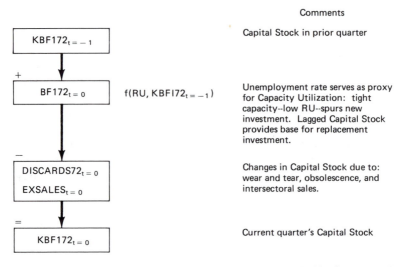

Comments

Capital Stock in prior quarter

Unemployment rate serves as proxy for Capacity Utilization: tight capacity--low RU--spurs new investment. Lagged Capital Stock provides base for replacement investment.

Changes in Capital Stock due to: wear and tear, obsolescence, and intersectoral sales.

Current quarter's Capital Stock

FIGURE 8-2   Changes in real business fixed capital stock. Net investment

fixed investment to construct a quarterly series for constant dollar gross business capital stock.

$$KBFI72_t = KBFI72_{t-1} + \Delta KBFI72_t \qquad (8\text{-}10)$$

where $$\Delta KBFI72_t = \frac{(BFI72_t - DISCARDS72_t \pm EXSALES72_t)}{4}$$

A virtue of this approach is that it closely approximates the more elaborate one that BEA follows. The quarterly change in the real capital stock ($\Delta KBFI72$) is derived from the actual data on business fixed investment flows, minus discards (DISCARDS72)—which can be estimated based on past depreciation schedules and current analysis—and the effect of sales to (purchases from) other sectors (EXSALES72)—which are relatively small under normal circumstances and can be estimated by interpolation and analysis of used car sales by the business sector.[20] Furthermore, because real business fixed investment will be estimated partly as a function of lagged capital stock, simultaneous estimation of real fixed investment and the real capital stock is not necessary. Figure 8-2 presents a flow diagram which shows how these variables interrelate.

To capture the cyclical effect on investment, the unemployment rate is used. The use of the unemployment rate has several advantages. The unemployment rate does possess strong cyclical characteristics. The unemploy-

[20] The National Income and Product Accounts contain data on net sales of used cars by the business sector on a constant dollar basis in Table 1.15, *"Auto Output in Constant Dollars."*

ment rate can be estimated outside the model, thus avoiding the problems of simultaneous estimation posed by using changes in real GNP. (Moreover, *ex post* forecasts using the unemployment rate yield better forecast results, with fewer econometric problems, than ones using the change in real GNP, or the lagged value of real GNP.) Finally, the unemployment rate, since it is a measure of under-utilized labor resources, can be viewed as a proxy for the capacity utilization rate, thus eliminating the need to forecast capacity utilization rates separately. Changes in real business fixed investment are assumed to be inversely related to changes in the unemployment rate.

Thus, the level of real business fixed investment is estimated using equation 8-11, in which the independent variables are: real business fixed capital stock lagged one quarter, and the unemployment rate in the current quarter.

$$BFI72_t = a + b_t * KBFI72_{t-1} + b_2 * RU_t \qquad (8\text{-}11)$$

coefficients	t statistics
$a = 2.693$	(0.37)
$b_1 = 0.105$	(20.62)
$b_2 = -7.651$	(−11.45)
rho $= 0.763$	(8.32)

$$\overline{R}^2 = 0.990 \quad D\text{-}W = 2.014 \quad SER = 2.049$$

The equation was estimated quarterly from 1968 through 1980. The estimated relationship explains much of the variation in real business fixed investment and each of the coefficients is highly significant except the constant term. The coefficient on the capital stock suggests an increase of $0.1 billion for each $1.0 billion increase in the prior quarter's capital stock. This result should not be taken quite so literally. It is not necessary to replace one-tenth of the prior quarter's capital stock in just three months. The coefficient, however, is consistent with the average rate of depreciation on business plant and equipment.[21] In the late 1970s-early 1980s quarterly changes in the real business capital stock have been about $20 billion. Thus, other conditions equal, real business fixed investment would rise by roughly $2

---

[21] Similar equations for real business fixed investment in structures and producers' durable equipment can be constructed separately. The coefficient on the lagged capital stock would then more closely approximate the average depreciation rates for each type of capital. However, this would require separate estimates for each class of capital stock discards, and *ex sector* sales. A more elaborate, but basically similar approach developed in a study by Clark, showed that there was little if any advantage to estimating structures and producers' durable equipment separately—the estimates of total business fixed investment yielded as good or better results. See Peter K. Clark, "Investment in the 1970s: Theory, Performance, and Prediction," *Brookings Papers on Economic Activity*, No. 1 (Washington, DC: The Brookings Institution, 1979), 73–113.

billion per quarter. The coefficient on the unemployment rate, on the other hand, shows what happens when other conditions are not equal. A one percentage point increase in the unemployment rate (worsening cyclical conditions) would result in a roughly $7.7 billion decline in real business fixed investment.

The summary statistics and forecast results for this equation are quite good. The value for R^2 indicates that 99% of the variation in real business fixed investment is accounted for by the relationship specified in equation 8-11. After a Cochrane-Orcutt correction is performed, the Durbin-Watson statistic indicates an absence of serial correlation, and the value of rho is not troublesomely high. The standard error of the regression suggests that 95% of the time the estimate would be within 2.4% of the actual value in 1983.

Forecast values for 1983 are contrasted with the actuals in Table 8-5. The errors are small except for the first quarter overestimate of $4.2 billion (2.6%). Moreover, the forecast captured the rapid surge in investment in the second half of 1983 (an estimated annual growth rate of 19.6% compared to actual growth of 22.9%). This largely reflected the impact of the declining unemployment rate (IQ: 10.4%, IIQ: 10.1%, IIIQ: 9.4%, IVQ: 8.5%). For the year as a whole, the actual and forecast growth rates were quite close.

Net exports.   The foreign sector is comprised of U.S. exports of goods and services less U.S. imports of foreign produced goods and services. When it is recognized that U.S. exports are foreign countries' imports, then the problem of describing changes in real net exports (real exports minus real imports, both from the U.S. view) reduces to one of describing import flows. Real imports are mainly a function of two sets of variables: (1) domestic absorption—real import demand is a function of real income; and (2) relative prices (including interest rates and exchange rates).

The greater difficulty is in forecasting real exports (X72). Since U.S. exports comprise a part of other countries' imports, a complete model requires forecasting the factors that effect import demand in these countries.

TABLE 8-5   Actual Versus Forecast Values for Real GNP Components: 1983 (business fixed investment)

| | QUARTERS | | | | ANNUAL AVERAGE | IV Q − IV Q GROWTH |
	I	II	III	IV		
	(BILLIONS OF CONSTANT 1972 DOLLARS)					
Actual	159.9	163.0	170.1	180.7	168.4	12.6%
Forecast	164.1	164.4	171.0	179.8	169.8	12.9
Error (Act − Fcst)	−4.2	−1.4	−0.9	0.9	−1.4	−0.3
-as % of Actual	−2.6%	−0.9%	−0.5%	0.5%	−0.8%	
	RMSE = $2.3 Billion		MAPE = 1.1%			

Such a task is beyond the resources of most forecasters. Instead it is recommended that exports be forecast on the basis of judgment. This should certainly involve analysis of recent export patterns and judgments about expected foreign demand for agricultural and nonagricultural exports. In addition, the forecaster may wish to use the OECD forecast of exports as a reference: this forecast does rely partly on an integrated set of national macroeconomic models.[22] Alternatively, real exports can be estimated using a simple time series method.

Real imports (M72) also pose a challenge to the forecaster. The absorption portion of import demand can be approximated by using a one-quarter lag on real GNP. Relative prices pose a greater problem, however, because, as in considering exports, price variables for a large number of foreign economies need to be estimated. Rather than attempt to forecast these variables explicitly, the present approach is limited to the absorption portion of real imports. This does, at least, capture some of the domestic economy's effects on the foreign sector. The forecaster should bear in mind, however, that other factors are important—namely relative prices—and, thus, the equation results should be adjusted judgmentally to reflect these other factors.

Equation 8-12 relates the level of real imports to the level of real GNP in the prior quarter.

$$M72_t = a + b * GNP72_{t-1} \tag{8-12}$$

coefficients	t statistics
a = −60.742	(−7.97)
b = 0.114	(18.59)
rho = 0.613	(5.70)

$$\overline{R}^2 = 0.973 \quad \text{D-W} = 2.04 \quad \text{SER} = 2.929$$

Equation 8-12 was estimated quarterly from 1967 through 1980. The coefficient on lagged real GNP states that real imports will increase by just over $0.1 billion for every $1 billion rise in real GNP. Alternative versions of this equation with longer lags provided no improvement in the overall fit and had insignificant coefficients for some of the lag periods. Including the percentage change in domestic prices (without regard to foreign prices) also resulted in an insignificant, small coefficient.

The value of $\overline{R}^2$ is surprisingly high, suggesting that this simple relationship accounts for 97.3% of the variation in real imports. The Durbin-Watson statistic indicates an absence of serial correlation after a Cochrane-

---

[22] Published semi-annually (July and December) in the *OECD Economic Outlook*, Organization for Economic Cooperation and Development Publications and Information Center, Suite 1207, 1750 Pennsylvania Ave., Washington, DC 20006.

Orcutt transformation is performed, and the value of rho is not unduly high. The standard error of the regression suggests the forecast value will be within ±4.6% of the actual 1983 value 95% of the time.

Ex post out-of-sample forecast values for 1983 are compared to the actuals in Table 8-6. The errors are quite large and indicate that the forecast values consistently under-estimated the actuals. Moreover, the forecast growth rate for the full year was markedly less than actual growth. These results suggest that some factor(s) other than domestic absorption exerted a strong positive effect on real U.S. import demand. A likely explanation was the surprising strength the dollar's foreign exchange value enjoyed in 1983. This largely reflected high relative inflation-adjusted interest rates in the U.S. and, partly, the role the dollar as a haven currency during a period of high international uncertainty. These are factors a forecaster should have taken into account to adjust the equation results.

Thus, as stated, the forecast levels for real imports should be judgmentally adjusted to correct for the exclusion of important price variables. Real net exports can then be determined by subtracting the adjusted forecast values for real imports from the judgmentally derived values for real exports. The resulting forecast for net exports is thus partly judgmental and partly equation based. The use of equation 8-12 to derive a forecast of real imports maintains some connection to the other equation-based values.

Government spending.   Judgment plays some role in the forecasts for consumption, residential construction, and business fixed investment, mainly in the construction of the error pattern. In forecasting net exports, judgment plays a larger role: real exports are derived judgmentally; while real imports are forecast partly on the basis of equation 8-12, the amount of judgmental adjustment (the relative size of the error term) is much larger than that for the other equation-based measures. Real spending on goods and services by federal, state, and local governments is based, in this approach, totally on the forecaster's judgment.

It is useful to forecast Federal government spending separately from state and local government spending. In general, these flows are forecast on

TABLE 8-6   Actual Versus Forecast Values for Real GNP Components: 1983 (imports)

	QUARTERS				ANNUAL AVERAGE	IV Q–IV Q GROWTH
	I	II	III	IV		
	(BILLIONS OF CONSTANT 1972 DOLLARS)					
Actual	116.8	123.9	129.2	137.8	126.9	21.4%
Forecast	111.2	114.6	122.3	126.4	118.6	8.0
Error (Act − Fcst)	5.6	9.3	6.9	11.4	8.3	13.4
-as % of Actual	4.8%	7.5%	5.3%	8.3%	6.5%	
	RMSE = $8.6 Billion			MAPE = 6.5%		

the basis of: (1) recent spending patterns, modified by (2) policy actions. The *Budget of the U.S. Government* is the starting point for forecasting Federal spending. Moreover, real Federal spending can be forecast separately for the defense and nondefense sectors. The *Budget* provides the basis for projections of real defense spending. If the forecaster chooses to accept the Budget projections, which are on a fiscal year basis (from October 1 to September 30), then judgments based on actual outlay patterns must be relied on to determine the quarterly flows. Nondefense spending often displays more volatility than defense outlays. One source of this volatility is the amount of the agricultural surplus purchased by the Commodity Credit Corporation. In recent years these purchases have been large, but subject to wide quarterly swings.[23] Fixing on an amount depends upon the forecaster's judgment about the size of the agricultural surplus, current and prospective agricultural policy, and analysis of past purchases.

State and local government purchases display a more trend-like pattern. Factors which should be considered are: the phase of the business cycle—in recessions, tax revenues rise more slowly, constraining the ability to spend; population growth—much of state and local spending is for such services as education and health care which are closely linked to both population growth over long periods and Federal policies towards revenue sharing.

The judgments a forecaster makes about government spending often comprise the main policy assumptions underlying a macroeconomic forecast. They require a great deal of thought and should result from careful analysis of recent and future policy. Clearly, the more detailed the analysis—even to the programmatic level—the sounder will be the judgments that result.

Final sales and the change in business inventories.   Real final sales equal real GNP less the change in real business inventories, or from equation 8-1a, the sum of consumer spending, residential construction expenditures, business fixed investment, net exports, and government spending (all expressed in constant dollar terms). At this stage in the estimation process, real final sales can thus be derived from the forecast values of its components. This measure, by itself, is an important aggregate of economic activity.

Table 8-7 contrasts actual and forecast values for real final sales in 1983. The forecast values in this *ex post* estimation are equal to the sum of the forecast values for personal consumption expenditures, residential construction, business fixed investment, less imports (all in constant dollar terms) from Tables 8-1 and 8-4 through 8-6, respectively, plus the *actual*

---

[23] For instance, in 1983 the real quarterly inventory changes for the Commodity Credit Corporation were: IQ − $0.5 billion; IIQ − $0.7 billion; IIIQ + $0.8 billion; and IVQ − $3.7 billion (all expressed at annual rates in constant 1972 dollar terms).

**TABLE 8-7   Actual Versus Forecast Values for Real GNP Components: 1983
(final sales)**

| | QUARTERS | | | | ANNUAL | IV Q–IV Q |
	I	II	III	IV	AVERAGE	GROWTH
	(BILLIONS OF CONSTANT 1972 DOLLARS)					
Actual	1505.5	1530.5	1549.7	1563.8	1537.4	4.0%
Forecast	1530.0	1536.0	1570.1	1578.6	1553.7	4.9
Error (Act − Fcst)	−24.5	−5.5	−20.4	−14.8	−16.3	−0.9
-as % of Actual	−1.6%	−0.4%	−1.3%	−1.0%	−1.1%	
	RMSE = $17.8 Billion		MAPE = 1.1%			

values for exports and government spending. The use of actual values in estimating final sales in Table 8-7 ignores one source of potential error— namely, the possibility that the judgmentally determined estimates of real exports and government spending may prove wrong.[24] Thus, the errors shown in Table 8-7 for the forecast values of real final sales only reflect the effects due to unexplained variation in the estimating equations. These errors are encouraging: ranging from an over-estimate of 1.6% in the first quarter to one of only 0.4% in the second quarter. The results consistently over-estimate final sales, although the error for the annual average and the growth during the year are small enough to appear acceptable. This conclusion is strengthened by the fact that a disproportionately large share of the total error was accounted for by the under-estimates of real imports (which, since they are subtracted from final sales, produce final sales over-estimates). It was noted above that these errors are likely due to foreign exchange rate developments that an alert forecaster should take into account in judgmentally adjusting the equation-derived estimates of real imports.

The estimates of real final sales can be used with assumed values for the inventory/sales ratio to determine the level and change in business inventories and, thus, to derive real GNP estimates. This process, however, requires considerable judgment on the part of the forecaster. There are at least three steps: (1) farm inventories and the annualized quarterly change in farm inventories should be estimated separately; (2) the final sales estimates must be refined further to focus just on the final sales of goods; and (3) values for the ratio of nonfarm inventories to final sales of goods must be assumed.

It is advisable to treat farm inventories separately because they are more related to conditions of agricultural supply—crop harvests—and demand than to the phase of the business cycle. A forecast of farm inventories should take into account: recent grain crop harvests, planting intentions,

---

[24] Of course, there is the possibility that these errors may either offset each other, or in combination offset the errors associated with the equation-derived estimates.

crop yield estimates,[25] and the recent state of agricultural stocks. As the late 1970s and early 1980s showed, farm inventories can move counter to the cyclical change in nonfarm inventories. A further important factor is the role of Federal agricultural policy; Government policies in recent years have attempted to support farm prices and incomes by inducing farmers to reduce plantings so as to limit crop surpluses. In addition, there have been a number of programs which have had the effect of limiting the supplies of grain already harvested which enter the market. While it is clearly difficult for the non-specialist forecaster to make accurate judgments about all these factors, the more thought given to their likely impact, the greater the prospects of an accurate forecast for the change in farm inventories.

Nonfarm inventories display a more cyclical relationship with final sales. However, nearly half of total final sales consist of services, for which there is not a strong relationship to inventories. Therefore, it is necessary to look separately at final sales of goods, structures, and services. In practice, it is easier to estimate the services component and subtract this from total final sales. There are three main service components in final sales: (1) consumer spending on services, (2) net exports of services, and (3) government spending on services. Consumer spending on services can be estimated from the forecast value for consumption of nondurable goods and services (CN&S72) by adjusting the trend growth rate for recent activity patterns. The U.S. nearly always records a large surplus on its real trade in services account (exports of services minus imports of services). Once again, the forecaster can estimate the portion of net exports accounted for by services based on recent activity analysis. Finally, total government spending for services has accounted for roughly 75% of all government spending in recent years. These guidelines, supplemented by judgments formed on the basis of recent activity, should result in close approximation of the value of total services in final sales. Subtracting estimated services results in an estimate of the final sales of goods and structures.

It is also desirable to back structures out of this total since inventories are mainly held against the sale of goods. Expenditure on structures is included in three GNP components: (1) residential structures, (2) business investment in nonresidential structures, and (3) spending by government entities—mainly at the state and local levels—on structures. Estimates of the value of structures in nonservice final sales can be made by applying analysis of recent trends to the explicit forecasts of residential construction, business fixed investment, and government spending.

The remaining portion of real final sales, thus, reflects sales of goods

---

[25] The U.S. Department of Agriculture provides data on planting intentions for most cash crops in the spring, and successive estimates of the likely crop yields as the growing season (usually the summer months) progresses in a series of publications: *Prospective Plantings, Acreage,* and *Crop Production,* published by the Crop Reporting Board (Washington, DC: U.S. Department of Agriculture.)

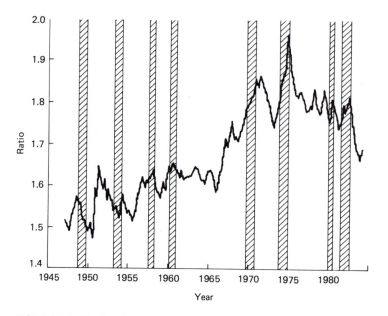

FIGURE 8-3   **Ratio of nonfarm inventories to final sales of goods (1972 dollar basis)**

alone. When the final sales of goods are divided by four—so as to express them at a quarterly rate—and then divided into the end-of-quarter levels of real nonfarm inventories, the inventory/sales ratios that result are similar to those examined in Chapter 7. This is roughly the way BEA constructs real inventory/sales ratios and provides a time series for past quarters. The problem is to forecast the level of real nonfarm inventories. If forecast values for the I/S ratio can be assumed, these can be multiplied by the forecast levels of real final sales of goods to derive values for the real level of nonfarm inventories.

Figure 8-3 presents a plot of the ratio of real nonfarm business inventories to final sales of goods from first quarter 1947 through fourth quarter 1983. Two features are striking: (1) on average, the level of the I/S ratio shifted upwards between 1965 and 1969;[26] and (2) the I/S ratio shows greater volatility during recessions and the first four quarters following the recession trough (which include the return to the past peak in activity—recovery) than during expansion periods. The average level of the I/S ratio since 1969 seems more relevant to near-term economic forecasting. (It seems unlikely that there will be a sudden return to the pre-1967 level.)

The expected cyclical pattern during the forecast period should be the

[26] From 1947 : 1 through 1965 : 4, the average of the I/S ratio was 1.584 with a standard error of +0.047; from 1970 : 1 through 1983 : 4, the average level of the I/S ratio was 1.800 with a standard error of +0.052.

forecaster's first consideration. If the other GNP components suggest that the economy will be in recession or recovery, then the I/S ratio is likely to follow a pattern similar to that for the average of the most recent four recessions, shown in the second to last column in Table 8-8. During recent recession-recovery periods (shown as the ten quarters following the peak in business activity), the I/S ratio has risen during the recession, reaching its high point roughly five quarters after the peak in activity—during this period the I/S ratio rises mainly because final sales decline and inventories are first run down and then grow more slowly than final sales.[27] During the four, eleven-quarter recession-recovery periods since 1969, the I/S ratio has generally been above its level in expansion periods. If the period being forecast appears to be an expansion period—including neither recession nor recovery—the average I/S ratio for such periods is the relevant benchmark.

The forecast levels for the ratio of real nonfarm inventories to real final sales of goods is, in the end, derived judgmentally. The difficulty of making these judgments can be eased, however, if the forecaster: (1) pays attention to the cyclical state of final sales, and (2) uses this evidence in conjunction with past evidence on I/S ratio patterns to derive the forecast pattern for the ratio.

Equation 8-13 shows how the level of real nonfarm business inventories (INVNF72) is determined by multiplying real final sales of goods (FSG72, expressed at quarterly rates) by the I/S ratio. The annual rate of change in nonfarm inventories (Δ INVNF72) is then equal to the annualized quarter-to-quarter change in the nonfarm inventory stock. Finally, the change in total business inventories (Δ INV72) is equal to the sum of the change in farm and nonfarm inventories.

$$\text{INVNF72} = (\text{FSG72}/4) * \text{ISRATIO} \qquad (8\text{-}13)$$
$$\Delta\text{INVNF72}_t = (\text{INVNF72}_t - \text{INVNF72}_{t-1}) * 4$$
$$\Delta\text{INV72} = \Delta\text{INVF72} + \Delta\text{INVNF72}$$

Real GNP.   The forecasts for all of the components of real final sales and for the change in real business inventories provide the data needed to forecast real GNP—which is simply the sum of these two aggregates.

$$\text{GNP72} = \text{FS72} + \Delta\text{INV72} \qquad (8\text{-}14)$$

The approach described above, while simple, provides a useful method for estimating real GNP and its main components at relatively low cost.[28]

---

[27] The exception was after the 1980 recession. The 1981–82 recession began only five quarters after the first quarter 1980 peak and four quarters after the second quarter 1980 trough.

[28] The Appendix to this chapter describes how this approach can be adapted to solution on a micro-computer.

TABLE 8-8 Ratios Nonfarm Inventories to Final Sales of Goods in Recession[a]

Peak Quarter Trough Quarter[b]	1948:4 1949:4	1953:2 1954:2	1957:3 1958:1	1960:1 1960:4	1969:3 1970:4	1973:4 1975:1	1980:1 1980:2	1981:2 1982:4	AVERAGES		
									FIRST 4 CYCLES	SECOND 4 CYCLES	ALL CYCLES
P	1.558	1.544	1.615	1.647	1.784	1.810	1.755	1.756	1.591	1.781	1.686
P + 1	1.558	1.548	1.622	1.633	1.792	1.850	1.812	1.764	1.590	1.811	1.701
P + 2	1.513	1.521	1.636	1.652	1.799	1.865	1.789	1.791	1.580	1.811	1.696
P + 3	1.520	1.560	1.614	1.645	1.812	1.874	1.775	1.773	1.585	1.808	1.697
P + 4	[c]1.491	1.579	1.587	1.639	1.817	1.961	[d]1.756	1.797	1.574	1.828	1.701
P + 5	1.498	1.555	1.575	1.624	1.855	1.913	1.764	1.811	1.563	1.834	1.698
P + 6	1.510	1.533	1.582	1.636	1.839	1.865	1.791	1.748	1.565	1.804	1.685
P + 7	1.471	1.545	1.606	1.617	1.866	1.844	1.791	1.733	1.560	1.808	1.684
P + 8	1.595	1.527	1.591	1.619	1.853	1.820	1.773	1.690	1.583	1.784	1.684
P + 9	1.574	1.517	1.626	1.622	1.835	1.814	1.797	1.653	1.585	1.782	1.684
P + 10	1.648	1.531	[d]1.647	1.621	1.826	1.825	1.811	1.665	1.612	1.782	1.697

Average for all other periods (67 quarters)

	1.569	1.716	
	20	47	
		Quarters	

(a) Final Sales of Goods at quarterly rates
(b) Peaks and troughs of real GNP, not reference dates of the National Bureau of Economic Research
(c) Trough quarter underlined
(d) New peak

There are three aspects of this approach which help to result in a well-considered economic forecast.

> First, the use of specific equations to derive estimates for the various sectoral activity values forces the forecaster to focus on the variables that affect each activity. This process requires two important sets of judgments by the forecaster: (1) the form of the equation—reflecting the theoretical view held by the economist-forecaster of the way the economy operates—must be determined; and (2) the forecast values for the exogenous variables must be determined.
>
> Second, combining these equations in a recursive model, at least, assures consistency among the forecasts.
>
> Third, the necessity to make judgmental forecasts for some sectors and judgmental adjustment of the error patterns for those sectors which are forecast on the basis of equations, forces the forecaster to be an economist, not merely a technician.

The forecaster does not approach a forecast *de novo,* with no prior expectations. Rather the forecaster is approaching the forecast problem with the benefit of a past forecast view and after having performed recent activity analyses. Thus, the mechanical aspects of this forecast approach only serve to test and quantify the economist-forecaster's basic view of the future.

The forecast of real economic activity on the product side can be used as a core around which to build forecasts of inflation and current dollar income flows. These two topics will be explored briefly in the rest of this chapter.

Implicit Price Deflators and Current Dollar GNP

The real economic activities measured by the National Product Account concepts discussed above differ from their market value—the amount of money which is actually spent on these goods and services—over time by the rate at which prices are changing: the inflation rate. In estimating GNP, BEA first compiles data on the market value of goods and services produced; that is, the *current dollar* GNP is estimated first. These estimates are then *de*flated to derive estimates of real, or *constant dollar,* GNP. Real GNP is then divided into the current dollar estimates to derive the *implicit* GNP deflator. The forecast approach discussed here reverses this process: forecasts of real GNP are prepared first; the inflation rate is determined next; and then the forecast values of real GNP are *in*flated to derive current dollar estimates.

The most often used inflation measure[29] in the National Product Ac-

---

[29] There is also a measure called the *chain price deflator,* which uses weights based on the relative importance of each spending sector to total GNP in the prior quarter; and there is a *fixed weight deflator,* which uses weights based on the relative importance of the spending sectors in 1972, the base year.

counts, the implicit price deflator, differs from other inflation measures—such as the consumer and producer price indexes. Whereas these other price measures are fixed-weight concepts, the deflator is a composite index (1972=100), which weights relevant price index components from the CPI and PPI by the proportion that each activity comprises of total GNP in each quarter. In other words, the implicit price deflator is a flexibly-weighted price index.[30]

As with real GNP, there are a range of forecast approaches from complex to simple which may be followed to derive forecasts for the GNP deflator. A complex—and costly—approach is to develop a detailed production-demand model to solve for prices at a disaggregated level. This is the approach followed by the large, commercial econometric models. For instance, the DRI model contains nearly 100 equations in the price block.[31] Alternatively, a single-equation model—based, for instance, on the relationship between real GNP and the money supply—can be used. While less costly than the full econometric model, such an approach limits the range of influences that the forecast inflation measure responds to and is, thus, likely to exclude some important influences. The impact of the 1973–74 and 1979 OPEC oil shocks on overall prices are examples of such influences. These are widely regarded to have resulted in one-time increases in the U.S. economy's aggregate supply curve.[32]

Once again, the approach described here takes a middle course: it is simpler than a full supply-demand price determination model, but it takes account—largely based on the forecaster's judgments—of more factors than a single-equation approach.

The factor costs-productivity analysis described in Chapter 6 can be used to derive an initial estimate of the "underlying" inflation rate. It may be recalled that the estimation of productivity required an estimate of real business output. A forecast of real GNP and its components, like that described above, permits such an estimate: real GNP less real government spending serves as a proxy for real business output. The inflation rate which results from a forecast based on the factor costs-productivity approach is narrower in scope than the implicit price deflator; it covers only the private business sector. Nevertheless, this measure provides an estimate of the "underlying" inflation rate, based on which, more detailed estimates of less aggregate price changes can be developed.

---

[30] For a fuller discussion of these differences the reader may wish to review the section in Chapter 3 on price indexes.

[31] This probably understates the process of price determination in the DRI model. The equations for explicitly determining prices, wages and productivity account for 94 out of a total 781 equations. However, these equations depend upon interaction with many of the others for solution. See Otto Eckstein, *The DRI Model of the U.S. Economy* (New York: McGraw-Hill, 1983), pp. 8–17.

[32] See J.A. Wilcox, "Why Interest Rates Were So Low in the 1970s," *American Economic Review* (Mar. 1983), for one view on this subject.

The second step requires the forecaster to prepare forecasts of the specific price indexes (deflators) for each major component of GNP. This process can, itself, be viewed in three parts. First, the forecaster must decide on how detailed the sectoral analysis is to be. Clearly, the sectoral price analysis can not be more detailed than the number of activity sectors forecast, but it may be less so. Among the considerations which will affect this decision are: the extent to which there are significant differences among the price trends of the different sectors; the ability to distinguish among these differing trends on the basis of data and judgment; and the use to which the forecast will be put—the carpet manufacturer will clearly want a detailed forecast for non-auto consumer durable goods prices. Second, the forecaster should analyze past sectoral price trends relative to the "underlying" inflation rate and other likely influences. It is partly on the basis of such analysis that the forecaster forms judgments about the future behavior of these price indexes. Third, forecast percentage changes (expressed at annual rates) for each sectoral price index are assumed.

A brief example of this process can be given. (A) It is decided to forecast the price deflator for residential construction expenditures. (B) Analysis of past price changes (expressed as annualized, quarterly percentage changes) shows that the deflator for residential construction spending (PRES) is subject to greater volatility than the deflator for total GNP (PGNP). Moreover, the percentage change in the residential construction deflator is shown to be smaller (and sometimes negative) than that for the GNP deflator or the "underlying" inflation rate in recessions and recoveries, and larger than the other measures in expansions. (C) The analysis of recent price trends—in both absolute terms and relative to the "underlying" inflation rate—in combination with the completed forecast of real economic activity serves as the basis for a judgmental forecast of the quarterly changes in the residential construction deflator. A similar process can be followed for each sectoral deflator to be forecast.

Once the sectoral price deflators have been forecast, they can be combined as a weighted average to form a forecast of the implicit GNP deflator. Equation 8-15 depicts this process for a simple four-sector example.

$$\dot{P} = (\dot{P}_c * w_c) + (\dot{P}_i * w_i) + (\dot{P}_x * w_x) - (\dot{P}_m * w_m) + (\dot{P}_g * w_g) \quad (8\text{-}15)$$

Where $\dot{P}$ = the annualized, quarterly percentage change in the GNP deflator.

$\dot{P}c$, $\dot{P}i$, $\dot{P}x$, $\dot{P}m$ and $\dot{P}g$ = the annualized, quarterly percentage changes in the deflator for consumption, investment, exports, imports, and government spending, respectively.

wc, wi, wx, wm, and wg = the share of real GNP in each quarter accounted for by each final spending sector (e.g., wc = C72/GNP72).

An example of this estimation process for 1983 is presented in Table 8-9. Forecast estimates of the main components of real GNP are used to estimate real GNP shares, the weights in equation 8-15.[33] Inflation rates are then estimated or assumed for the main components of final sales. (In Table 8-9, actual annualized percentage changes for the main components of final sales are used.) Note that the inflation rates by component do not include a value for the change in inventories. This acknowledges the complexity of deflating inventories.[34] As a result this method estimates the weighted percent changes in the deflator for final sales directly. Then, by converting the annualized percentage changes to quarterly rates and multiplying them by the value of the deflator in the previous quarter, the value of the final sales deflator can be estimated. If the simplifying assumption is made that inventory prices change at the same rate, on average, as the prices for final goods and services, the percentage changes for the final sales deflator can be used as a proxy to compute the GNP deflator. As can be seen from Table 8-9, the estimated percentage changes for both final sales and GNP provide close estimates of the actual values for the individual quarters and on a fourth quarter-to-fourth quarter basis (estimated changes of 3.9% for final sales and GNP compared to actual rates of 3.8% and 4.1%, respectively).[35]

Using forecast values for the real GNP components and the implicit deflators, the forecaster can compute the forecast values for current dollar GNP. This can be approached from two directions. First, the forecast values of real GNP can be multiplied by the forecast values for the implicit GNP deflator so as to compute values for current dollar GNP directly. Second, the forecast values for real activity in each of the final sales sectors can be multiplied by the associated deflator values, and the sectoral current dollar amounts summed to derive current dollar final sales forecasts. These values can then be contrasted with the previously estimated values for current dollar GNP in order to derive estimates of the current dollar values for the change in business inventories. At this point, the forecaster should evaluate all of the forecast results for reasonableness. If one result appears unlikely— say, the current dollar values for the change in business inventories imply

---

[33] The values for personal consumption, residential construction, business fixed investment, and imports are the equation-derived estimates from Tables 8-1, 8-5, and 8-6 respectively. The values shown for the change in inventories, exports, and government spending are actual. In an *ex ante* forecast these would be judgmentally derived exogenous estimates. The values shown for final sales and GNP, thus, reflect the summation of these judgmental and equation-derived estimates.

[34] There is no deflator for the change in business inventories. BEA does compute deflators for the stock of business inventories, however. It is also necessary to compute the Inventory Valuation Adjustment (IVA) to convert from the change in business inventories in current dollars to constant dollars.

[35] Of course, an *ex ante* forecast would be subject to greater error from at least two sources: (1) the values for real change in inventories, exports, and government spending would be estimates; and (2) all the inflation rates by component would be estimates.

TABLE 8-9 Estimation of Deflators

	1983 I	II	III	IV
		BILLIONS OF	1972 DOLLARS	
ESTIMATED REAL GNP COMPONENTS				
Personal Consumption	993.8	999.0	1024.7	1030.7
Residential Construction	53.0	59.0	60.9	61.7
Business Fixed Investment	164.1	164.4	171.0	179.8
Change in Inventories*	-15.4	-5.4	3.8	8.7
Net Exports	26.1	21.6	18.4	14.2
+ Exports*	137.3	136.2	140.7	140.6
- Imports	111.2	114.6	122.3	126.4
Government*	292.9	292.1	295.2	292.2
Final Sales	1529.9	1536.1	1570.2	1578.6
Real GNP	1514.5	1530.7	1574.0	1587.3
		PER	CENT	
ESTIMATED REAL GNP SHARES				
Personal Consumption	65.62	65.26	65.10	64.93
Residential Construction	3.50	3.85	3.87	3.89
Business Fixed Investment	10.84	10.74	10.86	11.33
Change in Inventories*	-1.02	-0.35	0.24	0.55
Net Exports	1.72	1.41	1.17	0.89
+ Exports*	9.07	8.90	8.94	8.86
- Imports	7.34	7.49	7.77	7.96
Government*	19.34	19.08	18.75	18.41
Final Sales	101.02	100.35	99.76	99.45

	1983 I	II	III	IV
		ANNUALIZED PERCE	NTAGE RATES	
*INFLATION RATES BY COMPONENT**				
Personal Consumption	2.2	4.6	4.2	2.8
Residential Construction	11.4	-1.6	8.6	-0.4
Business Fixed Investment	-4.2	-2.6	0.1	1.3
+ Exports*	4.3	3.6	3.9	6.6
- Imports	-17.5	8.3	11.3	-10.7
Government*	8.2	4.7	4.4	4.5
ESTIMATED DEFLATORS		*1972=100*		
Final Sales	212.96	214.67	216.46	218.72
Annualized Percent Change	4.60	3.25	3.38	4.24
Real GNP	212.38	214.08	215.87	218.12
Annualized Percent Change	4.60	3.25	3.38	4.24
ACTUAL DEFLATORS				
Final Sales	213.28	214.74	216.41	218.49
Annualized Percent Change	5.23	2.77	3.15	3.90
Real GNP	212.83	214.55	216.44	218.53
Annualized Percent Change	5.50	3.27	3.57	3.92

* Actual data used

inventory/sales ratios that are far out of line with recent trends—one or more of the results may need to be adjusted.

A final test of the likelihood of the forecasts of current dollar GNP—and, by implication, of the real and/or inflation components—is to compare forecast current dollar GNP growth with the likely growth in the monetary aggregates and velocity. This relationship is depicted in equation 8-16.

$$\dot{M} * \dot{V} = \dot{GNP} = \dot{P} * \dot{GNP72} \qquad (8\text{-}16)$$

where $\dot{M}$ = the growth rate for the relevant monetary aggregate
$\dot{V}$ = the growth rate for the related velocity measure
$\dot{GNP}$ = the growth rate for current dollar GNP
$\dot{P}$ = the growth rate for the implicit GNP deflator
$\dot{GNP72}$ = the growth rate for real GNP

All growth rates expressed in fourth quarter-to-fourth quarter terms.

Since October 1979, the Federal Reserve has aimed at slowing the growth of the monetary aggregates to specified fourth quarter-to-fourth quarter target growth rates. While there has been some slippage in meeting these targets, they have constituted a constraint on economic performance. As a practical matter, whenever forecast current dollar GNP growth is significantly greater than the rate implied by the monetary policy constraint, the forecast should be seriously questioned. Results in 1980–82 showed that the Federal Reserve's efforts to slow monetary growth constrained GNP growth in three phases: (1) current dollar GNP growth faster than was consistent with the money supply targets resulted in sharply rising interest rates and an acceleration in velocity; (2) the high, rising interest rates choked off real GNP growth—leading to the 1981–82 recession; and (3) eventually, the low level of economic activity slowed inflation, so that current dollar GNP growth conformed to the monetary growth targets. Indeed, as the recession lengthened and inflation slowed sharply (partly due to non-monetary forces—the oil glut and abundant food supplies), current dollar GNP growth fell below the target growth for money supply, velocity and interest rates declined, and real GNP growth picked up. Even a quasi-monetarist view of the 1981-83 cycle ends up attributing much of the cyclical forces—behind both the recession and the recovery—to monetary policy.

The entire process of estimating (a) real GNP, its components, and growth, (b) the aggregate inflation rate, (c) current dollar GNP and its growth, and (d) subjecting these results to a monetary policy constraint is an *iterative* process. It is unlikely that the first pass at a forecast will lead to a consistent result. However, this approach provides the forecaster with some criteria for adjusting the forecast and re-estimating it.

GNP Forecast: National Income Approach

The construction of a GNP forecast from the income side is less straightforward than a product-side forecast. Although the components of GNP on the product account represent a mixture of inflation and real economic activities, detailed forecasts for both the real quantities and price levels can be made using the forecaster's theoretical and judgmental insights. The National Income Accounts, however, are largely accounting relationships which distinguish those income flows—such as wage and salary income and corporate profits—which result from current production, from those income flows—such as transfers and contributions for social insurance—which are unrelated to current production.

Compiling a current dollar GNP forecast based on income flows is worth the effort for three reasons. First, the income flows are important and, as will be shown, can be used to refine forecasts of product-side activities. Second, the accounting relationship between product- and income-side GNP serves as a check on the product-side forecast. The forecaster is forced to insure that reasonable income flows can be derived to match the already forecast product-side GNP flows. Third, the additional information an income-side forecast provides allows the forecaster to develop a more detailed commentary about the likely performance of the economy.

The two components which account for most of GNP in the National Income Account are personal income and corporate profits. Table 8-10 lists the main components of the National Income Account and shows their relationships. As can be seen, most components are derived from either personal income or corporate profits. The role of these two important income flows, their composition, and their relationship to GNP will be briefly described in this section. Many of the components are estimated on the basis of judgment and recent activity analysis, *given a forecast of product-side GNP*.

Personal Income, Disposable Personal Income, Consumption, and Savings

Personal income accounts for more than 80% of total GNP. A detailed approach for preparing forecasts of personal income at a monthly frequency has already been described in Part II. Quarterly forecasts of personal income and its major components can be derived by averaging the monthly forecasts.

It is useful to separate personal income into its main outlay categories: tax and nontax payments, and disposable personal income. Disposable personal income, in turn, can be divided among: consumption, personal transfers, net interest payments, and personal saving. When disposable personal income is deflated by the personal consumption deflator, the resulting real

TABLE 8-10   Gross National Product: Income Account—Principal Components

	COMPONENTS		SOURCE
	Gross National Product	(1)	= (5) + (2)
Less:	Capital Consumption Allowance with Capital consumption adjustment	(2)	= (3) + (4)
	Capital Consumption allowance	(3)	KBFI72 & CP
	Capital Consumption adjustment	(4)	CP
Equals:	Net National Product	(5)	= (10) + (6) + (7) + (8) − (9)
Less:	Indirect Business Tax and nontax liability	(6)	CP
	Business Transfers Payments	(7)	CP
	Statistical Discrepancy	(8)	Exog.
Plus:	Subsidies less current surplus of government enterprises	(9)	Exog.
Equals:	National Income	(10)	= (19) + (11) + (12) + (13) + (14) − (15) − (16) − (17) − (18)
Less:	Corporate profits with inventory valuation and capital consumption adjustment	(11)	CP
	Net Interest	(12)	PI & CP
	Contributions for social insurance	(13)	PI & CP
	Wage accruals less disbursements	(14)	Exog.
Plus:	Government transfer payments to persons	(15)	PI
	Personal Interest Income	(16)	PI
	Personal Dividend Income	(17)	PI
	Business Transfer Payments	(18)	PI & CP
Equals:	Personal Income	(19)	PI

PI = Personal Income
CP = Corporate Profits

estimate can be used to compute an alternative estimate of real personal consumption expenditures (C72). In this way, an important component of real GNP, estimated on the product side, can be checked from the income side. Moreover, by subtracting the small amounts for personal transfer payments and net interest payments from the remainder of disposable personal income, the forecaster can derive an estimate of personal saving and the

TABLE 8-11   Personal Income and its Disposition: 1979–83

	1979	1980	1981	1982	1983
	(BILLIONS OF DOLLARS)				
Personal Income	1951.2	2165.3	2435.0	2578.6	2742.1
Less: Personal Tax and					
Nontax Payments	301.0	336.5	387.4	402.1	406.5
Federal	230.6	257.7	298.6	304.7	295.9
State and Local	70.4	78.8	88.7	97.4	110.5
Equals: Disposable Personal					
Income	1650.2	1828.9	2047.6	2176.5	2335.6
Less: Personal Consumption					
Expenditures	1507.2	1688.1	1857.2	1991.9	2158.0
Interest Paid by					
Consumers to Business	45.5	49.6	54.3	58.1	62.8
Net Personal Transfer					
Payments to Foreigners	0.8	1.0	0.9	1.1	1.2
Equals: Personal Saving	96.7	110.2	135.3	125.4	113.6
Personal Saving as a					
Percentage of Disposable					
Personal Income	5.9%	6.0%	6.6%	5.8%	4.9%

personal saving rate (personal saving divided by disposable personal income, expressed as a percentage)—two important economic measures. Table 8-11 presents annual data for 1979-83 for Personal Income and its outlay components.

The portion of personal income paid out in taxes is estimated judgmentally. It is useful, however, to separate tax payments[36] between those received by the Federal government and those received by state and local governments. The quarterly changes in Federal personal tax receipts reflect: (1) the growth in current dollar income, which drives income tax receipts; and (2) fiscal policy. The second of these two factors makes it desirable to forecast Federal personal tax receipts judgmentally. The forecaster must and should, make explicit assumptions about Federal tax policy. During periods of major tax policy changes—such as the tax rate cuts which occurred in fiscal years 1982 and 1983 as a result of the Economic Recovery Tax Act of 1981 and the Tax Equity and Fiscal Responsibility Act of 1982— such changes can significantly alter the relationship between income and

---

[36] Nontax payments include user fees and fines. These represent about 1% of Federal personal tax and nontax receipts and about 10% for state and local governments.

Federal tax receipts. Tax changes are likely to have important impacts on economic performance. Thus, considerable effort should be given to forecasting these flows: the forecast of Federal personal tax payments is one of the most important assumptions underlying a medium-term macroeconomic forecast. Personal tax payments to state and local governments, in general, display a more regular relationship to income trends.

Disposable personal income—personal income less tax and nontax payments to government entities—is an important economic aggregate, largely because of its basic role in the Keynesian consumption function. When deflated by the personal consumption deflator, the resulting measure of real disposable income (YD72) can be used to derive an alternative estimate of real consumption (C72) to that estimated from equation 8-2. This income-based estimate of real consumption can be derived using equation 8-17.

$$C72 = a + b * YD72 \tag{8-17}$$

coefficients	t statistics
a = −14.86	(−0.67)
b = 0.92	(35.57)
rho = 0.71	(7.23)

$$\overline{R}^2 = 0.9958 \quad \text{D-W} = 2.24 \quad \text{SER} = 6.93$$

Equation 8-17 was estimated from first quarter 1967 through fourth quarter 1980. The coefficient for real disposable income is consistent with expectations about the marginal propensity to consume: for each $1 billion increase in real disposable income, real consumption increases by just over $920 million. The summary statistics for equation 8-17 are quite good. The $\overline{R}^2$ indicates that 99.6% of the variation in real consumption is accounted for by the relationship. After a Cochrane-Orcutt correction, the Durbin-Watson statistic indicates a lack of serial correlation, and the standard error of the regression indicates that the estimated value will be within ±1.4% of the actual in 1983, 95% of the time.

Table 8-12 compares the forecast results for real personal consumption expenditures using equations 8-2 and 8-17. Each equation provides close estimates and each has advantages: the results using equation 8-2 provide closer estimates for 1983 as a whole, though the root mean square error is minimized using equation 8-17. It is desirable to follow both approaches. For instance, equation 8-2 performed slightly better than equation 8-17 over the estimation period: the standard error of the regression was lower ($4.94 billion) for the former than the latter ($6.93 billion) equation. Moreover, the independent variables used in equation 8-2 are also used for estimating other

TABLE 8-12   Alternative Forecasts of Real Consumption: 1983

	QUARTERS				ANNUAL	IV Q − IV Q
	I	II	III	IV	AVERAGE	GROWTH
	BILLIONS OF CONSTANT (1972) DOLLARS					
	Results based on Equation 8-2					
Actual	986.7	1010.6	1016.0	1032.2	1011.4	5.4%
Forecast	993.8	999.0	1024.7	1030.7	1012.0	5.4
Error (Act − Fcst)	−7.1	11.6	−8.7	1.5	−0.6	0.0
-as % of Actual	−0.7%	1.1%	−0.9	0.1	−0.1	
	RMSE = $15.3 Billion		MAPE = 0.7%			
	Results based on Equation 8-17					
Actual	986.7	1010.6	1016.0	1032.2	1011.4	5.4%
Forecast	983.2	991.8	1018.4	1030.8	1006.0	5.8
Error (Act − Fcst)	3.5	18.8	−2.4	1.4	5.4	−0.4
-as % of Actual	0.4%	1.9%	−0.2%	0.1%	0.5%	
	RMSE = $9.7 Billion		MAPE = 0.6%			

product-side GNP components.[37] The important point, however, is that using both equations provides the forecaster with two error patterns which can be used to refine the error pattern incorporated in the final forecast. Such an iterative process is recommended.

A further check on the forecast can be performed by estimating the remaining outlays from disposable income and deriving forecasts of personal saving and the personal saving rate.

Corporate Profits

The role of corporate profits in the National Income Accounts is complex. Moreover, although corporate profits comprise a small but volatile portion of GNP (ranging from just over 4% of GNP to just under 10% since 1970), forecasts for corporate profits and related flows are vital to constructing an income-side GNP forecast.

The approach to forecasting corporate profits and related flows described here requires the forecaster to make judgments about the main contributing factors, based on past trends and expected cyclical developments. Table 8-13 presents data for 1983 on corporate profits and related measures which can be used to derive such a forecast.

The first step is to derive a forecast of operating profits for nonfinancial corporations (line 6 in Table 8-13). This measure excludes inventory profits and values depreciation on the current replacement cost of capital assets rather than according to their original (historical) cost. Operating profits,

---

[37] It should be remembered that the forecasts of personal income values, from which the estimates of disposable personal income are made, depend on some of these same variables.

TABLE 8-13 Corporate Profits and Related Measures: 1983 (billions of dollars, unless otherwise stated)

	I	II	III	IV	ANNUAL AVERAGE
			QUARTERS		
(1) Gross National Product	3171.5	3272.0	3362.2	3436.2	3310.5
(2) Gross Domestic Product- Nonfinancial Corporations	1817.6	1892.4	1957.8	2019.0	1921.7
(3) -Share	57.3%	57.8%	58.2%	58.8%	58.0%
Nonfinancial Corporations Operating Profit Margins					
(4) -as percentage of GNP	4.2%	5.1%	5.8%	6.3%	5.4%
(5) -as percentage of GDP	7.4%	8.8%	9.9%	10.8%	9.3%
(6) Operating Profits	133.9	165.7	194.5	217.2	177.8
(7) Inventory Valuation Adjustment	-1.7	-10.6	-18.3	-6.3	-9.2
(8) Capital Consumption Adjustment	15.9	27.3	39.0	47.6	32.4
(9) Profits, Pretax	119.7	149.0	173.8	175.9	154.6
(10) -Profits tax liability	41.8	55.0	63.9	64.2	56.2
(11) -Effective profits tax rate	34.9%	36.9%	36.8%	36.5%	36.4%
(12) -Profits, Aftertax	77.9	94.0	109.9	111.7	98.4
Total Corporate Pretax Profits					
(13) Nonfinancial Corporations	119.7	149.0	173.8	175.9	154.6
(14) Other Corporations	29.8	33.8	31.9	30.6	31.5
(15) Total	149.5	182.8	205.7	206.5	186.1
(16) Depreciation (Replacement Cost)	228.3	229.8	233.1	235.2	231.6
(17) Depreciation (Historical Cost)	214.4	204.2	195.5	189.0	200.8
(18) Capital Consumption Adjustment	13.9	25.6	37.6	46.2	30.8
Corporate Profits Tax Liability					
(19) Nonfinancial Corporations	41.8	55.0	63.9	64.2	56.2
(20) Other Corporations	19.7	21.0	21.0	21.1	20.7
(21) Total	61.5	76.0	84.9	85.3	76.9
(22) Effective Corporate Tax Rate	41.1%	41.6%	41.3%	41.3%	41.3%
Aftertax Corporate Profits					
(23) Nonfinancial Corporations	77.9	94.0	109.9	111.7	98.4
(24) Other Corporations	10.1	12.7	10.8	9.5	10.8
(25) Total	88.0	106.7	120.7	121.2	109.2

thus, are a measure of corporations' profitability based on current operations. It is recommended that corporate profits be forecast for nonfinancial corporations and financial corporations separately; the former comprise a larger share of both output and total profits and can more easily be related to overall economic activity than the latter. Gross Domestic Product of nonfinancial corporations (GDPNF) measures the value of nonfinancial corporate output and has shown a fairly stable relationship to GNP: accounting for some 57% to 59% of GNP between 1967 and 1983 (line 3). This stable relationship—which is even more stable over one or two year spans—can be used to estimate GDPNF, given forecast values for GNP. It can be assumed that: (a) in normal times, corporations attempt to price their output so as to achieve some target profit margin relative to sales; but (b) during downturns—when demand unexpectedly weakens—these profit margins narrow. Thus, analysis of recent profit margin trends—line 4 from Table 8-13 shows operating profit margins as a percentage of GNP, line 5 as a percentage of GDPNF—and the expected cyclical performance of the economy can be performed to estimate nonfinancial corporate operating profits (line 6). An alternative approach is to estimate a regression relationship between nonfinancial corporate operating profits and either GNP or GDPNF. While such a relationship yields close estimates in normal times, it tends to overestimate them during downturns. For this reason, a carefully constructed judgmental forecast is more appropriate.

Operating profits of all corporations enter GNP directly. Before turning to operating profits for nonfinancial corporations, however, it is worthwhile to examine nonfinancial profits as reported for tax purposes (line 9). This measure differs from operating profits by including inventory profits and depreciation valued at the original (historical) cost of the assets. The inventory valuation adjustment (IVA, line 7) is a measure of inventory profits— the rise in revenue over costs due to the change in value caused by inflation and in the mix of goods held in inventory. Similarly, the capital consumption adjustment (CCAdj. line 8) measures the difference between the value of depreciated assets at historical and replacement cost. This value can be estimated using the deflator for business fixed investment and making explicit assumptions about changes in tax laws. Both the IVA and the Capital Consumption Allowance are frequently expressed as negative values representing the adjustments from "book" profits needed to derive operating profits.[38] In this approach, where the aim is to go from operating profits to book profits, the procedure is reversed: the negative values for IVA and CCAdj are subtracted from operating profits.

Book, or pretax profits (lines 9 and 13) are computed in order to calcu-

---

[38] The Capital Consumption Adjustment was positive in 1983, reflecting the effect of liberalized depreciation allowances as a result of 1981 and 1982 tax law changes.

late corporate income tax payments[39] and, thus, aftertax profits. As with forecasting personal tax payments, nonfinancial corporate tax liabilities (line 10 and 19) are estimated on the basis of past trends for the effective tax rate (line 11) and judgments about expected tax policy. Once again, the assumptions about tax policy—whether personal or corporate—are among the most important judgments a forecaster must reach. Aftertax profits (lines 12 and 23) are then the basis for dividends paid by nonfinancial corporations (not shown, but these can be estimated based on the assumed dividend payout ratio) and retained earnings.

Book profits for all other corporations (line 14) include the Federal Reserve (viewed as a corporation for national income accounting purposes), financial corporations, and "rest of the world" (ROW) profits (net profits received from foreign operations of U.S. corporations). These account for from 10% to 12% of total corporate book profits. Federal Reserve profits: (1) result from interest earned on U.S. Treasury securities, and so are related to interest rates on U.S. Treasuries; and (2) are taxed at a roughly 98% rate. Financial corporations' profits also largely depend on interest income, while ROW profits depend on both: (1) economic activity abroad, and (2) foreign exchange rate movements. While the Capital Consumption Adjustment applies to all corporations, IVA applies only to nonfinancial corporations.

The corporate profit concepts shown in Table 8-13 can be used for analysis of the corporate sector. In particular such concepts as retained earnings, cash flow, and corporate savings can be derived from those measures described in Table 8-13. These may be useful inputs, or checks, on capital spending and governmental budget deficit forecasts. More to the point, however, these corporate profit concepts can be combined with the personal income components to estimate GNP as in Table 8-10.

SUMMARY

The bulk of this chapter has been concerned with a detailed discussion of an eclectic model for medium-term GNP forecasting. It should be strongly restated that this model was not intended as definitive, or even "state of the art." There are much more sophisticated models for forecasting GNP. Rather, the model described here was used to illustrate an approach to GNP forecasting. Using (1) few simply derived, exogenous variables, (2) a few

---

[39] Other taxes paid by corporations—mainly excise, sales, and property taxes—are counted as pretax costs and not included in either operating or book profits. This item is, however, the major difference between National Income and Net National Product, see Table 8-10.

well-thought out relationships (depicted by regression equations), and (3) estimates based on judgment or external forecasts, the forecaster is able to build a simple, yet detailed, forecast model for real GNP. This model is more useful than a single-equation reduced form model of GNP because it allows the economist to draw conclusions about not only total real GNP, but also about its components. The more detail in a forecast, the more criteria there are for judging its likelihood. Moreover, this approach is not very costly: there are only a few regressions to be computed, which need only be updated annually; forecast updates can be computed manually, or at little more cost but at much greater speed, using a microcomputer. (See Appendix to this chapter.) The real GNP model can be viewed as the core of a broader forecast including: inflation, personal income, corporate profits, and current dollar GNP.

Finally, it should be noted that this need not be a static approach. Improvements should always be sought. Clearly, it is easier to improve a basic model than to have no model at all. Thus, the model described in this chapter might better be viewed as the starting point for the reader's own model building.

QUESTIONS FOR REVIEW AND RESEARCH

8-1 Real GNP, while a measure of output produced, is a broader measure of economic activity than industrial production because it includes the output of the private service sector, the government sector, and the output of domestic producers for export net of the output of foreign producers imported by the U.S. Industrial production, on the other hand, measures the total output of domestic manufacturers, mines, and utilities.

(a) Using the data in the table below, compare the trends in U.S. economic performance depicted by the quarterly percentage changes in these two measures from first quarter 1975 through fourth quarter 1979. To what extent can the differences be accounted for by the performance of real consumer spending on services, real government spending, and foreign trade flows?

(b) Estimate a relationship between real GNP (GNP72) and industrial production (INDPROD) over this period of the form:

$$GNP72 = a + b * INDPROD$$

Remembering that industrial production is a monthly measure, might this equation be useful for estimating a monthly measure of real GNP?

(c) Evaluate your estimated relationship by performing an *ex post* forecast for real GNP in 1980 and explain the results. Can you suggest additional economic measures which improve these results?

		REAL GNP	INDUSTRIAL PRODUCTION
		(BILLIONS OF 1972 DOLLARS)	1967=100
1975	I	1,204.3	113.2
	II	1,218.9	114.2
	III	1,246.1	120.5
	IV	1,257.3	123.4
1976	I	1,285.0	127.6
	II	1,293.7	129.9
	III	1,301.1	131.5
	IV	1,313.1	132.5
1977	I	1,341.3	134.8
	II	1,363.3	138.0
	III	1,385.8	139.3
	IV	1,388.4	140.3
1978	I	1,400.0	140.8
	II	1,437.0	145.1
	III	1,448.8	147.9
	IV	1,468.4	150.7
1979	I	1,472.6	152.7
	II	1,469.2	152.3
	III	1,486.6	152.6
	IV	1,489.3	152.5

8-2   The population 16 years old and over (POP16&) is included in equation 8-2—which estimates real consumption spending (C72)—as a measure of the trend rate of consumption growth. Using annual data from the latest issue of *The Economic Report of the President* construct a data series for the post-war period that is equal to this population measure times its coefficient in equation 8-2.

$$C72_{trend} = 10.79 * POP16\&$$

Plot and compare the annual growth rates for your constructed series with those for actual real consumption spending. How do the average annual growth rates over the full period compare? Can the deviations in the growth rate of C72 from those for $C72_{trend}$ be accounted for by movements in inflation and the unemployment rate? Discuss the relative importance of cyclical and trend forces on real consumption growth in the post-war period.

8-3   Contrast the annual percentage changes of real consumption of: (a) durable goods (CDMV&P72 + CDO72); (b) nondurable goods (CN72); and (c) services (CS72).

Estimate regression relationships at quarterly frequencies between real consumption expenditures for nondurable goods and for services, respectively, and the population 16 years and over.

$$CN72 = a + b * POP16\&$$
$$CS72 = a + b * POP16\&$$

Do these trend-based equations provide a useful basis for forecasting these consumption components?

8-4   The low value for the interest rate coefficient in equation 8-6 appears to suggest a weaker interest rate response for real residential construction spending than seems consistent with economic theory. It was stated that this may reflect the interest rate responses already captured by equations 7-26 through 7-28 for estimating housing starts (which, in turn, enter equation 8-6 as independent variables). E·aluate this suggestion. (You may find it useful to solve equation 8-6 algebraically in a reduced form after substituting the estimated forms of the housing starts equations. The resulting reduced form of equation 8-6, thus accentuates the role of interest rates.)

8-5   One notion of the accelerator is that businesses invest—increase the capital stock—in response to past increases in consumer demand. Analyze this concept using quarterly data for real consumption spending and real business fixed investment. Can a statistical relationship be established which supports this view and is useful for forecasting? If so, what other variables should also be considered?

8-6   Consult recent issues of the *Survey of Current Business* and the *Economic Report of the President* for data on U.S. exports by commodity and country. Compute and analyze the percentage of total exports accounted for by the (a) five most important export commodities, and (b) five largest trading partners of the U.S. What does this analysis suggest about the concentration of U.S. exports? Do these percentages reflect the volatility in exports or are these more important trading relationships more stable than total exports? Finally, explain how such an analysis may be useful in developing assumptions for the level of real exports in a GNP forecast.

8-7   The *Federal Reserve Bulletin* contains a Table on Foreign Exchange Rates (Table 3.28) which includes an index of the weighted average exchange value of the U.S. dollar against ten other major currencies. (This Table is summarized in the *Economic Report of the President*.) Re-estimate equation 8-12 including quarterly average values for this index and evaluate the performance of the new equation for estimating real imports (M72) in 1983 compared to the results shown in Table 8-6. Discuss the difficulties posed by having to forecast this index *ex ante*.

8-8   Compare the total on-budget U.S. government expenditures for 1983 to the current dollar Federal spending totals included in GNP. Construct a table which shows the translation from the Budget to the National Product Account. Compare the National Product Account totals for these items against the amounts originally projected for the Federal Government Budget in fiscal years 1983-84. (Remember, fiscal year 1983 includes fourth quarter 1982 and ends in third quarter 1983. Fourth quarter 1983 is included in fiscal year 1984.)

8-9   Construct a table for the period since 1970 showing quarterly percentage changes in: the implicit GNP deflator; the personal consumption deflator, and the Consumer Price Index-all urban (CPI-U). Analyze the extent to which any differences in the personal consumption deflator and CPI-U can be explained by the difference in weights on spending for durable goods, nondurable goods, and services. Discuss the steps necessary in translating forecast changes in the CPI-U into changes for the personal consumption deflator. Indicate some of the factors which should be considered in devising forecasts of the nonconsumption components of the implicit GNP deflator.

8-10   Construct a table similar to Table 8-13 using annual data for the past ten years. Analyze and discuss the performance of corporate profitability itself and relative to broader economic performance during this period.

8-11   Compare the regression results for equation 8-17—which estimates real consumption as a function of real disposable income from first quarter 1967 through fourth quarter 1980 (including a Cochrane-Orcutt correction)—with the similar simple regression equation estimated from first quarter 1970 through fourth quarter 1973 in Chapter 4. Indicate how the longer estimation period improves the equation results. Contrast forecasts for the 1981-83 period using the two equations. What conclusions do your results suggest about the optimal estimation period for a forecast equation?

APPENDIX
TO CHAPTER 8
Adapting the real GNP model for solution with a micro-computer

There has been a rapid acceptance of personal, or micro-computers for business use in recent years. Moreover, the development of "spreadsheet" software has greatly extended the business applications of micro-computers, while the comparatively low purchase cost (ranging from $1,000 to $10,000 for a complete system) and the near absence of operating cost has added to the appeal.

An economic model, like that developed in Chapter 8, can be adapted for routine solution on a micro-computer using a spread sheet program. Such a solution approach has a number of advantages over alternative methods.

> Calculation is far quicker than manual solution. As a result, it is easier to estimate alternative forecasts based on slight variations in assumptions. This, in turn, leads to clearer judgments about the truly critical assumptions: those for which small input changes result in large effects on outcomes.
>
> The results of forecasts and forecast versions are easily stored on floppy, or hard disks.
>
> The cost of this speed and versatility is far less than on-line solution on a time-sharing system, yet it retains the desirable interaction that time-sharing systems have, but that batch systems do not. As noted above, aside from the initial purchase price, almost the only other cost is the trivial expense of electricity.

There is a wide and growing range of micro-computers with compatible software that can be used as described below. The specific system on which the example in this Appendix was generated is an Apple III™ computer using a *VISICALC III*™ software package.[1] It should be noted that the micro-computer is used only for solving an already-estimated model; estimation takes place separately, and can be performed: (1) using some other software package designed for performing econometric analysis—such as

---

[1] *Apple III* is a registered trademark of Apple Computer, Inc. *VISICALC* and *VISICALC III* are registered trademarks of Personal Software, Inc.

TSP (Time Series Processor); (2) on a time-sharing system accessed through the micro-computer; or (3) using a different computer system altogether.

Table A8-1 presents a print out of a forecast solution, using the model portrayed in Figure 8-1 and composed of the equations derived in Chapter 8 for forecasting real GNP. This is an *ex post*, out-of-sample, solution for the eight quarters from first quarter 1982 through fourth quarter 1983. In general, the estimation period for the equations was first quarter 1967 through fourth quarter 1980.

For ease of discussion, the output shown in Table A8-1 can be viewed in seven parts or blocks. The first block, A, contains values for the independent variables—the population 16 years old and over (POP 16&), the unemployment rate (UNEMP RATE), the year-over-year percentage change in CPIU (INFLAT), the prime rate, unit sales of domestically produced autos (CARSDOM), unit sales of foreign autos (CARSFOR), housing starts (HUSTS) and the real capital stock (KSTOCK72)—and three key solution aggregates: real GNP (GNP72), current dollar GNP, and the implicit price deflator. The values for the first seven of the independent variables are input exogenously. Thus, by making slight changes in one or more of the independent variables, a different solution can be derived, and so the sensitivity of the assumptions can be tested. The values for the real capital stock are determined endogenously, quarter by quarter, as in equation 8-10. One of the attractive features of "spreadsheet" programs like this one is that a variable such as KSTOCK72 can be solved and presented near the top of the spreadsheet even though it requires solution of another variable, BFI72, which is performed near the bottom (line 70) of the table.

Block B of Table A8-1 contains the equations for estimating real consumption and its components. The estimation of real personal consumption expenditures (C72), based on equation 8-2, is shown in detail in lines 12 through 19. This estimation will be described in detail; most of the other equations are solved in a similar manner.

Lines 12 through 15 show the quarterly contributions of each of the terms in equation 8-2. Thus, line 12 is simply the constant term (−776.02) which is repeated in each column (or quarter). Line 13, however, shows the value which results from multiplying the coefficient for population from equation 6-2 (10.794) by the value for population 16 years old and over in each quarter. This is done in the program by specifying each cell (a column-row combination) in row 13 as equal to the product of the coefficient times the cell of the independent variable. (In this case, the matrix location is D1: first quarter 1982, POP 16&.) This method of showing the product of each independent variable and its coefficient is useful for gauging the relative contribution of each variable both at a particular time and over time. The unemployment rate (line 14) and inflation (line 15) variables are treated similarly.

Line 16, RHO ADJ, recalls the fact that in estimating equation 6-2 a

Cochrane-Orcutt adjustment was performed to remove the effects of serial correlation. As a result, a term, rho, was found which must be incorporated into the forecast estimation. This is done by multiplying the value of rho by the difference between the actual value of C72 in the prior quarter and the sum of the products of the estimated coefficients and independent values in the prior quarter.[2] This calculation is depicted in equation A8-2, using the same symbols as equation 8-2, and values for second quarter 1982.

$$\text{RHO ADJ}_t = \text{rho} * (\text{C72 ACT}_{t-1} - a - b_1 * \text{POP16\&}_{t-1} \\ - b_2 * \text{RU}_{t-1} - b_3 * \text{INFLAT}_{t-1}) \quad \text{(A8-1)}$$

$$\text{RHO ACT}_{82:2} = 0.66267 * (961.4 + 776.02 - 1874.54 + 91.64 + 28.31) \\ = -11.38$$

All lagged values must be input for the first forecast quarter, but in subsequent quarters the lagged variables can be cited by their matrix location. This makes re-estimating and updating easier.

The components of equation 8-2 are summed on line 17 to form an estimate of total real consumption, C72 EST—thus, for each quarter (column) the value on line 17 is equal to the sum of the values on lines 12 through 16. When this value is contrasted with the actual value (line 18, C72 ACT), the difference, or ERROR, can be determined (line 19). In an *ex post* forecast, as shown in Table A8-1 where all the actual values are known, the error terms are exactly known. These values may then be used to forecast the future error pattern. Either some mechanistic—average or moving average—or judgmental approach may be used to determine future errors. Thus, for an *ex ante* forecast, the estimated values for real consumption (C72 EST) and the forecast errors (ERROR) would be added to derive the "actual" forecast value (C72 ACT).

Real consumption of motor vehicles and parts (CDMV&P72) and of other durable goods (CDO72) are computed in similar fashion based on equation 8-3 (for CDMV&P72, lines 20 through 27) and equation 6-4 (for CDO72, lines 28 through 35). Real consumption of nondurable goods and services (CN&S72) are then derived as residuals.

CN&S72 EST = C72 EST − CDMV&P72 EST − CDO72 EST
CN&S72 ACT = C72 ACT − CDMV&P72 ACT − CDO72 ACT

This aggregate can then be split into its component parts (CN72, line 39; and CS72, line 40).

Most of the rest of the model is solved in a like manner. Block C shows

---

[2] See Robert S. Pindyck and Daniel L. Rubenfeld, *Econometric Models and Economic Forecasts* (New York: McGraw-Hill, 1976), pp. 111–12.

TABLE A8-1 Forecast of Real GNP and Components: 1982–83

			I 82	II 82	III 82
	(1)	POP 16&	173.67	174.19	174.71
	(2)	UNEMP. RATE	8.77	9.46	9.89
	(3)	INFLAT	7.60	6.79	5.77
	(4)	PRIME RATE	16.27	16.50	14.71
	(5)	CARSDOM	5.77	5.48	5.50
Block A	(6)	CARSFOR	2.24	2.03	2.22
	(7)	HUSTS	0.92	0.95	1.12
	(8)	KSTOCK72	2239.65	2257.60	2274.30
	(9)	GNP72	1485.80	1489.30	1485.70
	(10)	GNP	3021.40	3070.20	3090.70
	(11)	DEFLATOR	203.36	206.15	208.03
		EQUATIONS			
	(12)	CONSTANT	−776.02	−776.02	−776.02
	(13)	POP 16&	1874.54	1880.21	1885.82
	(14)	UNEMP. RATE	−91.64	−98.88	−103.37
	(15)	INFLAT	−28.31	−25.29	−21.49
	(16)	RHO ADJ	−17.51	−11.38	−7.43
	(17)	C72 EST	961.06	968.64	977.50
	(18)	C72 ACT	961.40	968.80	971.00
	(19)	ERROR (A-E)	0.34	0.16	−6.50
	(20)	CONSTANT	−113.58	−113.58	−113.58
	(21)	CARSDOM	24.93	23.70	23.79
	(22)	UNEMP. RATE	−7.64	−8.24	−8.62
	(23)	POP 16&	159.22	159.70	160.18
	(24)	PRIME RATE	−9.46	−9.59	−8.55
	(25)	CDMV&P72 EST	53.48	51.99	53.22
	(26)	CDMV&P72 ACT	56.40	56.50	56.40
Block B	(27)	ERROR (A-E)	2.92	4.51	3.18
	(28)	CONSTANT	−122.86	−122.86	−122.86
	(29)	POP 16&	229.57	230.26	230.95
	(30)	UNEMP. RATE	−17.68	−19.07	−19.94
	(31)	PRIME RATE	−2.89	−2.93	−2.62
	(32)	RHO ADJ	−0.93	−1.84	−1.09
	(33)	CDO72 EST	85.21	83.56	84.44
	(34)	CDO72 ACT	82.10	83.00	81.90
	(35)	ERROR (A-E)	−3.11	−0.56	−2.54
	(36)	CN&S72 EST	822.38	833.09	839.84
	(37)	CN&S72 ACT	823.00	829.20	832.90
	(38)	ERROR (A-E)	0.62	−3.89	−6.94
	(39)	CN72	362.60	363.50	364.70
	(40)	CS72	460.40	465.70	468.20
	(41)	CONSTANT	−34.80	−34.80	−34.80
	(42)	POP 16&	65.97	66.17	66.37
	(43)	PRIME RATE	−8.25	−8.37	−7.46
	(44)	HUSTS t = 0	4.38	4.53	5.32
Block C	(45)	HUSTS t = −1	10.18	10.82	11.20
	(46)	HUSTS t = −2	3.25	2.92	3.11
	(47)	RES72 EST	40.73	41.27	43.73

IV 82	I 83	II 83	III 83	IV 83	COEFFICIENTS
175.23	175.69	176.14	176.63	177.13	
10.66	10.37	10.09	9.39	8.49	
4.48	3.50	3.41	2.71	3.31	
11.80	10.86	10.50	10.79	11.00	
6.08	6.06	6.95	6.95	7.23	
2.53	2.31	2.28	2.36	2.67	
1.26	1.69	1.69	1.79	1.69	
2290.00	2305.50	2321.63	2339.33	2359.53	
1480.70	1490.10	1530.50	1553.40	1572.50	
3109.60	3171.50	3272.00	3362.20	3436.20	
210.00	212.83	214.55	216.44	218.53	
−776.02	−776.02	−776.02	−776.02	−776.02	−776.017
1891.43	1896.40	1901.26	1906.58	1911.97	10.794
−111.42	−108.39	−105.46	−98.15	−88.71	−10.4523
−16.69	−13.04	−12.70	−10.09	−12.33	−3.72499
−9.23	−5.11	−8.12	−2.34	−4.19	.662627
978.07	993.85	998.95	1024.66	1030.73	
979.60	986.70	1010.60	1016.00	1032.20	
1.53	−7.15	11.65	−8.66	1.47	
−113.58	−113.58	−113.58	−113.58	−113.58	−113.578
26.29	26.21	30.04	30.05	31.24	4.32363
−9.29	−9.04	−8.79	−8.18	−7.39	−.871305
160.66	161.08	161.49	161.94	162.40	.916824
−6.86	−6.32	−6.11	−6.27	−6.40	−.5915
57.21	58.36	63.06	63.96	66.27	
60.50	60.90	69.10	69.10	73.00	
3.29	2.54	6.04	5.14	6.73	
−122.86	−122.86	−122.86	−122.86	−122.86	−122.859
231.64	232.25	232.84	233.49	234.15	1.32191
−21.49	−20.91	−20.35	−18.93	−17.11	−2.01638
−2.10	−1.93	−1.87	−1.92	−1.96	−.177783
−1.65	−1.13	−0.70	−0.21	−0.45	.454948
83.53	85.42	87.07	89.57	91.78	
82.70	85.00	87.30	88.80	92.20	
−0.83	−0.42	0.23	−0.77	0.42	
837.32	850.07	848.83	871.13	872.68	
836.40	840.90	854.10	858.10	866.90	
−0.92	−9.17	5.27	−13.03	−5.78	
366.00	368.90	374.70	378.10	382.50	
470.40	472.00	479.40	480.05	484.40	
−34.80	−34.80	−34.80	−34.80	−34.80	−34.8034
66.57	66.74	66.91	67.10	67.29	.379873
−5.98	−5.51	−5.32	−5.47	−5.58	−.507039
5.97	8.06	8.03	8.50	8.06	4.75879
13.16	14.76	19.92	19.85	21.02	11.7637
3.21	3.77	4.24	5.71	5.69	3.3754
48.12	53.02	58.96	60.89	61.68	

(*Continued*)

TABLE A8-1 (*Continued*)

			I 82	II 82	III 82
	(48)	RES72 ACT	36.30	37.80	36.50
	(49)	ERROR (A-E)	−4.43	−3.47	−7.23
		REAL GOVERNMENT SPENDING			
	(50)	FED DEF	75.50	77.80	80.40
	(51)	FED NONDEF	39.10	32.50	36.50
Block D	(52)	FED TOTAL	114.60	110.30	116.90
	(53)	STATE & LOCAL	174.90	175.40	175.30
	(54)	TOTAL	289.50	285.70	292.20
	(55)	EXPORTS72	151.80	154.50	146.40
	(56)	CONSTANT	−60.74	−60.74	−60.74
	(57)	GNP72 t = −1	170.23	169.74	170.14
	(58)	RHO ADJ	7.44	4.36	7.42
	(59)	IMPORTS72 E	116.93	113.36	116.82
Block E	(60)	IMPORTS72 A	116.60	121.10	122.40
	(61)	ERROR (A-E)	−0.33	7.74	5.58
	(62)	(X-M) EST	34.87	41.14	29.58
	(63)	(X-M) ACT	35.20	33.40	24.00
	(64)	ERROR (A-E)	0.33	−7.74	−5.58
	(65)	CONSTANT	2.69	2.69	2.69
	(66)	KSTOCK72 t = −1	232.51	234.55	236.43
	(67)	UNEMP. RATE	−67.08	−72.38	−75.67
	(68)	RHO ADJ	4.06	4.18	1.71
Block F	(69)	BFI72 EST	172.19	169.04	165.16
	(70)	BFI72 ACT	173.60	167.10	163.30
	(71)	ERROR (A-E)	1.41	−1.94	−1.86
	(72)	STRUCT72	54.30	54.00	53.00
	(73)	PDE72	419.30	113.10	110.30
	(74)	FS72 EST	1498.35	1505.79	1508.17
	(75)	FS72 ACT	1496.00	1492.70	1487.00
	(76)	ERROR (A-E)	−2.35	−13.09	−21.17
	(77)	FSGOODS72	678.30	668.10	663.00
	(78)	I/S RATIONF	1.7733	1.7973	1.8112
	(79)	INV NF	300.70	300.20	300.20
Block G	(80)	INV FARM	44.50	44.20	43.80
	(81)	INV TOTAL	345.20	344.40	344.00
	(82)	INV CH	−10.20	−3.40	−1.30
	(83)	GNP72	1485.80	1489.30	1485.70
	(84)	% CH SAAR	−5.11	0.95	−0.96
	(85)	KSTOCK72 E	2239.65	2257.60	2274.30

Abbreviations:

POP 16& – Noninstitutional, civilian, population, 16 and over (millions)

UNEMP. RATE – Unemployment Rate as a % of Civilian Labor Force

INFLAT – Year-over-year % change in Consumer Price Index–All Urban

CARSDOM – Unit sales of domestically-produced autos (millions, annual rate)

IV 82	I 83	II 83	III 83	IV 83	COEFFICIENTS
40.60	45.50	52.60	56.80	55.80	
−7.52	−7.52	−6.36	−4.09	−5.88	
81.40	82.70	84.20	84.20	85.80	EXOG
43.00	35.70	33.40	34.70	30.50	EXOG
124.40	118.40	117.60	118.90	116.30	
175.20	174.50	174.50	176.30	175.90	EXOG
299.60	292.90	292.10	295.20	292.20	
136.50	137.30	136.20	140.70	140.60	EXOG
−60.74	−60.74	−60.74	−60.74	−60.74	−60.7418
169.73	169.16	170.23	174.23	177.47	.114242
7.98	2.77	5.14	8.84	9.64	.61349
116.96	111.18	114.63	122.33	126.37	
113.50	116.80	123.90	129.20	137.80	
−3.46	5.62	9.27	6.87	11.43	
19.54	26.12	21.57	18.37	14.23	
23.00	20.50	12.30	11.40	2.80	
3.46	−5.62	−9.27	−6.97	−11.43	
2.69	2.69	2.69	2.69	2.69	2.6934
238.18	239.82	241.44	243.13	244.99	.104725
−81.56	−79.34	−77.20	−71.84	−64.94	−7.65121
−0.11	0.91	−2.50	−3.00	−2.96	.763405
159.19	164.08	164.44	170.98	179.78	
160.50	159.90	163.00	170.10	180.70	
1.31	−4.18	−1.44	−0.88	0.92	
52.20	50.30	48.30	49.60	50.40	
108.30	109.60	114.70	120.50	130.30	
1504.52	1529.97	1536.02	1570.09	1578.62	
1503.40	1505.50	1530.50	1549.70	1563.80	
−1.12	−24.47	−5.52	−20.39	−14.82	
674.80	672.30	687.20	695.30	708.00	
1.7481	1.7326	1.6898	1.6827	1.6650	
294.90	291.20	290.30	292.50	294.70	
43.40	43.30	42.80	41.60	41.50	
338.30	334.50	333.10	334.10	336.20	
−22.70	−15.40	−5.40	3.80	8.70	
1480.70	1490.10	1525.10	1553.50	1572.50	
−1.34	2.56	9.73	7.66	4.98	
2290.00	2305.50	2321.63	2339.33	2359.53	

CARSFOR	– Unit sales of foreign-produced autos (millions, annual rate)
HUSTS	– Housing units started (millions, annual rate)
KSTOCK72	– Real stock of business fixed capital (billions of 1972 dollars)
GNP72	– Real GNP (billions of 1972 dollars, annual rate)
GNP	– GNP (billions of current dollars, annual rate)
DEFLATOR	– Implicit GNP price deflator (1972 = 100)

(*Continued*)

TABLE A8-1 (*Continued*)

GNP COMPONENTS:	All in billions of 1972 dollars, annual rates
C72	Consumption spending
CDMV&P72	Consumption of motor vehicles & parts
CDO72	Consumption of other durable goods
CN&S72	Consumption of nondurables & services
CN72	Consumption of nondurable goods
CS72	Consumption of services
RES72	Residential construction
FED DEF	Federal defense spending on goods & services
FED NONDEF	Federal nondefense spending on goods & services
STATE & LOCAL	State & local government spending on goods & services
(X-M)	Net exports of goods & services
BFI72	Business fixed investment
PDE72	Investment in producers' durable equipment
STRUCT72	Investment in nonresidential structures
FS72	Final sales (GNP72 − INV CH)
FSGOODS72	Final sales of goods (less services & structures)
I/SRATIONF72	Ratio of FSGOODS72 (at quarterly rates) to INV NF
INV NF	End-of-quarter stock of nonfarm inventories
INV FARM	End-of-quarter stock of farm inventories
INV TOTAL	End-of-quarter stock of total business inventories
INV CH	Quarterly change in total business inventories (annual rate)
RHO ADJ	Rho value, from Cochrane-Orcutt correction, times prior quarter's residual

the process for estimating real residential construction expenditures (RES72). It should be noted that lines 45 and 46 show the contributions by housing starts lagged one (line 45) and two quarters (line 46). It can be seen clearly that, for instance, the failure of housing starts to increase in second quarter 1983 had a slightly greater effect on real residential construction in third quarter 1983 and still exerted a dampening impact in fourth quarter 1983 through the lagged effects of housing starts.

Block D shows real government spending and its components, all of which are determined outside the model. By altering the assumed values for one or more of the government spending components it is possible to solve different versions of the overall GNP model. Thus, this spreadsheet approach to GNP forecasting can also be used for sensitivity analysis.

Block E computes real net exports. The values for real exports are determined exogenously, and again, as with government spending, the impacts of alternative assumed growth paths can be evaluated. Real imports are estimated using equation 8-12, based on a one quarter lag on real GNP. This is one of the points where feedbacks enter the model estimation process. As stated in the chapter, the error term (line 61) takes on a special significance because it may include price effects from foreign exchange rate changes.

Real business fixed investment is estimated in Block F. Because the model is solved one quarter at a time (that is, the calculations are performed for an entire column before moving to the next column), the estimates for the capital stock are updated (line 85) before contributions of the lagged capital stock (KSTOCK72 t = −1, line 66) are needed to calculate the next quarter's real business fixed investment (BFI72 EST, line 69). The forecast values for total business fixed investment after adjustment by the error term (BFI72 ACT, line 70) are split between real spending on structures (line 71) and producers' durable equipment (line 72).

Block G presents the estimates for real final sales, the real change in business inventories, and the levels and annual rates of change for real GNP. Final sales are found by adding the values for the component measures. Two totals are derived: one based on the uncorrected estimates (FS72 EST, line 74), and the other equal to the actual value or the estimated values plus the error (FS72 ACT, line 75).

Real final sales of goods (FSGOODS72, line 77) are calculated by excluding from final sales the value of services and structures. This amount is then divided into real nonfarm inventories (INV NF, line 79) to derive the real nonfarm inventory/sales ratio (I/S RATIONF, line 78). In this *ex post* forecast, the I/S ratio is reported at full (eight digit) precision. This reflects a limitation of the software: data can be reported only at (a) whole integer value, (b) two decimal place accuracy, or (c) full precision. Though awkward and overly precise,[3] this is the most useful way to examine recent values of I/S RATIONF; forecast values can be expressed with less precision. For forecasting *ex ante* it is desirable to forecast nonfarm and farm inventories separately. Line 81 shows total business inventories (sum of farm and nonfarm inventories). The real change in business inventories (line 82) is equal to the difference in total inventories (line 81) times four.

Finally, real GNP (GNP72, line 83) is equal to real final sales (line 75) plus the change in real business inventories (line 82). The seasonally adjusted annual rate of change is shown on line 84.

Such an approach is a useful way to perform the iterations needed to combine the exogenous and equation-derived estimates of real GNP into an overall forecast. Particular attention should be focused on the exogenous values and the assumed error terms in an *ex ante* forecast. Fortunately, the mechanics of observing the effects of changes in these values is quite simple with such a spreadsheet analysis. The judgments the forecaster must make, however, are not simplified. This remains the most complex part of economic forecasting.

Table A8-2 presents a summary table of the GNP forecast performed in Table A8-1. This table can be compiled as part of the same spreadsheet used to generate Table A8-1. It shows quarterly and annual values for current dollar GNP, the implicit price deflator, and real GNP and its components for

---

[3] It may be noted that most values in the table are expressed to two digits. It should not be concluded that such detail is a measure of the accuracy of the forecasting process. Again this is a result of the software's limitations. There is an old maxim in GNP forecasting that "the one 90% certainty is that whatever digit is to the right of the decimal point is wrong."

TABLE A8-2 GNP Forecast Summary

	I	II	III	IV	1982	1983	1982–83	1982 IV–1983 IV
GNP	3172	3272	3362	3436	3073	3310	7.73	10.50
Deflator	212.83	214.55	216.44	218.53	206.89	215.59	4.21	4.06
Real GNP	1490	1525	1553	1573	1485	1535	3.45	6.20
Real GNP Components								
Consumption	987	1011	1016	1032	970	1011	4.24	5.37
Motor Vehicles & Parts	61	69	69	73	57	68	18.41	20.66
Other Durables	85	87	89	92	82	88	7.16	11.49
Nondurables	369	375	378	383	364	376	3.25	4.51
Services	472	479	480	484	466	479	2.74	2.98
Residential Construction	46	53	57	56	38	53	39.35	37.44
Business Fixed Investment	160	163	170	181	166	168	1.38	12.59
Producers' Durable Equipment	110	115	121	130	113	119	5.34	20.31
Nonresidential Structures	50	48	50	50	53	50	-6.98	-3.45
Change in Business Inventories	-15	-5	4	9	-9	-2		
Net Exports	21	12	11	3	29	12		
Government Spending	293	292	295	292	292	293	0.46	-2.47
Federal	118	118	119	116	117	118	1.07	-6.51
Defense	83	84	84	86	79	84	6.92	5.41
Nondefense	36	33	35	31	38	34	-11.12	-29.07
State and Local	175	175	176	176	175	175	0.06	0.40
Final Sales	1506	1531	1550	1564	1495	1537	2.85	4.02

1983 in levels and annual percentage growth. Such a table is more suitable for presenting the results of a forecast.

SUGGESTED ADDITIONAL READINGS FOR CHAPTER 8

The four works listed each present detailed discussion of a macroeconometric model developed by the author(s).

DUESENBERRY, JAMES F., GARY FROMM, LAWRENCE R. KLEIN, AND EDWIN KUH. *The Brookings Quarterly Econometric Model of the United States.* Skokie, IL: Rand McNally, and Amsterdam: North-Holland Publishing Co., 1965.

ECKSTEIN, OTTO. *The DRI Model of the U.S. Economy.* New York: McGraw-Hill, 1983.

EVANS, MICHAEL K. *Macroeconomic Activity.* New York: Harper & Row, Pub., 1969. A brief description and full equation listing of an early version of the Wharton Econometric Forecasting Model is included.

FAIR, RAY C. *Specification, Estimation, and Analysis of Macroeconometric Models.* Cambridge, MA: Harvard Univ. Press, 1984. This book offers an in-depth treatment of the topics discussed in this chapter by one of the pioneers in macroeconometric forecasting, including a detailed description of his latest model.

9

FINANCIAL FORECASTING

INTRODUCTION

A number of the economic measures considered in earlier chapters were directly related to interest rate movements, which, in turn, result from the interaction of financial and nonfinancial market forces. Moreover, in the broader sense described in Chapter 2, a general macroeconomic model should encompass both "real" forces—income and production—and "money" forces.[1] Interest rates form the main linkage between the two sides of the economy, resulting from the interaction of the demand for and supply of credit, and monetary policy.

Financial market variables pose some of the most important, difficult, and frustrating challenges in economic forecasting. The importance of financial forecasting is indicated by the resources, time, and money both financial and nonfinancial firms devote to the effort. The difficulty is attested to by the range of forecast approaches that have been developed and which are used. The fact that no one approach has emerged as "best" partly reflects the different costs associated with the various methods, but to a greater extent reflects the failure of any one approach to achieve consistently better forecast results over time.

Estimating financial variables is most vitally important to financial firms whose main business revolves around movements in these variables. Consequently, the need by these firms for reasonable, reliable forecasts is especially pronounced. Indeed, firms which act as financial intermediaries— as lenders, traders, brokers, underwriters, and investors—may rely on financial forecasts as the basis for taking positions, and ultimately, for the difference between profits and losses.

Forecasts of financial conditions are also important to nonfinancial firms for at least two reasons. The experience of recent years has vividly shown that financial variables—particularly interest rates—strongly affect business activity both as a cost or obstacle to pursuit of a firm's basic business plan and as a determinant of the final demand for the firm's products or services. The second reason, already alluded to in prior chapters, is that interest rates are often inputs to other forecasts. For instance, estimates of personal income, housing starts, and a number of GNP components all depend in part on interest rate variables. Since the main theme of the prior four chapters was that forecasts of economic activity variables are an important input to management decisions, it follows that forecasts of some basic financial variables are equally vital.

This chapter is aimed, primarily, at developing forecasts of the financial side inputs necessary to supplement the overall economic forecast efforts of nonfinancial firms. The much greater importance of financial fore-

---

[1] The terms "real" and "money" market forces are often used to denote the nonfinancial and financial sides of the economy, respectively. So far in this text the term "real" has been used to denote a variable which has been adjusted to remove the effects of price changes. Thus, to avoid confusion, the more cumbersome terms "nonfinancial" and "financial" will be used.

casting to financial firms requires a more extensive treatment of this topic than can be provided in a single chapter. Nevertheless, it is hoped that forecasters whose main aim is to prepare financial forecasts may also derive some benefit.

The chapter is organized in three sections. The first provides an extensive overview of the main financial sectors and flows in the U.S. economy. The approach to forecasting nonfinancial variables in previous chapters recognized the interrelated nature of economic activities. Similar interrelationships exist among financial variables. In examining these relationships, moreover, a number of concepts arise that are different from those that affect income and output determination. The second section offers a representative cross section of some diverse approaches to financial forecasting. The aim is to highlight the range of forecast approaches developed and used, not to provide an exhaustive catalogue of all approaches. The final section describes in detail a simple model that can be combined with the forecast methods described in Chapters 5 through 8 to develop a more complete approach to short- and medium-term macroeconomic forecasting.

AN OVERVIEW OF THE FINANCIAL ECONOMY AND KEY CONCEPTS

The economic activity variables which were the focus of Part II and the product and factor income concepts which were the focus of Chapter 8 largely ignored the financial flows which, in a fundamental way, make these activities possible. The one exception to this was that for those variables for which a direct interest rate effect was important, this effect was included in the specification of the relationship while ignoring how the interest rate variable was itself determined. This chapter corrects that omission.

Interest rates should be viewed, however, as the result of a complex of forces affecting the supply and demand for credit. Thus, if useful forecasts of interest rates are to be derived, the complex of financial flows that combine to determine interest rate levels—and there is not one "interest rate," but rather a number of rates which apply to short- and long-term credit instruments, that differ from market to market—should be considered. In other words, it is necessary to view the financial side of the economy as a system.

The complicated nature of the financial flows suggest that it be viewed in phases. First, an overview of the interactions between the main classes of financial market participants, or sectors, is described. The financial sectors embrace the same broad groups that comprise the nonfinancial economy, namely: households, businesses, foreigners, and government entities. The relative importance of groups within some of these sectors, however, requires somewhat more detailed classifications. Thus, the first need is for an overview of the roles each sector plays as a source (supplier) and user (demander) of loanable funds (credit) and the main forms these credit flows take. Description of a simplified flow of funds provides this overview. The second phase of this discussion provides a brief description of some of the main credit instruments which bridge the supply and demand for credit. Third, the basic forces which account for the levels of interest rates and yields on these instruments are discussed. Finally, the important role played by monetary policy in the financial sector is discussed.

Financial Market Overview

In analyzing and forecasting the net flow of goods and services, the National Income and Product Accounts are used and the main classes of economic agents are grouped in sectors reflecting the similar motives under-lying the activities of the entities within a sector. Financial market activities involve basically the same sectors in their roles as sources (suppliers) and users (demanders) of loanable funds (credit). Each sector is potentially both a source and user of loanable funds. In fact, if a sectoral statement of sources and uses of funds is constructed for each sector, financial activity can be divided into five broad categories. There are three main *uses* for funds: (1) investment, (2) lending, and (3) uninvested money assets on hand—cash and unused checking account balances. There are two basic *sources* of funds: (1) saving, and (2) borrowing. If sources and uses accounts are compiled for the different sectors and combined into a total Sources and Uses of funds state-ment, the net flows of loanable funds within the economy can be analyzed. Thus, the Flow of Funds Accounts fulfill a similar role for the financial side of the economy to that the National Income and Product Accounts perform for the nonfinancial economy.[2]

A simplified version of the Federal Reserve Board's table, *Funds Raised in U.S. Credit Markets,* is presented in Table 9-1, showing annual data in billions of dollars for 1979–82. This framework can be used to discuss the sectoral relationships in the flow of funds. (Table 9-2 shows the percent-age shares of net credit, excluding equities, raised by each sector.)

Before discussing each sector, however, a number of points can be made about total credit market flows based on Table 9-1. First, the flows shown in Table 9-1 are net flows; some sectors, particularly private financial businesses, experience much greater gross flows, reflecting the role of these firms as financial intermediaries. Second, it is clear from the changes in Total Credit Raised during this four-year period that financial market flows are quite volatile. The sharp decline in 1980, for instance, reflects not only the falloff in credit demand that could be expected given the recession in that

---

[2] A good introductory overview of the Flow of Funds Accounts is offered by Lawrence S. Ritter, "The Flow of Funds Accounts: A Framework for Financial Analysis," in Murray E. Polakoff, ed., *Financial Institutions and Markets* (Boston: Houghton Mifflin Co., 1970), pp. 21–36.

TABLE 9-1   Funds Raised in U.S. Credit Markets by Sector (billions of dollars)

	1979	1980	1981	1982
Nonfinancial Sectors	*409.1*	*382.2*	*418.4*	*424.3*
Public	*57.6*	*106.5*	*109.7*	*208.5*
U.S. Government	37.4	79.2	87.4	161.3
State & Local Governments	20.2	27.3	22.3	47.2
Private	*351.5*	*275.7*	*308.7*	*215.8*
Households	176.5	117.5	120.4	85.1
Businesses	154.8	131.0	161.0	114.5
Corporate	99.0	82.8	104.1	77.0
Nonfarm Noncorporate	34.4	33.8	40.5	28.2
Farm	21.4	14.4	16.4	9.3
Foreigners	20.2	27.2	27.3	16.2
Financial Sectors	*80.8*	*61.3*	*80.7*	*64.3*
U.S. Government Sponsored Credit Agencies	24.3	24.4	30.1	13.2
Mortgage Pools	23.1	19.2	15.0	47.4
Private Financial Businesses	33.4	17.7	35.6	3.7
Total Credit Raised	*489.9*	*443.5*	*499.1*	*488.6*
New Equity Issues	−3.8	22.1	−2.9	26.7
Total Funds Raised	*486.1*	*465.6*	*496.2*	*515.3*

Source: Board of Governors of the Federal Reserve System, *Federal Reserve Bulletin,* Table A-44.

year, but also the effects of the Credit Restraint Program in place between March and June of 1980. A third point is that when Federal government demand for credit grows suddenly, private users get "crowded out." This fact will be discussed further below, but, in general, it largely reflects the fact that Treasury securities offer certain tax advantages, and the lowest risk of default of any investment, which combine to make them more attractive to investors than most other instruments.

There are two broad classifications used in Table 9-1. The first is a division between users of credit for nonfinancial purposes, and users for mainly financial purposes, generally financial intermediation—that is, borrowing so as to re-lend to other credit users. The nonfinancial sector can further be divided into public—or governmental sectors—and private sectors. This division takes into account the advantage public credit users enjoy as a result of their ability to grant tax relief on the resulting income to investors.[3]

[3] All foreign credit market participants are included in the private sector despite the fact that foreign government entities often raise funds and invest excess funds—especially, in recent

TABLE 9-2   Share of Total Credit Raised, by Sector (percent)

	1979	1980	1981	1982
Nonfinancial Sectors	*83.5*	*86.2*	*83.8*	*86.8*
Public	*11.8*	*24.1*	*22.0*	*42.7*
U.S. Government	7.6	17.9	17.5	33.1
State & Local Governments	4.1	6.2	4.5	9.7
Private	*71.7*	*62.1*	*61.9*	*44.1*
Households	36.0	26.5	24.1	17.4
Businesses	31.6	29.5	32.3	23.4
Corporate	20.2	18.7	20.9	15.8
Nonfarm, Noncorporate	7.0	7.6	8.1	5.8
Farm	4.4	3.2	3.3	1.9
Foreigners	4.1	6.1	5.5	3.3
Financial Sectors	*16.5*	*13.8*	*16.2*	*13.2*
U.S. Government				
Sponsored				
Credit Agencies	5.0	5.5	6.0	2.7
Mortgage Pools	4.7	4.3	3.0	9.7
Private Financial Businesses	6.8	4.0	7.1	0.8

The *U.S. Government* raises funds primarily to finance the Federal budget deficit—the difference between Federal revenues and outlays. In the postwar period, the Federal budget has been in deficit in all but eight years (1948–49, 1951, 1956–57, 1960, and 1969). The Treasury borrows through issuing bills (with maturities of one year or less), notes (one to ten year maturities), and bonds (maturities over ten years). These securities are sold in regularly scheduled auctions to about three dozen primary dealers in Treasury securities at competitive rates and to the wider public at the average price set in each auction.[4] The amount of Treasury borrowing fluctuates partly due to structural imbalances in the Federal budget, which in recent years have resulted in more rapid growth in outlays—reflecting such noncyclical expenditures as defense, and entitlement programs such as social security—than in revenues even under conditions of rapid economic growth.

---

years, OPEC nations—in U.S. credit markets. This convention reflects the absence of tax preferences on foreign government security income earned in the U.S. Thus, foreign government participants in U.S. credit markets compete more directly with domestic private participants.

    [4] Treasury bills are sold on a "discount" basis. That is, bills are bid for by investors in $10,000 face amounts so that the "interest" rate on the bill is equal to the face amount minus the amount actually paid (the auction price per bill times the number of bills bought) all divided by the amount paid, expressed at an annualized rate. Notes and bonds, on the other hand, are sold on a yield basis, where a specific interest, or coupon, rate is fixed but the actual yield to maturity is based on the amount paid for the security in the auction. Detailed discussions of these calculations can be found in Marcia Stigum, *Money Market Calculations: Yields, Breakevens, and Arbitrage* (Homewood, IL: Dow Jones-Irwin, 1981).

Of course, when economic conditions weaken—as they did briefly in 1980, in the second half of 1981 and throughout 1982—revenues slow, expenditures rise (for instance, total outlays for unemployment benefits rise with increases in unemployment), the deficit widens, and Federal government demand for credit increases.

Income from Treasury securities is generally exempt from tax by state and local governments. In addition, these securities carry the "full faith and credit of the U.S. government" and, thus have virtually zero risk of default. For both of these reasons, Treasury borrowings represent a strong claim on the sources of funds, are usually satisfied—at a price—and may at times "crowd out" other borrowers from the credit markets. (Note the sharp rise in the share of all credit raised going to the U.S. government between 1979 and 1980 in Table 9-2.) It should be noted, however, that this "crowding out" is not absolute and usually occurs in periods—cyclical downturns—when private credit demands decline by themselves because of the worsening in business prospects.

State and local governments raise funds chiefly to finance capital outlays and to a lesser extent to bridge the short-term gap between revenues and current outlays. A great variety of state and local government entities issue notes and bonds in U.S. credit markets. These securities also range in "quality," which is reflected in the credit ratings assigned by private authorities (mainly Moody's and Standard and Poor's) reflecting the amount of existing debt owed, fiscal conditions, and the revenue raising prospects of the issuing governmental entity. These securities do possess one notable advantage over privately issued securities: the income is generally exempt from taxes by Federal, state, and local governments. This attraction to investors usually results in lower yields for state and local securities (referred to as municipals, or "munies") than for corporate securities. One further difference between state and local governments and Federal government participation in the credit markets is that, due to the range of fiscal conditions enjoyed by the former, particular state and local governments sometimes act as a source of funds—when budget surpluses exist.

Households play a large role in the flow of funds. Credit is used mainly for home purchases and to finance consumption of durable goods. These uses of loanable funds are supplied by means of residential mortgages and loans from commercial banks, thrift institutions, finance companies, credit unions, and other financial businesses. Since households, individually, have little or no market power, these loans are usually at rates which are above money or capital market rates. Moreover, in periods of credit market tightness or declining economic activity, households are typically the first sector to have their credit demands squeezed or crowded out by other borrowing sectors.

Households also play an important role as sources of funds. This results chiefly from household saving which may take a variety of forms:

small time deposits, certificates of deposit, money market accounts, and purchases of public and private securities. Household saving also responds to cyclical forces; saving is a function of disposable income, and thus when disposable income declines or slows its growth, saving will mirror this.

Businesses play a fundamental role in the nonfinancial economy and a no less, but more complex, role in the financial economy. One way to reduce the complexity of the business sector's financial role is to treat nonfinancial and financial businesses separately. Nonfinancial businesses are those firms, including farms, mainly engaged in the production of goods, trade, and the provision of nonfinancial services. Financial businesses, on the other hand, function mainly as financial intermediaries, facilitating the flow of credit by taking deposits or borrowing so as to relend to other borrowers.

Nonfinancial businesses have two main uses for funds. The first use is to finance operating costs until revenues are received: in the case of goods producers, this includes meeting the costs of production and carrying inventories; in the case of wholesale and retail trade, the chief needs for funds are to finance inventories and provide trade credit. These needs can be referred to as commercial and industrial credit uses. In addition, businesses require long-term funding to finance capital spending. The uses of funds are similar in nature, though the scale may differ, for nearly all types of nonfinancial businesses. The sources of funds, however, vary among corporations, non-farm noncorporations, and farms.

Corporations can call upon the widest range of funding sources. Because corporations have a legal existence of their own, they have the option of using their own savings—depreciation and retained earnings—issuing equities (stock)[5] and/or corporate notes and bonds in order to finance capital spending. These sources all depend on a variety of financial and nonfinancial conditions: the amount of corporate savings at any time depends on revenues (determined partly by economic conditions), past investment, accounting practices, and tax laws; the decision to issue new stock is dependent on market conditions and the amount of outstanding stock of the corporations; and corporate bond issues are affected by a host of financial conditions—interest rates, the flow of new issues relative to investor demand and, importantly, the relative presence or absence of the Treasury in financial markets. In addition, corporations can negotiate commercial mortgages to finance investment in structures. Large, well-known, corporations may also obtain short-term funds in the commercial paper market. Finally, the usual form of short-term commercial and industrial credit is supplied by bank lending.

Noncorporations—proprietorships and partnerships—have more limited sources of funds: mainly savings, mortgages and bank loans. Farms

---

[5] Equities are not strictly credit instruments since the issuer assumes no liability. They are, nevertheless, a source of funds to corporations and, thus, are included in Table 9-1.

have a somewhat wider range of lending sources because of the existence of Federally sponsored credit agencies, particularly the Farm Credit Banks.

Nonfinancial businesses also serve as a source of funds, chiefly through short-term deposits and investment of temporary cash surpluses (for instance, accrued tax liabilities) in short-term instruments.

Before considering financial businesses, the discussion of the nonfinancial sectors can be completed by examining the *foreign* sector. Foreign governments and private entities are both users and sources of funds in U.S. credit markets.[6] These entities have basically the same uses for credit that their U.S. counterparts have. They are attracted to borrow in the U.S. by the volume and depth of the U.S. credit markets. This is particularly the case in the bond market, though loans negotiated in the U.S. by American banks have become an important source of credit to foreign official and private borrowers.

A special factor affecting short-term credit raised by foreigners is consideration of foreign exchange movements. International comparisons of interest rates are affected not only by domestic credit conditions, but also by movements in the exchange value of the currencies. Foreign exchange rate movements, particularly in the forward markets, are in turn largely the result of interest rate differentials. For instance, if short-term interest rates are 15% in the U.K. and 10% in the U.S., a British firm may be attracted to borrow in the U.S. However, at the end of six months, the loan will have to be either repaid or rolled over in dollars. If the six-month forward dollar-sterling exchange rate is less than a 5% annual rate (the interest rate differential) the British borrower may borrow dollars in the U.S., exchange them for sterling, and agree to purchase dollars in six months at the forward rate so as to remove any exchange risk.[7]

Foreigners also act as sources of funds in U.S. credit markets, once again attracted by its range and depth. Most often foreign sources of domestic credit are holders of dollars who wish to find a source of interest income for these dollar-denominated financial assets. A key source for such funding in the late 1970s was the OPEC nations. Since petroleum sold for dollars, the OPEC countries saw their dollar assets grow faster than their own domestic uses for these funds during the period of rapidly rising oil prices. As a result, they invested a large share of these funds in U.S. financial markets, mainly in short-term Treasuries. More usual, is the foreign private investor attracted to U.S. credit markets by the social and political stability with which they are associated.

---

[6] Foreign government credit market participants are included in the private nonfinancial sector because they do not offer the tax advantages to U.S. investors that the U.S. Treasury and state and local government borrowers offer.

[7] For a detailed discussion of this process, called covered interest arbitrage, see Dominick Salvatore, *International Economics* (New York: Macmillan, 1983), pp. 318–20.

The *financial* sectors use funds chiefly in order to fulfill their principal function as sources of funds. Nearly all members of this sector act as financial intermediaries: acquiring funds from depositors, lenders, or investors at relatively low rates, which are re-lent in some other market(s) to yield a higher return. These entities are able to acquire funds at cheaper cost than they relend them because they wield market power in both their roles as users and sources of funds. Financial entities also require funds for normal operating expenses. In particular, if security and loan portfolios are viewed like goods producers' inventories, then the need to finance these "inventories" is also similar. In general, the need for fixed capital (plant and equipment) is less in relation to the total business of these entities than for goods producers.

U.S. government-sponsored *credit agencies* are entities that, in general, do not rely on Budget receipts as the main source of their funds, but rather rely on their own abilities to raise funds. Some agencies, such as the Federal Savings and Loan Insurance Corporation (FSLIC), rely primarily on user fees for funds. A few, such as the Farmers' Home Administration, the Small Business Administration, and the Agency for International Development, are funded directly by the Treasury. Most, such as the Federal National Mortgage Association, issue securities directly in credit markets. These securities are guaranteed up to certain limits by the Treasury, but are not backed by the "full faith and credit of the U.S. government." Thus, they offer somewhat lower risk to investors than private securities but more than Treasuries.

Another key difference between the activities of Federal agencies and the Treasury is in the uses of the funds raised. The Treasury uses credit raised to supplement tax receipts in carrying out the general activities of the Federal government. Federal agencies use funds raised mainly to supplement private sector credits to specific credit uses, mainly home purchases, student loans, farm credit, and small business credit. The purpose is to smooth the market imperfections that arise between, generally, large lenders and small borrowers.

Mortgage pools include Federal agencies and private groups involved chiefly in buying mortgages in the secondary market—that is, mortgages which have already been granted to home buyers, but which the original mortgage granter does not wish to hold until maturity. This activity usually insures greater liquidity in the mortgage market and thus, aids homebuilding. The falloff in net funds raised by mortgage pools in 1981 (Table 9-1) reflects two related factors: (1) the sharp decline in both new and existing home purchases, and (2) the steep rise in interest rates that made purchases of existing mortgages (made at lower interest rates) unattractive compared to the higher cost of financing such purchases.

The *private financial business* sector performs the central role in facilitating the flow of credit. Included in this sector are the groups described below.

> *Commercial banks* (referred to as banks) which accept demand deposits (checking accounts) and make loans as their main business. Institutional changes in recent years have led banks to accept a greater variety of deposits, including: negotiated orders of withdrawal (NOW accounts) which pay interest so long as a minimum balance is maintained; super-NOWs; Money Market Deposit Accounts, which are like mutual funds based on money market instruments; certificates of deposit; and time deposits. In addition, most banks participate directly in the money and capital markets dealing in instruments that range from Federal funds sales and purchases to those banks which are primary dealers in Treasury and municipal securities. Banks' main lending activity is in making commercial and industrial loans to nonfinancial businesses. In addition, banks make consumer loans, mortgage loans, and loans to foreign private and official borrowers.
>
> *Thrift institutions* (Savings and Loan Associations, Mutual Savings Banks, and Credit Unions) accept time deposits and other savings-type deposits (NOWs, CDs, etc.) and mainly make mortgage and other consumer loans.
>
> *Finance companies* use their own and borrowed funds to make consumer-type loans. These companies may either be independent businesses, or tied to producers of durable goods (for instance, General Motors Acceptance Corporation, General Electric Credit Corporation). Large finance companies also raise funds in the commercial paper market.
>
> *Insurance companies* use the premiums paid to them to invest in securities, to make commercial mortgage loans, and to lend directly to large business borrowers.
>
> *Investment banks and brokerages* acquire funds either from customers or by direct borrowing in money markets so as to reinvest these funds in securities and debt instruments. These firms fulfill a classic speculative role in the financial markets. They offer a return to their sources of funds which is less than that they hope to obtain from their use of funds—which represent, in turn, a source of funds to other borrowers. Thus, these firms take on risks, for which they hope to be rewarded, and so, enhance the flow of funds generally.

This overview of financial sectors provides some insight to the flow of funds that lubricates U.S. economic activity. The discussion also introduced some terms and concepts specific to the financial economy. Most importantly, it presented the financial economy as a market in which the demand and supply for credit determines its price (interest rate). The focus of nonfinancial forecasters is mainly on nonfinancial economic forces. As already noted, however, interest rates have an important bearing on many of these activities. It is important, however, to remember that interest rates are the outcome of financial market forces. Financial flows should, at least, be considered before deriving an interest rate forecast, and should be considered carefully and in detail.

Financial Instruments

The main financial instruments, already referred to in passing, can be divided into five groups, ranging from longest to shortest maturities.

Corporate stock, or *equities,* are not in a strict sense credit instruments since the issuer assumes no liability to repay the funds raised. Instead the purchaser exchanges one financial asset—cash—for another—a title of ownership in the corporation. Equities do, however, relate fairly closely to credit instruments; they represent an alternative source of funds to credit instruments from the view of the corporate issuer, and they appeal to broadly the same class of investors as long-term credit instruments, and thus are substitutes for bonds in investor portfolios. Thus, equities can be viewed as "quasi-credit" instruments with an infinite maturity.

There are a number of considerations which affect corporate decisions to issue stock. First is the general state of the overall stock market; to insure the greatest possible flow of funds to the corporation it is desirable to issue new stock in a rising market. More specific are the implications for existing stockholders. In general, investors hold stocks both for long-term capital gain and for the dividend income they produce. Corporations, therefore, must be careful that: (1) new issues do not so lower the prospects for per share price appreciation as to make them unattractive to both new and existing investors, and (2) they maintain the dividend/price ratio (yield) to both new and existing shareholders. These conditions are more likely to be met when prospects are for rising economic activity and profits. Finally, demand for equities is often inversely related to bond yields. When bond yields are low, the prospects for capital gains and for increasing yields from equities are higher (partly because low interest rates usually signal a period of lower cost-higher profit) than when the reverse is true.

Mortgages represent one of the longest maturity forms of credit. Purchasers of residential and commercial buildings are the main users of mortgage credit. Thrift institutions, commercial banks, and insurance companies are the main sources. Mortgages are usually granted for a fixed term, 15 to 30 years, for a portion (on average, about 75%) of the purchase price of the building, with the building itself serving as security for the loan. In the past, mortgages were usually granted at fixed interest rates. While this remains the standard practice, in recent years because of increased volatility in other credit markets, variable rate mortgages tied to some money market interest rate have become more common. This option has reduced the reluctance of mortgage lenders to make mortgages in periods of volatile interest rates; there is less danger of getting "locked in" to a low-yielding asset (the fixed rate mortgage) funded by higher-yielding liabilities (deposits and borrowed funds).

More than two-thirds of total mortgage debt outstanding at the end of

1982 was for one- to four-family homes, of which some 42% was held by thrift institutions and some 27% by commercial banks. There is a more even distribution of commercial mortgage debt (accounting for nearly 15% of the outstanding total at the end of 1982) among commercial banks (34%) insurance companies (31%) and thrifts (22%).

Notes and bonds which pay a stated interest rate, the coupon rate, usually paid annually or semi-annually, are issued directly by the U.S. Treasury, Federal agencies, state and local governments, corporations, and foreign borrowers in the capital markets as a source of long-term funds. These interest bearing securities are usually issued in auctions, with the coupon rate set to reflect prevailing interest rates on issues with similar maturities. Interest bearing securities can be resold in secondary markets; thus, they are quoted in prices per $100 of face amount in dollars and 32nds. These prices relate the present value of the interest flow, if held to maturity, to present interest rates. For example, if a two-year note is issued with a 9% interest rate and this rate accurately reflects then current interest rates, then it is sold at par, a price of 100. If after one year interest rates rise so that a one-year (the term to maturity remaining on the two year note issued a year earlier) note is $9\frac{1}{2}$%, the price of the original note will decline so that the combined face value of the note at maturity and the remaining interest payments when divided by the new price equal 1.095, or in other words result in a $9\frac{1}{2}$% yield.[8] Under these conditions the note is said to be selling at discount. Conversely, if market interest rates decline, the price of the note must rise to bring it into line—the note would then be selling at a premium.

The attraction of interest bearing securities to the issuer is that they gain access to funds for a prolonged time at a fixed interest cost. Moreover, the corporate issuer gains this access without any directly adverse impact on shareholders. (Of course, the interest cost is a charge against revenues that must be met before profits are distributed, but presumably the use of the funds will produce a sufficient return to offset this.) There is the risk, how-

---

[8] The price in this example can be determined simply. If the interest is paid annually, and

F = face value of the note (usually $1000)
c = coupon rate (in this case 9%)
r = current market rate for one year ($9\frac{1}{2}$%)
P = current price, such that

$$P = F \times \frac{(1 + c)}{(1 + r)} = 1000 \times \frac{(1 + .09)}{(1 + .095)}$$
$$= 995.40$$

This is of course a very simple case if the note were a three-year note with two years to maturity; or even if, as usual, the interest were paid semi-annually, the solution would be somewhat more complicated, but the approach would be the same. For an extensive treatment of security price and yield calculation see Marcia Stignum, *Money Market Calculations: Yields, Break-Evens, and Arbitrage,* (Homewood, IL: Dow Jones-Irwin, 1981).

ever, that interest rates will decline subsequently and yet the issuer will be locked into the higher cost, long-term security and cannot easily avail itself of the lower rates. The attraction and concern of the investor are similar: the attraction is the yield on the security; the concern is that interest rates may rise, resulting in missed opportunities and price erosion if the investor wishes to sell the security. These conflicting concerns of note and bond issuers (borrowers) and investors (lenders) are among the principal market influences on yields.

Perhaps the most ordinary sources of financial sector credit are *loans,* other than mortgages, made by commercial banks, thrifts, insurance companies, and finance companies. These are the funds normally used by businesses to finance operating expenses and by households to finance consumption of durable goods.

The most important forms of such credit are the commercial and industrial loans made by banks to the business sector. These are usually short-term (one year or less) loans made at variable rates. In the past, the prime rate was the interest rate charged by banks to their best—most credit-worthy—customers; the rates to other customers was higher, reflecting higher risk, but related to and moving with the prime. In recent years, competition from money market sources, the greater volatility of market rates, and efforts by banks to achieve a better match between the cost of their liabilities (deposits and borrowed funds) and the return on their assets (loans), have changed the meaning of the prime rate. It is now mainly an indicative rate: large customers with access to the commercial paper market may negotiate "below-prime" loans, while loans to other customers continue to be priced based on—but not often equal to—the prime rate. Commercial and industrial loans, for the most part, are variable rate loans which fluctuate with the prime, which, in turn, moves in line with other market rates, and credit demand and supply conditions. Since commercial and industrial loans are a major source of financing for business operating costs—especially, for maintaining inventories—movements in the prime rate have a fundamental effect on business activity.

Commercial banks are also an important source of loans to individuals. These are mainly installment loans for one to ten years and include automobile loans (which are secured by the auto), credit card and other revolving credits, home improvement, mobile home, and other consumer related loans. Generally, these are fixed rate loans priced well above business borrowing rates. The higher interest rates charged individuals reflect: the greater risk of default, the higher cost of administering a greater number of smaller loans, and the lesser market power (ability to negotiate) of individual borrowers.

Thrift institutions' non-mortgage loans are mainly to individuals for similar purposes and at rates close to those charged by banks. Insurance companies grant loans to policyholders based on their paid up premiums at somewhat lower rates reflecting the reduced risk of default. Insurance companies also make longer term, negotiated loans to businesses. Finance companies mainly lend to individuals—either directly or in the form of credit cards—usually at higher rates than charged by banks.

Money market instruments generally are the most liquid—shortest maturity, from overnight to one year—forms of credit. Moreover, because of the role Federal funds borrowing and certificate of deposit issuance play as sources of commercial bank reserves, and the role that the commercial paper market plays as an alternative to commercial and industrial loans as a source of business credit, money market interest rates have a profound influence on the level of longer term interest rates. The main money market instruments are listed below.

Federal Funds are interbank loans of reserves of one bank which are temporarily in excess of the amount required to meet Federal Reserve reserve requirements to another bank whose reserves relative to deposits are less than the Federal Reserve required level. These loans (borrowings) are generally overnight—although over-the-weekend loans are three-, or in the case of a holiday weekend, four-day loans—quoted at an annualized interest rate.[9] Because of the basic impact that Federal funds loans have on bank reserves, the Fed funds rate is one of the most closely watched and most important interest rates for determining overall interest rate movements.

The *repurchase, or repo, rate* is similar to and closely tied to the Federal funds rate. Financial and nonfinancial businesses with temporary excess cash make commitments to buy short-term securities for a specified period—generally one to seven days—and promise to resell it to the same owner at the end of the period at a specified lower price. The difference between the two prices divided by the purchase price is the repo rate.

Treasury bills, most frequently issued in three-month (90 days) and six-month (180 days) maturities, are the main instruments used by the Treasury to finance the Federal deficit. Unlike notes and bonds, Treasury bills are sold at discount. That is, there is no stated interest rate; rather the bills are sold at weekly auctions in face amounts of $10,000 and the difference between the face amount and the auction price divided by the face amount and annualized on a 360 day year basis is the yield.

Certificates of deposit, or CDs, are instruments issued by banks in minimum amounts of $100,000, with maturities of at least 14 days, but most commonly 30, 90, or 180 days. Yields at issuance are quoted in simple interest terms on the basis of a 360 day year. CDs are negotiable and may be resold in secondary markets.[10] CDs represent an important alternative source of bank funding to borrowing in the Federal funds market, and the CD rate along with the Fed funds rate are principal determinants of the cost of funds, and thus lending rates for banks. Banks are most likely to resort to longer dated CD issues when

---

[9] Thus, an overnight loan of $1 million at a 10% annual rate implies a de-compounded one-day rate of 0.026%, or interest of $261.15 per million dollars of principal.

[10] For a detailed discussion of CD price and yield calculations see Stigum, *Money Market Calculations: Yields, Break-Evens, and Arbitrage,* pp. 71–86.

short-term interest rates—particularly the Fed funds rate—are expected to rise; CDs then represent a means of locking in a rate (for a particular term) that is likely to be cheaper than repeated Fed funds borrowings at increasing interest cost. In addition to CDs issued by U.S. Banks there are also active markets in Eurodollar CDs, issued by foreign branches of U.S. banks, and Yankee CDs, issued by U.S. branches of foreign banks.

Commercial paper borrowings are direct borrowings, generally by large, low risk, corporations, in money markets. Although commercial paper can be issued for up to 270 days without registering with the Securities and Exchange Commission (SEC), the usual term is 30 days. Commercial paper can be resold in secondary markets. It represents an alternative to short-term bank loans and the rates are, therefore, highly competitive to bank loan interest rates.

These and other money market instruments form an important source of short-term credit. The importance of the money market to credit markets is even greater. The volume of financing in money markets is immense, and the frequency of flows make the money markets an invaluable source of information on the demand, supply, and costs of credit on a daily basis.

Composition of Interest Rates

The provision of credit requires the lender to relinquish the use of the loaned funds for a time while the borrower benefits from the use of these funds. During the term of the loan the lender must accept not only the fact of parting with the use of the funds, but also uncertainty associated with the risks that the borrower may default or that when the loan is repaid the purchasing value of the funds is likely to be eroded by inflation. Interest rates, thus can be viewed as payments to lenders to compensate them not only for the foregone uses of their funds but also against the risk of default and erosion of purchasing power. Indeed, all interest rates can be viewed as composed of payments: (1) for the loss of liquidity, (2) against the risk of default, and (3) to offset the effects of inflation. Lenders and borrowers may have different views on the strength or weakness of each of these factors; these opposing views are resolved in the financial markets in the form of upward (lenders' concerns about the future overwhelm their own and the borrowers' hopes—the markets are bearish on interest rates) or downward (lenders' hopes about the future overpower their concerns and complement the desires of borrowers—the markets are bullish on interest rates) pressures on interest rate levels. These forces and their working are basic to an understanding of the interrelationships among interest rates. Such an understanding is even more essential when the purpose is to forecast future interest rates levels.

The *liquidity* preferences of lenders—the concept that lenders require a higher return the longer the term of the loan—is a basic factor underlying the *term structure* of interest rates—the normal relationship that shows interest rates on similar-risk instruments rise as term to maturity lengthens.

The concept of liquidity preference has been developed by among others, Alfred Marshall, Irving Fisher, Knut Wicksell, John Maynard Keynes, John Hicks, and Don Patinkin as an extension of utility theory. Simply stated, lenders require a greater return (higher interest rates) the longer the term of the loan because of the increasing disutility of parting with funds as the term of the loan lengthens. This theoretical relationship is confirmed in fact when loans of varying terms to similar borrowers (thus holding the risk of default constant) are viewed at a point in time.

Such a comparison is offered by the Treasury yield curve shown in Figure 9-1. This depicts average yields for a range of Treasury issues plotted against their term to maturity for the month of June, 1983. Normal yield curves conform to the general shape of the one shown in Figure 9-1: yields increase most steeply for short-term instruments (in this case for maturities from three months to about two years); an inflection point—or shoulder—develops, beyond which intermediate term securities continue to increase, but less rapidly; longer term issues rise only slightly before tapering off. (The curve shown actually declines, or inverts, between 20 and 30 years.) The much sharper rise in short-term rates partly reflects the greater trading volume in these issues. It also reflects, however, increased investor uncertainty about near-term monetary policy, economic, and inflation developments. Since these uncertainties are usually much greater in the near-term, short-term rates move further in reaction to them. Indeed, at times, the entire yield curve may invert, as shown in Figure 9-2, the Treasury yield curve for December, 1981. At that time, short-term rates were very high (3-month bills near 16.4%) reflecting concern about then-current inflation and the prospects

FIGURE 9-1   Treasury yield curve (June 1983)

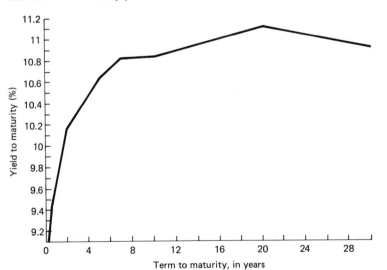

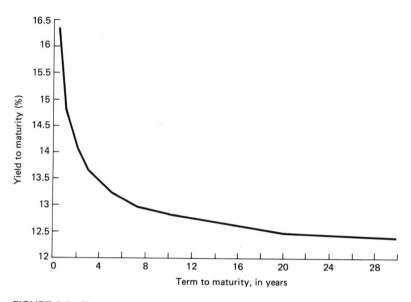

FIGURE 9-2   Treasury yield curve (December 1981)

for further tightening of monetary policy by the Federal Reserve. Interest rates declined as the term to maturity lengthened. (The yield on the 30 year bond was below 12.5%.) This reflected market sentiment that the adverse conditions then present would show some improvement; for instance, the Fed would tighten monetary policy, the economy would slow its growth, and inflation would slow—this is in fact what happened.

The main point is that the Treasury yield curve is a useful means of portraying how the financial market views the term structure relationship among interest rates at a point in time. Moreover, when yield curves for different dates are compared, it is possible to see how market sentiment has changed as a result of economic and other forces in the intervening period. Yield curves are not easily constructed for other classes of borrowers because the credit risks are more diverse.

As noted earlier, Treasury securities have the lowest risk of default because they are backed by "the full faith and credit of the U.S. Government." Virtually all other lending involves somewhat greater—though often still low—risk that the borrower may not repay on time. Table 9-3 presents a comparison of yields on Treasury short- and long-term securities for December 1982 with yields for a variety of money and capital market securities. As can be seen, similar-term, non-Treasury issues offer higher yields than the Treasury issues. This *quality spread,* measured in basis points (one basis point equals one hundredth of a percentage point of interest), reflects the market assessment of the increased risk of default associated with these borrowers. The quality spreads are widest in the capital (bond) market,

TABLE 9-3   Interest Rates and Quality Spreads for Selected Interest Rates (rates are average daily rates for December 1982)

		MONEY MARKET RATES[1]		
		FINANCE CO.	OTHER	
	TREASURY	COMMERCIAL	COMMERCIAL	CERTIFICATES
MATURITY	BILLS	PAPER	PAPER	OF DEPOSITS
3 month	8.21	8.47	8.82	8.66
6 month	8.63	8.67	9.01	8.80

QUALITY SPREAD AGAINST TREASURIES

3 month	—	.26	.61	.45
6 month	—	.04	.38	.17

BOND YIELDS

CORPORATE BONDS[3]

TREASURY[2]	Aaa	Aa	A	Baa
10.33	11.83	12.44	13.66	14.14

QUALITY SPREAD AGAINST TREASURY BOND COMPOSITE

	1.50	2.11	3.33	3.81

[1] Yields on Treasury bills and commercial paper have been converted to investment yield basis. Treasury bill and certificate of deposit rates used are secondary market yields.

[2] Unweighted averages of yields to maturity or call for all outstanding notes and bonds neither due nor callable in less than 10 years.

[3] Daily figures from Moody's Investor Service. Based on yields to maturity on selected long-term bonds.

Source: *Federal Reserve Bulletin* (Washington, DC: Board of Governors, Federal Reserve System), Table A28.

where there are fairly wide spreads among the corporate bond classes themselves (from Aaa, the highest credit rating to Baa, the lowest credit rating shown). The much wider quality spreads in the capital market compared to the money market reflect the increased risk of default as maturity extends into the more uncertain future.

Analysis of quality spreads lessen the problems raised by the absence of non-Treasury yield curves. If quality spreads are carefully analyzed, the term structure for non-Treasury interest rates can be derived; for instance, from high grade commercial paper at the short end through highly rated corporate bonds with varying terms to maturity or call. Moreover, if future quality spreads can be determined,[11] a forecast of the Treasury yield curve could be used to derive forecast values for a variety of other interest rates. (Indeed, such an analysis will serve as a part of the interest rate forecasting approach described in the final section of this chapter.)

Irving Fisher attributed the level of nominal interest rates to a "real" component—including term structure and quality considerations—and an *inflation premium.*[12] Lenders are concerned that when repaid, the proceeds of the loan will have the same purchasing power as when the loan was made. Thus, they attempt to include their expectations for the future rate of inflation in the interest rate they charge. For instance, if a lender assesses the loss of liquidity, risk of default, and attendant costs on a one-year loan as equivalent to two percentage points (200 basis points) and expects six percent inflation rate over the next year, then an eight percent interest rate would be desired.

Table 9-4 presents annual average interest rates for five credit instruments: new 6-month Treasury bills, high grade commercial paper, bank loans made at prime, long-term Treasury bonds, and long-term, high grade corporate bonds. The interest rates are shown on a yield basis in nominal and inflation-adjusted terms (the nominal rate minus the year-to-year percent change in the consumer price index). Several points emerge from analysis of this data.

Between 1953 and 1972[13] inflation remained relatively low (ranging from −0.4% in 1955 to a high of 5.9% in 1970) and all of the inflation-adjusted rates were relatively stable. One measure of this stability is provided by the low standard errors for the various interest rates during the period shown in Table 9-5. The inflation-adjusted interest rates show far less stability during the 1973–82 period: the standard errors are all three to four times greater than in the earlier period. Between 1973 and 1982, inflation was again variable, but in a higher range (from a low of 5.8%—which nearly matched the high in the earlier period—to a high of 13.5%). Indeed, many of the inflation-adjusted annual average interest rates were negative during the 1970s. The high standard errors and the prevalence of negative inflation-adjusted interest rates suggest that the inflation expectations of lenders were less accurate in anticipating actual inflation in the later period—when inflation was high—than in the earlier, lower inflation, period. Most attempts to proxy inflation

---

[11] These may depend on present and expected economic conditions and market supply-demand conditions.

[12] Irving Fisher, *The Theory of Interest* (New York: Macmillan, 1930). For a seminal discussion of the inflation premium see William P. Yohe and Denis S. Karnosky, "Interest Rates and Price Level Changes, 1952–69," in *Federal Reserve Bank of St. Louis Review* (Dec. 1969), pp. 18–38.

[13] The six-month Treasury bill was introduced in 1959. Between 1959 and 1972 stability in inflation-adjusted interest rates similar to that in the longer 1953–72 period existed. See Table 9-5.

TABLE 9-4 Selected Interest Rates, Nominal and Adjusted for Inflation Yearly Averages (investment yield basis): 1953–1982

	INFLA-TION[1]	6 MONTH[2] TREASURY BILL		4-6 MONTH[3] COMMERCIAL PAPER		PRIME RATE		10-YEAR[4] TREASURY BOND		MOODY'S Aaa CORPORATE BOND	
		NOMINAL	ADJUSTED	NOMINAL	ADJUSTED	NOMINAL	ADJUSTED	NOMINAL	ADJUSTED	NOMINAL	ADJUSTED
1953	0.8%			2.48	1.68	3.17	2.37	2.85	2.05	3.20	2.40
1954	0.5			1.61	1.11	3.05	2.55	2.40	1.90	2.90	2.40
1955	-0.4			2.23	2.63	3.16	3.56	2.82	3.22	3.06	3.46
1956	1.5			3.41	1.91	3.77	2.27	3.18	1.68	3.36	1.86
1957	3.6			3.94	0.34	4.20	0.60	3.65	0.05	3.89	0.29
1958	2.7			2.53	-0.17	3.83	1.13	3.32	0.62	3.79	1.09
1959	0.8	3.962	3.162	4.11	3.31	4.48	3.68	4.33	3.53	4.38	3.58
1960	1.6	3.347	1.747	3.98	2.38	4.82	3.22	4.12	2.52	4.41	2.81
1961	1.0	2.676	1.676	3.06	2.06	4.50	3.50	3.88	2.88	4.35	3.35
1962	1.1	2.992	1.892	3.36	2.26	4.50	3.40	3.95	2.85	4.33	3.23
1963	1.2	3.353	2.153	3.67	2.47	4.50	3.30	4.00	2.80	4.26	3.06
1964	1.3	3.808	2.508	4.11	2.81	4.54	3.20	4.19	2.89	4.40	3.10
1965	1.7	4.197	2.497	4.54	2.84	4.54	2.84	4.28	2.58	4.49	2.79
1966	2.9	5.288	2.388	5.79	2.89	5.63	2.73	4.92	2.02	5.13	2.23
1967	2.9	4.807	1.907	5.31	2.41	5.61	2.71	5.07	2.17	5.51	2.61

1968	4.2	5.704	1.504	6.17	1.97	6.30	2.10	5.65	1.45	6.18	1.98
1969	5.4	7.198	1.798	8.27	2.87	7.96	2.56	6.67	1.27	7.03	1.63
1970	5.9	6.881	0.981	8.13	2.23	7.91	2.01	7.35	1.45	8.04	2.14
1971	4.3	4.680	0.380	5.32	1.02	5.72	1.42	6.16	1.86	7.39	3.09
1972	3.3	4.633	1.333	4.91	1.61	5.25	1.95	6.21	2.91	7.21	3.91
1973	6.2	7.552	1.352	8.62	2.42	8.03	1.83	6.84	0.64	7.44	1.24
1974	11.0	8.372	-2.628	10.50	-0.50	10.81	-0.19	7.56	-3.44	8.57	-2.43
1975	9.1	6.405	-2.695	6.62	-2.48	7.86	-1.24	7.99	-1.11	8.83	-0.27
1976	5.8	5.485	-0.315	5.56	-0.24	6.84	1.04	7.61	1.81	8.43	2.63
1977	6.5	5.747	-0.753	5.85	-0.65	6.83	0.33	7.42	0.92	8.02	1.52
1978	7.7	7.983	0.283	8.44	0.74	9.06	1.36	8.41	0.71	8.73	1.03
1979	11.3	10.698	-0.602	11.71	0.41	12.67	1.47	9.44	-1.86	9.63	-1.67
1980	13.5	12.236	-1.264	13.29	-0.21	15.27	1.77	11.46	-2.04	11.94	-1.56
1981	10.4	15.054	4.654	16.17	5.77	18.87	8.47	13.91	3.51	14.17	3.77
1982	6.1	11.905	5.805	12.83	6.73	14.86	8.76	13.00	6.90	13.79	7.69

(1) Inflation measured by the year-to-year percentage change in the Consumer Price Index

(2) Rates on new issues converted to investment yield basis

(3) Rates on 4-6 month paper prior to November 1979 converted to investment yield basis assuming 6-month maturity, after November 1979 rates are for 6-month maturity

(4) Yields on the more actively traded issues adjusted to constant maturities by the Treasury Department

Source: *Economic Report of the President* (Washington, DC: U.S. Government Printing Office, 1983), Tables B-52 and B-67

TABLE 9-5   Selected Interest Rates Adjusted for Inflation: Period Averages (percent, investment, yield basis)

	1953–72	1959–72	1973–82	1953–82	1959–82
6-Month Treasury Bill	n.a.	1.85 (0.67)	0.38 (2.69)	n.a.	1.24
4–6 Month Commercial Paper	2.03 (0.87)	2.37 (0.57)	1.12 (2.79)	1.75	1.88
Prime Rate	2.39 (0.82)	2.48 (0.65)	2.36 (3.25)	2.38	2.43
10-year Treasury Bond	2.18 (0.86)	2.44 (0.65)	0.60 (2.86)	1.62	1.67
Moody's Aaa Corporate Bond	2.55 (0.87)	2.82 (0.62)	1.20 (2.89)	1.67	2.15

Source: Data from Table 9-4, inflation adjusted rates n.a. (not applicable); 6-month Treasury bill introduced in 1959. Numbers in parentheses are standard errors.

expectations assume they are formed on the basis of past inflation experience; thus, a distributed lag of past inflation rates is used.[14] The volatile and high inflation experienced in the 1970s, however, probably made recent inflation rates less useful as a guide to future inflation. Thus, lenders underestimated inflation early in the period and, so nominal interest rates were too low. The very high inflation-adjusted interest rates in 1981 and 1982, on the other hand, suggest that by that time lenders were unwilling to believe that

[14] The study by Yohe and Karnosky focused on two hypothesized relationships:

$$(1)\ rn_t = \dot{P}^e_t + rr_t$$

and

$$(2)\ \dot{P}^e_t = \sum_{i=0}^{n} w_i * \dot{P}_{t-i}$$

where rn_t = nominal interest rate at time t
   rr_t = real interest rate at time t
   $\dot{P}^e_t$ = expected inflation rate at time t
   $\dot{P}_{t-i}$ = actual inflation rate at time $t - i$

See Yohe and Karnosky, "Interest Rates and Price Level Changes, 1952–69," p. 19. One problem with this approach is that inflation expectations are measured indirectly. Gibson used survey data compiled by Joseph Livingston for the 1947–70 period as a source of actual inflation expectation in William E. Gibson, "Interest Rates and Inflationary Expectations: New Evidence," *American Economic Review* (Dec. 1972), pp. 854–65. For a discussion of other approaches to developing measures of inflation expectations see Kajal Lahiri, "Inflationary Expectations: Their Formation and Interest Rate Effects," *American Economic Review* (Mar. 1976), pp. 124–31.

the slowdown in inflation—brought on by tight monetary policy and two recessions—would persist. This is in contrast to the 1975–1976 experience when inflation slowed and nominal interest rates declined partly in anticipation of lower inflation than did not persist.

The prime rate is an exception to the other rates shown. The inflation-adjusted prime rate was relatively high with no more variation than other rates during the 1953–72 period. This probably reflected its role as an administered rate—indeed from 1959 through 1965 the nominal prime rate hardly changed. Between 1973 and 1982 the average inflation-adjusted prime rate was higher than the other rates shown (see Table 9-5) though the variation was also greater as shown by the standard error. These results suggest that banks actively managed the prime rate and quickly responded to changes in inflation trends and, thus, expectations.

The data do suggest that inflation adjusted interest rates maintained the expected term relationships (shown by the differences between the Treasury bill and Treasury bond yields and between the commercial paper and corporate bond yields) and the quality spread (measured by the differences between the commercial paper and Treasury bill rates and between the corporate and Treasury bond rates). The term relationship flattened, however, in the 1973-82 period. (The Treasury bill-bond rate differential narrowed from 59 basis points on average in 1959–72 to 22 basis points in 1973–82, while the commercial paper-corporate bond differential narrowed from 52 basis points on average in 1953–72 to only 8 basis points in 1973–82.) This flattening of yield curves mainly reflects the sharper relative rise in nominal short-term rates. At the same time, quality spreads widened. (The commercial paper-Treasury bill spread widened on average from 55 basis points in 1959–72 to 74 basis points in 1973–82, while the corporate-Treasury bond spread widened from 37 basis points in 1953–72 to 60 basis points in 1973–82.)

The three relationships described above together comprise the components of nominal interest rates. Treasury bills are the most nearly riskless, most liquid, credit instruments. Thus, the Treasury bill rate[15] mainly reflects inflation expectations (and a measure of the premium investors require to absorb the "excess supply" of bills in times of tight credit conditions). The increased return demanded by lenders in compensation for the decrease in utility which accompanies longer term lending can be seen in the Treasury yield curve. Finally, the measure of risk associated with loans to lower quality, higher risk, borrowers is captured by the quality spread.

Demand and Supply of Money and the Role of Monetary Policy

The demand and supply of money and the control of the latter by the Federal Reserve exert a profound influence on financial markets which has not yet been discussed. When demands for money are readily accommo-

[15] Ideally, this should be the shortest term to maturity bill, not the six-month bill.

dated by the amount of money the Fed is willing to supply, the cost of credit—interest rates—is determined mainly by those private factors already considered. Alternatively, when the Fed attempts to limit the supply of money to a level well below that suggested by sectoral credit demands, this restraint introduces further upward pressure on interest rates.

The general aim of Federal Reserve monetary policy is to maintain monetary and financial conditions conducive to noninflationary economic growth. The more rapid inflation during the 1970s and increased research on the quantity theory of money over the past twenty five years have resulted in a narrower focus: to slow monetary growth to a less inflationary pace. This has, in turn, led to a shift in the Fed's operating procedures. In particular, since October 1979, the Fed has focused on controlling the growth of bank reserves in order to contain monetary growth within specified target ranges.[16] Essentially the combined growth of money and its velocity (assuming velocity follows some stable trend path over long periods) should be constrained so that nominal GNP growth—the product of real economic growth and inflation—is noninflationary, or during the transition to noninflationary growth, produces a slowing in the rate of inflation. This process is exemplified by the equation of exchange.

$$\dot{M} \times \dot{V} = \dot{Y} = \dot{P} \times \dot{y} \qquad (9\text{-}1)$$

where the dots over the variables indicate growth rates. Thus,

$\dot{M}$ = growth in the money stock
$\dot{V}$ = growth in velocity, assumed to follow a stable trend
$\dot{Y}$ = growth in current dollar GNP
$\dot{P}$ = inflation rate measured by the GNP deflator
$\dot{y}$ = growth in real GNP

Indeed, with stable trend velocity and in the absence of inflation ($\dot{P} = 0$, $\dot{Y} = \dot{y}$), noninflationary monetary growth will be based on the potential growth rate for real output. In reality, however, the trend rate of velocity is not stable,[17] and inflation had not been absent when the new, more explicitly monetarist, policy was begun in late 1979.

[16] For a survey of the Federal Reserve's operating procedures prior to October 6, 1979 see Henry C. Wallich and Peter M. Keir, "The Role of Operating Guides in U.S. Monetary Policy: A Historical Review," *Federal Reserve Bulletin* (Sept. 1979), pp. 679–91. The new procedures were described in a mimeographed release, "The New Federal Reserve Technical Procedures for Controlling Money," (Washington, DC: Board of Governors of the Federal Reserve System, Jan. 1980). Recent evaluations of, and changes in, these policies can be found in the regular Federal Reserve reports to Congress reprinted in issues of the *Federal Reserve Bulletin*.

[17] This is especially so for narrow money supply velocity (Vl) which has shown frequent bouts of instability, most recently in 1981–82 when growth was negative. This may be partly a

A key result that emerged during the first few years of the new policy approach was that, starting in a period of rapid inflation, restraining monetary growth did indeed restrain current dollar GNP growth. However, a restrained monetary growth policy under these circumstances could only affect current dollar GNP growth; it could not discriminate between inflation and real growth. In fact, during 1980–82, the policy seems to have had its effect in three stages. First, the abrupt slowing in money supply growth confronted continued rapid money demand, thus driving up interest rates. Second, the sharp rise in interest rates early in 1980 and again in late 1980-early 1981 choked off the economic activities that underlay money demand, resulting in the short 1980 recession and the longer one from July 1981 through November 1982. Third, largely as a result of the decline in real GNP, inflation slowed sharply.

Clearly, the attempt to control inflationary pressures through monetary policy has important general and specific effects on the sectors of the financial economy and, indeed, on the production of goods and services. Before examining these effects, a brief discussion of views about the nature of money, its demand, and supply is useful.

The classic statement of the role of money is as: (1) a medium of exchange, (2) a store of value, and (3) a standard of account. Anti-inflationary monetary policy aims at facilitating the first role by preserving the other two. In its narrowest sense, money takes the form of currency held by the public and demand deposits, or checking accounts (referred to by Keynes as bank money[18]). In recent years, financial innovation has resulted in a number of new deposit forms—NOW accounts (Negotiated Orders of Withdrawal), super NOWs, and Money Market Deposit Accounts—which pay interest on deposits (unlike demand deposits). The first two of these "other checkables" are now included in the Federal Reserve's definition of the narrowly defined money stock (M1). Other "near monies"—which possess less liquidity and, thus, are less useful as mediums of exchange—such as time (savings) deposits and certificates of deposit, are included in the Fed's broader money aggregates.

The demand for money[19] focuses on the first two roles of money. Money is demanded for three reasons: (1) for transactions, (2) for precautionary reasons, and (3) as an alternative to other financial assets. These

---

measurement problem (velocity is a residual measure, derived by dividing current dollar GNP by the seasonally adjusted quarterly average level for the money stock), and it is at least partly due to the introduction of new accounts (other checkables) which occasioned deposit shifts. More aggregate measures of the money stock, however, show greater stability.

[18] John Maynard Keynes, *A Treatise on Money* (London: Macmillan, 1930), pp. 20–29.

[19] This section and that on the supply of money draw on the discussion in Ronald L. Teigen, "The Demand for and Supply of Money," in Ronald L. Teigen, ed., *Readings in Money, National Income, and Stabilization Policy* (Homewood, IL: Richard D. Irwin, 1978), pp. 54–81.

demands are met out of balances which are either already owned or loaned. It is through the latter form, specifically bank loans, (and Federal Reserve purchases of Treasury securities for its own portfolio—monetization of government debt) that monetary growth occurs. Demands for transactions purposes are quite straightforward, and relate closely to measures of economic activity, such as retail sales, personal income, or GNP. These relationships focus on money's role as a medium of exchange; as transactions rise with economic activity, the public's demand for money balances to carry out these transactions also rises. Baumol and Tobin[20] have also hypothesized a relationship between the transactions demand for money and interest rates, which states that individual economic units may economize on their money holdings as interest rates and yields on securities rise. (The opportunity cost of holding idle cash balances increases.) The precautionary demand is fairly stable, though it has some relationship with economic conditions. In particular, when conditions weaken—as measured, for instance, by a rising unemployment rate—precautionary balances may increase. The asset demand for money has long posed problems for economists. Keynes' original concept of the speculative demand, developed in *The General Theory*,[21] assumed that economic factors hold all their assets either in cash or bonds. This was too limiting an assumption. Friedman, on the other hand, disputes the existence of any relationship between money demand and interest rates.[22] Tobin has proposed one of the more plausible explanations for the asset demand for money.[23] He assumes that economic actors may hold portfolios of both cash and securities as wealth, reflecting the desire for the return from securities (both income and the prospect for a capital gain) weighed against risk (capital loss). Thus, as yields rise, cash assets may decline in part because of the greater return from interest bearing assets, and in part because the risk of a capital loss lessens. (Remember, as the yield rises the price of the security declines, thus lessening the prospect of further price declines.)

The demand for money can thus be related to the level of economic activity directly and interest rates indirectly. This can be shown as in 9-2.

$$Md = f(Y, r) \qquad\qquad (9\text{-}2)$$

[20] William J. Baumol, "The Transactions Demand for Cash: An Inventory Theoretic Approach," *Quarterly Journal of Economies* (Nov. 1952), pp. 545–56; and James Tobin, "The Interest-Elasticity of Transactions Demand for Cash," *Review of Economics and Statistics* (Aug. 1956), pp. 241–47.

[21] John Maynard Keynes, *The General Theory of Employment, Interest, and Money* (London: Macmillan, 1936), pp. 170–74.

[22] Milton Friedman, "The Demand for Money: Some Theoretical and Empirical Results," *Journal of Political Economy* (Aug. 1959), pp. 327–51.

[23] James Tobin, "Liquidity Preference as Behavior Toward Risk," *Review of Economic Studies* (Feb. 1958), pp. 65–86.

where

$$\frac{\Delta Md}{\Delta Y} > 0, \quad \frac{\Delta Md}{\Delta r} < 0$$

Whether or not the separate demands can be isolated is less important than recognizing that total money demand responds to both economic activity and interest rates.

The stock of money grows chiefly through deposit growth resulting from loan creation at commercial banks. (When a bank makes a loan— particularly a commercial and industrial loan—it credits the proceeds to a checking account, thus increasing the money stock.) The Federal Reserve attempts to control this rate of money growth through its reserve supplying operations. Depository institutions must maintain reserves against deposits varying from 1% for long-term deposits to $16\frac{1}{2}$% at banks with total demand deposits in excess of \$400 million.[24] Thus, in order to increase loans either excess reserves must be available, or reserves must be obtained in the money and capital markets, or borrowed from the Federal Reserve discount window. Total reserves may be viewed in a number of ways. From the viewpoint of the banks' use of reserves, total reserves (TR) consist of required reserves (RR) and excess reserves (RE).

$$TR = RR + RE \tag{9-3}$$

The sources of reserves are either a result of borrowing through the Fed's discount facility (B) or from other sources (new cash deposits or the money market, particularly Fed funds purchases) referred to as nonborrowed, or unborrowed reserves (UR).

$$TR = B + UR \tag{9-4}$$

Banks desire to optimize their excess reserves: some cushion is desirable so as to meet increases in loan demand, but at the same time excess reserves earn no return, so too much excess is too much. Moreover, banks generally try to limit discount borrowings and instead resort to the Fed funds market to meet sudden increases in reserve needs (or to lend excess reserves). Thus, free reserves (FR)—excess reserves less discount borrowings—are the focal point of banks' reserve optimization.

$$FR = RE - B \tag{9-5}$$

[24] For detail on reserve requirements see Table 1.15, "Reserve Requirements of Depository Institutions," in issues of the *Federal Reserve Bulletin.*

or $$NBR = B - RE$$

In general, it can be assumed that free reserves fall when market interest rates rise, as banks attempt to respond to increases in loan demand, which partly account for the rise in interest rates, and to economize on money market borrowings to supplement reserves. At the same time, the level of free reserves will tend to rise with increases in the Federal Reserve discount rate because discount borrowings will decrease.

The Fed targets unborrowed reserves—the portion of reserves over which it has the greatest control—as the practical means of regulating money growth. The reserve target is translated into active policy through open market operations: purchases or sales—either permanently, or temporarily through repurchase agreements—of Treasury securities with bank and nonbank primary dealers.[25] When the Fed sells (buys) securities to (from) a bank dealer it debits (credits) the bank's reserve account at its local Federal Reserve Bank, thus draining (adding) reserves to the banking system. When the transaction is with a nonbank dealer the effect is the same; the dealer's clearing bank's reserve account is affected. The effect of open market operations on the banking system's reserves is quickly translated into interest rate effects. Usually, the rates on the Treasury securities involved are affected. The Federal funds rate, however, is almost always affected: sales of securities drain reserves, reduce the amount of excess reserves in the system, and thus cause the funds rate to rise—the Fed is said to have tightened; Fed purchases of securities, on the other hand, inject reserves, leading the funds rate to decline—the Fed is said to have eased.

These conclusions are not always correct. The Fed conducts open market operations not only to effect policy changes, but also merely to offset seasonal or aberrational changes in reserves. There are a number of such changes which occur with some regularity and which must be offset just to maintain the money stock at a desired level. For instance,

> The Fed supplies reserves near corporate tax dates to offset the drain that occurs when tax payments flow from corporate accounts (included in the money stock) to the Treasury (excluded);
>
> Conversely, reserves are drained in the spring when tax refunds are flowing from the Treasury to taxpayers;
>
> The Fed supplies reserves at Christmas time when transactions demands rise sharply;
>
> And, disruptions to the check clearing process—often caused by severe weather—swell interbank float and are commonly offset by draining operations.

---

[25] An excellent discussion of this topic is offered in Paul Meek, *Open Market Operations* (New York: Federal Reserve Bank of New York, 1979), available upon request from Federal Reserve Bank of New York, Public Information Department, 33 Liberty St., New York, NY 10045.

Routine operational reserve adjustments can briefly obscure the Fed's policy-directed operations. One clue to the true intent of open market operations is the biweekly report on the average level of free reserves (or, when discount borrowings exceed excess reserves, net borrowed reserves). A more conclusive insight is gained from the minutes of the Federal Open Market Committee (FOMC) meetings, usually reported with just over a one-month lag. Finally, financial market observers and others can and do judge the likely Fed reaction to monthly economic and inflation reports, given recent Fed open market actions and available information (including FOMC minutes) to anticipate the likely policy response.

Both the demand for and supply of money respond to interest rate changes. Moreover, the monetary policy actions of the Federal Reserve affect the level of interest rates, not as the direct result of interest rate targeting as once was the case, but rather as a result of the Fed's efforts in adjusting reserves in the banking system. Thus, the demand for money, its supply by the banking system, and its regulation by the Federal Reserve all affect or are affected by interest rates.

SUMMARY

Financial flows among the various sectors of the economy are the basic forces determining the levels of interest rates. The uses of credit largely mirror the demands for real durable consumption, homebuilding, and business spending for inventories and fixed investment. The ultimate source of loanable funds is the saving of various sectors. These saving flows are channeled to borrowers through financial mediation—loans and market purchases of securities. Interest rates measure the relative strength of financial flows. However, there is no one interest rate that does this, but rather a complex of rates and yields reflecting the variety of debt instruments. All interest rates are composed of three elemental components: a liquidity, or term structure component, that usually rises as the term to maturity lengthens; a quality component that reflects the risk of default of the various classes of borrowers; and an inflation premium which incorporates the inflation expectations of lenders. Federal Reserve monetary policy is a further influence on the level of interest rates, which aims at insuring stable financial conditions. In recent years, monetary policy has mainly been directed at achieving less inflationary monetary growth by controlling nonborrowed reserve growth. The need to resist stronger monetary demand associated with inflation and demands for funds stemming from real economic activities has led to record high interest rates which first choked off real growth, but in time produced a slowdown in inflation.

All of these factors should be considered in preparing interest rate forecasts. Indeed, one of the main points to emerge from the discussion above is that interest rates are the result of these forces; they are the end of a forecasting process, and cannot be considered in isolation.

THREE APPROACHES TO FINANCIAL FORECASTING

This section discusses three different approaches to financial forecasting developed in the early 1970s by Hunt, Hendershott, and Nelson.[26] These approaches use, in order, a multi-equation econometric model of which the fifty equation financial model is a portion; a flow-of-funds multi-sector model in which nonfinancial variables are exogenous; and a linear stochastic equation which explains the term structure of interest rates. Thus, the three approaches present a range of methods and expose the strengths and weaknesses of each.

Hunt's model resulted from his work in developing the financial market model for the Chase Econometric Associates monthly econometric model of the U.S. economy. As such, it integrates nonfinancial demand and supply variables with the demand and supply of credit and the determination of interest rate levels and vice versa. Hunt indicates five distinguishing characteristics of this model.[27] First, the primary exogenous monetary policy variable is the nonborrowed monetary base (i.e., currency and nonborrowed commercial bank reserves). Second, it contains a completely developed market for Federal funds, borrowed reserves, excess reserves, currency held by nonmember banks, and currency held by the nonbank public. Consequently, it is possible to derive values for all of the major reserve aggregates. Third, the components of the U.S. Government budget—the supply of Treasury debt outstanding and its cash assets—enter into the determination of various interest rates and the private sector's stock of financial assets and liabilities. Fourth, each key interest rate is determined by the basic supply and demand factors operating in its market. (They are not based on the term structure, as in other models.) Fifth, foreign money markets are treated endogenously.

The model is carefully built up from theoretical and empirical relationships underlying the financial cycle and from relationships between financial cycles and general business cycles. Detailed equations are presented for seven credit demand sectors: (1) the net change in commercial bank loans, (2) new issues of corporate bonds (3) new issues of municipal bonds, (4) the

[26] Lacy H. Hunt, *Dynamics of Forecasting Financial Cycles: Theory, Technique, and Implementation* (Greenwich, CT: JAI Press, 1976); Patric H. Hendershott, *Understanding Capital Markets: A Financial Flow of Funds Model* (Lexington, MA: Lexington Books), 1977; and Charles R. Nelson, *The Term Structure of Interest Rates* (New York: Basic Books, 1972).

[27] Lacy H. Hunt, *Dynamics of Forecasting Financial Cycles: Theory Technique, and Implementation* (Greenwich, CT: JAI Press, 1976), pp. 8–10.

net change in the debt of Federally sponsored credit agencies, (5) the net change in mortgage debt outstanding, (6) the net change in nonbank commercial paper, and (7) the Governmental budget deficit.

The model was tested in two ways for the February 1974 through February 1975 period. First, thirteen one-month simulations were performed, in each case using actual data for the moving base months. The second, more rigorous, test was a thirteen-month simulation using calculated values for all endogenous variables. Both tests showed that the model performed well over this difficult period.

Hunt derived six overall conclusions about financial cycles from the model.

(1) The Fed funds rate is the key money market interest rate. An increase in the Fed funds rate will raise Treasury bill rates, CD rates, commercial paper rates, and the prime rate. The main influence comes not from the Federal Reserve but from loan demand at banks and market expectations of commercial bankers: increased loan demand leads to upward pressure on the funds rate and, in turn, on the prime rate, ultimately resulting in a decline in loan demand—hence, financial cycles.

(2) The discount rate plays a very minor role. Its main direct influence is on member bank borrowing from the Fed which in turn impacts the money supply and other bank deposits.

(3) The money market process is determined by the complex interaction of numerous real and financial variables. In the end it represents results of decisions of banks, the nonbank public, and the Treasury.

(4) U.S. money markets are linked to Eurodollar markets.

(5) While Eurodollar rates and demand are influenced by conditions in the U.S., they are also influenced by trade flows, economic conditions in Europe, and financial market conditions in Germany and the U.K.

(6) The Treasury and corporate bond markets are the main components of the capital markets. The municipal bond and mortgage markets are more isolated in their influence.

Hunt's model suffers somewhat from being dated. Moreover, by this point, other equally elaborate econometric models relating the financial and nonfinancial sectors exist. Nevertheless, the book remains one of the most extensive treatments of econometric financial forecasting and sheds much useful and still-relevant light on the area. In the end, the approach described is too elaborate, and expensive, to be emulated by most forecasters, but the insights gained may help in constructing simpler econometrically-based forecasts.

Hendershott developed a 48-equation econometric model based on a flow of funds framework using quarterly data estimated over the 1959–71 period. He cites three distinguishing characteristics.[28] First, the entire finan-

---

[28] Hendershott, *Understanding Capital Markets* p 2.

cial behavior of each sector is consistent with the given (exogenous) nonfinancial behavior of the sector. Second, the balance sheet constraint—sources-equal-uses identity—is enforced explictly at all times; there are no "residual" categories floating about to pick up any needed slack. Third, the primary security rates in the model are determined by the other fundamental identity in the flow-of-funds accounting structure, the constraint that issues equal purchases in each security market.

There are eight sectors and nine financial instruments and associated yields analyzed. The eight sectors are: (1) households, (2) nonfinancial businesses, (3) state and local governments, (4) commercial banks, (5) thrifts, (6) other finance (largely insurance companies and pension funds), (7) the Federal government, and (8) the rest of the world. The disaggregation of finance into banks, thrifts, and others reflects the importance of liability management by commercial banks and differences in portfolio preferences. The Federal government sector includes the Treasury, the Federal Reserve, and federally sponsored credit agencies. Because only the mortgage purchase behavior of the agencies is endogenous, the Treasury and the Fed are effectively exogenous. The rest of the world is explictly treated as exogenous. The nine financial instruments and yields are: (1) money (no yield); (2) savings accounts at banks (average of CD and passbook rate); (3) savings accounts at nonbank financial institutions (average of effective yields on savings and loan shares and mutual savings bank deposits); (4) contractual savings (no yield); (5) insurance policy loans (constant); (6) home mortgages (mortgage rate); (7) all other short-term securities (commercial paper rate); (8) all other long-term securities (20-year Aa utility corporate bond rate); and (9) liabilities to foreign branches (Eurodollar rate).

A sources and uses statement is constructed for each sector, with the general structure as shown in Figure 9-3.

Uses	Sources
ΔFA_1	ΔFL_1
.	.
.	.
.	.
$\Delta FA_x - CG$	ΔFL_y
INV$_1$	SAV
.	
.	
INV$_z$	

FIGURE 9-3
Hendershott's generalized sources and uses of funds statement
Source: Patric H. Hendershott, *Understanding Capital Markets.*

ΔFA equals the change in financial assets for assets 1 through x less the capital gain (CG) on equities, ΔFL is the change in financial liabilities on liabilities 1 through y, INV is investment in real assets for real assets 1 through z, and SAV is saving. Investment in real assets and savings are treated as exogenous to each sector. Equations are then estimated for net issues of the y financial liabilities, and the net purchases of the x financial assets, estimated in linear form, and regressed on the exogenous sources and uses (SAV, INV_1 . . . INV_z) past equity capital gains (ΣCG), the difference between current and expected yields on long-term liabilities (R^*), changes in the yields on financial assets held by the sector (ΔR), and changes in sectoral income (Δy).

Hendershott compared his model with the MIT-PENN-SSRC bank-reserves model in simulations forecasting three interest rates—commercial paper, mortgage, and corporate bond rate—two ways. These included an in-sample dynamic simulation for the period from first quarter 1966 through fourth quarter 1971 (in which calculated values in one quarter are used as lagged endogenous variables in subsequent quarters), and an out-of-sample forecast for the four quarters of 1972. The overall performance of the two models was approximately equal. For the in-sample simulation, the flow of funds model was better at predicting levels (particularly the corporate bond rate) while the bank-reserves model was better at predicting changes (particularly for the commercial paper rate). In forecasting, the flow of funds model again tracked the corporate bond rate more closely, while the bank-reserves model was better for the mortgage rate. The main advantage of the flow of funds model over a bank-reserves model is the greater information provided by the former regarding financial flows. The model is explicitly designed to explain the various security issues and purchases of the sectors. The aggregate sector and instrument results were good. Unfortunately, to be useful, Hendershott noted, less aggregate results may be needed. Moreover, forecasting solely on the basis of coefficients estimated on past data implies a degree of stability in the financial structure that may be unrealistic. Thus, judgment must still be relied on to make the aggregate model results useful.

Hendershott's model, like Hunt's, is large, sophisticated, and would be costly to maintain. Moreover, Hendershott's model requires an extensive amount of exogenous data. Its greatest virtue is in examining the purely financial relationships of the sectors as financial relationships.

Nelson's model designed to analyse the term structure of interest rates may be used for forecasting. The model is based on two key hypotheses. First, that spot yields for multi-period securities can be interpreted as a series of forward interest rates. Thus, a two period yield can be viewed as the one-year forward rate one year in the future. Second, Nelson shows that these term structure relationships can be estimated by linear stochastic (time series) processes that are either autoregressive (AR) for the stationary case, or integrated moving averages (IMA) for the nonstationary case.[29]

---

[29] He uses the methods developed by Box and Jenkins, see G.F.P. Box and G.M. Jenkins, *Time Series Analysis for Forecasting and Control* (San Francisco: Holden-Day, Inc., 1970). A less difficult introduction to time series forecasting is contained in Charles R. Nelson, *Applied Time Series Analysis For Managerial Forecasting* (San Francisco: Holden-Day, Inc., 1973).

The sequence of one-period forward rates, $_t r_{t+i}$ may be derived from the spot rates, $R_{i,t}$, using the relationship

$$_t r_{t+i} = \frac{(1 + R_{i+1,t})^{i+1}}{(1 + R_{i,t})^i} - 1 \tag{9-6}$$

These rates can then be used in an AR or IMA process to estimate the term premium, $_t \hat{T}_{t+n}$, the difference between the forward rate and the expected value of the future rates. The forecast results proved quite good.

Nelson's approach has the virtue of economy of data; past yield curve data provide sufficient information. As with all time series approaches, however, the estimation of the correct stochastic process requires experience akin to art. Moreover, the information provided about financial market forces is very limited. The method does have value as a control forecast on any other approach. The results can be contrasted to evaluate the reasonableness of econometrically- or judgmentally-produced forecasts.

A FINANCIAL FORECASTING METHODOLOGY

This section describes an approach to forecasting interest rates, and the money stock which is less complex than the models developed by Hunt and Hendershott, but which yields more economic information than the time series approach of Nelson. The core of the approach is a set of equations which produces an indicative interest rate forecast—in this case, for the six-month Treasury bill rate—based on the reserve supplying actions of the Federal Reserve, the reactions of the banking system, and the money demand of the non-bank public. A number of other interest rate forecasts are then generated using spread relationships to the basic six-month Treasury bill rate.

The subjective judgments of the forecaster play at least as important a role as the objective equation results in developing the final forecasts. There are two main reasons for this. First, the policy actions and goals of the Federal Reserve exert a vital, often determining, influence on interest rates and the financial sector variables. The Fed's actions are in response to a host of economic forces, however, which are themselves subject to change; at one time the main thrust of policy may be to reduce inflation; at another it may be directed at inducing economic recovery; and at still another time it may be aimed at calming international financial markets. These changing aims of monetary policy can lead to changes in the Fed's monetary growth targets and, in turn, can effect changes in operating procedures, such as the change from interest rate targeting to reserve targeting in October 1979, and then to a temporary reemphasis of interest rate targets in October 1982.

Consequently, a fixed objective (i.e. mechanistic) approach to forecasting all reserve variables endogenously is unlikely to respond quickly enough, or at all, to either subtle or pronounced changes in monetary policy. It is, instead, necessary to forecast at least some of these variables exogenously, reflecting the forecaster's appraisal of the likely conduct of Fed policy.

A second reason for the importance of judgment is in recognition of Hendershott's point that reliance on fixed coefficient equations, derived from past activity, implies a greater confidence in the stability of financial behavior than seems consistent with actual experience. The main value of the equation-based results is the information they supply about the interrelationships among the various economic forces included. The forecaster, however, must avoid being enticed into believing the results simply because they are produced by econometrically derived equations. The economist-forecaster's own analysis of the economic processes should always dominate mere statistical results.

This section describes: (1) a statistical model used to derive forecasts of an indicative interest rate; (2) a process for developing other interest rate forecasts based on the indicative forecast of the six-month Treasury bill rate and past spread relationships; and (3) some of the points where judgment is most needed, and some advice on how these judgments can be formed.

An Indicative Interest Rate Forecast Model[30]

This approach derives forecasts of the six-month Treasury bill rate based on separate estimates of the supply of and demand for narrowly defined money. The six-month Treasury bill rate is chosen as the indicative interest rate because: (1) six-month Treasury bills are actively traded instruments, popular with both banks and the nonbank public; (2) as a Treasury issue, quality considerations can be ignored; (3) it is often an instrument that the Fed buys or sells in conducting open market operations; and (4) this rate has recently acquired a special importance as the base rate that banks and thrifts use to set the rates they pay on six-month savings certificates. Cases can be made for using some other short-term rate—such as the Federal funds rate, the three-month Treasury bill rate, or a CD or commercial paper rate—such a change would not affect the nature of the analysis, only the specific coefficients.

It is vital to recognize that the estimates of the narrow money stock (Ml) which the Federal Reserve tracks and publishes, when viewed over time, are not strictly either the supply of money (Mls) or the demand for

[30] Much of the material in this section benefitted from discussion and earlier work done by one former and two present colleagues at Chemical Bank: James P. Winder (now at The Bank of New York), Carl A. Batlin, and Jeffrey R. Leeds, respectively. It is difficult to tell where their excellent insights leave off and the author's begin. Their generous help is gratefully acknowledged.

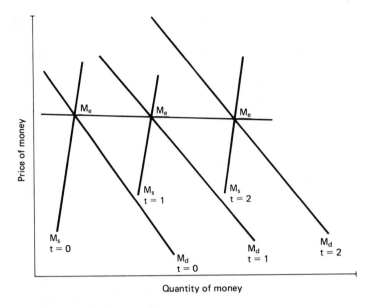

Quantity of money

FIGURE 9-4   Money supply and demand over time

money (Mld). Instead, the time series on the money stock represents equilibrium points on the shifting supply and demand schedules for money. (See Figure 9-4.)[31] Of course, *ex post* these values are all equal. However, the approach detailed here looks at the supply of and demand for money *ex ante* and, thus, differences between these desired levels and actual levels of the money stock do occur and create upward or downward pressure on interest rates.

The money supply (Mls) is a function of the reserve supplying activities of the Fed and, to a lesser extent, the reaction of member banks to the state of reserve availability. Furthermore, if currency is assumed to follow a stable trend, then changes in the money supply can be viewed as reflecting changes in checkable deposits against which reserves must be held. Thus, the amount of reserves determines the money supply as in 9-7.

$$UR_t - FR_t = RR_t = rreq_t * Mls_t \qquad (9\text{-}7)$$

where UR_t = unborrowed (nonborrowed) reserves at t
FR_t = free reserves (excess reserves minus discount borrowings) at time t; when this term is negative, net borrowed reserves exist (discount borrowings exceed excess reserves)

---

[31] For a more detailed discussion of this point see Ronald L. Teigen, "The Demand for and Supply of Money," in Ronald L. Teigen, ed., *Readings in Money, National Income, and Stabilization Policy* (Homewood, IL: Richard D. Irwin, 1978), pp. 59–62.

RR_t = required reserves at time t

Mls_t = money supply at time t

$rreq_t$ = the effective reserve requirement at time t, equal to the observed money stock (Ml_t) divided by required reserves at time t.

Unborrowed reserves is the key reserve variable the Fed can control. As such, it must be regarded as a policy variable, and therefore be determined exogenously.

The amount of free reserves, on the other hand, partly reflects the desires of the banking system. When loan demand is strong, market interest rates are likely to be rising, and excess reserves will be minimized so that banks can both meet the rising quantity of loan demand and benefit from the increases in prices received (interest rates). The rising market interest rates also imply an increasing opportunity cost to holding idle excess reserves. Thus, an inverse relationship between free reserves and interest rates can be posited. In addition, since discount borrowings can be assumed to have an inverse relationship to the Federal Reserve discount rate (rd), free reserves are assumed to relate directly to the discount rate.[32]

$$FR_t = f(r_t, rd_t) \tag{9-8}$$

where
$$\frac{\Delta FR}{\Delta r} < 0, \quad \frac{\Delta FR}{\Delta rd} > 0$$

This equation is shown in stochastic form with estimated coefficients in 9-8a.

$$FR_t = a + b_1 * r_t + b_2 * rd_t + e_t \tag{9-8a}$$

coefficients	t statistics
a = 0.673	(1.19)
b_1 = −0.285	(−6.17)
b_2 = 0.109	(1.44)
rho = 0.879	(19.03)

$\overline{R}^2 = 0.8345$ D-W = 1.94   SER = 0.33

---

[32] In fact, the important policy relationship should be that market interest rates (r_t) respond to the amount of free reserves the Federal Reserve is willing to allow. Carl Batlin has stressed that the level of free (net borrowed) reserves, as a result of lagged reserve accounting which was phased out in 1984, reflected an excess supply (demand) for reserves, reflecting changes in the money stock two weeks earlier, thus exerting downward (upward) pressures on interest rates as banks adjusted their reserves. The relationship is viewed as in equation 9-7 in order to be of more direct use in estimating the interest rate in equation 9-15.

The equation was estimated using monthly data for the period January 1973 through December 1981. The coefficients all have the expected signs. The coefficient on the discount rate was only significant at the 90% level, but since the residuals were smaller using 9-8 than a variant without the discount rate it was decided to ignore the usual criteria of a 95% confidence test.

Substituting 9-8a for free reserves in equation 9-7, and dividing each side by the effective reserve requirement, an estimating equation for the narrow money supply (Mls) can be derived.

$$Mls_t = \frac{UR_t}{rreq_t} - \frac{FR_t}{rreq_t} \qquad (9-9)$$

$$= \frac{UR_t}{rreq_t} - \frac{(0.673 - 0.285 * r_t + 0.109 * rd_t)}{rreq_t}$$

When actual data from 1973 through 1982 were substituted in this equation and the resulting estimates contrasted against the published money stock (Ml), the results were close. (See Figure 9-5.) The root mean square error for the full ten-year period was $6.9 billion, while the mean absolute percentage error was 1.66%. As can be seen from Figure 9-5, the errors were particularly large in 1973–74 and 1981–82. It has been suggested that disintermediation in the former period and the introduction of new deposit accounts in the

FIGURE 9-5   Money stock versus estimated money supply

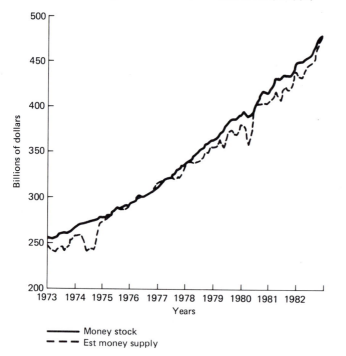

Money stock
Est money supply

latter period may have led to a greater degree of change in the actual effective reserve requirements than is picked up by the rough approximation (RR_t/Ml_t) used here.[33]

In an *in vitro* forecast situation there are likely to be other sources of error. An unborrowed reserve path must be assumed based on the forecaster's assessment of Federal Reserve policy. Similarly, changes in the discount rate must be anticipated. The market interest rate used, the six-month Treasury bill rate, will be solved for below. The need to assume values for unborrowed reserves and the discount rate, however, suggest a number of alternative forecasts—ranging from optimistic to pessimistic—should be assumed so that different interest rate forecasts, or simulations, can be solved for.

The demand for money is assumed to respond directly to a transaction demand (T_t) and indirectly to the opportunity cost of holding money balances versus interest-bearing assets, represented by an indirect relationship with a lagged interest rate.[34]

$$Mld_t = f(T_t, r_t) \tag{9-10}$$

where $\quad \dfrac{\Delta Mld}{\Delta T} > 0 \quad$ and $\quad \dfrac{\Delta Mld}{\Delta r} < 0$

The transactions demand is represented by retail sales (RS) in the current and prior months. The opportunity cost is represented by the lagged interest rate. A fitted version for the 1973-81 period of this equation is shown in 9-10 where all variables except the interest rate are in natural logarithms.[35]

$$Mld_t = a + b_1 * RS_t + b_2 * RS_{t-1} + b_3 * r_{t-1} \tag{9-11}$$

coefficients	t statistics
a = 4.037	(3.87)
b_1 = 0.180	(4.29)
b_2 = 0.260	(6.33)
b_3 = −0.0024	(−3.99)
rho = 0.99998	(56.190)

$$\overline{R}^2 = 0.9991 \quad D\text{-}W = 1.24 \quad SER = 0.005$$

[33] The author is grateful to Jeffrey Leeds for this suggestion.

[34] Interest rates are lagged on the plausible premise that investors wait some period for confirmation that opportunity costs really have changed—a process of signal extraction—and, thus, that it is worthwhile to alter portfolios.

[35] The interest rate also fulfills a role as a proxy for velocity in this equation. That is the change in velocity can be related to some constant raised to the power of the interest rate.

$$\dot{V} = 1 + a^r$$

Thus, while other variables are shown in log form the interest rate is not.

The high value of rho, nearly equal to one, and the still-low Durbin-Watson statistic pose problems, particularly if the equation is to be used for forecasting. One interpretation of the high rho is that the equation would be better estimated in first differences. It is expected that a regression in first difference form will have a lower adjusted coefficient of determination ($\overline{R}^2$). This can be overlooked, however, because of the high $\overline{R}^2$ in equation 9-10 (even before Cochrane-Orcutt correction, $\overline{R}^2 = 0.9991$). Once, again, all variables except the interest rate are in natural logarithms and the regression is fitted for 1973–81.

$$Mld_t - Mld_{t-1} = a + b_1 * (RS_t - RS_{t-1})$$
$$+ b_2 * (RS_{t-1} - RS_{t-2}) + b_3 * (r_{t-1} - r_{t-2}) \quad (9\text{-}12)$$

	coefficients	t statistics
	$a = 0.004$	(7.28)
	$b_1 = 0.054$	(1.42)
	$b_2 = 0.132$	(3.54)
	$b_3 = -0.0025$	(−5.16)

$$\overline{R}^2 = 0.26 \quad D\text{-}W = 1.54 \quad SER = 0.004$$

The Durbin-Watson statistic is still low, but it was decided not to correct for this by Cochrane-Orcutt because the equation was already in difference form. By moving the lagged money demand to the right-hand side (using the actual money stock) this equation can be used to estimate the log of the demand for money and, by exponentiation, the level of the demand for money.

$$Mld_t = Mld_{t-1} + a + b_1 * RS_t + (b_2 - b_1) * RS_{t-1}$$
$$+ b_2 * RS_{t-2} + b_3 * r_{t-1} - b_3 * r_{t-2} \quad (9\text{-}13)$$

or

$$Ln(Mld_t) = Ln(Mld_{t-1}) + 0.004 + 0.054 * Ln(RS_t)$$
$$+ 0.078 * Ln(RS_{t-1}) - 0.132 * Ln(RS_{t-2}) - 0.0025 * r_{t-1} + 0.0025 * r_{t-2}$$

When contrasted with the actual money stock (see Figure 9-6) the estimated results are very close (root mean square error of $1.5 billion, mean absolute percentage error of 0.30%). These results are much closer to published money stock data than those for estimating the money supply.

Ex ante, equilibrium is achieved when the money stock exactly equals both the supply of money and the demand for money.

$$Ml = Mls = Mld \quad (9\text{-}14)$$

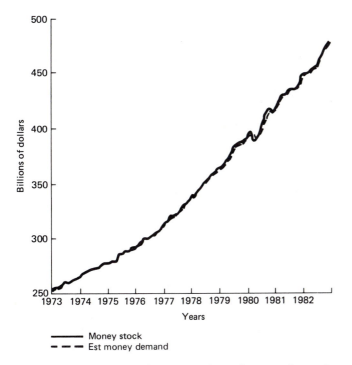

—— Money stock
– – – Est money demand

FIGURE 9-6   Money stock versus estimated money demand

Substituting 9-9 and 9-13 for this condition

$$\frac{UR_t}{rreq_t} - \frac{(0.673 - 0.285 * r_t + 0.109 * rd_t)}{rreq_t} = Mld_t,$$

so that the interest rate can be solved for directly by rearranging terms.

$$\hat{r}_t = 2.366 + 3.515 * ((rreq_t * \hat{Mld}_t) - UR_t) + 0.384 * rd_t \qquad (9\text{-}15)$$

When this equation is solved for 1973–82 the results show large errors (actual and estimated interest rate levels and the errors are shown in panel A of Table 9-6).[36] The mean absolute error for the 1973–81 estimates is 187 basis points and for 1982 it equals 222 basis points. It was thought that since equation 9-8 contained an estimate for rho (0.879), the effects of which were excluded from 9-15, this might account for some of the error. Thus, it

---

[36] Since this equation is not estimated directly there are not, strictly speaking, in-sample and out-of-sample periods. However, two of the terms—the demand for money and free reserves—are substituted for by fitted equations estimated over the 1973–81 period. Thus, 1982 can be loosely regarded as an out-of-sample period.

TABLE 9-6   Six-Month Treasury Bill Rates, Actual and Estimated: 1982 (percent, discount basis)

A. $\hat{r}_t = 2.366 + 3.515 * ((rreq_t * \hat{M}ld_t) - UR_t) + 0.384 * rd_t$

	ACTUAL	ESTIMATED	ERROR
Jan.	12.83	9.10	3.73
Feb.	13.61	12.21	1.40
Mar.	12.77	11.57	1.20
Apr.	12.80	12.16	0.64
May	12.16	9.59	2.57
June	12.70	10.90	1.80
July	11.88	7.92	3.96
Aug.	9.88	6.98	2.90
Sept.	9.37	7.90	1.47
Oct.	8.29	5.68	2.61
Nov.	8.34	6.41	1.93
Dec.	8.16	5.80	2.36
Mean Absolute Error			2.215

B. $\hat{r}_t' = 0.879 * (r_{t-1} - \hat{r}_{t-1}) + \hat{r}_t$

	ACTUAL	ESTIMATED	ERROR
Jan.	12.83	12.11	0.72
Feb.	13.61	15.49	-1.89
Mar.	12.77	12.80	-0.03
Apr.	12.80	13.21	-0.41
May	12.16	10.16	2.00
June	12.70	13.16	-0.46
July	11.88	9.50	2.38
Aug.	9.88	10.46	-0.58
Sept.	9.37	10.45	-1.08
Oct.	8.29	6.97	1.32
Nov.	8.34	8.71	-0.37
Dec.	8.16	7.49	0.67
Mean Absolute Error			0.992

was decided to perform a second-stage estimate of the six-month Treasury bill rate (r_t') equal to the value of rho times the one-month lagged error from equation 9-15 plus the estimate of the current month's interest rate from 9-15.[37]

$$\hat{r}_t' = 0.879 * (r_{t-1} - \hat{r}_{t-1}) + \hat{r}_t \qquad (9\text{-}16)$$

[37] The decision to use the rho value from equation 10-8 was somewhat arbitrary. Other values could be tried, including exponential smoothing, to derive a coefficient for the error term in 10-16.

The results produced a pronounced improvement for both the 1973–81 period and for 1982: the mean absolute errors decreased to 94 basis points and 99 basis points, respectively. Figure 9-7 presents plots of the actual and estimated six-month Treasury bill rates, while panel B of Table 9-6 presents actual and estimated interest rate levels and the errors for 1982. One striking result from Figure 9-7 is that the estimated Treasury bill rates (dotted line) show greater volatility than the actuals (solid line).

The forecast errors are somewhat larger in the second half of 1982, when the Fed began actively to ease policy, than in the first half (mean absolute errors of 107 basis points and 92 basis points, respectively). The mean absolute errors remain uncomfortably large, however, for all periods. Mean errors (with regard to sign) are much smaller: 2 basis points for the 1973–81 period, 19 basis points for 1982. This suggests that when the estimated results are viewed as indications for, say, a full year they are fairly useful. When the purpose is to get precise monthly estimates, however, the equation results must still be tempered by the economist-forecaster's judg-

FIGURE 9-7   6-month T-bill actual versus estimated

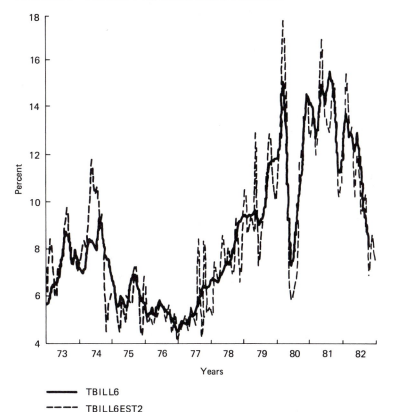

ment. Nevertheless, the equation results do provide information which, on average, provides useful indications of the movement over time for the six-month Treasury bill rate.

Deriving an Array of Interest Rate Forecasts

The detailed approach outlined above to forecast the six-month Treasury bill rate could just as easily be used to forecast some other money market rate;[38] obvious alternatives are: the Federal funds rate, a commercial paper rate, a certificate of deposit rate, or even the three-month Treasury bill rate. However, it would be inefficient, and theoretically pointless, to reproduce the estimation procedure described above for more than one rate. Nevertheless, it is desirable to have forecasts for other interest rates. For instance the mortgage rate on new homes is an input in the estimation of housing starts described in Chapter 7, while the prime rate (and the mortgage rate indirectly through use of housing starts as an exogenous input) is an exogenous input to the real GNP forecast approach described in Chapter 8.

A desired approach is to link other interest rate forecasts to the base interest rate. This assures consistency. Ideally, there should be some stable, objective relationships that can be used. In fact, the relationships are not stable and there is no single objective (i.e., mechanistic) method to derive other interest rates even if the forecast of the six-month Treasury bill rate is accurate. The judgment of the forecaster remains essential.

Figures 9-8 through 9-12 portray spreads between the six-month Treasury bill rate[39] and, respectively: the Federal funds rate, the prime rate, the Treasury bond rate, the corporate Aaa bond rate, and the mortgage rate. The solid line represents the actual spread—a positive spread means that the indicated interest rate was greater than the Treasury Bill rate, a negative spread implies a higher level for the Treasury Bill rate than for the indicated instrument. (For instance, in 1974, the Federal funds rate exceeded the Treasury Bill rate, while by 1976 the Treasury Bill rate was higher than the Fed funds rate.) The dotted lines represent twelve-month centered moving averages of the spreads. If the spread relationships were highly stable, then the actual spread and its moving average would virtually coincide and show little variation over time. In fact, this is nearly so from 1976 through mid 1979, but not in other periods. In particular, the 1980–82 period is characterized by pronounced volatility, with a number of wide swings in the spreads. These swings reflect: (1) the effects of the Federal Reserves' switch from interest rate to reserve targeting, which led to wider, less coordinated swings in interest rates; and (2) the consequently greater importance of specific credit market forces on individual interest rate movements.

---

[38] The base rate should be a money market (i.e. short-term) rate in order to provide an "anchor" for yield curve analyses.

[39] The six-month Treasury bill rate was converted to an investment yield basis in each case.

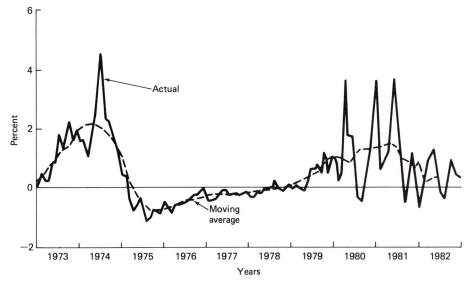

FIGURE 9-8   Fed funds—T-bill spreads

The spread between the six-month Treasury bill rate and the Federal funds rate underwent the greatest volatility during these years. In particular, there were three sharp swings in 1980–81. Early in 1980 the Fed funds rate rose more steeply as the Federal Reserve tightened monetary policy. The onset of the 1980 recession produced a sharp slowing in the growth of both

FIGURE 9-9   Prime—T-bill spreads

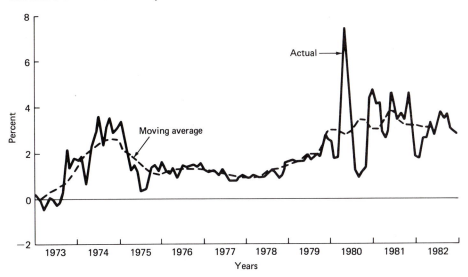

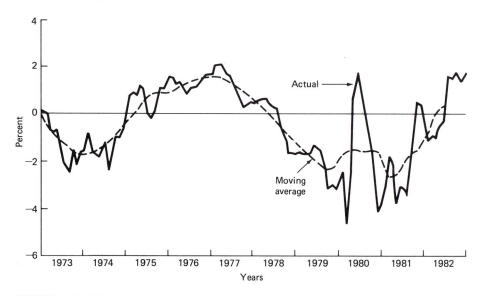

FIGURE 9-10 **Government bond—T-bill spreads**

the money stock and the demand for money so that by mid 1980 the Fed eased and both the Fed funds rate and the Treasury bill rate fell sharply. By late 1980, money stock and demand were growing rapidly again and the Fed funds rate reached a new high in early 1981 while the bill rate rose less rapidly. Monetary policy and market fears eased briefly in the spring of 1981,

FIGURE 9-11 **Corporate bond—T-bill spreads**

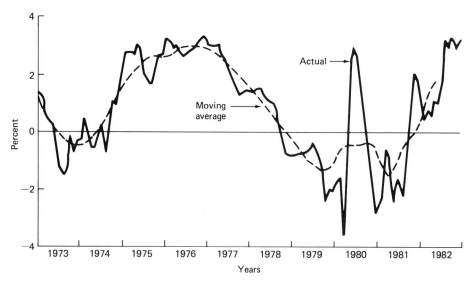

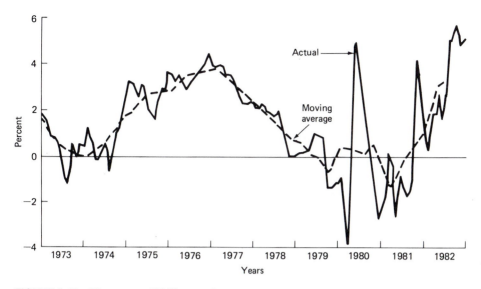

FIGURE 9-12   Mortgage—T-bill spreads

but by mid year a further tightening move pushed the Fed funds rate back to a new high on a monthly average basis (19.1% in June 1981), while the Treasury bill rate rose less. Thereafter, the deepening recession and slow-down in inflation produced narrower swings, gradually moving the spread near zero.

The spread between the *prime rate* and the Treasury bill rate followed the pattern of the Fed funds rate into early 1981. (On a monthly average basis, the prime rate reached an all-time high of 20.5% in August 1981—just as the 1981–82 recession began.) Thereafter, the prime rate maintained a higher-than-historical and less volatile spread to the bill rate.

The spread between the *Treasury bond* and bill rates increased sharply through mid 1980 reflecting worsening fears about inflation and concerns about the widening Federal budget deficit. During 1981, the spread was again negative as investors were deterred from investing in the longer term bonds by stubborn, high inflation—the yield curve inverted. The slowing of infla-tion in 1982 returned the yield curve (spread relationship) to its normal upward sloping shape (bond rates exceeded bill rates).

The broadly similar movements for the spreads between Treasury bill rates and corporate bond and mortgage rates, respectively, reflected: (1) similar factors to those cited above; and (2) reduced borrowings by corpora-tions and home buyers during the 1981–82 recession.

It is clear from the discussion above that the forces that affect various interest rate spreads are varied. Knowledge of past spread relationships provides the forecaster with a basis for forming judgments about the likely behavior of spreads in any period. In the end, however, forecasts of particular interest rates rely heavily on judgment.

The Role of Judgment Summarized

A purely objective or mechanistic approach to interest rate forecasting would be desirable. The foregoing discussion, however, repeatedly points out the failure of such an approach. Interest rate forecasting (as is true of all economic forecasting) is not merely a technical exercise; the judgments of an economist are needed.

Three key points in the approach that has been described require the economist-forecaster to make judgmental adjustments.

1. The growth path for unborrowed reserves must be exogenously assumed. This represents the effective aim of Federal Reserve policy and is, thus, a central determinant of monetary tightness or ease. One way to minimize the effects of a mis-forecast is to develop a number of different reserve path forecasts—ranging from accomodative to restrictive growth in the supply of reserves. This simulation approach allows the forecaster to provide management with a base forecast and alternatives and criteria for monitoring actual reserve growth relative to the forecast. In the event that one of the alternatives proves correct, the implications for the overall economic forecast can, then, be anticipated.
2. The indicative interest rate forecast that emerges from the equation is likely to require adjustment even if the reserve path is forecast correctly, due to the effects of exogenous factors. The recent tracking behavior of the model results provides some insight to the direction and magnitude of adjustments. In addition, the policy announcements of the Federal Reserve should be analyzed. Close attention should be paid to the minutes of Open Market Committee meetings and to the regular Congressional testimony of the Chairman of the Board of Governors.
3. Spread relationships can be subject to violent swings. Attention to the economic forces and credit demands which underlie particular·credit instruments can provide insight into the likelihood and direction of such swings. For instance, when home building is weak the mortgage rate spread is likely to narrow.

Economists who are full-time money market forecasters observe monetary policy and credit market conditions in minute detail, and their forecasts are mainly based on well-informed judgments. The nonfinancial forecaster does not typically have the time or resources to duplicate these efforts. Nevertheless, the multitude of published financial forecasts and credit market commentaries can serve as a useful aid in developing one's own forecast.

QUESTIONS FOR REVIEW AND RESEARCH

9-1   It was stated that "interest rates form the main linkage between the two sides of the economy." Using the sectoral components from the National Income and Product Accounts and the Flow of Funds Accounts, indicate: (a) how demands for real goods and services (from the Product Accounts) are translated into demands for credit (in the Flow of Funds Accounts); (b) how the disposition of personal income and profits (from the Income Accounts) affects the supply of credit; and (c) how these effects surface in interest rate movements. An answer may be developed in general terms and/or for a specific year, say 1982.

9-2 The Federal government borrows in credit markets mainly to finance its budget deficit. As a result of the government's willingness to pay any price for credit, low risk of default, and tax advantages on interest earned by investors (lenders), this borrowing may "crowd out" other borrowers. Discuss the effects of a $50 billion dollar increase in Federal borrowing (due to an equal widening in the deficit) on private nonfinancial borrowing and associated interest rates and yields when the economy is: (a) falling into recession, and (b) expected to continue to grow near its trend rate ($2\frac{1}{2}\%$ per annum) in real terms.

9-3 The recent trend towards variable interest rates on residential mortgage loans has the intent of making mortgage lending less volatile in response to sharp interest rate swings. Discuss this concept in terms of the differing effects on housing start activity under conditions of fixed-rate and variable-rate mortgages.

9-4 To convert a discount-basis interest rate to a simple (365 day basis) interest rate one can use the formula

$$r = \frac{365 * d}{360 - d * t_{sm}}$$

where d   = rate of discount (decimal)
       r   = equivalent simple interest rate (decimal)
      t_{sm} = days from settlement to maturity.

(See Stigum, *Money Market Calculations*, p. 32.)

Using this formula, convert the discount rates shown below for Treasury bills as of September 9, 1983 to simple yield bases.

MATURITY DATE	BID (DISCOUNT)	YIELD
10/13/83	8.68%	
11/17/83	9.03	
12/15/83	9.16	
1/19/84	9.22	
2/16/84	9.33	
3/8/84	9.34	

9-5 Discuss what the short-term yield curve for one-to-six-month Treasury bills, described by the rates in problem 9-4 above, suggests about investor expectations.

9-6 In a particular month (say September) the Consumer Price Index rises by 0.7%, which expressed at a compound annual rate is 8.7%. In the two prior months the increases were 0.5% in July (6.2%) and 0.3% in August (3.7%). Thus, over three months, the compound annual rate of increase has been 6.2%, while over the twelve months through September the CPI has risen 5.2%. What is the likely impact of the acceleration in prices on a 20-year Treasury bond yield if it had been trading at a yield of 8.0% prior to the release of the

September CPI? What does this say about the inflation expectations of investors?

Suppose that two-tenths of a percent of the rise in the CPI in September was due to a one-time rise in gasoline taxes. Would this make a difference in the impact on the bond yield?

9-7   Increasing demand for bank loans by corporations can lead to upward pressure on interest rates from two sources: (1) the increased credit demand itself puts upward pressure on bank loan interest rates; and (2) the resultant tightening of bank reserves is likely to lead to increased bank borrowing in the Fed funds market, thus putting upward pressure on the Fed funds rate and, ultimately, on all other interest rates. Discuss this point with special reference to the Federal Reserve's role in regulating the supply of reserves through open market operations.

9-8   Indicate some exogenous factors which may account for the errors between the actual and estimated Treasury bill rates in panel B of Table 9-6.

10

LONG-TERM MACROECONOMIC FORECASTING

OVERVIEW

Chapter 8 examined the development of medium-term macroeconomic fore-casting for use in business *operational* planning. It was stated that longer term forecasts—looking out five, ten, or more years—serve as a basis for business strategic planning. This chapter identifies some of the differences between long-term and other forms of forecasting, reviews the principal theoretical long-term economic relationships, and describes a model based on these relationships that can be used as a core around which a long-term forecast can be constructed.

The starkest differences between the two approaches relate to the degree of certainty which can be attached to the results and the specificity of the forecasts. In particular, medium-term forecasts emphasize the effects of policy and other forces on aggregate demand and its main components dur-ing the forecast period. These effects are introduced through assumed values (or values determined outside the main model, as with the unemployment rate and interest rates) and through judgmental adjustments of results. Such assumptions and adjustments are made on the basis of the economist-fore-caster's expert intuition about likely behavior over the next one or two years and with the recognition that any errors are likely to be small and can be corrected in periodic updates. Long-term forecasting, however, focuses mainly on the economy's production possibilities, reflecting likely growth and utilization of the factors of production. Less attention is paid to the effects of policy changes or minor fluctuations in demand:[1] these become increasingly difficult to foresee as a forecast horizon lengthens—for one thing, presidential administrations and, thus, economic policies are likely to change in unpredictable ways during the course of ten years.

The value of a long-term forecast to business planners is that it pro-vides two types of insights to the future. First, it shows the economy's potential performance given existing amounts of labor and capital and the likely growth if full resource employment prevails throughout the forecast period. Second, and more important, it shows the *probable central growth trend,* recognizing that: the forecast is unlikely to be starting from a position of full resource employment and it is even less likely, given past perfor-mance, that such a condition would persist for long. The importance of the phrase "probable central growth trend" is a recognition that: (1) cycles in economic growth have dominated postwar U.S. economic performances; (2) exact dating of these cycles more than, at most, two or three years in the future is virtually impossible; but (3) the trend growth over prolonged peri-ods may be forecast with a fair degree of confidence, even though estimates for individual periods may deviate from the trend.

There are five steps or processes recommended for preparing a long-term forecast.

[1] See Lawrence A. Mayer, "Long-Term Economic Projections," in William F. Butler, Robert A. Kavish, and Robert B. Platt, eds., *Methods and Techniques of Business Forecasting,* (Englewood Cliffs, NJ: Prentice-Hall, Inc., 1974), pp. 365–72.

An existing medium-term forecast, incorporating the forecaster's best judgments on policy and demand effects, serves as a useful starting point. There are two reasons for this. First, the forecaster is likely to "know" more about these forces in the near-term, and this knowledge should be used. Second, the early performance of a long-term forecast will be evaluated first against actual outcomes, affecting confidence in the forecast values further out, and thus, should reflect the fullest information available.

Trends in the most important economic variables over long periods should be reviewed. This does not imply that these trends can simply be extrapolated. Nevertheless, past trends do suggest likely future limits and permit analysis of any recent changes. Moreover, some variables can be forecast by "ageing" past data—as in forecasting working-age population, given past population growth and mortality rates—or by extrapolating past averages—as with labor force participation rates.

Econometric methods are used to combine theoretical relationships with past trends to forecast future trends. It should be noted that these procedures are performed at a more aggregate level in long-term forecasting, both in terms of the economic measures themselves and their frequency—usually forecasts are done at an annual rather than a quarterly or monthly frequency.

There are important shifts in long-term trends due to: already-instituted policy changes, demographic, sociological, and technological conditions that can be anticipated and should be incorporated into the forecast. Examples of each of these four types of changes can be cited. The major shift to a more explicitly monetarist monetary policy in late 1979 set the stage for continued monetary targeting in the years to follow. The maturing of the "baby-boom" generation (those born between 1946 and 1961) pointed to a high rate of labor force growth in the 1970s, but a lower rate in the 1980s. An increased influx of women to the labor force from the mid 1960s occurred as a result of societal changes and is likely to persist. A pronounced shift towards energy conservation followed the 1973–74 and 1979 OPEC oil price rises.

Finally, as with all other forecasts, the economist-forecaster must adjust forecast results to reflect the forecaster's own judgment of the likely outcome.

The remainder of this chapter discusses the major variables and their relationships in long-term forecasting and provides an example of a "core" long-term forecasting model. The next section discusses the main theoretical relationships and examines the postwar trends for these measures. A model developed for forecasting these measures is described in the third section.

LONG-TERM MACROECONOMIC RELATIONSHIPS

As noted above, long-term macroeconomic forecasting is approached somewhat differently than medium-term forecasting. In particular, the emphasis shifts from factors affecting brief fluctuations in demand to those determining the trend growth in production. In fact, there are two main macroeconomic activities which are the focus of the long-term forecasting approach described below. The first is the trend rate of growth likely in the production of total goods and services resulting from utilization of the two main productive factors—labor and capital—both of which have grown over time. The second focus is the rate of increase in production costs—and thus output prices. The approach described in this chapter is largely restricted to these two macroeconomic forces. In practice, however, it is possible to forecast other more industry-specific measures, using production and cost trends as a basic or "core" forecast. Examples will be shown for two such measures: housing starts and new automobile demand.

The Trend Rate of Production Growth

Output is produced by utilizing available factor supplies. It is usual to regard the variable factors as labor and capital.[2] Thus, production or output (Q) is a function of available labor (L) and capital (K), as in 10-1.

$$Q = f(L,K) \qquad (10\text{-}1)$$

In fact, there are two relevant production functions: (1) potential output (Q^*) measures production when both labor (L^*) and capital (K^*) are fully employed;

$$Q^* = f(L^*,K^*) \qquad (10\text{-}1a)$$

while (2) actual output (as in 10-1) shows the level of production that results from actual employment and capital utilization levels. Output can be measured in terms of the yearly level of real GNP, labor in terms of the employed labor force,[3] and capital by the level of the capital stock in real terms. The postwar trends for potential[4] and actual output are shown in Figure 10-1. As can be seen, actual output has been equal to or less than potential in most years, with the major exception of the 1965–69 period when the combined

---

[2] For a detailed theoretical discussion of this relationship see R.G.D. Allen, *Macro-Economic Theory: A Mathematical Treatment* (New York: St. Martin's Press, 1968), Ch. 3, especially pp. 33–52.

[3] An alternative measure would be total employee-hours (employment times average hours worked per week). The use of only the number of employed workers infers a fairly constant proportion between number of workers and the average workweek. This inference appears justified by the empirical results and avoids the need to forecast the average workweek.

[4] Estimates of potential real GNP were formerly prepared by the Council of Economic Advisors, see *Economic Report of the President* for 1977, 1978, 1979, and 1980; but are now updated by the Bureau of Economic Analysis, U.S. Department of Commerce. See Frank de Leeuw, Thomas H. Holloway, Darwin C. Johnson, David S. McClain, and Charles A. Waite, "The High-Employment Budget: New Estimates, 1955–80," *Survey of Current Business* (Nov. 1980), pp. 13–43; and Frank de Leeuw and Thomas M. Holloway, "The High-Employment Budget: Revised Estimates and Automatic Inflation Effects," *Survey of Current Business* (Apr. 1982), pp. 21–33.

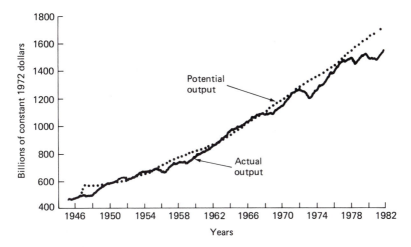

FIGURE 10-1   Potential output versus actual output
Source: U.S. Department of Commerce, *Survey of Current Business*

effects of the Viet Nam war and strong domestic economic growth pushed real growth above potential. The shortfall between potential and actual GNP is referred to as the GNP gap, and provides a measure of the extent of underutilized resources (or cyclical forces).

A long-term forecast should include expected trends for both potential and actual output, and thus for both potential and actual resource utilization. Figure 10-2 shows a flow chart of this dual forecasting approach. The starting points for both forecasts are estimates for the labor force and capital stock. The lower half of the chart depicts the way in which potential output results from high resource utilization, while the upper half follows the path by which actual output is generated.

Labor as a Factor of Production

The amount of labor employed in production at any time is dependent on the labor force available for employment and the state of economic activity. The size of the labor force, in turn, is determined jointly by the working-age population and the participation rate—the portion of the working age civilian population which is either employed or actively seeking employment at any time. Figure 10-3a depicts historical trends for the civilian working-age population, labor force, and employment, while Figure 10-3b shows the behavior of the participation rate. These concepts and their estimation are briefly described below.

The civilian working age population encompasses the noninstitutional population sixteen years of age and over outside the armed forces. This is the population segment available for work. Estimates for this group can be

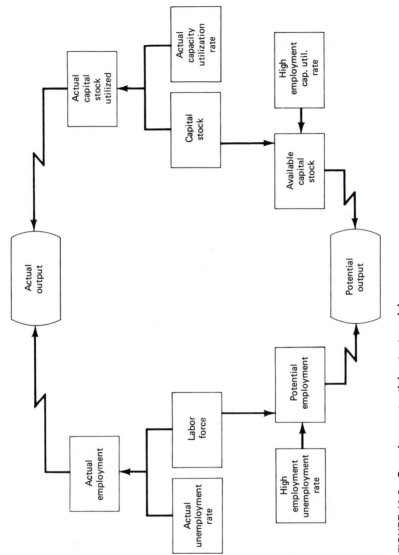

FIGURE 10-2 Overview: potential output model

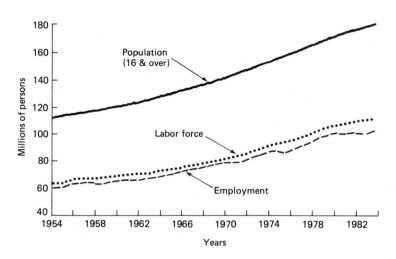

FIGURE 10-3A   Relationship of population, labor force & employment
Source: Bureau of Labor Statistics, U.S. Department of Labor

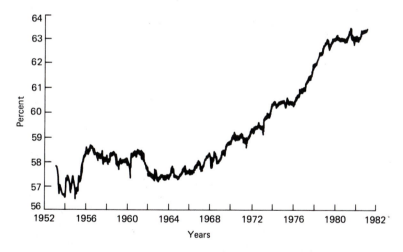

FIGURE 10-3B   Participation rate as percentage of working age population.
Source: Bureau of Labor Statistics, U.S. Department of Labor

made for fairly long periods by "ageing" past population data. That is, by adding the number of youths reaching the age of sixteen each year (based on age group population data) and the number of new immigrants (a fairly constant amount) and subtracting expected deaths (based on past mortality data) the net increase in the change in the working-age population can be estimated.[5] It is desirable to derive estimates for a number of age-sex groups. At a minimum, male and female teenage (16–19 years old) and male and female adult (20 years and over) population groups should be derived so that the differing growth rates and participation rates for these groups can be analyzed.

Civilian labor force participation rates have followed different trends for the various age-sex population groups during the postwar period. Some of these differences have been due to cyclical forces which are beyond the scope of the long-term forecasting approach described here.[6] The most important secular trends, on the other hand, have been a gradual decline in the adult male participation rate and the steady increase in female participation rates for all age groups. This latter trend is likely to persist, though likely at a less rapid rate than from 1960 through 1980.[7] The trend for participation rates can thus be judgmentally derived, based on past trends and the forecaster's expectations about future social forces.

Estimates for the civilian labor force can then be made by summing the products of the population and participation rate in each year for each age-sex group as in 10-2.

$$LFC_t = \sum_i (POP_{i,t} * RP_{i,t}) \tag{10-2}$$

where LFC = Civilian labor force (millions)
       POP = Noninstitutional civilian population (millions)
       RP   = Participation rate (decimal)
       i   = age-sex classification.

While these labor force estimates are determined through a largely judgmental method, the margin for error is small because: (1) the population component grows quite steadily, with any variations due chiefly to lagged effects of changing birth rates which can be discerned well in advance; and (2) the secular trend in labor force participation changes slowly. Thus, the civilian labor force can be derived exogenously in a long-term model.

Once the labor force has been determined the next step is to derive the

---

[5] Assumptions about the size of the armed forces should also be made, which can be based on Budget projections.

[6] For a discussion of one approach to dealing with such forces see Richard Anders, Christopher Caton, and Christopher Probyn, "Labor Force Projections and Potential Output," in Allen R. Sanderson, ed., *DRI Readings in Macroeconomics* (New York: McGraw-Hill, 1981), pp. 110–28.

[7] If the female participation rate did continue to rise as rapidly as it did between 1960 and 1980, then female labor force participation would surpass the male participation rate by the end of the century. It seems unlikely that social roles would change to that extent.

split between employed and unemployed labor force participants. This represents the first dividing point between the paths for potential and actual output. It is reasonable to follow the path for potential output first. Potential output assumes a high-employment unemployment rate (where the unemployment rate equals the number of unemployed expressed as a percentage of the civilian labor force).

The concept of high-employment unemployment recognizes two aspects of U.S. labor market conditions. First, there is a certain amount of structural and frictional unemployment even when the economy is operating at full potential. The former reflects a segment of low-skilled, poorly-educated persons who, for mainly sociological reasons, cannot gain employment despite the state of economic activity; the latter reflects workers who are between jobs and thus, out of work voluntarily. This rate has been assessed as roughly 4% of the labor force by the Council of Economic Advisors (CEA).[8] The second factor, which caused the official estimate of the full employment rate to rise to 5.1% by 1975–82, has been the steady influx of first-time teenage and female jobseekers reflecting: (1) the increase in teenage new entrants due to the maturation of young people born in the "baby boom" years 1946–61, and (2) the increase in female labor force participation. Because these new entrants lack prior work experience and possess lower job skills than experienced workers it is assumed they will have a longer job search.[9] Accepting the CEA's definition of a 5.1% full-employment unemployment rate (RUFE), the levels of full-employment employment (EFE) and unemployment (UFE) can then be estimated using the previously derived labels for the civilian labor force as in 10-3a and 10-3b.

$$EFE = (1 - RUFE) * LFC \qquad (10\text{-}3a)$$

$$UFE = (RUFE) * LFC \qquad (10\text{-}3b)$$

where   LFC = Civilian labor force (millions)
RUFE = Full-employment unemployment rate (decimal)
EFE = Full-employment employment (millions)
UFE = Full-employment unemployment (millions)

Many economists regard the CEA estimate of RUFE as too low, implying

[8] See Geoffrey H. Moore, *Business Cycles, Inflation, and Forecasting* (Cambridge, MA: Ballinger Publishing Co. for the National Bureau of Economic Research, Inc., 1980), pp. 126–35, for a discussion of the rationale behind this evaluation.

[9] A seminal article which analyzes adjustments to the unemployment rate in order to separate the cyclical from secular affects is by George L. Perry, "Changing Labor Markets and Inflation," *Brookings Papers on Economic Activity*, No. 3 (1973), 411–41.

that full employment is reached at some higher unemployment rate. An alternative, four-step method for deriving RUFE has been suggested.[10]

(1) It is assumed that 1973 was a year of full resource utilization. Thus, the full-employment unemployment rate (RUFE) and the actual unemployment rate (RU) can be set equal for that year at 4.9%; and the full-employment capacity utilization rate for manufacturing (UCAPMFE) can be set equal to the actual capacity utilization rate for manufacturing (UCAPM) at 87.6%.

(2) Since

$$\frac{RU}{RUFE} = \frac{UCAPFE}{UCAP} = 1 \text{ in } 1973,$$

then

$$RUFE_t = RU_t * \left[\frac{UCAP_t}{UCAPFE_{73}} \right]$$

or, substituting for $UCAPFE_{73}$,

$$RUFE_t = RU_t * \left[\frac{UCAP_t}{87.6} \right] \tag{10-4}$$

(3) Yearly estimates of RUFE can then be derived using data for RU and UCAPM.

(4) Because RUFE calculated in this way is quite variable, a five-year moving average is used to smooth it. Table 10-1 compares the CEA estimates to the estimates of RUFE derived from equation 8-4 for 1955–82.

The approach to forecasting actual labor force employment derives employment first and treats unemployment as a residual, given labor availability as represented by the size of the labor force. The actual level of employment reflects employers' demand for labor services in producing planned output. If it is assumed that planned output is related to past output levels, then employment should also be related to the past level of output as in 10-5a.

$$E_t = f(Q_{t-1}) \tag{10-5a}$$
$$U_t = LFC_t - E_t \tag{10-5b}$$

Capital as a Factor of Production

Capital is the other main factor used in production. Specifically, the concept which the Department of Commerce refers to as "fixed, reproducible, tangible, private, nonresidential capital stock."[11] The capital input to

---

[10] This method was suggested by a former colleague of the author's, Michael P. Niemira (now at Paine Webber), and is used in the model we constructed at Chemical Bank.

[11] Each of the adjectives in this term narrows the concept and distinguishes it from the other forms of capital. "Fixed" indicates that inventories are not included. "Reproducible" excludes land and natural resources. "Tangible" excludes human capital—education, skills,

TABLE 10-1   Estimates of the Full-Employment Unemployment Rate (percent)

	OFFICIAL[1]	ALTERNATIVE[2]
1955	4.0	3.7
1956	4.0	3.9
1957	4.0	4.1
1958	4.0	4.7
1959	4.1	4.7
1960	4.2	4.8
1961	4.2	5.2
1962	4.2	5.4
1963	4.3	5.3
1964	4.3	5.3
1965	4.4	5.2
1966	4.5	4.8
1967	4.4	4.6
1968	4.5	4.2
1969	4.6	3.9
1970	4.7	3.8
1971	4.8	4.1
1972	4.9	4.4
1973	4.9	4.7
1974	5.0	5.1
1975	5.1	5.6
1976	5.1	5.9
1977	5.1	6.2
1978	5.1	6.4
1979	5.1	6.4
1980	5.1	6.3
1981	5.1	6.3
1982	5.1	6.5

[1] See deLeeuw et al, "The High-Employment Budget: New Estimates 1955–80," *Survey of Current Business* (Nov. 1980), p. 17.
[2] Derived using equation 10-4.

production is dependent on the capital stock and the capacity utilization rate—the amount of capital actually utilized, a concept that fulfills a role for capital similar to that which the unemployment rate fulfills for labor as a measure of resource utilization.

---

and training—a concept included in at least one study of the capital stock. See John W. Kendrick, *The Formation and Stocks of Total Capital* (New York: Columbia Univ. Press for the National Bureau of Economic Research, 1976). "Private" excludes government capital. While "nonresidential" excludes the residential capital stock. Thus, this concept includes the stock of business structures and producers' durable goods.

The capital stock is estimated by a perpetual inventory method, equal to the cumulative flow of gross business fixed investment from the National Income and Product Accounts less the cumulated value of investment that has been discarded.[12] For any year, this estimate is represented by the identity shown in 10-6.

$$K72_t = BFI72_t - D_t + K72_{t-1} \qquad (10\text{-}6)$$

where $K72$ = Fixed, reproducible, tangible, private, nonresidential capital stock in constant (1972) dollars.
   $BFI72$ = Business fixed investment in constant (1972) dollars
   $D72$ = Discards of worn out capital in constant (1972) dollars.

Figure 10-4 presents the post-war trends for these measures. As can be seen from Figure 10-4 (and as was noted in Chapter 8) business fixed investment, which measures the flow of gross changes in the capital stock, has had the most volatile trend—showing a pronounced cyclical response—and is the key determinant of the growth of the capital stock. Real investment, in turn, responds to three main forces over the long term. The level of the capital stock in the prior year represents the need for replacement investment. The gap between potential and actual output $(Q^* - Q)$ in the prior year proxies cyclical conditions in the period when investment decisions are likely to be made. (This recognizes the lag that exists between the time when an investment decision is made and that when the bulk of spending actually occurs). Finally, interest rates (r) in the prior year can be assumed to affect investment decisions adversely. This relationship is shown in 10-7.

$$BFI72_t = f(K72, (Q^* - Q), r)_{t-1} \qquad (10\text{-}7)$$

The real level of discards has followed a smoother trend than investment during the post-war years and has maintained a close relationship to the capital stock: equaling between $3\frac{1}{2}\%$ and 4% of $K72$ in most years. It is completely reasonable that discards should relate to the lagged capital stock, and they can be estimated this way as in 10-8.

$$D72_t = f(K72_{t-1}) \qquad (10\text{-}8)$$

---

[12] The basic source for these estimates is U.S. Department of Commerce, *Fixed Reproducible Tangible Wealth in the United States, 1925–79* (Washington, DC: Superintendent of Documents, U.S. Government Printing Office, Mar. 1982), updated annually in the *Survey of Current Business*. A detailed description of the methods and concepts behind these estimates is provided in Allan H. Young and John C. Musgrave, "Estimation of Capital Stock in the United States," in Dan Usher, ed., *The Measurement of Capital* (Chicago: Univ. of Chicago Press, 1980), pp. 23–81. A further small deduction is made to account for sales by the business sector of used capital to other sectors.

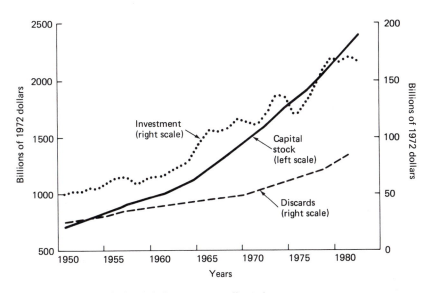

FIGURE 10-4   Capital stock, investment, discards
Source: Bureau of Economic Analysis, U.S. Department of Commerce

Finally, once real investment and discards are estimated, then the capital stock can be estimated recursively.

The existing capital stock determines the amount of productive capacity. However, just as the concept of full employment does not imply 100% of the labor force is employed, so full capacity utilization does not imply 100% of available capacity is utilized. Allowance must be made for "down time," service, and the slack producers desire so as to respond to unexpected events. In fact, capacity utilization has only exceeded 90% once since 1948 (91.6% in 1966), while the most recent high was the 87.6% rate recorded in 1973. If this capacity rate is regarded as full utilization then the capital variable for estimating potential output is the capital stock times the full capacity utilization rate (RCAPFE)

$$K_t^* = (K72_t * RCAPFE)$$

while the capital variable used for estimating actual output is the capital stock times the actual capacity utilization rate (RCAP).

$$K_t = (K72_t * RCAP_t)$$

Thus, equations 10-1 and 10-1a can be stated somewhat more precisely. Actual output is a function of the employed labor force and the utilized capital stock as in 10-9,

$$Q_t = f(E_t, (K72_t * RCAP_t)) \tag{10-9}$$

and potential output is a function of the full employment levels for these variables as in 10-9a.

$$Q_t^* = f(EFE_t, (K72_t * RCAPFE)) \tag{10-9a}$$

Production Costs and Output Prices

Just as the trend rate of growth in real output results from utilization of an economy's available factor resources, so the rate of change in output prices—inflation—reflects trends in factor input costs. Perhaps the most frequent request a business economist receives from management is for an inflation forecast. It is a vital input for projecting both costs and revenues in planning. The approach described here uses analyses and forecasts of labor costs and nonlabor payments as a basis for an output price forecast.

Unit labor cost (ULC)—the labor costs incurred in producing a constant dollar's worth of real output—is the more variable and basic input cost. This is a complex concept combining (1) the cost of a standard unit of labor services, and (2) the amount of labor services needed to produce one constant dollar's worth of output. As was seen in Chapter 6, unit labor costs are equal to labor compensation per hour (COMP/H) divided by productivity or output per hour (Q/H), all in index terms (1977 = 100). Figure 10-5a presents annual percentage changes in productivity, while Figure 10-5b presents annual percentage changes for unit labor costs and hourly compensation from 1948 through 1982. Table 10-2 presents summary growth rates. Two points are notable from the Graphs and Table: (1) the rate of increase in hourly compensation was greater on average from the mid 1960s onward (8.0%) than in the earlier years (5.1%); and (2) productivity gains were more volatile and, on average, less than half as rapid in this latter period (1.5%) than in

TABLE 10-2   Trends in Hourly Compensation, Productivity, and Unit Labor Costs 1947–82 (average annual percentage changes)

	COMPENSATION PER HOUR	OUTPUT PER HOUR	UNIT LABOR COST
1947–1982	6.5	2.4	4.0
1947–1965	5.1	3.3	1.8
1965–1982	8.0	1.5	6.5

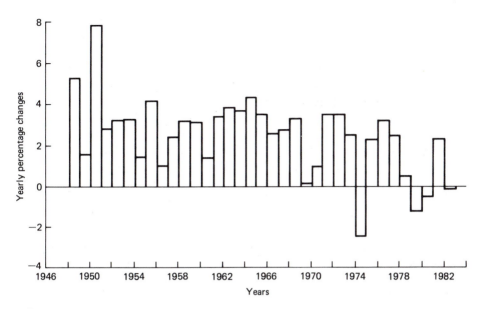

FIGURE 10-5A   Productivity
Source: Bureau of Labor Statistics, U.S. Department of Labor

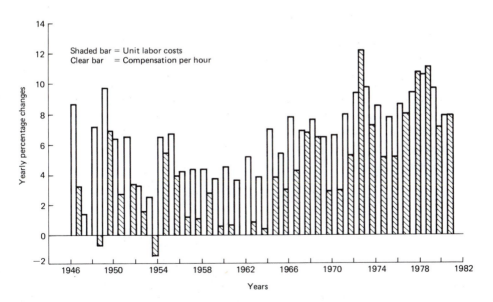

FIGURE 10-5B   Unit labor cost, & hourly compensation
Source: Bureau of Labor Statistics, U.S. Department of Labor

earlier years (3.3%). The combined effect of these two developments was a rate of increase in unit labor costs between 1965 and 1982 that was more than three times as rapid (6.5% per year) as that between 1947 and 1965 (1.8%).

Hourly compensation is a broader measure than hourly wages, including in addition: benefits and employer contributions to social security. Wages supply most of the thrust behind compensation gains, however, and so those forces which affect the variation in wage rates also affect hourly compensation. There appear to be two main sets of forces which have been found in past studies[13] to be the main sources of wage rate variation: (1) the degree of labor market tightness (or slack), and (2) "cost of living" effects. Labor market tightness can be proxied by the annual change in the unemployment rate ($\Delta RU_t = RU_t - RU_{t-1}$). This relationship is similar to the Phillips Curve relationship[14] and implies an inverse relationship: when ΔRU is positive, the labor market is in a state of excess supply and upward pressure on wage rates (and compensation per hour) should ease; when the change in the unemployment rate is negative, excess supply is lessening and upward pressure on wages (and compensation per hour) is likely to increase. The "cost of living" effect refers to the observed tendency for workers to seek to maintain the spending power of their wages. Thus, as output prices increase—as inflation occurs—wage rates are likely to increase. This effect can be captured by the annual percentage change in the consumer price index ($\%\Delta CPIU$).

These relationships are shown in 10-10.

$$(COMP/H)_t = f(\Delta RU_t, \%\Delta CPIU_t) \tag{10-10}$$

where $\quad \dfrac{\Delta(COMP/H)}{\Delta RU} < 0 \text{ and } \dfrac{\Delta(COMP/H)}{\%\Delta CPIU} > 0$

Productivity measures the real output produced per hour worked. Thus productivity is used to translate hourly compensation (in dollars per hour) into dollars per unit of output (unit labor costs). Productivity can be shown to be a function of the percentage change in real output and a time trend as in 10-11.

$$(Q/H)_t = f(\%\Delta Q_t, TIME) \tag{10-11}$$

---

[13] For instance, William D. Nordhaus, "The Worldwide Wage Explosion," *Brookings Papers on Economic Activity, (BPEA)*, No. 2 (1972), 431–64; George L. Perry, "Changing Labor Markets and Inflation," *BPEA*, No. 3 (1973); Robert E. Hall, "The Process of Inflation in the Labor Market," *BPEA*, No. 2 (1974) 343–410; George L. Perry, "Determinants of Wage Inflation Around the World *(BPEA)*, No. 2 (1975), 403–35; and Michael L. Wachter, "The Changing Cyclical Responsiveness of Wage Inflation," *BPEA*, No. 1 (1976), 115–59.

[14] A. W. Philipps, "The Relationship Between Unemployment and the Rate of Change in Money Wages in the United Kingdom 1861–1957," *Economica* (Nov. 1958), pp. 283–99.

The slowdown in productivity growth since the mid 1960s reflects both: slower real output growth from 1965 through 1982 (2.8% per year) compared to 1947–65 (3.9% per year) and the more rapid growth in hours worked in the latter period (1.2% per year) than in the earlier years (0.4%).[15] Equation 10-11, by stating productivity as a function of real output growth—which in turn is partly a function of labor force utilization (employment)—captures the effects of changes in the relative utilization of the factors of production. This involves some simultaneity in solution, a topic that will be addressed in section III of this chapter.

With functional relationships established for hourly compensation and productivity, unit labor costs can be estimated using the identity in (10-12).

$$ULC_t \equiv (COMP/Q)_t = \frac{(COMP/H)_t}{(Q/H)_t} \qquad (10\text{-}12)$$

Unit nonlabor payments (UNLP) measure the costs of all other inputs in the production of a constant dollar's worth of output. For the total private business sector,[16] these costs consist of: depreciation, interest, rent, indirect business taxes, and profit. Two key points can be made about unit nonlabor payments. First, the name itself reflects the subordinate relationship it bears to unit labor costs; unit nonlabor payments are treated by BLS as a residual. Second, within the unit nonlabor payments concept, the largest components—and the ones that are the source of most of its variation—are depreciation, interest, and profits which relate to the role of capital in production.

Both of these points are useful in estimating unit nonlabor payments. A relationship to lagged unit labor costs emphasizes the primary impetus which labor costs apply to all costs and prices. In addition, it is likely that as labor costs rise producers will attempt to substitute capital in production, thus increasing demand for capital and exerting upward pressure on the depreciation and interest components of unit nonlabor payments. To reflect this pressure more directly unit nonlabor payments are also assumed to be directly related to the lagged real capital stock. Thus, unit nonlabor payments can be estimated as in 10-13.

$$UNLP_t = f(ULC_{t-1}, K72_{t-1}) \qquad (10\text{-}13)$$

[15] The productivity showdown has been analyzed in Edward F. Denison, "Explanations of Declining Productivity Growth," *Survey of Current Business* (Aug. 1979), pp. 1–24. This article was based on a more detailed study, Edward F. Denison, *Accounting for Slower Economic Growth: the United States in the 1970s* (Washington: The Brookings Institution, 1979). Denison was unable to account for roughly 70% of the slowdown in productivity growth by conventional forces. The role of TIME in equation 10-11 is an attempt to capture this "X factor."

[16] The unit labor cost measures already examined and the unit nonlabor payments discussed in this section refer to the domestic private business sector. This sector accounts for roughly 85% of GNP. This is the largest sector for which these cost data are compiled.

Figure 10-6a shows trends for output prices, Figure 10-6b for unit labor costs and unit nonlabor payments for 1947–82 (all indexed to 1977 = 100). It can be seen that, while the trends differ slightly in some years, for the entire time span there is considerable similarity. This is confirmed by the summary data in Table 10-3.

FIGURE 10-6A   Output prices 1947–82
Source: Bureau of Labor Statistics, U.S. Department of Labor

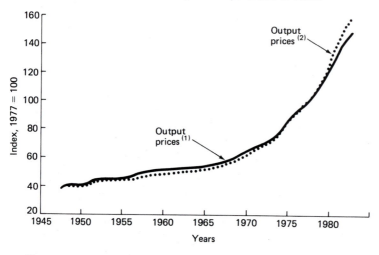

(1) Implicit price deflator for domestic private business sector
(2) Consumer price index (all urban)

FIGURE 10-6B   Unit labor cost, unit nonlabor payments, 1947–82
Source: Bureau of Labor Statistics, U.S. Department of Labor

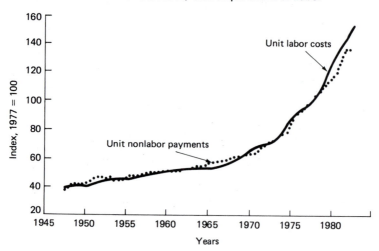

TABLE 10-3 Trends for Unit Labor Cost, Unit Nonlabor Payments, and Output Prices 1947–1982 (average annual percentage changes)

	ULC	UNLP	OUTPUT PRICES
1947–82	4.0	3.8	4.0
1947–65	1.8	2.2	2.0
1965–82	6.4	5.4	6.0

Once unit labor costs and unit nonlabor payments are estimated, output prices can be estimated from them. The approach described above focused on factor shares of total output based on the National Income and Product Accounts. Consequently, the appropriate measure of output prices is the GNP implicit price deflator (PGNP). This relationship is shown in 10-14.

$$PGNP_t = f(ULC_t, UNLP_t) \qquad (10\text{-}14)$$

The more widely followed consumer price index (CPIU) can then be estimated from the deflator as in 10-15.

$$CPIU_t = f(PGNP_t) \qquad (10\text{-}15)$$

SUMMARY

The relationships described above provide the basis for a set of core long-term forecasts for output and prices and their determinants. A specific estimating model based on these functional forms will be described in the next section. Before turning to this model, however, some limitations and further uses of the approach described above are discussed.

The components of a forecast based on the output and price concepts described above provide a "bare bones" look at future economic performance. These measures—factor and output growth, and the change in costs and prices—are important and provide a great deal of information about the economy's potential and probable performance over the longer term. Moreover, estimation requires relatively few exogenous inputs, while constructing assumed values for those which are required causes the forecaster to focus on these important measures.

It is likely, however, that other variables may be important to business management. In general, the forecast model described here can be used to develop forecasts for other variables through "satellite" models. For instance, a carpet manufacturer may sell carpeting for new homes, existing homes, and new cars. Thus, in addition to the variables in the core model an economist forecasting carpet demand may desire measures of new home construction, the total stock of homes, and the demand for new domestically produced autos. Analyzing these variables, the economist concludes that relationships can be derived using variables already forecast plus one other important determinant: interest rates. Thus, in addition to the core model four additional equations must be derived: (1) an interest rate, (2) housing starts, (3) the stock of residential structures, and (4) new U.S.-made car sales.

In the long term, interest rates (in this case the prime rate) can be hypothesized to be determined by the difference between the growth in the money supply (M, assumed to be exogenous, but to follow some pre-determined growth path which reflects continued monetary control by the Federal Reserve) and growth in the components of the demand for money. The demand for money can be assumed to include: (1) a direct relationship to real output growth, (2) a direct relationship to inflation, and (3) an inverse relationship to the GNP gap. Thus, the interest rate (r) would be estimated as in 10-16.

$$r_t = f(\%\Delta M_t, \%\Delta Q_t, \%\Delta CPIU_t, (Q * - Q)_t) \qquad (10\text{-}16)$$

Housing starts (HUSTS) can then be hypothesized to be a function of: (1) per capita real output (Q/POP), and (2) inflation adjusted interest rates as in 10-17.

$$HUSTS_t = f\left((Q/POP)_t, \left(r - \frac{CPIU}{100}\right)_t\right) \qquad (10\text{-}17)$$

The stock of residential structures then can be derived by a perpetual inventory method where total stock (KR) equals the stock of existing houses (HEXT$_t$ = KR$_{t-1}$) plus new starts as in 10-18.

$$KR_t = f(HEXT_t, HUSTS_t) \qquad (10\text{-}18)$$

Car sales (CARS) can be estimated using the same variables as housing starts, namely: per capita real output, and inflation adjusted interest rates, plus the GNP gap to capture the extreme cyclical response of auto demand.

$$CARS_t = f\left((Q/POP)_t, \left(r - \frac{CPIU}{100}\right)_t, (Q * - Q)_t\right) \qquad (10\text{-}19)$$

Finally, carpet demand (CARP72) can be estimated as a function of (1) housing starts, (2) existing homes, and (3) new U.S.-made car sales as in 10-20.

$$CARP72_t = f(HUSTS_t, HEXT_t, CARS_t) \tag{10-20}$$

Thus, a satellite model consisting of five equations can be constructed and used with the core model to construct a forecast for a particular industry. Clearly, the more detailed the requirements, the larger the satellite model will have to be.

A LONG-TERM FORECASTING MODEL

The long-term macroeconomic relationships described in Section II are transformed into empirical relationships and brought together in this section to form a "core" long-term forecasting model.[17] This model provides estimates of the basic macroeconomic variables which determine the U.S. economy's trend growth path. Other specific activity measures—such as those described at the end of Section II for forecasting carpet demand—can then be derived using "satellite" relationships to the core model.

A key difference between this model and the short- and medium-term models described in earlier chapters is its focus. As stated at the beginning of the chapter, the long-term model is mainly concerned with the economy's aggregate supply path—its production possibilities and probabilities—while shorter-term forecasting focuses on fluctuations in aggregate and sectoral demand. A related difference is that the model and the resulting forecasts are at an annual, rather than a quarterly, frequency. This is appropriate to the aim of providing information on broad economic trends rather than on precise periodic movements. While the mechanics of forecasting at a quarterly instead of an annual frequency do not present insurmountable obstacles, such an approach at least runs the risk of merely "refining ignorance" when extended beyond two years, and may raise the more serious problem of suggesting that more is known about future cyclical patterns than is the case.

A further difference pertains to the way in which the model is solved. The short-term indicator forecasts described in Part II are mainly single-equation models, while the medium-term macroeconomic forecast approach described in Chapter 8 and the interest rate model in Chapter 9 are recursive.

---

[17] The model described here reflects the extensive efforts of Michael P. Niemira, a former colleague in the Economic Research Department of Chemical Bank, in revising and improving an earlier version developed by the author. His contributions greatly extended the information provided by the model and increased its *ex post* forecasting accuracy, for which Niemira deserves full credit. The remaining limitations reflect the constraints imposed by the author.

That is, the forecast variables are solved sequentially in a series of equations which use exogenous and/or lagged endogenous variables as determinants, and then the solution is adjusted until the forecaster is satisfied with the results based on error analyses. Lagged endogenous variables are used in some equations in the long-term model, but in many other cases the annual frequency of the model makes lagged relationships less suitable. As a result, solutions of some of the relationships described in Section II require values for unlagged endogenous variables in other relationships. For instance: the consumer price index (CPIU) is a function of the GNP implicit price deflator (PGNP); however, the deflator is partly a function of unit labor costs (ULC), which is an identity partly determined by hourly compensation (COMP/H), which itself is partly a function of the percentage change in consumer prices. To deal with this problem of *simultaneity,* some of the equations must be solved using a simultaneous equation method.[18]

Once estimating equations are derived, they must be combined, or ordered, in a way that insures the most efficient solution of the total simultaneous model.[19] The equations of the model are ordered in three "blocks," or groups: (1) a pre-recursive block which contains identities and equations based on exogenous or lagged variables; (2) a simultaneous block which contains those identities and equations requiring simultaneous solution; and (3) a post-recursive block which consists of those identities and equations which use lagged variables from the other two blocks as inputs.

Before describing these solution blocks one further point must be clarified. A number of the measures of economic activity described in general form in Section II can be represented by several different conceptual measures. For instance, real output (Q) can be expressed in terms of: potential real GNP (GNP72FE), real GNP (GNP72), potential real gross domestic product (GDP72FE), real gross domestic product (GDP72), or the index of industrial production (JQIND). The choice of which measure to use in a particular equation depends: primarily, on the most suitable measure for the activity being estimated; and secondly, on empirical-econometric considerations. A general criterion is to minimize the number of different measures that need to be estimated. This satisfies the goal of simplicity that has been a feature of all the estimation approaches described in the text, and also limits the sources of error in estimation.

Table 10-4 lists the functional forms of the model equations in terms of

---

[18] An accessible discussion of simultaneous equation estimation is provided in Salvatore, *Theory and Problems of Statistics and Econometrics* (New York: McGraw-Hill, 1982), Ch. 10. Successively more advanced discussions are provided in: Pindyck and Rubinfeld, *Econometric Models and Economic Forecasts* (New York: McGraw-Hill, 1976, Ch. 9; and Intriligator, *Econometric Models, Techniques, and Applications* (Englewood Cliffs, NJ: Prentice-Hall, Inc., 1978), Chs. 10–13.

[19] In the case of the model described here, this was done in the *EPS* environment of the Data Resources Inc. system. This uses a Gauss-Seidel algorithm to order the equations. The Gauss-Seidel method is described in Walter C. Labys, *Dynamic Commodity Models: Specification, Estimation, and Simulation* (Lexington, MA: Lexington Books, 1973), pp. 208–12.

the measures actually used, ordered by economic activity. The model is estimated for the years 1955–81.[20] There are thirty-one variables used in the model, of which six are exogenous, twelve are identities, one is a quasi-identity, and the remaining twelve are stochastic equations. The six exogenous variables are: (1) working-age population, derived by ageing population data; (2) the civilian labor force, which is determined based on population and participation rates determined by exponential smoothing; (3) the high-output capacity utilization rate, assumed to equal the rate in 1973; (4) rest of the world real GNP, which has been a fairly constant percentage (around 2%) of real GNP; (5) the narrow money supply is determined judgmentally based on past Federal Reserve policy and the forecaster's expectations of its future direction; and (6) a time trend which merely assigns an ordinal number to the years included in the estimation and forecast periods. The twelve identities are: (1) high-output real GNP, (2) real GNP, (3) current dollar GNP, (4) the GNP gap, (5) the GDP gap, (6) high-output employment, (7) the high-output unemployment rate, (8) unemployment, (9) the unemployment rate, (10) the real capital stock, (11) the capacity utilization rate, and (12) unit labor costs. High-employment real GDP is a quasi-identity in that it uses the estimated coefficients for actual real GDP. These thirteen relationships are all depicted in Table 10-4.

The solution order of the model variables, arranged in four blocks (exogenous, pre-recursive, simultaneous, and post-recursive), is presented in Table 10-5. Detailed estimation results for the twelve stochastic equations are presented in Table 10-6 in the order in which they are solved in the model. The overall results are quite good.

The adjusted coefficients of determination ($\overline{R}^2$) for nine of the twelve equations exceed 0.9, indicating that at least 90% of the variation in the dependent variables is accounted for by variation in the explanatory variables. (Indeed, in seven cases the $\overline{R}^2$ exceeds 0.99.) The three equations with $\overline{R}^2$s of less than 0.9—these are for productivity, hourly compensation, and the prime-rate—are each specified in a transformed manner: productivity and hourly compensation are solved for in percent change form, the prime rate in natural log form. When the fitted values are transformed back into levels, the estimated levels are much closer to the actuals.[21]

---

[20] The model equations are re-estimated each year to take account of the annual National Income and Product Account benchmark revisions. It is desirable to estimate the model for one less year than the latest data cover (for instance the version estimated in mid 1983 did not include 1982 data in the estimation) in order to be able to conduct an out-of-sample, *ex post* dynamic simulation to test the forecast accuracy of the model.

[21] The mean absolute errors (MAE) and coefficients of determination for the fitted levels compared to the actuals are shown in the Table below.

	MAE	$\overline{R}^2$
Productivity	0.74%	0.9943
Compensation Per Hour	0.34	0.9996
Prime rate	0.49	0.8927

TABLE 10-4 Long-Term Macroeconomic Forecasting Model Equation Forms

ACTIVITY MEASURES	FUNCTIONAL FORM	TYPE OF FUNCTION
A. OUTPUT		
POTENTIAL REAL GNP	GNP72FE = GDP72FE + GNPROW72	Identity
REAL GNP	GNP72 = GDP72 + GNPROW72	Identity
CURRENT DOLLAR GNP	GNP = GNP72 * PGNP	Identity
POTENTIAL GDP	GDP72FE = f(EFE,(K72 * UCAPFE), TIME)	Quasi-Identity
REAL GDP	GDP72 = f(E,(K72 * UCAP), TIME)	Log-Log
REST OF WORLD GNP	GNPROW72	Exogenous
INDUSTRIAL PRODUCTION INDEX	JQIND = f(GNP72)	Quadratic
GNPGAP	GNPGAP = 100 * ((GNP72FE-GNP72)/GNP72)	Identity
GDPGAP	GDPGAP = 100 * ((GDP72FE-GDP72)/GDP72)	Identity
B. POPULATION, LABOR FORCE, AND EMPLOYMENT		
WORKING AGE POPULATION	N16&	Exogenous
LABOR FORCE	LCF = f(Σw_i * LCF_i)	Exponential Smoothing
HIGH-OUTPUT EMPLOYMENT	EFE = (LCF * (100-RUFE))/100	Identity
EMPLOYMENT	E = f($GNP72_{t-1}$)	Level
HIGH—OUTPUT UNEMPLOYMENT RATE	RUFE = RU * (UCAP/87.6)	Identity
UNEMPLOYMENT	U = LCF − E	Identity
UNEMPLOYMENT RATE	RU = (100 * U)/LCF	Identity

C. CAPITAL STOCK, UTILIZATION, AND INVESTMENT

CAPITAL STOCK	$K72 = (K72_{t-1} - D72) + BFI72$	Identity
NONRESIDENTIAL INVESTMENT	$BFI72 = f(K72_{t-1}, GDPGAP_{t-1}, PRIME_{t-1})$	Levels
CAPACITY	$CAP = f(K72_{t-1}, \underline{TIME})$	Quadratic
HIGH-OUTPUT CAPACITY		
UTILIZATION	$\underline{UCAPFE} = 87.6$	Exogenous
CAPACITY UTILIZATION	$UCAP = JQIND/CAP$	Identity
DISCARDS	$D72 = f(K72_{t-1})$	Level

D. COSTS, PRODUCTIVITY, AND PRICES

HOURLY COMPENSATION	$(COMP/H) = f(CPIU, RU)$	Percent Change
OUTPUT PER HOUR	$(Q/H) = f(GDP72, \underline{TIME})$	Percent Change
UNIT LABOR COST	$ULC = (COMP/H)/(Q/H)$	Identity
UNIT NONLABOR PAYMENTS	$UNLP = f(K72_{t-1}, ULC_{t-1})$	Level
GNP DEFLATOR	$PGNP = f(ULC, UNLP)$	Percent Change
CONSUMER PRICE INDEX	$CPIU = f(PGNP)$	Percent Change

E. INTEREST RATE

PRIME RATE	$\Delta PRIME = f(\Delta CPIU, \Delta MNY1, GNPGAP, \Delta GNP72)$	Log-Log
MONEY SUPPLY	$\underline{MNY1}$	Exogenous

TIME is an exogenous counter.
Underlined variables are exogenous.

**TABLE 10-5   Solution Order Long-Term Macroeconomic
                Forecasting Model**

I. Exogenous Variables
   1. Working-Age Population (N16&)
   2. Civilian Labor Force (LFC)
   3. High-Output Capacity Utilization Rate (UCAPFE)
   4. Rest of World Real GNP (GNPROW72)
   5. Money Supply (MNY1)
   6. Time Trend (TIME)

II. Pre-Recursive Block
   1. High-Output Employment (EFE)   Identity
   2. Employment (E)   Equation
   3. Capacity (CAP)   Equation
   4. Unemployment (U)   Identity
   5. Unemployment Rate (RU)   Identity
   6. Unit Nonlabor Payments (UNLP)   Equation
   7. Real Nonresidential Fixed Investment (BFI72)   Equation
   8. Real Discards (D72)   Equation
   9. Real Capital Stock (K72)   Identity
  10. Potential Real GDP (GDP72FE)   Quasi-Identity

III. Simultaneous Block
   1. Capacity Utilization Rate (UCAP)   Identity
   2. Real GDP (GDP72)   Equation
   3. Real GNP (GNP72)   Identity
   4. Industrial Production (JQIND)   Equation
   5. Productivity (Q/H)   Equation
   6. Unit Labor Costs (ULC)   Identity
   7. Implicit GNP Price Deflator (PGNP)   Equation
   8. Consumer Price Index (CPIU)   Equation
   9. Hourly Compensation (COMP/H)   Equation

IV. Post Recursive Block
   1. Potential Real GNP (GNP72FE)   Identity
   2. GNP Gap (GNPGAP)   Identity
   3. Current Dollar GNP (GNP)   Identity
   4. GDP Gap (GDPGAP)   Identity
   5. High-Output Unemployment Rate (RUFE)   Identity
   6. Prime Rate (PRIME)   Equation

The Durbin-Watson statistics are significant at the five percent level,
indicating the absence of autocorrelation, for eight of the equations. For two
others—real GDP and the GNP deflator—the Durbin-Watson statistics are
in the "grey area" where the test is inconclusive. In two cases—capacity
and discards—the Durbin-Watson statistics indicate positive autocorrelation. Low Durbin-Watson statistics for some equations are common with

TABLE 10-6 Long-Term Model Equations: Estimated Coefficients and Summary Statistics

Employment

$$E_t = 34.345 + 0.0433 * GNP72_{t-1} \quad Rho = 0.787$$
$$(12.81) \quad (17.52) \qquad\qquad (6.13)$$

$$\overline{R}^2 = 0.9925 \quad D\text{-}W = 1.93 \quad SER = 1.07$$

Capacity

$$CAP_t = -0.536 + 3.83 \times 10^{-4} * K72_{t-1} + 2.12 \times 10^{-6} * (K72_{t-1})^2$$
$$(-4.74) \quad (1.28) \qquad\qquad (4.38)$$
$$+ 0.090 * TIME + 6.99 \times 10^{-3} * (TIME)^2 - 2.66 \times 10^{-4} * (K72_{t-1} * TIME)$$
$$(4.66) \qquad\quad (5.18) \qquad\qquad (-5.07)$$

$$\overline{R}^2 = 0.9993 \quad D\text{-}W = 0.61 \quad SER = 0.01$$

Unit Nonlabor Payments

$$UNLP_t = -0.016 + 7.61 \times 10^{-5} * K72_{t-1} + 0.910 * ULC_{t-1} \quad Rho = 0.407$$
$$(-0.71) \quad (1.62) \qquad\qquad (12.11) \qquad\qquad (2.09)$$

$$\overline{R}^2 = 0.9947 \quad D\text{-}W = 1.80 \quad SER = 0.02$$

Real Nonresidential Fixed Investment

$$BFI72_t = -12.690 + 0.103 * K72_{t-1} - 1.819 * GDPGAP_{t-1}$$
$$(-1.09) \quad (9.59) \qquad\quad (-3.41)$$
$$- 2.819 * PRIME_{t-1} \quad Rho = 0.705$$
$$(-3.04) \qquad\qquad (3.51)$$

$$\overline{R}^2 = 0.9784 \quad D\text{-}W = 1.71 \quad SER = 5.23$$

Real Discards

$$D72_t = -0.155 + 0.039 * K72_{t-1} \quad Rho = 0.929$$
$$(-0.05) \quad (18.96) \qquad\qquad (14.95)$$

$$\overline{R}^2 = 0.9977 \quad D\text{-}W = 0.68 \quad SER = 0.71$$

Real GDP

$$Ln(GDP72) = 2.036 + 0.511 * Ln(K72 * UCAP) + 0.175 * Ln(E) + 0.183 * Ln(TIME)$$
$$(11.67) \quad (8.16) \qquad\qquad (1.63) \qquad\qquad (9.65)$$

$$\overline{R}^2 = 0.9975 \quad D\text{-}W = 1.34 \quad SER = 0.01$$

Industrial Production

$$JQIND = -0.343 + 1.47 \times 10^{-3} * GNP72 - 1.56 \times 10^{-7} * (GNP72)^2$$
$$(-3.78) \quad (8.24) \qquad\qquad (-1.87)$$

$$\overline{R}^2 = 0.9924 \quad D\text{-}W = 1.65 \quad SER = 0.03$$

Productivity

$$\%\Delta(Q/H) = 2.675 + 0.367 * \%\Delta(GDP72) - 0.089 * TIME$$
$$(3.53) \quad (3.58) \qquad\qquad (-2.82)$$

$$\overline{R}^2 = 0.4539 \quad D\text{-}W = 1.91 \quad SER = 1.20$$

(Continued)

TABLE 10-6 (*Continued*)

Implicit GNP Price Deflator

$$\%\Delta(PGNP) = 0.505 + 0.610 * \%\Delta(ULC) + 0.329 * \%\Delta(UNLP)$$
$$(5.45)\quad\;(40.34)\qquad\qquad\quad(20.99)$$

$$\bar{R}^2 = 0.9908 \quad D\text{-}W = 1.22 \quad SER = 0.26$$

Consumer Price Index

$$\%\Delta(CPIU) = -1.250 + 1.308 * \%\Delta(PGNP)$$
$$(-3.21)\quad\;(17.73)$$

$$\bar{R}^2 = 0.9233 \quad D\text{-}W = 1.78 \quad SER = 1.03$$

Hourly Compensation

$$\%\Delta(COMP/H)_t = 4.098 + 0.558 * \%\Delta(CPIU_t) - 0.247 * (RU_t - RU_{t-1})$$
$$(15.64)\quad(12.46)\qquad\qquad\quad(-1.60)$$

$$\bar{R}^2\; 0.8643 \quad D\text{-}W = 1.68 \quad SER = 0.78$$

Prime Rate

$$Ln(\Delta PRIME) = 4.998 * Ln(\Delta CPIU) - 3.629 * Ln(\Delta MNY1)$$
$$(5.37)\qquad\qquad\qquad(-2.46)$$
$$- 0.043 * GNPGAP + 2.884 * Ln(\Delta GNP72)$$
$$(-4.84)\qquad\qquad\quad(2.39)$$
$$\bar{R}^2 = 0.6803 \quad D\text{-}W = 1.47 \quad SER = 0.11$$

Figures in parentheses are t statistics

simultaneous models[22] and are usually ignored if the overall model produces good results.

The equations for capacity and industrial production are in quadratic form so as to capture more of the extreme cyclical response of these measures than a strictly linear form would, using annual data. In all cases the coefficients conformed to *a priori* expectations as regards sign where such expectations existed. Moreover, in the vast majority of cases, the coefficients were significant at the five percent level.

The ultimate test of any forecast model is how well it forecasts. To test the forecast properties of the model an *ex post,* dynamic, out-of-sample simulation[23] was performed for 1982. Table 10-7 compares the actual to the estimated values of the key measures in the forecast and shows the errors

---

[22] See, for instance, James S. Duesenberry, Edwin I. Kuh, and Lawrence R. Klein, eds., *The Brookings Quarterly Econometric Model of the United States* (Skokie, IL: Rand McNally, 1965); and Otto Eckstein, *The DRI Model of the U.S. Economy* (New York: McGraw-Hill, 1983); both of these include equations with low Durbin-Watson statistics.

[23] That is, the equations were simultaneously solved using exogenous, lagged endogenous, and simultaneously derived, unlagged, endogenous inputs as if the 1982 values were not known. This test duplicates actual forecast conditions for the first year of a forecast.

TABLE 10-7   Ex Post, Out-of-Sample, Dynamic Simulation, 1982

	ACTUAL	ESTIMATED	ERROR (A-E)	PERCENT ERROR
Employment (millions)	99.530	101.180	−1.65	−1.66%
Unemployment Rate (%)	9.7	8.2	1.5	
Real Investment (Bil. 1972 $)	165.75	167.16	−1.41	−0.85
Real Discards (Bil. 1972 $)	86.5	86.7	−0.2	−0.23
Real Capital Stock (Bil. 1972 $)	2390.95	2392.36	−1.41	−0.06
Capacity (1967 = 100)	197.0	197.7	−0.7	−0.36
Capacity Utilization Rate (%)	69.8	80.7	−10.9	
Real Gross Domestic Product (Bil. 1972 $)	1453.6	1551.6	−98.0	−6.74
Real Gross National Product (Bil. 1972 $)	1476.85	1574.85	−98.0	−6.63
Industrial Production (1967 = 100)	137.5	159.7	−22.2	−16.15
Hourly Compensation (1977 = 100)	154.5	155.0	−0.5	−0.32
Productivity (1977 = 100)	100.9	102.3	−1.4	−1.39
Unit Labor Cost (1977 = 100)	153.0	151.6	1.4	0.92
Unit Nonlabor Payments (1977 = 100)	138.8	142.8	−4.0	−2.88
Implicit GNP Deflator (1972 = 100)	207.1	207.2	−0.1	−0.05
Consumer Price Index (1967 = 100)	284.6	284.6	0.0	0.0

(actual less forecast value) and the percent errors (the error as a percentage of the actual value).

The errors for the output measures—real GDP, real GNP, and industrial production—are large and unacceptable. This reflects a simultaneity problem. Real GDP is a function of employment and the product of the real capital stock and the capacity utilization rate. The errors for employment and the real capital stock are not serious. The error for the capacity utilization rate is serious, as UCAP is a function of industrial production, which is in turn a function of real GNP (see Table 10-4). This type of error pattern is common in simultaneous models and is one reason why *ex post* dynamic tests should be run: such errors emerge and are apparent either because actual data exist for part of the year and/or the results of a shorter-term (demand oriented) forecast can be contrasted. The usual way to address this problem is by use of *add factors*, exogenous variables added to the stochastic equation to force the results to converge toward a desired level. For instance an add factor for the capacity utilization rate (UCAPADD) such that

$$UCAP = (JQIND/CAP) + UCAPADD$$

where $$UCAPADD = 7.5$$

greatly improves the results and by itself moves the estimates of real GDP, real GNP, and industrial production much closer to the actuals. This is an important example of the use of an economist's judgment in transforming raw econometric results into a usable forecast. The errors for the cost and price measures, on the other hand, are much smaller, suggesting that any add factors should be very small.

This example illustrates the need to analyze a model's results outside the forecast period. The role of judgment is shown again to be the primary factor that the economist uses in converting mere statistical and theoretical techniques into a usable forecast.

A NOTE ON CYCLICAL BEHAVIOR

It has been noted that long-term forecasting is concerned more with long-term growth potential than brief fluctuations in economic activity. The emphasis on the supply aspects of the U.S. economy in the approach described is a further reason for largely ignoring demand-related cycles in a long-term forecast. Moreover, the large commercial models have had a poor track record at anticipating cyclical turning points even four quarters ahead.

Nevertheless, the near certainty that during a ten-year forecast period there is likely to be at least one cyclical swing makes it desirable for the forecaster to note their occurrence and suggest something about the probable timing. The National Bureau of Economic Research (NBER) and the Bureau of Economic Analysis (BEA) Department of Commerce have classified thirty business cycles since 1854, of which eight have occurred since 1945.[24] For the postwar period, the eight downturns have averaged eleven months, while the expansions have averaged 45 months. Thus, the U.S. economy has, roughly, grown nearly four years for every one year of contraction. As a rough approximation, therefore, a ten-year forecast period can be assumed to contain two years of recession and these can be approximately dated to occur after four years of expansion from the last cyclical trough.

QUESTIONS FOR REVIEW AND RESEARCH

10-1   A number of long-term economic assumptions which might have been made (and in some cases were made) in 1970, 1975, and 1980 proved wrong over the next five years. Identify such assumptions made in each of these periods and explain why they were faulty. Is there a common concept to these assumptions which provide a guide to long-term forecasting?

[24] These are listed in *Business Conditions Digest* (July 1983), p. 103.

10-2 Examine and plot annual data for the post-war period on the birth rate, death rate, and immigration. Discuss how these trends affect your expectations for population growth over the next (a) five and (b) ten years.

10-3 Estimate and plot annual capital-to-labor ratios for the post war period. (Evaluate the differences using (a) the number of employed and (b) total employee-hours worked as the denominator.)

    (a) How stable has this ratio been? Can you offer reasons for periods of instability?

    (b) Does this relationship offer insights to productivity and price trends?

10-4 Identify the additional variables needed and the functional forms of additional equations to derive a satellite model for a long-term forecast relevant to one of the industries listed below.

    (a) China dishes
    (b) Typewriters
    (c) Refrigerators
    (d) Domestic airlines

10-5 It was stated that the role of government economic policies is less in a long-term forecast because they are subject to sharp changes—in part reflecting unpredictable changes in the political orientation of the Administration in power. Indicate some of the shifts in economic policy (both fiscal and monetary) that have occurred in the past ten years and contrast present policy orientation with that existing during the 1960s.

10-6 For the postwar period the U.S. economy has averaged 45-month expansions and 11-month recessions. Plot actual real GNP quarterly on a IQ: 1946 = 100 index. Contrast this actual performance with an index based on average cyclical patterns. Evaluate the usefulness of this technique in preparing a 10-year economic forecast.

11

ECONOMIC FORECASTING AT THE FIRM AND INDUSTRY LEVEL

INTRODUCTION

The earlier chapters in this text stress general macroeconomic forecasting. This emphasis reflects the importance of these forecasts to the activities of a corporate economic forecaster. Two reasons can be cited. First, analyses and forecasts of overall macroeconomic conditions constitute the most expert contribution the economist makes to a firm's planning and general business operations. Other managers may have more detailed knowledge of firm-specific topics—such as production methods, capacity, and product market conditions—but the performance of the overall economy is where the economist's knowledge is greater. Second, specific macroeconomic measures—whether estimated as part of an integrated forecast or directly themselves—often are key inputs to the firm's own planning.

Nevertheless, forecasts of firm- and industry-specific variables—costs, resource needs, market demand conditions, product demand, and market share—are the more vital function of a business economic forecaster. While it is useful to provide an array of general macroeconomic forecasts, the true test of an economic forecaster's value to the firm is the accuracy of these "bottom-line," firm-specific variables. If the economist only provides forecasts of how the overall economy will perform and does not translate these into their impact on the sales, costs, and profitability of the firm, the economist's function is reduced to that of a curiosity rather than the more important role of a shaper of management decisions.

Because forecasting at the firm, or even the industry level, is necessarily quite particular to the conditions faced by an individual firm or industry there are greater limits on the guidelines and approaches which can be described in this chapter than was true for the general forecasting situations described in Chapters 5 through 10. There are, nevertheless, some general guidelines and forecast situations. Section I offers pointers on the purposes and scope of industry and firm forecasting that are general enough to be useful for all business economists. Section II provides examples of six forecasting situations covering a broad range of industries and markets. These examples stress the interrelationships that exist between macroeconomic and firm forecasting and indicate some of the specific needs and modifications required. Section III offers guidelines on presenting forecast results. This is a crucial part of the economic forecaster's role: a technically expert forecast is useless unless its findings and implications are clearly communicated to the managers who will have to make decisions based on these results.

I. PURPOSES AND SCOPE OF BUSINESS FORECASTING

The ultimate purpose of economic forecasting in a business setting is to provide senior management and line managers with expert advice about the current and future behavior of the economy with special emphasis on how these developments are likely to impact the firm's business. Other roles include responding to specific requests to interpret economic developments and policy changes, and helping to mold the firm's external position on economic issues. The business economist's role is thus a staff position, and whether it is performed within a separate economic research department, an economics and planning department, or submerged within the corporate planning department, the economist(s) generally report at a high level in the corporate hierarchy.[1]

An essential condition for the economic forecaster to be effective is the development and maintenance of a two-way communication channel with management. On the economist's part this requires that the needs of management be fully understood. The first step towards this understanding is detailed knowledge on the economist's part of the firm's operations. By clearly understanding the operations of the firm, the economist can anticipate and propose ongoing economic analyses and forecasts that complement and enhance these operations. Initially, this is likely to require meeting with the managers of the line divisions to learn how they operate. This willingness to learn at the outset will later make it easier for the economist to propose specific projects which these same line managers can readily perceive as aids rather than regard as pointless interference from on high. It is equally important that the economist learn the concerns and goals of senior management. These will often have a broader scope than those of line managers. In this regard the economist's role is nothing less than providing the economic advice needed to insure the firm's continued health and survival.

It is helpful to recall the three roles of business economic forecasting alluded to earlier in this text. The first role is in providing *strategic* or *long-term* planning inputs to corporate management. Long-term planning is helped by long-term economic forecasts, but long-term forecasts cannot be prepared in isolation. The long-term is a succession of short-terms, and so, the long-term forecast should be integrated with a short-term forecast. Otherwise, management's response to the long-term forecast results is, quite rightly, likely to be "you can't get there from here."

The second role is providing *support to line operations*. This support includes: demand and supply forecasts (including estimates of input costs and product price trends): analyses in response to specific "what if" requests; regular product line forecasts; and early warnings of changes in economic conditions. Regular weekly, quarterly, or monthly economic reports—detailing changes in the macroeconomic environment, their likely impact on the firm's operations over the next one-two years, and the associated risks—can play a major role in communicating the economic fore-

---

[1] A somewhat dated but still useful survey of corporate economic functions is in the report by David I. Fisher, *The Corporate Economist* (New York: The Conference Board, Inc., 1975).

caster's view throughout the firm. In addition, such reports may anticipate concerns of managers while, at least, maintaining awareness of the economic forecaster's function and providing a stimulus for line operatives to respond to.

The third role is the *presentation of the firm's view on economic questions* to the wider audience comprised of the business community, government, and the public at large. As business/economic policy questions have become more intertwined and complex, the need for expert statements by business leaders has enhanced the economic advisor role of the business economist. Moreover, in many cases a firm's customers will view requests of the firm's economic forecast as part of a business relationship. (Working in a large commercial bank, the author frequently receives requests from both large and small customers for "the Bank's" forecasts of economic variables which the customer will then use as inputs to its own planning.)

The communication channel must also run from management, at all levels, to the economist. The economic forecaster should not, however, be passive in allowing this to happen. One of the most important contributions the economic forecaster can make towards stimulating this dialogue is to make clear both the uses and limits of the forecasting process. As economic forecasting has become a more common part of overall business management, a sense of frustration has risen at its failures and some resulting under-appreciation of its successes. Thomas H. Naylor has pointed out that this is partly a result of economic forecasters "over-selling" their ability to predict the future.[2] The tendency to "over-qualify" forecasts is a common criticism of economic forecasters (giving rise to the old joke that "if all the economists in the world were laid end to end they would never reach a conclusion"). The fact remains, however, that economic forecasts deal with uncertainty, and so it is prudent and honest to set out the risks that may cause a forecast to err.

One way of making management aware of the risks to a forecast and yet not appear to be building alibis for future errors is to involve managers at the outset in setting the assumptions that will underlie the forecast. Such an exercise not only highlights the greatest risks, but may also reduce those risks by utilizing the expert insights of those managers closest to the particular business situation. Naylor also warns that the forecast errors which are tolerable to an economist may seem intolerable to management. For this reason he advises economic forecasters to "under-sell" rather than "over-sell" the accuracy of econometrically derived forecasts.[3]

A. Gilbert Heebner, Senior Vice President and Chief Economist at the

[2] Thomas H. Naylor, "The Politics of Corporate Economics," *Business Economics* (Mar. 1981), pp. 6–12.

[3] Naylor, "The Politics of Corporate Economics," p. 9.

Philadelphia National Bank, has offered four guidelines for business economic forecasters.[4]

(1) "Get the viewpoints of others in the company and endeavor to gain their concurrence in the forecast." It is better to tackle potential disputes head on before the forecast is issued. The wider the participation in a forecast exercise, the less opposition there will be to its final results.

(2) "Don't just project a set of numbers; provide also a discussion of assumptions and rationale." Without supporting discussion of the underlying assumptions, a forecast must succeed or fail on the basis of the absolute accuracy of the quantitative results. Keynes once pointed out that it is better to be vaguely right than precisely wrong. It is only possible to be vaguely right if some qualitative guidelines for interpreting the quantitative results of a forecast are provided.

(3) "Give a range of forecast figures." This is perhaps the most difficult advice to follow in practice. Management usually dose not want the range of probable outcomes for a forecast, but rather the actual value(s) the forecaster expects. Identifying the risks of a forecast and providing some indication of what the likely impact on the forecast results will be if those risks occur may be preferable to providing range forecasts. (Heebner points out that one implication of providing a range forecast is that management may justifiably expect a greater degree of accuracy than with a point forecast—the results of a range forecast should fall within the range.)

(4) "Update the forecast periodically." Macroeconomic conditions and policies change, risks may become more likely, and small errors emerge. The forecast can be constantly adjusted to reflect increased certainties or uncertainties. Clearly, not every change is noteworthy. If the forecast is updated regularly, however, these changes can be communicated to management in a calm, useful manner.

An important message in the foregoing discussion is that the economic forecaster's role in a firm should not be taken for granted, either by the economist or by management. The responsibility for developing this role, however, lies mainly with the economist. The question, "How can my contribution as an economic forecaster enhance the profitable operations of my firm?" should constantly be re-examined.

II. SIX BUSINESS FORECASTING SITUATIONS

The forecasting situations a business economist is likely to confront vary greatly from industry to industry and from firm to firm within industries depending on market structure and the size and organization of the firm, to

---

[4] A. Gilbert Heebner, "Making Forecasts More Useful to the Company," *NABE NEWS*—the newsletter of the National Association of Business Economists (Jan. 1978), pp. 2–5.

name just the most important factors. This fact poses a serious problem to describing how firm-specific forecasting should be conducted. This section, nevertheless, attempts to address this issue by describing six varied forecast situations which, while not exhaustive, do provide an extensive cross-section of forecast situations. Each case details: the objective of the forecast, some of the distinguishing industry, firm, or market features of the forecast exercise, and the forecast methods used. The six forecast situations described are for:

(1)   An international petroleum company.
(2)   An integrated paper company.
(3)   A carpet manufacturer.
(4)   A marketing company selling toothpaste.
(5)   An electric utility company.
(6)   Contributions to not-for-profit organizations.

An International Petroleum Company

In a large petroleum company, which produces and refines crude petroleum, and markets the products internationally, the main objective of the economic forecasting staff is to forecast demand for products by regional and end-use markets so these forecast demands can be balanced against crude oil supplies and refining capacity. The formal forecast is performed once a year in the early autumn and includes detailed monthly demand estimates by product and country for the following calendar year, with annual estimates for the four succeeding years. While the forecast is only published annually, the process occupies the staff throughout the year. For one thing, it is necessary to monitor constantly national macroeconomic trends in each country.

There are three distinguishing features about the forecasting situation. First, crude oil supplies can be assumed to be assured and abundant. The assumption that these supplies are assured must be questioned periodically, but this is an evaluation made by senior management based on the assessment of regional managers. Thus, the assumption of assured supply is exogenous to the economic forecasting process, although the chief economist may be consulted and have an important input to the evaluation.

The second feature is the need to forecast demand in up to fifty countries. As a result, macroeconomic forecasts for each of these economies are required. This function accounts for the main activity of the economics staff during the year. Econometric models are developed and maintained for the larger, more developed countries. For some nations, however, poor or inadequate data make this activity impossible. External analyses and forecasts are monitored and used to help form judgmental forecasts for these latter nations and to adjust econometric forecasts.

TABLE 11-1   Petroleum Product Output (volume percentages of a barrel of crude input)

Type of Crude:	HEAVY CRUDE		MEDIUM CRUDE	
Refinery Configuration	A	B	A	B
Fractions				
Gas	4.3%	4.3%	2.1%	2.1%
Gasoline	2.1	5.1	5.5	9.1
Benzine	11.3	4.8	14.0	6.0
Naphtha	4.3	9.5	5.3	12.4
Kerosine	1.9	3.9	2.6	5.2
Light Diesel Oil	23.0	16.0	27.2	18.4
Heavy Diesel Oil	4.5	9.8	5.2	11.1
Fuel Oil*	48.8	46.6	38.1	35.7

* Includes residues which can be refined into parafin, lubricating oils, and asphalt.

Source: British Petroleum Company, *Our Industry Petroleum* (London: The British Petroleum Company Ltd., 1977). p. 257.

The third feature is the need to optimize refinery facilities according to two constraints. The first constraint is that there is only limited flexibility in the end-product mix that can be obtained from a barrel of crude oil, reflecting its chemical properties. Such flexibility as exists reflects (a) the chemical properties of the particular crude used, and (b) the configuration of the refinery. Table 11-1 depicts the percentage of products which can be derived from a heavy versus a medium crude using, in each case, two alternative refinery configurations.[5] The second constraint is the need to minimize the distance between refineries and end markets. It is more efficient to ship crude over long distances in bulk tankers from source to a refinery near the end market than to transport a range of products individually over long distances. The role of the economists, then, is to estimate the demand for each product in each market so that the supply department can then optimize the refinery runs around the world.

The approach followed for deriving aggregate product demand is to forecast demand for each of six groups of product in each country. This is done on the basis of statistical relationships between product demand and a number of standard macroeconomic variables. As a general rule, an attempt is made to keep the relationships standard across countries, though there are two exceptions: (1) in the case of a few highly developed nations extensive macroeconomic data permit the development of more elaborate relationships; while (2) at the other extreme, statistical data are so scanty in some countries that purely judgmental forecasts are needed.

[5] Data are from British Petroleum Company, *Our Industry Petroleum* (London: The British Petroleum Company, Ltd., 1977), pp. 255–58.

The six broad product demand-macroeconomic measure relationships can be briefly described.

Liquified petroleum gas, benzine, and naptha are mainly used as petrochemical feedstocks, though they also have other industrial uses. Where these products are used they can be estimated based on a relationship with the level of industrial production.

Motor gasoline demand is largely a function of automobile usage. Depending on the availability of data, gasoline demand can be estimated as a function of auto registrations, income, and population.

The main use of *kerosene* in developed nations is as jet fuel. This demand can be estimated on the basis of jet travel, which in turn, can be estimated from population, income, and a trend factor. In less developed countries, kerosene is frequently used for home cooking and heating. This demand can be estimated as a function of population.

Diesel fuel is used both for fueling trucks and heavy equipment and for home heating. The former use can be estimated as a function of industrial production and the latter related to population.

Heavy fuel oil is mainly used in industry and its demand can be estimated as a function of industrial production.

Finally, *asphalt,* which is a residual in the refining process, is mainly used in construction and road paving. Asphalt demand can be estimated on the basis of residential and nonresidential construction and government spending. This is also an area where knowledge of large planned construction projects can suggest judgmental adjustments to the forecast.

Once preliminary product demand forecasts are completed for each country, these "first-pass" forecasts are submitted for comment to managers on location. These comments can be a valuable source of information to the forecaster and the process of managerial review helps commit the line management to the forecast. After integrating the comments from the field, the country demand forecasts can be finalized and aggregated by region. These total product demands then have to be refined to arrive at company demand forecasts through market share analysis. When company regional product demand forecasts are finalized, they are forwarded to the supply planning department where refinery operating schedules are determined through an elaborate system of linear programming.[6]

Thus, the role of the economic forecasting group in a large petroleum company is but a part, albeit an important one, of the overall supply-demand planning process. The economists have the primary responsibility for maintaining macroeconomic forecasts for a large number and range of economies that are then used as the bases for the product demand forecasts. The con-

---

[6] The linear programming technique is widely used in the petroleum industry to determine the optimum refinery configuration to produce the required product mix given the crude inputs. A linear program for one refinery can have 5000 arguments.

sensual nature of the demand forecast is highlighted by the interchange between the centralized economic forecasting staff and the regional managers.

An Integrated Paper Company[7]

The Corporate Planning department semi-annually forecasts demand for a variety of products over the next five years and uses these demand forecasts along with input cost and product price forecasts for planning marketing strategy, and financial and capacity needs for both the next year and the longer term.

This section focuses on one product line, fiber boxes—more widely referred to as cardboard boxes. Fiber boxes are an intermediate good. That is, the demand for fiber boxes is related to the demand for final products that are packaged in them, and is thus driven by activity in these end-use markets. The forecasting process is conducted in three main phases. First, a "first-pass" total demand forecast is prepared based on a relationship between shipments and macroeconomic activity. The second phase—which may be conducted concurrently with the total demand forecast—is a forecast of supply conditions: an evaluation of available and likely capacity, costs, and competitive conditions. Third, these results are then discussed by the Corporate Planning staff with the operating divisions in order to update information on current and expected market conditions and to get the line reaction to the forecast results.

Fiber box shipments have been found to have a close relationship with the index of industrial production in manufacturing. Such a relationship is intuitive, reflecting the fact that much manufacturing output is shipped in fiber boxes. Figure 11-1a shows the trends for manufacturing production and fiber box shipments from first quarter 1978 through fourth quarter 1981. The similar cyclical behavior of the two series is particularly vivid for the short cycle from second quarter 1980 through third quarter 1981. This historical relationship is the basis for a simple, but highly accurate forecasting relationship, which shows fiber box shipments (FIBTOTSHP) as a function of industrial production in manufacturing (JQINDM) as in 11-1.

$$FIBTOTSHP = a + b * JQINDM \qquad (11\text{-}1)$$

coefficients	t statistics
a = 7,867.62	(1.91)
b = 36,228.1	(11.60)
rho = 0.658	(6.16)

$$\overline{R}^2 = 0.9383 \quad D\text{-}W = 1.62 \quad SER = 1403$$

[7] The author wishes to thank A.C. Veverka, General Manager, and K.F. McAuley, Director Strategic Planning, St. Regis Company for their valuable assistance on this section.

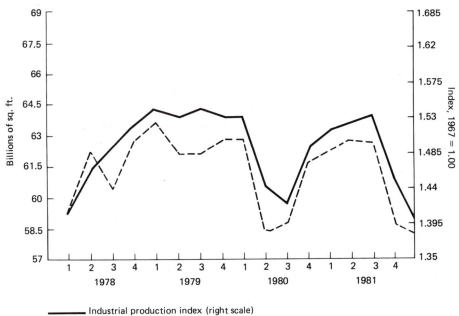

FIGURE 11-1a   Industrial production—mfg. versus fiber box shipments

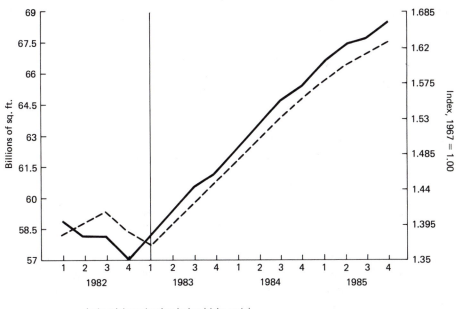

FIGURE 11-1b   Industrial production—mfg. versus fiber box shipments

The input variable, industrial production in manufacturing, is supplied by the Corporate Planning department's macroeconomic forecast, which in turn is derived from a modified version of a large commercial econometric forecasting model.[8] Figure 11-1b shows the results of this "first-pass" forecast prepared in the second quarter of 1983. One further adjustment is necessary; estimates of inventories on hand are deducted from the total demand forecast. This was a particularly important factor in the early quarters of the forecast; as the economy emerged from the 1981–82 recession these stocks were high but were expected to decline to more normal levels as recovery progressed.

There is a special feature of the industry that must be taken into account in assessing the supply situation. Current technology and capacity are such that box production offers no constraint: existing plant and equipment are ample and can be run at variable rates which encompass virtually all feasible demands. Linerboard—a basic raw material input in box production—does, however, impose a constraint. Linerboard supply is a function of capacity, which, in turn, is determined by expected demand and profitability–the margin between price and costs. Linerboard costs are determined by three components: (1) fiber cost, (2) labor cost, and (3) energy cost. Fiber cost is forecast using the department's extensive long-term study of total fiber demand and supply. Labor and energy costs are forecast using macroeconometric model results. When these cost forecasts are input into a linerboard model, the supply of linerboard and its costs can be estimated.

Integrating the results from the demand and supply forecasts, a detailed fiber box forecast can be derived containing total shipments and prices. These results are then presented to the divisional managers for their reaction and to derive feasible production and sales plans.

The fiber box case provides an example of how a forecast of an intermediate product can be derived from a satellite model which uses inputs from a more general macroeconomic model. As was the case with the petroleum company example, the fiber box case also shows the importance of line inputs to the overall forecasting and planning process.

A Carpet Manufacturer

A full-line carpet manufacturing company produces a line of durable goods, the demand for which is highly cyclical. Indeed, the cyclical nature of carpet demand is the main feature of this forecasting exercise. Insuring adequate productive capacity is an important, though secondary, objective. Thus, the Economic Planning Department in the carpet manufacturing case must focus on demand and supply conditions with special emphasis on the cyclical nature of demand.

---

[8] In this case, the Data Resources Inc. (DRI) U.S. model was used, modified by changed exogenous assumptions developed by the Department's economist, Charles Shih.

The end-market demands for carpeting are five: (1) carpeting for new homes, (2) replacement carpets for existing homes, (3) nonresidential carpeting (mainly for offices and stores), (4) carpeting for new cars, and (5) all other demands. The first four of these demands (accounting for roughly 95% of total demand) can be forecast on the basis of econometric relationships between past demands for each category and macroeconomic variables.

The demand for carpeting for *new homes* has been estimated to account for roughly 20% of total carpet sales.[9] A regression on a distributed lag of housing starts captures much of the movement in this demand. (A lagged rather than unlagged relationship is preferred since new homes are furnished at various stages of completion, but presumably not at the start of construction.) Steiner found that total carpet demand could be estimated quite well with a single equation including a distributed lag of real residential construction, a relative price index, and a weighted unemployment rate measure.[10] This appears to be an unduly aggregate approach for a comprehensive carpet manufacturer. The use of a relative price index appears warranted, but the unemployment rate merely captures cyclical forces which are more appropriately captured by housing starts. (When an equation containing both housing starts and the unemployment rate was tested, the unemployment rate was found to be insignificant.) Equation 11-2a shows carpet demand for new housing (CARPNH) as a function of lagged housing starts ($\Sigma HUSTS_{t-1}$), and an index of carpet prices relative to the consumer price index (PCARP/CPIU).

$$CARPNH = f\left(\sum_i HUSTS_{t-1}, \frac{PCARP}{CPIU}\right) \qquad (11\text{-}2a)$$

Carpet demand for *existing homes* is more complex than for new homes. The demand is again for a high-priced, durable good and, thus, cyclical. However, it may be partly counter cyclical; if households are deterred from building a new house they may wish to refurbish their existing house. Thus, an inverse relationship to housing starts can be posited. There also appears to be a strong trend component that must be taken into account. Equation 11-2b shows carpet demand for existing houses (CARPEH) as a function of current housing starts (an inverse relationship is expected), relative prices, personal income per capita (YP/POP) as a measure of affordability, and population (POP) as a measure of trend.

$$CARPEH = f\left(HUSTS, \frac{PCARP}{CPIU}, (YP/POP), POP\right) \qquad (11\text{-}2b)$$

---

[9] Pierre Steiner, "Using Econometrics to Forecast Demand," *Carpet and Rug Industry* (Apr. 1979), pp. 27–31.

[10] Pierre Steiner, "Using Econometrics to Forecast Demand," p. 29.

Carpet demand for *nonresidential structures* is partly for furnishing newly built structures and partly for refurbishing existing structures. The former demand is likely to be more cyclical than the latter, which may be regarded as trend-like, reflecting the ongoing upkeep of business plants.

For these reasons, nonresidential carpet demand (CARPNR) can be represented as a function of real investment in nonresidential structures (ICNR72) and of the log of time, as a trend measure, as in 11-2c.

$$CARPNR = f(ICNR72, \log(TIME)) \qquad (11\text{-}2c)$$

Demand for carpeting for *new automobiles* (CARPCARS) is also highly cyclical, but can be directly estimated as a function of new domestically produced car sales (CARSD) as in 11-2d.

$$CARPCARS = f(CARSD) \qquad (11\text{-}2d)$$

Thus, carpet demand can be forecast using a satellite model which is based on variables derived from a general macroeconomic forecasting model. The only industry-specific variables are the demands for different carpeting (in millions of square feet) and an index of carpet prices.

Supply conditions are determined by production costs and capacity. Capacity can be estimated on the basis of a long-term carpet demand forecast. Thus, capital costs can be regarded as fixed over the near term though great weight should be placed on the cyclical phase of the economy and its effects on capacity utilization and financing costs. The two main variable costs are then labor and raw material costs. Labor costs can be forecast by modifying a macroeconomic labor cost forecast to specific industry conditions. Material input cost estimates can be worked out with line managers close to market conditions.

The distinguishing feature of the carpet manufacturer case is the importance of cyclical demand shifts. Once again, however, the forecasting process is greatly aided by the availability of general macroeconomic forecasts.

A Toothpaste Marketing Firm

Companies which produce and market personal products, such as soap and toothpaste, have a quite different focus than the manufacturing companies examined in the first three cases. These products are relatively inexpensive nondurable goods so total demand is subject to fairly stable secular growth due mainly to demographic factors (population and the number of households). There is some evidence[11] that toothpaste demand is related to

---

[11] See Roger D. Carlson, "Demand Analysis for Toothpaste," *Business Economics* (Sept. 1977), pp. 61–66 which updates an earlier study by Kristian S. Palda and Larry M. Blair, "A Moving Cross-Section Analysis of Demand for Toothpaste," *Journal of Marketing Research* (Nov. 1970), pp. 439–49.

cross-sectional, socio-economic forces (family income, race, education, and profession of family head), but no evidence of cyclical relationship. Consequently, economists in such firms are often found in the Marketing Research department where they concentrate on microeconomic analyses of market composition and price elasticity.

One macroeconomic forecasting concern, however, relates to the market share a particular toothpaste may attain. In marketing firms, the actual cost of producing the toothpaste is small relative to the costs of advertising and promotion. Advertising is the main way in which such a product gains and maintains market share. Thus, a critical task in the successful marketing of a brand of toothpaste is determining the advertising budget which is optimal for the brand to gain and maintain desired market share. This is a topic on which economic forecasting can be helpful.

The forecast approach is in two stages. First, the total market for toothpaste sales must be forecast. This demand can be forecast on the basis of forecast demographic characteristics—population by age: youths 5 to 16 years old (POP516), and adults 16 years old and over (POP16&); and the number of households (HH)—and basic economic measures—per capita income (YP/POP) and relative price (PTP/CPIU). These variables can be derived from an existing macroeconomic forecasting model[12] with estimates of the price index for toothpaste (PTP) estimated internally. Thus, total toothpaste demand (TP) can be estimated from equation 11-3a.

$$TP = f\left(POP516, POP16\&, HH, (YP/POP), \left(\frac{PTP}{CPIU}\right)\right) \quad (11\text{-}3a)$$

Once total toothpaste demand is estimated, sales of the particular brand can be forecast given a range of advertising budgets. A series of articles by Carlson, Schreiber, and Bourgo[13] have focused on a relationship between sales of Crest toothpaste and advertising budgets. All three articles recognize that the impact of advertising on sales is cumulative, has diminishing returns, and that current advertising has a minimal impact on current sales, but at low levels advertising has only a limited ability to reach the target audience. To address all these problems Bourgo has specified a nonlinear (transformed) model shown in equation 11-3b.[14]

---

[12] Forecasts of some of the basic demographic features—population by age group and the number of households—can be derived from the Census Bureau's *Current Population Reports* which supply annual long-term projections.

[13] Roger D. Carlson, "Advertising and Sales Relationships for Toothpaste," *Business Economics* (Sept. 1981), pp. 36–39; Max M. Schreiber, "Forecasting Sales on the Basis of Advertising Budgets: The Case of Crest Toothpaste," *Business Economics* (May 1982), pp. 43–45; and Donald G. Bourgo, "Forecasting Crest Sales," *Business Economics* (Jan. 1983), pp. 48–50.

[14] Bourgo, "Forecasting Crest Sales," pp. 48–49.

$$TPS_t = a + b_1 * (1/Ad_{t-1}) + b_2 * (1/Ad_{t-2}) \qquad (11\text{-}3b)$$

where

$$b_i < 0, i = 1, 2$$

TPS = Toothpaste brand sales in millions of dollars
Ad_{t-1} = Advertising budget lagged one period, millions of dollars
Ad_{t-2} = Advertising budget lagged two periods, millions of dollars

coefficients	*t statistics*
a = 409.5	(15.29)
b_1 = −1578.1	(−3.08)
b_2 = −2478.3	(−4.46)

$\overline{R}^2 = 0.951$ Forecast error = $3.7 million
Percent error = 1.5%

These analyses were somewhat hampered by having to rely on publicly available data. In reality, a toothpaste marketing firm could expect better results by using more precise company data (including unit sales). The approach, however, highlights the special nature of forecasting sales of a heavily advertised, low priced, nondurable good. Unlike the oil, fiber box, and carpet cases, supply factors—production costs and capacity—are less important considerations than finding the optimal advertising budget to achieve a desired sales-advertising cost balance.

An Electric Utility Company[15]

Electric utility companies differ from the firms treated above because they are regulated monopolies supplying an essential service to a regional market. The objective of forecasting in an electric utility company is twofold: (1) to forecast the amount of generating capacity required over the next ten or more years (the time new construction may take) to assure adequate service to the market; and (2) to forecast the rates necessary to finance ongoing operations and new capital spending during the forecast period.

The need to forecast long-term electricity demand is complicated by the necessity to request rate increases from the regulatory authority early in the financing period and the fact that unexpected increases in inflation may require supplementary requests if the initial request looks likely to be insuffi-

---

[15] The author thanks Thomas W. Moore, Chief Economist for the Tampa Electric Company, for his assistance on this section.

cient or if the forecast of generating needs changes. As a result, the economic forecaster may be subjected to critical review not only internally, but also by the regulatory authorities which may prove professionally embarrassing.

There are three distinct phases of the forecasting process in an electric company. First, the long-term growth in electricity demand due to general economic forces must be forecast. Electricity demand can be viewed as stemming from two sources: consumer residential demand, and business, commercial, and industrial demand. A first pass at forecasting these demands is made based on external and internal forecasts of national macroeconomic measures. For instance, residential demand is a function of population (as a measure of trend), housing starts (representing new net demand), and relative prices which in addition to measuring affordability, serve as a proxy for energy conservation (as the price of electricity increases relative to other prices, consumers are more likely to conserve on electricity usage). Business demand can be viewed as a function of industrial production, retail sales growth (as a proxy for new retail establishments), nonresidential construction, and relative prices.

The second phase involves modifying the forecast trends for these national macroeconomic measures to reflect local conditions. This involves developing a regional forecast model based on available data and anticipating differences in local versus national trends. Useful regional data include: state and metropolitan area employment and income, and, importantly, past data on electricity demand itself.

Also in many states, including Florida, regional economic models have been developed.[16] Special features which are addressed at this stage include: state immigration/emmigration and seasonal patterns in electricity demand, both of which are highly important in Florida. After modifying the forecast for local influences, a long-term forecast of local electricity demand is derived.

The third phase of the process involves the economists working with the engineering and finance departments to determine what the demand forecast implies for generating capacity. If added capacity is indicated, then a financing program must be devised. The economist's role at this point is secondary, although much will depend on the accuracy of the demand forecast.

The case of forecasting electricity demand emphasizes the use of long-term economic forecasting. In addition, there is also the special need to adapt a national macroeconomic forecast to capture local trends.

---

[16] See Donald L. Koch and Nathaniel J. Mass, "The Florida Economy—Elements of a System Dynamics Approach," *Business Economics* (Jan. 1981), pp. 21–25. There is also a state econometric model project at the University of Florida.

Private Charitable Contributions to Not-for-Profit Organizations

An unusual case is presented by the studies conducted by Chemical Bank which forecast private charitable contributions to not-for-profit organizations over five-year periods.[17] Not-for-profit organizations rely on contributions from individuals, corporations, foundations, and bequests to finance a substantial portion of their operations. Information about the likely future flow of contributions is a necessary basis for the financial and operational planning of these organizations. In an effort to aid its customers in this sector Chemical Bank's Not-for-Profit Group requested the Economic Research Department to prepare five-year forecasts of the flow of contributions based on expected economic conditions.

Private contributions were analyzed by three major contributor groups: (1) individuals, accounting for roughly 85% of the total; (2) corporations, which give between 5% and 6% of the total; and (3) foundations and bequests combined, which account for the remainder. Annual data on contributions from 1955, through 1979 for the first study, through 1982 for the second study, compiled by the American Association of Fund-Raising Counsel, Inc., were used to estimate relationships with a number of economic relationships for each contributor group. One operating constraint was a decision to restrict the economic determinants to the few most significant ones that could be forecast with the lowest likelihood of forecast error in the independent variables. There was also an explicit decision to avoid using tax policy variables as they introduced uncertainty about both long-term direction and impact.[18]

Contributions by individuals (INDCON) displayed the most regular trend, a quality that was proxied by including the population 16 years and over (POP16&) in the relationship. The major economic influence on individual giving was found to be personal income (YP). A highly significant relationship was found using these variables as shown in 11-4a.

$$INDCON = a + b_1 * YP + b_2 * POP16\& \qquad (11\text{-}4a)$$

coefficients	t statistics
$a = -4.32$	(-4.53)
$b_1 = 0.018$	(70.55)
$b_2 = 0.041$	(4.86)

$$\overline{R}^2 = 0.9996 \quad D\text{-}W = 1.45 \quad SER = 0.25$$

---

[17] *Giving and Getting: A Chemical Bank Study of Charitable Contributions Through 1984* (New York: Chemical Bank, Jan. 1981); and *Giving and Giving: A Chemical Bank Study of Charitable Contributions 1983 Through 1988* (New York: Chemical Bank, Dec. 1983).

[18] Indeed, the absence of any explicit assumptions about the major tax changes that occurred between the two studies appeared to have little impact on the interim forecast results.

The fact that such a significant relationship was found for individual contributions was particularly encouraging because this group accounts for such a large share of total giving.

Corporate contributions (CORPCON) have shown much greater variation over time. This reflects the primary role played by corporate before-tax profits (ZBT) in determining the ability of corporations to make contributions. Corporate profits are among the most cyclical of macroeconomic measures. There were two modifications made to the basic relationship between corporate contributions and profits in developing an estimating equation. First, real before-tax profits were used (profits were deflated by the implicit GNP deflator, PGNP) to remove the artificial swelling of profits by inflation which corporations would be likely to discount. Second, it was found that the best relationship occurred when estimated in percent change form as in 11-4b. Thus, it was necessary to transform the results into level form.

$$\%\Delta(\text{CORPCON}) = a + b * (\%\Delta(\text{ZBT}) - \%\Delta(\text{PGNP})) \qquad (11\text{-}4\text{b})$$

coefficients	t statistics
a = 6.08	(3.07)
b = 0.63	(4.32)

$$\overline{R}^2 = 0.4555 \quad \text{D-W} = 1.83 \quad \text{SER} = 9.66$$

(When transformed back into levels, estimated corporate contributions showed a much closer fit to the actual levels than the low $\overline{R}^2$ for the percent change form suggested.)

Contributions from foundations and bequests were combined not because they are similar (they are not), but because attempts to find significant relationships to economic variables separately proved unsuccessful. The trend for the combined groups, called other contributions (OCON), showed great variation which appeared to be related to business cycle effects. This category was accordingly estimated as a function of two cyclical variables: the inverse of the unemployment rate in the prior year $(1/RU_{t-1})$, and the level of real GNP (GNP72).[19] One further modification was that other contributions were forecast in real terms (divided by the implicit GNP deflator) as in 11-4c. Thus, in this case the forecast levels had to be transformed back into current dollar terms. In this case, the low $\overline{R}^2$ and poor Dubin-Watson statistic represented more serious problems. Alternative estimating equa-

---

For one thing, it is still far from clear whether the net effects were favorable or unfavorable. The preliminary judgment is that they were neutral.

[19] One other variable that seemed on an *a priori* basis to be important, the performance of the stock market, was excluded because it did not seem likely that it could be forecast with a low enough forecast error. Moreover, analysis did not show that it was clearly helpful in explaining the past trend.

tions, however, were worse. Thus, it was decided to use equation 11-4c recognizing the potential for error it posed.

$$\left(\frac{\text{OCON}}{\text{PGNP}}\right)_t = a + b_1 * (1/RU_{t-1}) + b_2 * GNP72_t \qquad (11\text{-}4c)$$

coefficients	t statistics
a = −1.81	(−2.04)
b_1 = 11.33	(3.97)
b_2 = 0.0026	(5.05)

$$\overline{R}^2 = 0.5718 \quad \text{D-W} = 0.95 \quad \text{SER} = 0.61$$

The values for the explanatory variables in equations 11-4a, 11-4b, and 11-4c were taken from the Economic Research department's long-term macroeconomic forecast model. The forecast performed well over the three interim forecast years (1980–82) between the two studies despite a worse-than-expected economic performance, resulting in a cumulative underestimate of 3.8%.

Once the forecast levels for the contributor groups were estimated, it was possible to evaluate which groups would experience the fastest growth over the forecast period. It was then possible to derive implications for funding the six main recipient categories of not-for-profit organizations.[20] Importantly, those recipient groups which historically had been most dependent on contributor groups forecast to grow rapidly, could expect to see their funding grow more rapidly than those recipients which had historically been more dependent on those sources forecast to grow more slowly.

The results of the first study proved useful to the Not-for-Profit Group in advising their customers in two ways. First, the existence of a contributions forecast provided these organizations with a better basis for financial planning. Second, those organizations which had an adverse funding mix could take steps to alter it. Indeed, the intense fund-raising efforts that many not-for-profit organizations embarked on may have been a factor in producing the better-than-forecast growth in total contributions in 1980–82.

This case presents a nonstandard use of a long-term macroeconomic forecast and application of basis forecasting techniques in addressing a particular need for an economic forecast.

III. PRESENTING FORECAST RESULTS

A set of forecast results which satisfy the economic forecaster's aims will seldom be in a form for immediate presentation to management and other intended users. One need only conjure a picture of an economist rushing out

---

[20] These are: religious organizations, education, health and hospitals, social welfare organizations, arts and cultural organizations, and civic, public, and other organizations.

of the office trailing a mass of computer print out shouting "Eureka!" to recognize this fact. Forecasts have to be presented in prose, tabular, graphic, and oral form to be understood and useful. The most basis guiding rule for forecast presentation is that the results should serve the needs of those who will use them to make decisions.

Forecast presentation *should not* be a showcase for the economist's expertise. A frequent criticism of economists is that they do not speak the language of business.[21] As a result, important points are lost, and an economist's otherwise good advise may be ignored because it is not understood.

A starting point, already referred to earlier in this chapter, which may help the economic forecaster avoid this pitfall, is to ascertain in advance the concerns of the forecast user and the use the forecast is intended to serve. The forecast can then be better focused on these concerns and uses. For example, suppose a lumber company's management is chiefly concerned with the number of new housing units that will be built over the next twelve months. It is likely that the quarterly changes in real GNP are key determinants of housing construction. The economist must spell this connection out clearly to management for it to be of use. Otherwise, management's response may be: "Why are you telling me about GNP? I want to know what housing construction will be." The economist should take advantage of the opportunity to instruct management about economic relationships. But the instructions: must be clear in making these connections thoroughly understood; and must not lose sight of the basic aim of the forecast exercise—in this case, to give management a forecast of likely housing start activity.

Forecasts can be presented in at least four ways: prose, numerical tables, graphs, and orally. These are all related and may all be required to present a forecast. This section offers guidelines for developing all four types of presentation. It is appropriate to begin with the written report since this is the most basic way in which a forecast and its implications are communicated.

A written report accompanying an economic forecast should relate an easy to read, logical story. One way to accomplish this is to think of the few major points the forecast makes and work from an outline that carefully builds support for these points. The writer should attempt to keep in mind the readers' interests and to anticipate questions. The report should relate directly to any supporting tables and graphs by integrating them into the story. The writing itself should aim for a high standard. Grammatical errors will distract the reader's attention and sabotage an otherwise important message. Economic writers should be thoroughly versed in the rules of writing

---

[21] For a discussion of pitfalls in this regard see the excellent article by Marina von Neuman Whitman, "Economics from Three Perspectives," *Business Economics* (Jan. 1983), pp. 20–24.

as laid out in a book like Strunk and White's *The Elements of Style*.[22] There are also a number of special guidelines for business writers. Use short words, in short sentences, in short paragraphs. These are more effective in holding a reader's attention and communicating complex ideas. Economists should always avoid jargon. A writer of a report on which action may be taken should avoid using the first person singular. Either the first person plural or third person narrative are better. Finally, unless writing a textbook, the normative word, should, should be avoided.

Since economic forecasts are by nature quantitative, it is almost certain that some of the quantitative results will be presented in tabular form. Tables should be as concise as possible. Extra information detracts from the basic quantitative message. If supporting data are to be included, the table should be constructed so that the reader proceeds through the data in a logical manner. For instance, Table 11-2 presents data for a housing start forecast. There are several points which can be made about tabular presentation shown in this table. The variables should be fully labelled, economist mnemonics should be avoided. The units each variable is measured in should be noted, and they should be expressed in manageable terms. (Housing starts are expressed in millions, not in units which would require six to seven significant digits.) One should avoid false precision. George McKinney, formerly Chief Economist and Senior Vice President at Irving Trust Company and now Professor at the University of Virginia, once pointed out that in a forecast "the forecaster knows that nine times out of ten whatever digit is to the right of the decimal point is wrong." Changes in measurement—such as from annual to quarterly frequency expressed at annual rates—should be noted. Finally, it may be appropriate to include confidence ranges or an alternative forecast.

A limited number of graphs of key variables may help to emphasize the key points of a forecast. A guideline in using graphs is that they should be virtually self explanatory. If it takes a thousand words to explain a graph, its use does not save exposition. Graphs are best used when they are a standard part of the presentation—for instance, monthly or quarterly graphs which are constantly updated and used to track the changes between forecasts. Line graphs are used to depict trends, bar graphs to show levels, and pie charts to show distributions. Formal presentations can be enhanced by expert advice from graphic designers whose professional skill is presenting data in graphical form.

Finally, almost all forecasts eventually have to be presented orally; either informally or in a formal, sometimes public, presentation. An oral presentation should be just as thoroughly prepared as a written report. Successfully delivered oral presentations can either be in the form of fully devel-

---

[22] William Strunk, Jr. and E.B. White, *The Elements of Style* (New York: Macmillan, 1979).

TABLE 11-2 Housing Starts and Related Indicators (history and forecast)

	YEARS			QUARTERS			
	t-2	t-1	t	I	II	III	IV
Population (millions)	227.7	229.8	232.0	230.5	231.5	232.5	233.5
Real GNP (billions of 1972 $)*	1474.0	1502.6	1475	1495	1460	1465	1480
Personal Income (billion $)*	2160.4	2415.8	2569	2510	2550	2590	2625
Mortgage Rate (%)	12.66	14.70	15.14	15.35	15.71	15.45	13.97
Housing Starts (millions)*	1.29	1.08	1.06	0.92	0.95	1.12	1.25
single-family (millions)*	0.85	0.71	0.66	0.59	0.61	0.65	0.79
multi-family (millions)*	0.44	0.37	0.40	0.33	0.34	0.47	0.46

* Quarterly data expressed at seasonally adjusted annual rates.

oped speeches or based on an outline of key points. If the speech approach is followed, the speaker must decide whether to memorize it or read it. In general, a well-delivered, well-paced speech made without reference to a text or notes makes a more favorable impression on the audience. However, if the speaker is doubtful that such a feat can be achieved without stumbling, then a seemingly off-the-cuff talk based on a brief outline may be more effective. A special warning should be made about the use of jokes. If a speaker is at all uncertain of being able to tell a joke successfully then it should not be attempted. Moreover, even if jokes are included, they should be brief, pertinent, and few, and never at the expense of the audience. In general, it should be remembered that an economic forecast is a serious matter with serious implications and jokes may well undermine this message.

THE ATTRACTIONS OF ECONOMIC FORECASTING

At the end of this text, a reader might wonder "Why become an economic forecaster?" This question allows me to step outside the impersonal role of author and hazard some answers.

First, economic forecasting allows a trained economist to apply skills to real life situations and be financially remunerated. In the end, I believe salaries do reflect an economist's success as a forecaster. While it may often seem that salaries reflect tenure in the job more than forecasting accuracy, the two are related. Poor forecasters are not kept around long.

A second attraction of economic forecasting is that it offers the economist the opportunity to influence corporate policy at a fairly high level. The economist can often trace policy actions based on a forecast and see how successful they are.

A third factor appeals to the competitive instinct. Forecasting economic measures provides many opportunities to be wrong—sometimes colossally. But there are also coups, and they are very gratifying.

Finally, a totally personal view: it's fun.

NAME INDEX

SUBJECT INDEX

A

Accelerator principle, 261–63
Adaptive expectations, 202
Add factors, 383
Affordability, housing, 229
Age-sex classification, 362
Aggregate demand and supply, 10–11, 20–26
Aggregate price level, 11, 21
Aggregate short-run production functions, 22
Aggregate supply path, 375
Agricultural Prices, 59–60
Annualized growth rates, 92
Annual rate, compound. *See* Compound annual rate.
A priori assumptions, 143
Assets, liquid. *See* Liquid assets.
Assumptions, 2–3, 248, 385
Auto-regressive integrated moving average (ARIMA) method, 105, 112–16
Average hourly earnings, 166, 168–71, 207–9
Average workweek, 166, 168–71

B

Balance of payments, 80
"Baseline" forecast, 197, 239
Benefits, non-wage, 43
Bonds, 18, 311–12, 316–17, 321–27
"Bottom-up" approach, 163–64, 169, 183
Brown's linear exponential smoothing, 109. *See also* Exponential smoothing
Budget of the United States Government, 7, 248, 252
Bureau of the Census, 40, 48–49, 53–59, 66–68, 149, 183, 187
Bureau of Economic Analysis (BEA), 34–36, 40, 47–48, 52, 65–69, 73, 100, 170, 176, 180, 263, 278
Bureau of Labor Statistics (BLS), 47, 50, 66, 85–86, 95, 98–99, 103, 150–53, 155, 157–58, 160, 163–65, 167–68, 170, 211–16
Business Conditions Digest, 62–65, 100
Business fixed investment, 261–67. *See also* Investment, nonresidential fixed
Business Statistics, 53